Phenomenology and Educational Theory in Conversation

Phenomenology and Educational Theory in Conversation challenges the abstract-technical understanding of education to orient the reader to the importance of relationality, intersubjectivity, and otherness to renew and reclaim the educational project.

This book treats education as a matter of existence, relationality, and common human concerns. It offers readers an alternative language to reveal and challenge the humanistic encounters that often disappear in the shadows of neoliberalism. The phenomenologists, and educational theorists featured here, offer insights that connect fully and concretely with the everyday lives of educators and students. They offer another language by which to understand education that is counter to the objectifying, instrumentalist language prevalent in neoliberal discourse.

This book will be of great interest for academics, researchers, and post-graduate students in the fields of pedagogy, phenomenology, educational theory, and progressive education.

Patrick Howard is Professor of Education at Cape Breton University in Sydney, Nova Scotia, Canada. He is co-editor of the open access journal *Phenomenology & Practice*.

Tone Saevi is Professor of Education at VID Specialized University, Bergen, Norway. She is the main editor of the open access journal *Phenomenology & Practice*.

Andrew Foran is Professor of Education at St. Francis Xavier University, Canada. He is co-editor of the open access journal *Phenomenology & Practice*.

Gert Biesta is Professor of Public Education in the Centre for Public Education and Pedagogy, Maynooth University, Ireland, and Professorial Fellow in Educational Theory and Pedagogy, Moray House School of Education and Sport, University of Edinburgh, UK.

Theorizing Education Series
Series Editors

Gert Biesta
Maynooth University, Ireland and University of Edinburgh, UK

Stefano Oliverio
University of Naples "Federico II", Italy

Theorizing Education brings together innovative work from a wide range of contexts and traditions which explicitly focuses on the roles of theory in educational research and educational practice. The series includes contextual and socio-historical analyses of existing traditions of theory and theorizing, exemplary use of theory, and empirical work where theory has been used in innovative ways. The distinctive focus for the series is the engagement with educational questions, articulating what explicitly educational function the work of particular forms of theorizing supports.

Religious Education and the Public Sphere
Patricia Hannam

Art as Unlearning
Towards a Mannerist Pedagogy
John Baldacchino

Education in the Age of the Screen
Possibilities and Transformations in Technology
Edited by Nancy Vansieleghem, Joris Vlieghe and Manuel Zahn

Manabi and Japanese Schooling
Beyond Learning in the Era of Globalization
Masamichi Ueno, Yasunori Kashiwagi, Kayo Fujii, Tomoya Saito and Taku Murayama

Phenomenology and Educational Theory in Conversation
Back to Education Itself
Edited by Patrick Howard, Tone Saevi, Andrew Foran, and Gert Biesta

For more information about this series, please visit: www.routledge.com/Theorizing-Education/book-series/THEOED

Phenomenology and Educational Theory in Conversation

Back to Education Itself

Edited by Patrick Howard, Tone Saevi, Andrew Foran, and Gert Biesta

LONDON AND NEW YORK

First published 2021
by Routledge
2 Park Square, Milton Park, Abingdon, Oxon OX14 4RN

and by Routledge
605 Third Avenue, New York, NY 10017

First issued in paperback 2022

Routledge is an imprint of the Taylor & Francis Group, an informa business

© 2021 selection and editorial matter, Patrick Howard, Tone Saevi, Andrew Foran, and Gert Biesta; individual chapters, the contributors

The right of Patrick Howard, Tone Saevi, Andrew Foran, and Gert Biesta to be identified as the authors of the editorial material, and of the authors for their individual chapters, has been asserted in accordance with sections 77 and 78 of the Copyright, Designs and Patents Act 1988.

All rights reserved. No part of this book may be reprinted or reproduced or utilized in any form or by any electronic, mechanical, or other means, now known or hereafter invented, including photocopying and recording, or in any information storage or retrieval system, without permission in writing from the publishers.

Trademark notice: Product or corporate names may be trademarks or registered trademarks, and are used only for identification and explanation without intent to infringe.

Publisher's Note
The publisher has gone to great lengths to ensure the quality of this reprint but points out that some imperfections in the original copies may be apparent.

British Library Cataloguing-in-Publication Data
A catalogue record for this book is available from the British Library

Library of Congress Cataloging-in-Publication Data
A catalog record for this book has been requested

ISBN: 978-0-367-20988-9 (hbk)
ISBN: 978-0-367-52313-8 (pbk)
ISBN: 978-0-429-26469-6 (ebk)

DOI: 10.4324/9780429264696

Typeset in Bembo
by Apex CoVantage, LLC

Contents

List of contributors viii
Acknowledgements xiii

Introduction to book 1

PART I
On education: the phenomenon of education reconsidered 7

1 On the givenness of teaching: encountering the educational phenomenon 11
   GERT BIESTA

2 Uncovering what educators desire through Kierkegaard's loving phenomenology 23
   SCOTT WEBSTER

3 Approaching education on its own terms 34
   JORIS VLIEGHE AND PIOTR ZAMOJSKI

4 Pedagogical practice 45
   ANDREW FORAN

PART 2
Children, adults, voice and agency: on the problem of seeing education from children's perspective 59

5 More than measurement: education, uncertainty, and existence 63
   PETER ROBERTS

6 Paulo Freire and living a non-neoliberal life in education 75
WALTER OMAR KOHAN

7 A phenomenology of reading: textual technology
and virtual worlds 88
EVA-MARIA SIMMS

8 Reality-testing subjectivity, naivety, and freedom – or on
the possibility of educational moments 100
TONE SAEVI

PART 3
The existentials – lived time, body, space, and relations 111

9 Bildung and embodiment: learning, practicing, space
and democratic education 115
MALTE BRINKMANN

10 Time, individuality, and interaction: a case study 128
HERNER SAEVEROT AND GLENN-EGIL TORGERSEN

11 The school building and the human: an intertwined
relationship 140
EVA ALERBY

12 Active and interactive bodies 151
STEPHEN J. SMITH

13 "Awakening to the world as phenomenon": the value of
phenomenology for a pedagogy of place and place making 164
DAVID SEAMON

14 From *kairos* to *chronos*: the lived experience of time
in education 179
ERIKA GOBLE

15 Educational possibilities: teaching toward the
phenomenological attitude 197
MARCUS MORSE AND SEAN BLENKINSOP

PART 4
To have been educated 211

16 Deceptively difficult education: a case for a lifetime
    of impact 215
    ALAN BAINBRIDGE

17 Education as pro-duction and e-duction 227
    STEIN M. WIVESTAD

18 Focal practices and the ontologically educated citizen 239
    DYLAN VAN DER SCHYFF

19 Between having and being: phenomenological reflections
    on having been educated 252
    PATRICK HOWARD

    Index 264

Contributors

Eva Alerby is Professor of Education and holds a chair at the Department of Arts, Communication and Education, Luleå University of Technology, Sweden. Her research interests are relations, identity and diversity in education, as well as philosophical and existential dimensions of education, such as place and space, time and temporality, silence and tacit knowledge.

Alan Bainbridge is Chartered Psychologist, Doctor of Clinical Science and Senior Lecturer in Education at Canterbury Christ Church University having previously taught in secondary schools for 18 years. He is interested in the contested space between psychoanalytic thought and practices to education in its widest sense and is a co-coordinator of the European Society for Research on the Education of Adults Life History and Biography Network. He uses his experience as a UKCP registered psychoanalytic psychotherapist to inform his research and works qualitatively to provide opportunities and spaces where participants can provide rich contextual data of their life experiences.

Gert Biesta is Professor of Public Education at the Centre for Public Education and Pedagogy, Maynooth University, Ireland; Professorial Fellow in Educational Theory and Pedagogy at the Moray House School of Education and Sport, University of Edinburgh; and NIVOZ Professor for Education at the University of Humanistic Studies, the Netherlands. He is co-editor of the *British Educational Research Journal* and associate editor of the journal *Educational Theory*. His recent books include *The Rediscovery of Teaching* (2017); *Obstinate Education: Reconnecting School and Society* (2019) and *Educational Research: An Unorthodox Introduction* (2020). His work has appeared in 20 different languages.

Sean Blenkinsop is Professor in the faculty of education at Simon Fraser University, Vancouver, BC, Canada. His current research focus is on education for cultural change in a time of environmental crisis. He has been involved in starting and researching several nature-based public schools in Canada. He was an author and editor for the recent book *Wild Pedagogies: Touchstones* *for Re-negotiating Education and the Environment in the Anthropocene* published by Palgrave.

Malte Brinkmann teaches General Educational Studies at the Institute for Educational Studies at Humboldt University, Berlin. He represents a phenomenologically oriented pedagogy, regularly attends the International Symposium on Phenomenological Educational Studies, and is editor of a book series on this subject. His research focuses on Bildung, educational and social-theoretical questions, in particular on a theory of embodied learning and practising (Üben) and aesthetic Bildung and Education. A further focus is on qualitative research in teaching and learning, in particular on phenomenological video analysis.

Andrew Foran began his teaching career as a secondary geography teacher and outdoor educator, and currently, he is Professor of Education at St. Francis Xavier University in Canada. The focus of his teacher education practice is service learning, experiential applications within public-school programmes, and K–12 curriculum development in outdoor education. Andrew's research examines teachers and students engaged in experiential courses and instruction outside of school settings. Andrew has developed numerous teacher education programmes, workshops, and courses, and has published nationally and internationally. Dr. Foran is leading a certificate programme in outdoor education for physical education teachers through St. Francis Xavier University, and he is co-editor of the open access journal *Phenomenology & Practice*.

Erika Goble is the Associate Dean of Research at NorQuest College, an Adjunct Assistant Professor with the Faculty of Rehabilitation Medicine, University of Alberta., and a Policy Fellow with the Education Policy Research Initiative, University of Ottawa. Her current research interests include moral distress in higher education and how ethics and aesthetics intersect in lived experience. Committed to community-based, community-driven applied research, she also supports a range of local community and healthcare organizations to plan, undertake, and evaluate social innovation projects.

Patrick Howard is Professor of Education at Cape Breton University in Canada. His research and writing explore how our defining human abilities, creativity, language, and imagination, as products of nature, are mediums by which we may grow in our relationships with the living places we inhabit. A common theme of his work is how teaching and learning can deepen the human–nonhuman interrelationship to provide a vital vision of education based on life values. Dr. Howard is an associate editor of the open source journal *Phenomenology & Practice*.

Walter Omar Kohan is Professor of Philosophy of Education at the State University of Rio de Janeiro since 2002. He is Director of the Center of

Studies in Philosophy and Childhood at the State University of Rio de Janeiro. Dr. Kohan is a visiting professor at different universities in Italy, France, Argentina, Mexico, and Chile and co-editor of *Childhood & Philosophy*. He has published over 100 peer reviewed articles, chapters and books in Spanish, Italian, Portuguese, and French and books in English that include *Childhood, Education And Philosophy: New Ideas For An Old Relationship* (2015); *The Inventive Schoolmaster* (2015).

Marcus Morse is Director, Outdoor Environmental Education in the School of Education at La Trobe University, Australia. His current research interests are in the areas of outdoor environmental education, dialogue in education, wild pedagogies, and forms of paying attention within outdoor environments.

Peter Roberts is Professor of Education and Director of the Educational Theory, Policy and Practice Research Hub at the University of Canterbury in New Zealand. His primary areas of scholarship are philosophy of education and educational policy studies. His most recent books include *Education and the Limits of Reason: Reading Dostoevsky, Tolstoy and Nabokov* (with Herner Saeverot, 2018), *Happiness, Hope, and Despair: Rethinking the Role of Education* (2016), *Education, Ethics and Existence: Camus and the Human Condition* (with Andrew Gibbons and Richard Heraud, 2015), *Better Worlds: Education, Art, and Utopia* (with John Freeman-Moir, 2013), and *The Virtues of Openness: Education, Science, and Scholarship in the Digital Age* (with Michael Peters, 2011).

Herner Saeverot is Professor of Education at the Department of Education, Western Norway University in Bergen, Norway. He is also Professor II at NLA University College in Oslo, Norway. His primary research interests include education and risks, existential education, and literature and education. Recent and forthcoming books include *Indirect Pedagogy* (2013); *Education and the Limits of Reason* (with Peter Roberts, 2018); *Meeting the Challenges of Existential Threats through Educational Innovation: A Proposal for an Expanded Curriculum* (2021). In 2019 he was appointed member of The Royal Norwegian Society of Sciences and Letters and All European Academics (ALLEA).

Tone Saevi works as a teacher and researcher in education at VID Specialized University, Norway. Her work has a special focus on Continental education (Allgemeine Pädagogik/Didaktik), educational philosophy, hermeneutic phenomenological methodology, and phenomenology of practice. She is the main editor of the open access journal *Phenomenology & Practice*. Saevi has published widely on basic educational questions like pedagogical relationality, responsibility, asymmetry and care, and phenomenological methodology (e.g. Learning in pedagogic relationships, published in *Sage Handbook of Learning* in 2015, Å skrive hermeneutisk fenomenologisk "fra mening til metode." Et pedagogisk eksempel på praksisens fenomenologi, *Fenomenologi i praktiken – Fenomenologisk forskning i et skandinaviskt perspektiv*, an article published in 2019).

David Seamon is Professor of Environment-Behavior and Place Studies in the Department of Architecture at Kansas State University in Manhattan, Kansas, USA. Trained in humanistic geography and environment-behavior research, he is interested in a phenomenological approach to place, architecture, and environmental design as place making. He edits *Environmental and Architectural Phenomenology*, which in 2019 celebrated 30 years of publication. His most recent book is *Life Takes Place: Phenomenology, Lifeworlds, and Place Making* (2018).

Eva-Maria Simms is Adrian van Kaam Professor of Psychology at Duquesne University in Pittsburgh. Her research group, PlaceLab, develops philosophical concepts and qualitative methods for researching the intersection of community, nature, and place in collaboration with community organizations that steward local neighbourhoods and green spaces. Dedicated to community engaged research, social justice, and recovering the attachment between people and place, PlaceLab gives voice to children's and adults' experiences of their local commons and enhances the connection between people and place. Dr. Simms has published widely in the areas of child psychology (*The Child In The World: Embodiment, Time, And Language In Early Childhood*, 2008).

Stephen Smith is Professor in the Faculty of Education at Simon Fraser University in Canada. His scholarly work, informed by phenomenological theories of embodiment, focuses on curricular and instructional matters of health and physical activity promotion. An ongoing line of scholarship concerns interspecies relations and, in particular, the training of horses and other companion animals. His interests in active and interactive bodies are grounded in movement practices that include partnered dance, martial arts, and circus arts, as well as equestrian disciplines.

Glenn-Egil Torgersen is Professor of Education at the University of South-Eastern Norway and professor II at NLA University College, Norway. He holds a PhD in Psychology and a Master's in Educational Science. In addition, he has professor (docent) competence in Educational Leadership, and holds a teacher license for primary school. His key research interests are pedagogical theory construction and practical implications for learning and training design, specifically aimed at professional education and emergency-preparedness. He is appointed member of the Academy of the Royal Norwegian Society of Sciences and Letters, and has many scientific publications, including the anthologies *Pedagogikk for det uforutsette* [*Pedagogy for the Unforeseen*] (Fagbokforlaget, 2015) and *Interaction: "Samhandling" Under Risk: A Step Ahead of the Unforeseen* (Cappelen Akademics, 2018).

Dylan van der Schyff is Senior Lecturer in Music at the Melbourne Conservatorium of Music, University of Melbourne. He received his PhD from Simon Fraser University, Canada, and holds postgraduate degrees in humanities (Simon Fraser University) and music psychology (University of Sheffield). His postdoctoral work was hosted by the Faculty of Music at the University of Oxford. Dylan is an active performer and has appeared on close to 200 recordings as a drummer/percussionist.

Joris Vlieghe is Assistant Professor of Philosophy and Theory of Education at KU Leuven (Belgium). With Naomi Hodgson and Piotr Zamojski he recently published a *Manifesto for a Post-critical Pedagogy* (2017) and with Zamojski, *Towards an Ontology of Teaching: Thing-centered Pedagogy, Affirmation and Love for the World* (2019). He is also interested in the impact of digital technologies on education, and more specifically in how fundamental notions such as schooling, attention, community, transformation, literacy, and creativity change when a culture of the screen is (rapidly) substituted for a culture of the book.

R. Scott Webster is Associate Professor of Education (Curriculum and Pedagogy) at the School of Education, Deakin University, Australia. Scott began his career in 1986 in North Queensland as a secondary HPE, Science and Maths teacher. He has also worked and studied in the UK and USA, and obtained his PhD from Griffith University, Australia, in 2003. He is the author of *Educating for Meaningful Lives* (2009), co-author, with Ann Ryan, of *Understanding Curriculum: The Australian context* (2014, 2019), and co-editor, with John Whelen, of *Rethinking Reflection and Ethics for Teachers* (2019).

Stein M. Wivestad started his career as a primary school teacher and since 1984 he has taught at NLA University College in Bergen, Norway. His research focuses on questions related to Continental general pedagogic (Allgemeine Pädagogik). He has published articles in *Phenomenology & Practice*, *Journal of Philosophy of Education*, and in *Studies in Philosophy and Education*. Professor Wivestad currently leads the research project "Upbuilding examples for adults close to children." The goal is to help adults become aware of how they are as role models and how they ought to be. The research group has developed a free internet database which describes pictures, films, music, and texts to facilitate discussion and learning.

Piotr Zamojski is Assistant Professor of Theory of Education and Didactics at University of Gdańsk (Poland). With Naomi Hodgson and Joris Vlieghe he recently published *Manifesto for a Post-critical Pedagogy* (2017) and with Vlieghe, *Towards an Ontology of Teaching: Thing-centered Pedagogy, Affirmation and Love for the World* (2019). He has also published on issues of the bureaucratization of education, totalitarianism and educational theory, building a public sphere around education, and the role of cultural codes in schooling.

Acknowledgements

As editors of this eclectic collection we invited contributors to dwell on what it means for education to "get back to the things themselves." This project took shape over cups of coffee at kitchen tables, and during late-night chats at conferences in Norway, Canada, and the United States. It was born out of chance meetings and meaningful conversations during airport layovers. The seeds germinated in dialogue with friends and colleagues deeply concerned with the *state of things* in our field and a sense of urgency to reconnect education with the experiential, the whole, the personal, and what it may mean to *get back to education itself*. This book has its own history connected to people, place, time, and our individual phenomenological journeys. It can be traced to teachers, mentors, individuals, and formative texts that orient us to lived experiences foundational to our becoming philosophers, phenomenologists, and educators.

We are thankful for those in our lives who nurtured this project and who encouraged us to question the taken-for-granted in a complex world, and to determine what is most essential in education. We are forever grateful for our students who give us reason to push back against neoliberal ideology in its many forms.

Introduction to book

Globally, over the past four decades, education has become almost synonymous with learning, achievement, and the attainment of predetermined outcomes, with schooling practices cloaked in quantifiable indicators of knowledge, skills, and attributes in the guise of personal growth. On hearing the premise for this collection, an esteemed colleague asked incredulously, "Hasn't that been done? Is there anything new that can be said?" Certainly, there is an impressive body of research that explores neoliberal effects on contemporary educational discourse. Many writers have taken up the critique of educational reforms which have dramatically altered the goals and purposes of education to align with economic and national-political interests. And there is considerable research that exists describing how powerful agendas, often external to schools, serve to standardize curricula, increase competition to achieve higher test scores, regulate greater accountability in classroom practices, and fundamentally transform what we understand about teachers and students in the complexity and richness of the pedagogical relationship.

In response to our colleague, the editors and the contributors in this collection, believe something new, and important, remains to be said. Contemporary educational discourse shaped by neoliberalism, along with globalization have moved beyond hegemony to become a dogma, the unquestioned public orthodoxy that operates as if it were objective reality (Patrick 2013, p. 1). From a societal perspective, one might now question, if neoliberalism has become part of the natural attitude; our taken-for-granted assumptions and experiences relevant to education. And now due to persistent conditioning, educators are simply no longer able to rise to the level of reflective awareness. Giroux (2019) argues that neoliberal ideals, and ways of knowing and being, have become "normalized" (p. 34). The project to commodify education, regulating learners, producing knowledge workers has resulted successfully in our understanding of education in strictly economic terms. However, Giroux (2019) goes a step further to say neoliberalism has provided a foundation on which an emergent authoritarian social order is being built, and this post-neoliberal "fascist populist political formation" (2019, p. 27) is increasingly evident around the world. Thus, neoliberalism continues to threaten liberal democracies and remains interested in hyper-individualism, competition, and instrumentalist approaches to education. Yet, it is not merely interest, neoliberalism is obsessed with education: fixated with measurement and quantification with the ultimate end of education being the creation of the knowledge worker and ultimate control of the democratic power of education.

And perhaps, it may not be overstating matters to express a sense of urgency in saying that this book is yet another stand against the attacks on education at all levels. To do so, we turn to educational theorists and phenomenologists who understand education as an existential project of human life. Existential education is a moral interest in the lifeworld of children and young people, and in adult attention to the lived meaning of the pedagogical relationship with the young. The existential dialogue of education never ends. It is an ongoing commitment and responsible attention to human life and its concerns. The editors of this book, and the invited contributors, support a phenomenological-existential orientation that offers another vision for education. Van Manen (2016) says the original sense of phenomenology did not reflect an erudite, philosophical pursuit uncoupled from people's lives and daily concerns. Phenomenology was

> the source for questioning the meaning of life as we live it and the nature of responsibility for personal actions and decisions . . . to struggle to dislodge and confront unexamined assumptions of our personal, cultural, political and social beliefs, views, and theories.
>
> (p. 13)

The contributors in this collection see beyond education as the skills, knowledge, and dispositions obtained by attending school. Rather, education is a matter of existence, relationality, common moral and human concerns, concerns for that which is more than human, for life as the human condition. Pedagogy is not mere instructional strategy, but an embodied practice of being oriented to the life of the child and young person in a thoughtful sensitivity for what is in their best interest. This book has an orientation counter to the doctrine of the abstract, technical rationalism dominant in contemporary educational discourse. Teachers, parents, students, and all those deeply interested in education require a new language through which to re-imagine the educational project. Over the past four decades neoliberal values and social relations have normalized ideas of human capital, students as consumers, and knowledge as that which is consumed. Teaching is facilitation, education is learning, and teachers meet learners' needs narrowly defined as prescribed inputs designed to reinforce pre-specified outcomes (Biesta 2011).

Different voices – existential conditions

The orientation of the writers is rooted in Continental education that is a broad moral, complex, and multidimensional inter-generational discipline and practice. For example, Mollenhauer (1983) purposely, in his thinking and writing, keeps a distance between school and education. He posits schools have become specialized institutions and education has become a branch of science. The result is that the threads of upbringing, of human becoming, have been gathered in too few hands and are no longer shared in the common texture of culture. Today, this concern is truer, and education in the Western cultures has been made over; it is hegemonic, monocultural and now infused with the last of Anglo-American neoliberal ideals (Biesta 2011). Today's educational practice has forgotten the existential and original aspects of pedagogy; thus, we start anew to understand what education is actually about (Masschelein 2011, Saevi 2012).

While we *believe* we know what education is about in contemporary evidence-based research and practice, we do not really know much about how children and young people inherit, transform, and recreate society, cultures, and common life. In fact, much of what we believe we know for sure in life is not sure at all, but as Lingis (2018) invites us to realize,

> all the major events in our lives are due to chance – our birth; a teacher who captivated us and engaged us in mathematics or nursing, music, or football; the person we happened to meet and fall in love with; the job opportunity that abruptly opened; our child who was born or who was autistic or who died; the car crash that crippled us; the tumor that grew silently in our inner organs. There is . . . an element of chance and risk in every relation with another human being. We never really know what someone might think or might do. We can only trust him or her. Chance is the unpredictable, the incalculable, the incomprehensible, surprise, shock, good, or bad luck.
>
> (p. 6)

Nevertheless, we continue to determine, rationalize about, and attend to causalities that may promote or hinder our wellbeing and plans. We transfer to our children the attitude that life should be manageable and successful, and if not, then something is wrong *with* them or *in* them.

The counter movements to the rationalized "knowledge society" intend to revive traditions of rich plurality and complex indefinite discourses and practices that were traded away by European governments 20 years ago in the 1999 Bologna Declaration followed by Quality Reform 2003, and the work of the Organisation for Economic Co-operation and Development (OECD) on reforming general education through its Programme for International Student Assessment (PISA) and Teaching and Learning International Survey (TALIS). The OECD effort has resulted in a world-wide functional and economically based system aiming at educational control and success. "The cultural-existential discussion that used to be the point and the end of education, increasingly found solutions in a specialized interdisciplinary and professionally oriented education locked up in educational institutions" (Saevi 2012, p. 180).

Where do we want to go or where *can* we go with this new educational reality? Education has become a commodity and a means for economic interests; therefore, the alternative response might be seen as a moral, existential one for the humanity of the next generation. Historically, European education "had stronger structures of a rather contradictory human existential reflection on what education was and should be, and a certain moral hesitation toward how we as educators influence and socialize the child" (Saevi 2012, p. 180). This hermeneutic attitude to life, life forms, actions, and intents is a quality also of the re-imagined existential education represented in this volume. An educational hierarchy is not one of dominion, of human resources as knowledge and skills, but of educational structures that give "priority of human existence and humanity above objects and issues, personal responsibility above social conventionality, and the experiential common moral distinctions between right and wrong, good and evil" (Saevi 2012, p. 182).

A new language is required to name, challenge, and reveal that which disappears as common sense to educationists overshadowed by neoliberalism. The phenomenologist and educational theorists featured here reject objectifying language in ways that connect fully and concretely with the everyday lives of educators and students. Language that is evocative and rich restores the unique, dismantles the technical articulations designed to control education processes, and offers instead a language that engages us, involves us, and opens spaces for self-reflection, so we may see more clearly the neoliberal landscape we face in our relationships with broader social forces. Reflection is not just thinking and it is never enough just to think critically. We need to be moved and motivated to understand education, classrooms, schools, and the pedagogical lives of children and youth differently than on offer by the neoliberal narrative.

This book opens a space for reflection by allowing us to reclaim human *becoming* at the heart of the educational project. In contributing an alternative language for education, we believe something new can be said.

Structure of the book

The book has been structured as four distinct parts to feature phenomenologists and educational theorists responding to overarching themes that speak to education as central to the human story in all its contingencies and messiness. Education and how we speak of it is inherently dialogical – an intergenerational and complex process. So, too, is this book designed to be attuned to the dialogical nature of hermeneutics. Educational theorists and phenomenologists problematize contemporary socio-political educational change and offer an alternative story for education and raise important questions to bring the practical, every-day life world of educators and students into recognizable focus.

Authors representing a diversity of theoretical/philosophical and phenomenological approaches contribute chapters to each of the four sections organized around general themes. One of the unique features of this volume is that each of the sections is introduced to the reader in a manner that explicates and contextualizes the contributions as not simply theoretical endeavours but truly practical conversations that open up new avenues of interpretation and inquiry, to re-imagine a new language for education by taking up Husserl's call of going "back to the things themselves" (Husserl 2001, p. 168) and re-engaging with that which is originary in education, to what it means to educate, to teach, to learn, and thereby bring up the next generation.

References

Biesta, G.J.J., 2011. Disciplines and theory in the academic study of education: A comparative analysis of the Anglo-American and Continental constructions in the field. *Pedagogy, Culture and Society*, 19 (2), 175–192. doi:10.1080/1468/366.2011.582255

Giroux, H., 2019. Neoliberalism and the weaponizing of language and education. *Race & Class*, 61 (1), 26–45.

Husserl, E., 2001/1900/1901. *Logical Investigations*. Edited by D. Moran. 2nd ed. 2 vols. London: Routledge.

Lingis, A., 2018. Cause, choice, chance. *Phenomenology & Practice*, 12 (2), 5–14.

Masschelein, J., 2011. Experimentum Scholae: The world once more . . . but not (Yet) finished. *Studies in Philosophy and Education*, 30, 529–535. doi:10.1007/s11217-011-9257-4

Mollenhauer, K., 1983. *Vergessene Zusammenhänge. Über Kultur und Erziehung*. München: Juventa.

Patrick, F., 2013. Neoliberalism, the knowledge economy, and the learner: Challenging the inevitability of the commodified self as an outcome of education. *ISRN Education*. Available from: http://dx.doi.org/10.1155/2013/108705

Saevi, T., 2012. Why Mollenhauer matters. A response to Klaus Mollenhauer's book Forgotten Connections. On Culture and Upbringing. Translated into English, edited and with an introduction by Norm Friesen. *Phenomenology & Practice*, 6 (2), 180–191.

Van Manen, M., 2016. *Phenomenology of practice. Meaning-giving methods in phenomenological research and writing*. New York: Routledge.

Part I

On education
The phenomenon of education reconsidered

Gert Biesta

It may seem obvious for a book on education to start with a section on education and, for a book that seeks to bring education and phenomenology into conversation, to start with a section on the *phenomenon* of education. Some may argue that this is actually not needed, because education is such a widespread and omnipresent phenomenon that we already know what it is, and that from there we should swiftly move to the study of education rather than focusing on the phenomenon that is supposed to be studied. Others may argue that a book on education should not pay that much attention to education, because what really matters nowadays is not education but learning.

The first line of argument will be familiar to readers in the English-speaking world and in countries influenced by developments there, because in the English-speaking world the study of education, at universities, colleges, and other institutions, is generally seen as a multi-disciplinary effort that has "education" as its object (see Biesta 2011). In those countries and settings, therefore, the psychology of education, the sociology of education, the philosophy of education, and the history of education have become established ways to conduct the study of education. While these approaches have generated and are continuing to generate interesting insights, the question that is often "forgotten" is what education "itself" is actually about or, to put it differently, what kind of assumptions need to come into play before education can actually become an object of study.

Even if one is able to find a school, college or university – which may have become more of a challenge nowadays given the way in which schools, hospitals, prisons, shops, and office blocks have become almost indistinguishable from each other; they all seem to be based on a similar architectural grammar – there is still the question what one would focus on, and why, if one has the intention to study the education happening in those buildings. Should the focus be on teachers and, if so, how can they be identified? Or on students? Would it be relevant to include janitors? Should the building itself be brought in as an educational actor? Is everything that teachers do educationally relevant? Such questions show that the study of education cannot skip over the question of education itself and, more specifically, the question of the phenomenon of education.

Yet here the second line of thought comes to the fore, as many nowadays would argue and do actually argue that education is all about learners and their learning. The "learnification" (Biesta 2010) of educational discourse and practice has indeed been hailed by some as a liberating paradigm shift (see, for example, Barr and Tagg 1995) that has helped education and educators to focus on what really should matter in education. That this shift is seen as liberating is particularly due to a prevalent but nonetheless misleading idea that education can only be enacted as a process in which teachers control students, where teachers and their teaching are seen as the major culprit and the turn towards learners and their learning as an emancipatory "escape" from this set-up.

While it cannot be denied that people can learn and do learn, the simple fact that people can do so and will do so without education and without the efforts from educators already indicates that learning is not enough if we wish to capture what education is about. One might say that it only takes one to learn, but that it takes two for education to happen: an educator and what in some languages, but not that often in English, is referred to as an "educandus," that is, the one being educated or receiving education. What the "educandus" is supposed to do with the education that is directed at him or her, what the relationship between educator and educandus actually is and is about, whether these are necessarily relationships between human beings or whether other actors can come into play, how intentional or not the actions of educator and educandus are or should be, what the purposes are that should "frame" the interaction, are all questions that need to be asked in order to begin to get a sense of the phenomenon of education, particularly when we acknowledge that this phenomenon "occurs," so we might say, beyond learning (Biesta 2006).

All this is not helped by the fact that the English word "education" carries an ambivalence with it, as it can refer to a process, to an (intentional) activity, to a practice, and to an institution, to name but a few options. It is particularly the difference between education as process and education as (intentional) activity that matters here, because when we use the word education to refer to a process, it is quite easy to claim or suggest that this is essential to a process of learning. Bearing in mind, therefore, that education can also refer to an intentional activity – something an educator does – it becomes possible to see a difference between education and learning and thus to raise different questions about the phenomenon of education itself.

It is for all these reasons, then, that this book opens with four chapters that seek to focus on the phenomenon of education, providing some groundwork against which other contributions in this collection can be read. Gert Biesta opens this section with a chapter on the "givenness of teaching," in order to move closer to an "encounter" with the educational phenomenon. He does this against the background of the recent turn in educational theory and practice towards the *language* of learning and towards the *practice* of learning, where the learner has been put in the centre of the educational endeavour and the teacher has been moved sideways. In his contribution he argues that the educational phenomenon cannot be captured in terms of learning but needs a notion of teaching and, more specifically, a notion of teaching that stands on itself and cannot be reduced to or deduced from learning; a notion of teaching, therefore, as something that is radically *given*. In his chapter he tries to argue why this is so and why this matters educationally. In his discussion on the work of Jean-Luc Marion he also shows why the question of the givenness of teaching goes to the heart of phenomenology itself so that, through the exploration of the givenness of teaching, we may actually come closer to an encounter with the educational phenomenon itself.

Scott Webster's contribution, "Uncovering what educators desire through Kierkegaard's loving phenomenology," situates the discussion with the impact of neoliberalism on contemporary educational practices; an impact, as he argues, that actively marginalizes *education* and opposes democracy. The expansion of the neoliberal agenda is not only being achieved by authoritative top-down policies being imposed upon educational institutions, but the agenda is also being furthered through educators themselves, perhaps unknowingly. As with all ideologies, neoliberalism can be embodied, and demonstrated by those who willingly enact reform requirements with their incentives, desiring to attain personal advantages and rewards for successfully doing so. By drawing primarily on Kierkegaard's understanding of phenomenology as repetition, involving love as a way-of-being, Webster argues that his insights can be utilized to confront any inadvertent self-interested ontology of *homo economicus* which may have become embodied by educators.

Joris Vlieghe and Piotr Zamojski continue the discussion with a further attempt at "approaching education on its own terms," as they put it in the title of their chapter, offering a phenomenological analysis. Vlieghe and Zamojski follow Hannah Arendt in her attempt to address the central question in philosophy of education: *What is the essence of education?* Put in more phenomenological terms this question reads: what exactly does it mean to educate and to be educated? They show that this question can be approached from two radically different and mutually opposed perspectives, and that it makes an immense difference which side one takes. The opposition, so they argue, is one between transcendence and immanence – a distinction they explore through the work of Giorgio Agamben. Although the transcendent perspective is today the most dominant, Vlieghe and Zamojski suggest that phenomenology can help to counter this dominant (meta)theoretical position that regards education merely as a means. In relation to this, they make an attempt at fleshing out what it would mean to approach education from a purely immanent perspective, which they briefly illustrate through a discussion of three essential educational issues: schooling, freedom, and love for the world.

Andrew Foran, in his chapter on "Pedagogical Practice," concludes the first section of the book. Taking his starting point in the observation that hundreds of years of institutionalized education have solidified a global hold on how children and young people are schooled, he argues that this comparative and competitive educative process has impacted significantly on the teacher's world, absorbing educators by *everydayness* in competing professionalized tensions and pressures of standardization. He shows that teacher education in Canada has tended to ignore pedagogical practices in teacher preparation in favour of government initiatives that promote the value of testing scores and government-controlled curricula. For the last 25 years, teacher education thus has shifted from building a practice on relational encounters with pupils to that of being a manager directing learning services. As a result, teachers are largely ignoring the personal and non-professional significance implied in the term "*pedagogy*." By reviving a pedagogical practice in teacher education, and exploring the lived experiences of teachers, phenomenology can position pedagogical priorities over social and psychological norms and academic outcomes, precisely because a phenomenological examination will challenge an outcomes-based and assessment driven education that is not oriented to an open future for the child but forecloses on multiple possibilities by insisting on pre-established criteria, percentiles, and performance norms. In his chapter he focuses on what many teachers still will claim as essential in the educational exchange – pedagogy – namely the value of relationality between teachers and pupils.

References

Barr, R.B. and Tagg, J., 1995. From teaching to learning: A new paradigm for undergraduate education. *Change* (Nov/Dec), 13–25.

Biesta, G.J.J., 2006. *Beyond learning. Democratic education for a human future*. Boulder, CO: Paradigm Publishers.

Biesta, G.J.J., 2010. *Good education in an age of measurement: Ethics, politics, democracy*. Boulder, CO: Paradigm Publishers.

Biesta, G.J.J., 2011. Disciplines and theory in the academic study of education: A Comparative Analysis of the Anglo-American and continental construction of the field. *Pedagogy, Culture and Society*, 19 (2), 175–192.

Chapter 1

On the givenness of teaching
Encountering the educational phenomenon

Gert Biesta

Introduction

When, about ten years ago, I coined the word 'learnification' (see Biesta 2009), it was first of all to denote the problematic impact of the rise of the 'new language of learning' on the discourse and practice of education. My main concern at the time was that the emergence of notions such as 'learner,' 'learning environment,' facilitator of learning' and 'lifelong learning' were all referring to education in terms of learning, without asking what the learning was *about* and, more importantly, what it was supposed to be *for*. It was particularly the absence of a vigorous debate about the purpose of education that worried me most. It prompted me to propose that education should always be concerned with and orientated towards *three* domains of purpose, which I referred to as qualification, socialisation and subjectification respectively.

I think that, ten years on, the learnification-thesis still stands.[1] Talk about learning is still rife in educational circles, new expressions such as 'deep learning,' 'brain-based learning' and 'machine learning' have entered the conversation, and policy makers continue to produce remarkable sentences such as that schools should "deliver at least one year's growth in learning for every student every year."[2] While there is evidence of a growing interest in the question of the purpose(s) of education (see, e.g., Hattie and Nepper Larsen 2020. Onderwijsraad 2016), much of what can be found in policy, research and practice continues to have a rather one-dimensional focus on learning, also due to the dominance of the frameworks promoted by the global education measurement industry.

There was, however, a further dimension to the learnification-thesis which was less prominent in my initial argument but which, over the past decade, has become an important strand in my thinking, writing and teaching. The key point here is the insight that teaching (and the whole spectrum of intentional educational endeavours more generally) *should not necessarily result in learning*, which also means that teaching *should not necessarily aim at learning*. The idea, in other words, is that there is more to teaching than learning, just as there is more to education than learning. In order to bring this 'more' to the fore, it is important to 'free' teaching from learning (Biesta 2015). I found helpful suggestions for exploring this dimension of the learnification-thesis in work from American analytic philosophy of education which, interestingly, largely predated the rise of the new language of learning.

The most explicit position here was taken by Paul Komisar who argued that "learning is not what the 'teacher' intends to produce" (Komisar 1968, p. 183) but that the intention of teaching might better be captured in terms of the 'awareness' of an 'auditor' – not a learner or student for Komisar – "*who is successfully becoming aware of the point of the act* [of teaching]" (Komisar 1968, p. 191; emphasis in original). And this awareness may cover a whole range of different responses, of which learning is only *one* possibility, but neither the sole nor the only destination. One important reason for creating a distance between teaching and learning has to do with the fact that there is more to *life* than learning. There is a range of ways in which human beings exist and the task of education should rather be about opening up this range of 'existential possibilities' (Biesta 2015) for our students, rather than only providing them with the position of the learner. The point here is also political, particularly with reference to attempts by policy makers and politicians to force people into 'the learning position,' most notably through the 'politics' of *lifelong* learning (see Biesta 2018).

It is against this background that, in recent years, I have started to make an explicit case for the re*dis*covery of teaching, which I also see as a recovery of teaching (Biesta 2017a). This is partly in order to restore teaching to its proper place in the educational endeavour – to give teaching back to education[3] (Biesta 2012) – and not see it as something outdated and of the past that we should be embarrassed about. And it is partly in order to highlight that what is distinctive about education is *not* the phenomenon of learning – which, after all, can also happen outside of education and can occur without teaching – but precisely the presence of and the encounter with teaching. Whereas learning is *accidental* to education, teaching, so I wish to suggest, is *essential* to education, albeit that the question what teaching is and how it might or should be enacted does, of course, need careful consideration in order not to fall back on narrow and naive notions of teaching as one-directional instruction or teaching as authoritarian control.

Whereas learning in some way always originates from the learner, that is, from the one who seeks to acquire knowledge, skills and understanding and approaches the world as a 'resource' where this can be found – like an act of foraging – teaching moves in the opposite direction as it comes to the student from 'elsewhere' (and again the question of what this 'elsewhere' is requires further consideration, also because it is not necessarily the teacher who is the origin of teaching; on this see also Prange 2005). Earlier (Biesta 2013), I have explored the latter dynamic in terms of the *gift* of teaching, arguing that it is important to make a distinction between *learning from* (someone or something) and *being taught by* (someone or something). In this chapter I wish to extend the exploration of teaching, by highlighting three dimensions of the way in which the 'givenness' of teaching manifests itself and by showing why and how this givenness matters educationally. In my earlier explorations writings from Levinas, Derrida and Kierkegaard have been particularly helpful. In the next section I will discuss some ideas from the work of Jean-Luc Marion who, in my view, provides a helpful and important 'next step' in the philosophical discussion at stake.

Being given

Over the past four decades Jean-Luc Marion has made major contributions in a number of fields, including the history of philosophy, theology and phenomenology. Even a proper reconstruction of Marion's contributions to phenomenology – articulated in three main volumes and numerous other publications (see particularly Marion 1998, 2002a, 2002b, 2011, 2016) – lies well beyond the scope of this chapter. More modestly, I will pick up one theme from Marion's writing and will utilise one particular 'way in,' in order to shed light on the phenomenon of givenness which, for Marion, also has to do with the givenness of the phenomenon.

The question Marion has been pursuing consistently in his writings is whether and, if so, how we can make sense of givenness – although even phrasing the question in that way raises a problem, because if we really try to make sense of givenness, then such givenness does precisely *not* depend on our acts of sense making. This already indicates, first, that Marion's question has an epistemological dimension, namely whether knowledge is constructed by us – either fully or partially – or given to us. Second, Marion's question has a theological dimension, which has to do with the question whether revelation is possible or whether everything that comes to us from 'beyond' is in some way of our own making. This indicates, third, that Marion's question also gets us into the field of hermeneutics in terms of whether the human being is first and foremost an interpreting being – a meaning-making animal, as some might say (see, e.g., Burke 1966) – or whether there is something that precedes and must precede our acts of meaning-making. This, fourth, means that Marion's question is also the question of phenomenology, starting from Husserl's ambition to go back to the things themselves rather than our interpretation of these things. Which, and this is the fifth dimension, also raises the question whether everything starts from the 'I' or whether something 'precedes' the 'I.'

One has to admire Marion for his ambition to engage with this cluster of questions, because they are not only the big questions of modern philosophy but perhaps first and foremost the big questions of human existence itself. In one sense, they therefore are of all times, but they also speak to major contemporary issues. They speak, for example, to neoliberalism by asking whether the self is indeed in the centre of the world and the world is just there for the 'I' to conquer and master – which means that Marion's questions speak both to the ecological crisis and the crisis of democracy. But they also ask whether a religious worldview, a 'belief' in transcendence, is outdated superstition, or whether the encounter with transcendence is more difficult to shrug off than many might think. And from an educational perspective, Marion's 'intervention' is important because it asks whether teaching is actually possible, or whether the reduction of everything educational to learning is inevitable.

On givenness

One of the shortest formulations Marion provides of his thoughts on givenness is through the 'principle' that "everything that shows itself must first give itself" (Marion 2011, p. 19).[4] The phrase already contains an important epistemological point, because it suggests that before any intentional 'act' of knowing can take place, something must have given itself to the knower. Marion emphasises that his principle does not articulate an interest in *what* is given but in the *how* of givenness. Marion is interested in "givenness as *a mode of phenomenality*, as the *how* or *manner* of the phenomenon" (Marion 2011, p. 19). This is not about "the immediate given, the perceptive content, or the lived experience of consciousness – in short, of some*thing* [emph. GB] that is given, but instead of the style of its phenomenalization *insofar as* it is given" (Marion 2011, p. 19). This means that Marion is after a phenomenology of the phenomenon of givenness, so to speak, not an ontology or metaphysics of givenness (see Marion 2011, p. 20).

An ontology or metaphysics of givenness would not only try to specify the exact nature of the 'what' that is given, but would also try to specify *what it is that gives* this 'what.' The problem with such an ambition is that it goes 'beyond' givenness itself and would therefore cease to be an 'account' of givenness. Moreover, it would, in its ambition to go 'behind' the phenomenon of givenness, deny the very idea that what shows itself must first give itself. It would, in a sense, *refuse* givenness. This is why givenness 'needs' a phenomenology, so to speak.

What is exciting about Marion's work is that he pursues this 'agenda' in the strictest way possible. One important line of argumentation challenges the (epistemological) assumption that everything that shows itself is supposed to show itself to a pre-existing consciousness. It will not be too difficult to see that on such a view the phenomenon begins to disappear – or actually disappears completely – because its manifestation, its givenness, is made totally dependent upon the activities of a knowing consciousness. This is the Kantian view of knowledge which starts from a 'transcendental ego' that comes 'before' the world and that sees phenomena as objects that appear according to the conditions of experience (see Marion 2016, p. 47). That is why Marion argues that taking givenness seriously means that we have to assume – or perhaps 'accept' is a better word here – that the phenomenon "shows itself in itself and from itself" (Marion 2016, p. 48) which also means that it "gives itself from itself"

(Marion 2016, p. 48), and is not given or assumed to be given by something or someone else.

A third reduction

It is here that the connection with phenomenology becomes apparent, because "in its most radical ambitions, philosophy, in the form of phenomenology, has had no other goal than this one: to allow the phenomenon to broaden out itself in itself, and to show itself from itself" (Marion 2016, p. 48) – or, in the words of Husserl: back to the things themselves! This reveals a second original theme in Marion's work that has to do with the status of 'reduction' in phenomenology and, more specifically, with his claim that phenomenology needs a 'third' reduction – not just a reduction to the given object (Husserl) or to be being of the given object (Heidegger) but to givenness *itself*. Reduction, as Marion explains, "consists in not taking everything I perceive for granted and in not receiving everything that happens to me with the same degree of evidence and thus of certainty but in each case to question what is actually given in order to distinguish it from what is only pieced together, inferred, or, so to say, acquired in a roundabout way, indirectly" (Marion 2017, pp. 72–73). This was central to Husserl's 'return to the things themselves,' and also to Heidegger's attempt at articulating the difference between things and their existence (beings and their Being [in German: sein]). Yet Marion's main point is that, in a sense, Husserl and Heidegger didn't go far enough with their reductions of the given. Husserl 'stopped' at the object, and Heidegger at the being of the object, but for Marion "objectness (Husserl) and beingness (Heidegger) only offer specific and possible cases, but surely not the most legitimate ones, of the naming of givenness" (Marion 2017, p. 78). Hence the need "for a third, more original reduction . . . namely the reduction to givenness" (Marion 2017, p. 79).

Two attitudes to things

I don't have the space to discuss the detail of Marion's phenomenology of givenness, but wish, in concluding this section, to say a bit more about the encounter with the phenomenon of givenness in more practical or everyday language, also in order to draw out some of the implications for the 'I.' And all this is important 'groundwork' for the exploration of teaching because the very possibility of a notion of teaching – or perhaps we can begin to say: of the phenomenon of teaching – depends in some way on the answer to the question whether givenness can exist in itself, or remains dependent on the cognitive acts of the ego (in educational terms: the 'learner'). How, then, can we 'make sense' (with the caveat mentioned earlier) of what is happening here, and also, what does taking givenness absolutely seriously imply for the self?

Marion's response starts from the suggestion that we can have two 'attitudes' towards things. One attitude, and this is "the most widespread attitude, the one for which we are trained" (Marion 2017, p. 83), consists in "reducing the chances that those [objects] around us will surprise us; consequently, we continually learn how to better control them" (Marion 2017, p. 83). In this attitude "we really count on being able to anticipate situations and accidents, to be able to react, to control, to correct, to secure" (Marion 2017, p. 83). This is a world where we find ourselves surrounded by objects, "which, being essentially functional, function because they are intended and conceived to function to our advantage," and this is done "so that we are in the centre" (Marion 2017, p. 83). Through this attitude "we live in a world that we organize such that we retain from it only those things that can be constituted as objects, only what we can grasp with our intelligibility, under the control of a quasi-master and possessor of nature." (Marion 2017, p. 83) We constitute such an object-ive world in order to rule out danger. Yet, so Marion asks, "what does ruling out danger mean if not keeping away from the unexpected," from that "which cannot be constituted as object, that against which one cannot protect oneself?" (Marion 2017, p. 83).

While this attitude is all good for thinking ahead, for what can be anticipated, "this rationality . . . does not want any of the rest [but] only retains this layer of reality that one can call the object" (Marion 2017, p. 84). "But the object offers a very thin and superficial layer of things. It leaves to the side . . . everything it cannot foresee, everything it cannot anticipate, what is said to be unknowable" (Marion 2017, p. 84). Yet it is precisely here "that the given is displayed because it characterizes what among things resists objectification and is given by its own initiative" (Marion 2017, p. 84). It is not so much – and probably not at all – for us to 'find' the given, that what gives itself. Rather, as Marion explains, "in the given, in the phenomenon inasmuch as it gives itself according to its character as nonobject . . . a place and moment are described where the ego must know how to allow itself to be found and which it does not decide" (Marion 2017, p. 85). In this way the ego leaves its central position, "obeys the event, and sees without foreseeing," as Marion puts it, which is precisely the opposite from the seeing-of-objects. Thus we encounter a reversal of our objective relation to the world. "In the case of the given, we find ourselves commanded by the thing, summoned to come experience it" (Marion 2017, p. 85).[5]

Although 'givenness' so conceived may give the suggestion that it requires passive receptivity from the side of the ego, Marion stresses that the term 'passivity' is not good enough precisely "because I cannot remain passive in front of the event: I make myself available or I avoid it, I take a risk or I run away, in short, I still decide, and I respond even by refusing to respond" (Marion 2017, p. 85). This means that in order to 'become passive' in such an encounter, "a certain kind of activity is required; one must leave oneself exposed to things with a certain amount of courage" (Marion 2017, pp. 85–86; see also Biesta 2017b). This, then, opens up "a different regime of phenomenality imposed on a different regime of subjectivity," as Marion puts it. Here the subject is no longer *before* the world, *before* the phenomenon – in space and in time – but rather "receives itself from what it receives" (Marion 2017, p. 86). The word that Marion uses for this different 'stature' of subjectivity, is, in French, the *adonné*, usually translated as the 'gifted.'

This reveals that Marion's attempt to 'think' givenness in its own terms – but perhaps we can now say: Marion's attempt to expose himself to givenness and encourage us to expose ourselves as well – is not just a matter of epistemology, and not just a matter of phenomenology, although the question of givenness opens up these fields in new ways as well, but is also an existential matter, a matter that concerns the existence of the 'I' or self or subject. That is why Marion emphasises that "everything takes on a different meaning if what happens to me is given to me from elsewhere" (Marion 2017, p. 38). If what happens to me "is a duplication and a product of myself, then even the most marvellous things lose their meaning," but if one instead thinks of the world as "essentially an experience of heteronomy, in other words as election, then everything is worth being lived, being expected, being desired, everything merits making an effort on its behalf" (Marion 2017, p. 38). Yet before trying to respond to the call "there is the more difficult thing, which is . . . to discover that there is a call, that is to say, being able to interpret what is as what comes to us" (Marion 2017, p. 39). And "this decision to take things as calls . . . decides everything else" (Marion 2017, p. 39).

The givenness of teaching: Three examples

I have already referred to the redefinition of teaching as facilitating learning; a redefinition that is part of a more general shift from teaching to learning and one instance of the ongoing learnification of education. The shift from teaching to learning is itself not entirely without reason. It is a response to authoritarian forms of education in which teaching is enacted as a form of control. The shift from teaching to learning is also a response to rather poor and unimaginative educational practices that are nowadays often referred to as traditional, didactic or transmissive teaching, although these three qualifications are often misleading. And the shift from teaching to learning is also the result of the influence of constructivist theories of learning and social-cultural approaches to education that all, in some way, argue that everything hangs on the activities of 'the learner,' with or without some scaffolding. In this regard we might say that contemporary education is still remarkably Kantian, and has perhaps even become more Kantian in recent years at least, that is, where it concerns its epistemological underpinnings.

All this has moved 'the learner' to the centre of the educational endeavour and has manoeuvred the teacher to the side-line – coach, facilitator, fellow-learner, friend, critical or otherwise, but hardly ever teacher. And it has given the impression that teaching is outdated, undesirable and, according to constructivist 'dogma,' even impossible. While for some this can mean nothing but the end of teaching, I wish, in this section to point at three dimensions or 'manifestations' of teaching that are not that easy to dispense with, at least not from an educational angle which, as I will argue as well, is fundamentally different from and hence not reducible to learning.

Being given what you didn't ask for

In learner-centred education we don't just hear that the work of the teacher should focus on learners and their learning, we also increasingly hear that learners should take responsibility for their own learning, should self-regulate their learning, and should take ownership of their learning, as all this will supposedly make the learning better. Such arguments are not just given in relation to the *process* of learning, but also with regard to its *content*. When it is suggested, for example, that students should set their own learning goals, it often also means that students decide about what they should be learning, for example because they have come to the conclusion that this is their specific 'learning need.' This line of thinking is further amplified because of the impact of neoliberal, market-driven reforms of education in which students – or their parents – are increasingly positioned as customers in the learning market and teachers and educational institutions as the providers. The key idea is that the responsibility of teachers, schools, colleges and universities is to satisfy their customers by giving them what they ask for.

Yet here the argument begins to break down, because an important rationale for education is precisely to give students what they *didn't* ask for, first and foremost because *they didn't even know they could ask for it*. This is the good old and nonetheless still relevant rationale of liberal education which always seeks to bring students "*beyond* the present and the particular" (Bailey 1984). But it also has to do with the important distinction between *servicing* the needs of 'customers' – which is what shops should do – and contributing to the *definition* of such needs – which characterises the work of professionals (on the distinction see Feinberg 2001). Whereas everyone is of course free to learn what they want to learn, the whole point of education is to give students *more* than what they ask for, that is, give them what they didn't ask for, were not looking for, were not even aware they might be looking for, and so on. This has to do with teaching as turning (Plato) or teaching as pointing (Prange) or attention formation (Stiegler), that is with the 'gesture' where as teachers we say, in all kinds of ways: look, there is something there that may be important for you to encounter, explore, have a look at, engage with, stay with, let into your life, and so on.

Teaching as double truth giving

The givenness of teaching not only plays a role in the 'what' of education – the question of curriculum – but also in the 'how' – the question of 'didactics' (to use a Continental notion), which has to do with Kierkegaard's suggestion that teaching is a matter of 'double truth giving' (see Kierkegaard 1985, Westphal 2008). Put simply, the idea here is that teaching is not just about giving students the truth, as Kierkegaard puts it, but also about giving them the conditions "of recognizing it as truth" (Westphal 2008, p. 25; see also Kierkegaard 1985, p. 14). There is a complex philosophical discussion in the background (which is actually first of all a theological discussion about the possibility of revelation; see Westphal 2008), but the point Kierkegaard is making here is actually remarkably practical and 'down to earth' as well, as Kierkegaard is providing a very effective critique of the idea that teaching is simply about the transmission of knowledge or information.

Kierkegaard's point is that in order to recognize something *as* knowledge one doesn't just need the 'material' itself but also needs to have, and be on the inside of, the 'frame' within which something makes sense, can be appreciated as knowledge, and so on. The difficult work of teaching is not that of providing students with information but is actually that of pulling them 'inside' the frame within which information can begin to make sense. It is precisely this latter act of 'pulling' that goes fundamentally *beyond* what students themselves can do because it is about encountering something that lies precisely *beyond* their current understanding. It is therefore something students can construct themselves from their current understanding, but is something that 'breaks through,' so we might say; something that is literally given (rather than taken).

Being given yourself

If the first and second manifestation of the givenness of teaching can be said to belong to the domains of qualification and socialisation, the third dimension of givenness has to do with the domain of subjectification. Put simply, subjectification refers to the existence of the student as subject and not as object. The word 'existence' is important here, because subject-ness is precisely to be understood as a way of existing. It is located, in other words, on the existential plane which means that it is a first-person matter – my existence as subject is something no one else can do for me.

This means that subjectification as an educational dynamic has nothing to do with psycho-socio-neurological development, or with enculturation or cultivation. While such processes contribute to the formation of individuals and can even be understood as a process of individuation, our existence as subject is of a different 'order.' To put it briefly, the question of our existence as subject is not about who we become but about what we will do with who we have become. If the first question is the question of who we are, the second question – that of subject-ness – is the question of how we are, how we will exist, how we will lead our life, how we will respond to the challenges that come our way.

Whereas in the English language these differences tend to disappear rather quickly under the one word of 'education,' the German tradition has the interesting distinction between two modalities of education, that of Bildung and that of Erziehung. Following Benner (2015) we might say that Bildung is about education as cultivation, whereas Erziehung is about education as subjectification. And the interesting and in my view very helpful phrase Benner uses in this context is to define Erziehung as 'Aufforderung zur Selbsttätigkeit.' This literally translates as summoning to self-action but the injunction here is not to be active, and also not to just be *you*rself, but rather to be *a* self – rather than just someone. Positively we might say that subject-ness emerges in response to the question 'Hey, you there, where are you?' – and this simple phrase captures the 'essence' of 'Erziehung' rather well (see also Biesta in press). Negatively I am reminded of an interesting formulation Jacques Rancière (2010) has given of the work of the emancipatory schoolmaster, namely as the one who forbids his students the pleasure of *not* being a subject – as it is indeed much easier to let other people decide for you than to have to decide for yourself. The point I am making here is that our subject-ness is not something that we construct from the inside-out, so to speak, but that it is in response to this question – which can take many different forms and manifestations of course – that the self is given to itself, as Marion might put it. And this is the third way in which we encounter a radical givenness in teaching.

Conclusion

In this chapter I have tried to make a case for an understanding of the educational phenomenon in terms of teaching – in terms of what comes to us rather than what emanates from us. I have discussed this in the context of the ongoing learnification of educational discourse and practice, have indicated some underlying philosophical issues, and have provided three examples of the manifestation of givenness of teaching that suggest why education cannot be reduced to or deduced from learning, but needs the 'gesture' of teaching as the encounter with what necessarily comes from 'elsewhere.' I do not expect that the ideas presented in this chapter will resolve these issues once and for all – the learning industry is powerful and extensive – but I do hope that I have managed to come a little closer to an encounter with the educational phenomenon itself.

Notes

1 The term seems to have spread, with, to date, close to 10,000 hits in google and close to 700 items in google scholar (last accessed 8 August 2019).
2 I read this in *Through growth to achievement: The report of the review to achieve educational excellence in Australian schools*, Department of Education and Training, 2018, p. xii.
3 Note that this is different from the ambition to give education back to teachers.
4 The sentence continues, in brackets, with "even if everything that gives itself nevertheless does not show itself without remainder."
5 Marion mentions a painting in the cloister of the convent of Trinity-on-the-Mount which has a secret point where one must be situated to see the painting. This point "is

determined by the painting and not by the spectator" so that "the spectator must obey the painting in order to see it" (Marion 2017, pp. 84–85). Marion calls the principle at stake here 'anamorphosis.'

References

Bailey, C.H., 1984. *Beyond the present and the particular: A theory of liberal education.* London: Routledge.
Benner, D., 2015. *Allgemeine Pädagogik. 8. Auflage.* Weinheim/München: Juventa.
Biesta, G.J.J., 2009. Good education in an age of measurement: On the need to reconnect with the question of purpose in education. *Educational Assessment, Evaluation and Accountability*, 21 (1), 33–46.
Biesta, G.J.J., 2012. Giving teaching back to education. Responding to the disappearance of the teacher. *Phenomenology and Practice*, 6 (2), 35–49.
Biesta, G.J.J., 2013. Receiving the gift of teaching: From 'learning from' to 'being taught by.' *Studies in Philosophy and Education*, 32 (5), 449–461.
Biesta, G.J.J., 2015. Freeing teaching from learning: Opening up existential possibilities in educational relationships. *Studies in Philosophy and Education*, 34 (3), 229–243. doi:10.1007/s11217-014-9454-z
Biesta, G.J.J., 2017a. *The rediscovery of teaching.* London/New York: Routledge.
Biesta, G.J.J., 2017b. *Letting art teach: Art education after Joseph Beuys.* Arnhem: ArtEZ Press.
Biesta, G.J.J., 2018. Interrupting the politics of learning, changing the discourse of education. In: K. Illeris, ed. *Contemporary theories of learning. Learning theorists . . . in their own words. Second revised edition.* London/New York: Routledge, 243–259.
Biesta, G.J.J., in press. Can the prevailing description of educational reality be considered complete? On the Parks-Eichmann paradox, spooky action at a distance, and a missing dimension in the theory of education. *Policy Futures in Education.*
Burke, K., 1966. *Language as symbolic action.* Oakland, CA: University of California Press.
Feinberg, W., 2001. Choice, autonomy, need-definition and educational reform. *Studies in Philosophy and Education*, 20 (5), 402–409.
Hattie, J. and Nepper Larsen, S., 2020. *The purposes of education: A conversation between John Hattie and Steen Nepper Larsen.* New York/London: Routledge.
Kierkegaard, S., 1985. Philosophical fragments. In: H.V. Hong and E.H. Hong, eds. *Kierkegaard's writings VII.* Princeton, NJ: Princeton University Press.
Komisar, P., 1968. Teaching: Act and enterprise. *Studies in Philosophy and Education*, 6 (2), 168–193.
Marion, J.-L., 1998. *Reduction and givenness: Investigations of Husserl, Heidegger, and phenomenology.* Evanston, IL: Northwestern University Press.
Marion, J.-L., 2002a. *Being given: Towards a phenomenology of givenness.* Stanford, CA: Stanford University Press.
Marion, J.-L., 2002b. *In excess: Studies of saturated phenomena.* New York: Fordham University Press.
Marion, J.-L., 2011. *The reason of the gift.* Charlottesville, VA: University of Virginia Press.
Marion, J.-L., 2016. *Givenness and revelation.* Oxford: Oxford University Press.
Marion, J.-L., 2017. *The rigor of things. Conversations with Dan Arbib.* New York: Fordham University Press.
Onderwijsraad, 2016. *De volle breedte van onderwijskwaliteit.* Den Haag: Onderwijsraad.

Prange, K., 2005. *Die Zeigestruktur der Erziehung: Grundriss der operativen Pädagogik.* Paderborn: Ferdinand Schöningh.

Rancière, J., 2010. On ignorant schoolmasters. *In*: C. Bingham and G.J.J. Biesta, eds. *Jacques Rancière: Education, truth, emancipation.* London/New York: Continuum, 1–24.

Westphal, M., 2008. *Levinas and Kierkegaard in dialogue.* Bloomington/Indianapolis: Indiana University Press.

Chapter 2

Uncovering what educators desire through Kierkegaard's loving phenomenology

Scott Webster

Introduction: embodied neoliberalism

Neoliberalism is the all-pervasive ideological influence behind the rise of globalisation which has been described by Giroux (2014, p. 47) as perhaps 'the most dangerous ideology of our time'. Neoliberalism values individuals and individual corporations to grow in materialistic wealth and influence and thus is understood as promoting 'private goods'. Such growth is enhanced through an acceptance of capitalistic 'free' markets and is stymied by collectives and governments which in contrast can value public goods over private goods. Consequently Harvey (2005, pp. 66, 69) identifies that neoliberalists are 'profoundly suspicious of democracy', discouraging opportunities for people 'to construct strong collective institutions' and seeking to put limits on 'democratic governance'. What may have begun as a 'suspicion' of democracy by neoliberalists, has, according to Giroux (2014), morphed into a 'war' against democracy and education. This ought to be of huge concern for educators, particularly for those who envision that education is inextricably linked with participatory democracy and the public good. Democracy, along with freedom and justice, are not ideologies like neoliberalism but are ideals which are characteristics of a public if its members desire what is 'good' for all, and especially so if they desire to be emancipated from ideological oppression.

What is significant about this rise of neoliberalism is that this 'war' has not simply consisted of neoliberalists triumphantly fighting against an opposition who are committed to the public good. Giroux (2014, p. 43) suggests that too many educators 'are willing to depoliticize their work by insulating theory, teaching, and research from the discourse, structures, and experiences of everyday life' and by desiring what the power elites want them to desire – which is characteristic of totalitarian states. Wolin (2017) has argued that western democracies have actually become quite tyrannical in character. Tyrannical regimes not only seek to control institutional practices of our societies, but they also seek to control everyone's way-of-being. As Dewey (2008a, pp. 70, 98) observed, a 'totalitarian regime is committed to control the whole of life of all its subjects by its hold over feelings, desires, emotions, as well as opinions' and therefore he claimed that democracies are not so much threated by foreign powers but by 'the existence within our own personal attitudes' of anti-democratic selfish desires devoid of commitment to the public good. Neoliberal totalitarianism has lured educators into uncritically accepting and conforming to its agenda by adopting self-interested desires which lead them to depoliticise their work as evidenced, for example, by 'value-free' practices and policies which have contributed to the 'evidence-based' movement, which are unable to challenge neoliberalism or promote democracy.

Education is clearly connected to political life because it intervenes in the lives of people to lead them to live a particular sort of societal life (Dewey 1981). In light of this connection Apple (2004, pp. 95–96) argues that educators ought to expose hegemonic ideologies such as neoliberalism, otherwise they will continue to 'work through them'. It is significant to note that ideological values work *through* educators who have their ways of thinking and valuing influenced by them. People don't tend to think *about* the content of hegemonic ideologies but instead think *with* them, employing the embedded ideas and values to give sense to the world and to their own activities within it. Chomsky (2017, p. 58) similarly argues that such a disclosure is important because ideas and values operate as 'social levers' which can be employed to either maintain the status quo of society, or to transform it. This has clear and important implications for the agency of educators which can unknowingly be harnessed by an ideology which has come to be embodied. In such an event, one's agency is likely to be limited only to furthering the agenda of the ideology and is unlikely to be able to resist it or to actively promote alternatives.

Dewey (1989a, p. 136) refers to the notion of 'personal disposition' to represent *desire* and *will* as being key attributes of agency. It is not sufficient to simply 'know' rationally what might be best but agency includes *wanting* to enact particular actions because one *desires* and *values* their expected consequences. In order to perform the actions of an educator one's agency must be moved by the desires which are appropriate for education (Webster 2017). An understanding of one's disposition must also incorporate one's being, including one's aspirations, emotions and desires. Dewey (1989b, p. 40) explains this through his example of 'the greatest philosopher' who, although well practiced in clear logic and rational thinking, 'exercises an animal-like preference to guide his thinking to its conclusions'. Here he provokingly seems to be indicating that rationality is always at the service of some other non-rational and even 'animal-like' desire for a particular outcome. He continues to explain that '"[r]eason" at its height cannot attain complete grasp and a self-contained assurance. It must fall back upon imagination – upon the embodiment of ideas in [an] emotionally charged sense' (Dewey 1989b, p. 40). In response to this particular explanation of Dewey's, Garrison (2010, p. 173) concludes that good teachers not only use 'rational rules' and 'effective instructional strategies and management techniques' but they also 'imagine noble ideals' which help empower their sense of agency. Therefore agency, understood to be founded in personal dispositions, is animated by aspirations for ideals which can either prioritise the public good such as pursuing democratic freedom for all, or they can prioritise self-interest such as pursuing private goods as emphasised with neoliberalism.

With reference to Dewey's notion of 'dispositions', Skourdoumbis (2019, p. 12) argues that in this current neoliberal 'age of audit', '[t]eaching practice is . . . narrowly defined towards particular performance dispositions, which are easily described and measured'. He argues that teachers are being encouraged to adopt particular dispositions which serve the interests of competition causing 'teacher agency [to be] often limited by the formalised rules and codes of standards and policy specifics'. Consequently, such a disposition restricts one's agency, motives and desires to be aligned with neoliberalism. Many educators accept they must work within neoliberal structures, but in doing so they can inadvertently promote the neoliberal agenda. Such a corporatisation of educators themselves should not come as a surprise because neoliberalism, like other ideologies, affects how people think, reason and are motivated. As Ball (2012, p. 18) observes, 'neoliberalism gets into our minds and our souls, into the ways in which we think about what we do'. Through such embodiment, educators can actually come to participate in the neoliberal systems in such a manner that they come to primarily value and *desire* the personal gains offered to them personally by the system over and above commitment to the public good. While it is acknowledged that educators need to function within neoliberal institutions, what is of concern is that there is the potential for them to adopt the reasoning associated with '*homo economicus*: the rational, competitive, self-interested individual consumer' (Roberts and Peters 2008, p. 78) and thus become motivated by, and *desirous* of, the allurement of private goods such as tenure, promotion and prestige, over and above the public goods of social justice, democracy and education. Therefore, it is argued in this chapter that educators ought to examine their most fundamental desires which form the basis of their agency. Such an examination is considered necessary to uncover potential inadvertent embodiment of neoliberalism. To undertake this self-examination, a phenomenological engagement, understood as existential dialectics as recommended by Kierkegaard, can be valuable.

Uncovering desires phenomenologically through Kierkegaard's *repetition*

Kierkegaard describes two different approaches to phenomenology. The first is exemplified by a philosophical knight desiring to conquer the essence of a phenomenon and who wants to be personally rewarded by taking possession of the essence to satisfy his desire to 'know'. The second approach describes a lover who desires what is best for his beloved and who pays intimate attention to how he may actually contribute towards this in a continual manner which is what Kierkegaard referred to as *repetition*. This does not mean repeating the same event or meaning *ad nauseam* but rather one is continually open to making sense in relation to a phenomenon one is seriously valuing, as will be explained later. When introducing these two different approaches of phenomenology, Kierkegaard (1989, p. 9) states:

> Now it is fitting for the phenomenon, which as such is always *foeminini generis* [of the female gender], to surrender to the stronger on account of its feminine nature, then in all fairness one can also demand of the philosophical knight a deferential propriety and a profound enthusiasm.

While Kierkegaard playfully refers to the philosopher as a conquering knight who ought to defer and submit to the phenomenon, this however, is not often achieved. Instead, Kierkegaard (1989, p. 9) suggests with reference to hyper-masculinity that 'one sometimes hears too much the jingling of spurs and the voice of the master' which represents that the philosopher is too quick or too confident in his ability to bring the presumed essence of a phenomenon into submission so that he can know it. This is the first manner of attempting to do phenomenology to which Kierkegaard warns against.

His playful reference for understanding phenomena as 'female' and the attainment of a certainty of knowledge as 'masculine' in a knightly and sometimes heroic sense, is also taken up by Nietzsche (1996, p. 15) who provokingly refers to 'hard won' truths and certainties as being 'manly' achievements. Both Kierkegaard and Nietzsche refer to these hyper-masculine types of philosophers being filled with too much self-interest and self-importance as they intend to 'conquer' various phenomenon. Dewey too was opposed to such an approach because it doesn't acknowledge the *relation* experienced between the philosopher and the phenomenon.

All three of these philosophers were against the separation of the knower from the phenomenon to be 'known', because such separation produces 'the dogma of two orders of Being, existence and essence' (Dewey 1929, p. 161). This typically leads to a positivistic and objective understanding of knowledge involving 'appropriation, acquisition . . . also possession' (Kierkegaard 1989, p. 46) which represents something which people seek to *have* and overlooks their interconnection that exists if one understands them as being in *relation* as is characteristic of his *repetition*.

Kierkegaard (1989, pp. 45–46) argued that the philosopher, as a *lover* of wisdom, ought to be more like an amorist who *loves* as a way-of-being and refers to the biblical definition that 'God is love' in the sense that 'he is the infinitely self-communicating . . . continuing in love . . . [and] participation in a fullness' to make the case that love can be understood as a way-of-being. Love can be represented via the Greek *eros* which is central to individual agency as it is recognised as being inclusive of intentionality, devotion and passion. This is encapsulated through Alexander (2013, p. 394) who bases much of his idea upon Dewey's work in *Experience and Nature*, and concludes that '[h]uman existence, I maintain, is driven by a desire, an Eros, to experience life with a sense of meaning and value'. Similarly, Garrison (2010, p. 88) claims that Dewey's approach to '[i]nquiry involves eros' and all the more so when inquiring into one's dealings with other people – such as the vocation of educators. He goes on to explain that when working 'in the caring professions' such as teaching, selves cannot be 'fixed' but must dynamically 'grow in relationships with others' (Garrison 2010, pp. 40–41). This is echoed in the work of Peck (1978, p. 85) who describes love as the 'will to extend one's self for the purpose of nurturing one's own or another's spiritual growth'. This aligns extremely well with how Kierkegaard depicts the lover who is phenomenologically enamoured with his beloved, being devoted to her growth and being willing to attend to this by adjusting himself holistically including his desires.

The agency of the lover is energised by his desire to serve his beloved's interests – not in a pandering manner but rather by being devoted to a critically thoughtful shared understanding of what might be 'good'. Importantly, loving does not involve applying a depoliticised one-size-fits-all template of do's and don'ts. Love requires a great deal of attentive and inquisitive listening and a shared sense of promoting a particular shared vision of societal life. Kierkegaard refers to the lover as being enamoured by the unique nuances that only he can notice and appreciate because, by being devoted to her, he is constantly listening and is open to discovering more. Such is the phenomenological approach of the lover, where the philosopher's way-of-being is *love*. This dynamic and active agency of love is associated with Kierkegaard's (1990, p. 21) repetition because he describes a 'true love affair . . . [as] restless'. He was against the Hegelian dialectic of unity which inevitably leads to a synthesis of conclusions in an objective sense and insists instead that life itself consists of an ongoing existential dialectic through his conception of *repetition* for which one is constantly present in a relation and is never able to conclude in an detached and objective manner.

This concept of *repetition* is explained in his book of the same title. In this he contrasts repetition with *recollection* which refers to a movement backwards, possibly as a reflective thought which looks over one's shoulder, drawing upon a meaning established in the past. Due to its nature of having its location in the past, its essence is fixed. It can no longer be revisited and adjusted. It has already happened. In contrast, repetition is a movement forwards. It too can be regarded as a form of reflective thinking but rather than seeking to remember or recollect a meaning from the past, it seeks to give sense and meaning dialectically with the present with an interest for future fulfilment. Repetition is reflexive in the sense that the one involved in this activity always includes *how* one is relating to the phenomenon and therefore one is able to adjust oneself and the meanings that one is giving to the phenomenon in one's ongoing relation with it. Kierkegaard (1992) argued that truth is to be found in *relations* rather than in the presumed essences of objects. He argued that 'subjectivity is truth' meaning that one needs to focus on *how* one is making sense and meaning through how one relates to a phenomenon. Kierkegaard (1983, p. 149) explains that 'repetition is the *interest* [*Interesse*] of metaphysics, and also the interest upon which metaphysics comes to grief'. By this he meant that the notion of first principles and abstract concepts are forms which lend themselves to recollection, but for repetition they cannot be simply remembered and 'transferred' into one's current relations with phenomena as one cannot draw upon a universal understanding to genuinely love a particular individual.

This notion of Kierkegaard's repetition is taken up by Caputo (1987, p. 40) who explains that '[t]he only way to stay with the given as given is to appreciate that it is always more than it gives itself out to be'. Here Caputo captures the contrast between the philosophical knight compared with the lover, who is continually attentive to the beloved. This is what Kierkegaard means by *repetition*. It consists of an ongoing dialectic between: what one thinks one understands; why things are understood in a particular way; what is one's earnest concerns for the future and how these understandings might need to be re-evaluated in the face of yet further interactions with and disclosure of the phenomenon. This is why, continuing the theme of the lover and the beloved, Kierkegaard (1983, p. 132) explains that 'repetition is a beloved wife of whom one never wearies'. Being an existentialist, Kierkegaard was very much against essentialism as it represents what is able to be fully disclosed and known. But in contrast he claims that 'life is a repetition' and '[r]epetition – that is actuality and the earnestness of existence' (Kierkegaard 1983, pp. 132–133). Kierkegaard suggests that to be able to endure this existential dialectic of repetition as a way-of-being without the satisfying closure of a Hegelian synthesis, requires both maturity and courage.

Continuing with the playful usage of gender for describing the phenomenon and the philosopher or observer who comes to conquer and know, Kierkegaard turns the table on the one who might aspire to be a philosopher knight, by claiming that such an inquirer ought to become feminine in character in the sense of being able to be impregnated by a new idea. He argues, '[i]f a person lacks this feminine quality so that the idea cannot establish the proper relation to him, which always means impregnation, then he is not qualified to be an observer' (Kierkegaard 1983, p. 146). Here Kierkegaard challenges us to take off any hyper-masculine pretensions we might have of desiring to conquer out of self-interest and self-ambition which excludes any acknowledgement that we may humbly need to change ourselves for the benefit of others.

Uncovering our desires through confronting them with Kierkegaard's repetition

In order to challenge neoliberal norms and pursue democracy and social justice through education, it has been argued that educators ought to have their agency constituted by the desires which they ought to have. These desires should demonstrate love and wholehearted dedication for enabling others to grow and flourish, and for society to become more socially just and democratic. In short, one ought to find public goods desirable. However, desires tend to be 'unseen' and therefore unarticulated so it is important to invest the time and effort to uncover what desires we have, and to evaluate them with a particular concern for the consequences which are produced via the activities which they initiate. Dewey recognised the importance of evaluating our desires and argued:

> The 'desirable', or the object which *should* be desired (valued), does not descend out of the a priori blue nor descend as an imperative from a moral Mount Sinai. It presents itself because past experience has shown that hasty action upon uncriticised desire leads to defeat and possibly to catastrophe. The 'desirable' as distinct from the 'desired' does not then designate something at large or a priori.
>
> (Dewey 2008b, p. 219)

Similarly, Biesta (2017, pp. 16–18) warns educators not to become '*subjected* to one's desires' uncritically but rather to develop a relationship with one's desires by having them *interrupted* in order to evaluate 'whether what we desire is desirable for our own lives and the lives we live with others'. Along the same lines Dewey (2008b, p. 221) warns us not to become subjected to our habits by 'continually interrupting' them 'to inquire' into them intellectually and through introducing some 'conflict' to examine the value of one's desires. This confronting provides both challenge and opportunity for one to uncover and articulate one's desires which may not have been previously raised for scrutiny. For example, one's motives, will and desires can be confronted by asking the 'hard questions' to which Apple refers, which lead one to examine one's habits and *raison d'etre*. Kierkegaard argued that religious scriptures which encourage contemplation similarly offer a 'mirror' for self-examination. Such reflections can be experienced as confrontational as one's fundamental beliefs are called into question. However, Sennett (1998, p. 75) warns that typically 'people can suffer from superficiality' and thereby tend to avoid such reflexive thinking. In this case, Vygotsky (1986, p. 243) suggests that a 'conversation with others' might be necessary to confront one's taken-for-granted assumptions. In order to un-conceal motives, educators and counsellors in particular, can interrupt or confront one's way-of-being by calling some aspect into question.

Kierkegaard's repetition, the experience of existential dialectics involving confronting ourselves, can be achieved in two ways. First, by a form of introspection. This is recognised by Apple (2013, p. 29), who argues that we should be 'asking the hard questions' which typically relate to our ideals and desires towards freedom and democracy. This is because these aspirational ideals are necessary attributes of the public good. Such confronting of 'hard' questions requires that we reflect upon whether we honestly are devoted to these ideals and desire pursuing them in our work. Are our desires for the public good indicative that we are lovingly committed to them? Do we display the characteristics of Kierkegaard's lover who is enamoured with democracy, justice and the public good in such a way that we are willing to change ourselves to *grow in relationships* in order to help their actualisation? Questions such as 'what do I value and desire the most?', 'what achievement am I most interested to attain?' and 'who will benefit the most if this were achieved?' are recommended questions for articulating and evaluating desires, and challenging any potentially self-interested motives typical of embodied neoliberalism.

In addition to reflecting introspectively upon our ideals the second aspect of Kierkegaard's phenomenological approach involves evaluating the actual consequences of our actions and anticipating the furthering of these consequences. This has been recognised by Kierkegaard (1983, pp. 274–275) who explained that 'consciousness emerges precisely through the collision [of ideality and reality]. . . . As soon as the question of *repetition* arises, the collision is present.' Such a 'collision' between our actual activities and ideals may reveal the value of our desires which drive our actions and what we really *want*. Dewey (2008b, p. 238) explains that the value of our desires is 'tested by consequences that actually ensue' and hence are not just abstract or idealistic but are existential and have very practical implications. Such consequences not only include long-term results but importantly they also include the micro-moments of life. These are often understood as the interactions that are experienced with others such that one is always keen to sense the apparent effects of one's actions upon others, such as for example, whether their non-verbal reactions indicate what we are communicating is being understood or whether it is confusing, boring or confronting. Such an approach of on-going dialectical reflexivity may therefore prevent desires from 'becom[ing] exclusive and selfish' (Dewey 2008c, p. 73). Reflecting on the question 'are my activities realistically enabling public life to be made more fulfilling and meaningful?' can be valuable in this regard. In short, the phenomenological engagement of Kierkegaard's repetition not only may uncover what educators desire but also may disclose what sort of person we are, and whether some of our taken-for-granted traits may be vices rather than virtues.

Dewey argued that a virtuous disposition is integrated and he offered three characteristics which include: open-mindedness, including curiosity; wholeheartedness in the sense of being 'thoroughly interested', absorbed and enthusiastic; and third, having responsibility which involves giving careful consideration to anticipated consequences of one's conduct (Dewey 1989a, pp. 136–138). In short, he sums up a virtuous disposition as 'love' where 'love, signifies completeness of devotion to the objects esteemed good' (Dewey 2008a, p. 259). In a similar manner, Kierkegaard referred to a purity of heart, where he claimed that such desirable purity can only come about by willing one thing – the good – which must necessarily be the 'public good' due to the inescapable consequences that attainment of goods have. He warns against double-mindedness where 'the person who wills the good for the sake of reward does not will one thing but is double-minded' (Kierkegaard 1993, p. 37) which is considered here to be symptomatic of the 'corporate educator' who is motivated by self-interest for the private goods offered to him personally through neoliberalism, even although he may articulate himself to be moved by more altruistic motives.

Conclusion

If educators are to guard themselves against inadvertently embodying neoliberalism into their 'common-sense' desires and understandings of the world, their work and even themselves, Kierkegaard's phenomenological understanding of *repetition* may offer some important insights. The embodiment of neoliberal ideology is primarily identified through desires which are self-interested because success is recognised through gaining private goods. This can be regarded as being merely a matter of common sense within a neoliberal context, where there is little to prompt an uncovering and re-evaluation of one's primary desires. While one might proclaim that one also aspires to ideals such as freedom and democracy, this could be an indication of what Kierkegaard refers to as double-mindedness. However, understanding our lives as a dynamic of existential dialectics between one's actions and the environment as per Kierkegaard's repetition, can raise awareness of our desires. This can be experienced as confrontational in the sense that what is often perceived as being the 'core' of our identity — our will, values and desires — is called into question. Such a confrontation is possible through reflexivity, as we consider whether our desires are what one ought to desire.

Through Kierkegaard's repetition, one can assess whether one is genuinely in love with public goods such as justice, democracy and education. If one is indeed committed to these ideals, then they ought to be evident in the consequences of one's activities. Such potentially confronting reflections should not just involve intellectual and political ideals but ought to include the ultimate concerns regarding making life meaningful (Webster 2009). Such confrontations can be experienced as existential crises where 'a person is plunged into doubt . . . regarding the very worth of life itself' (Dewey 1977a, p. 213). The potential value of this is that such crises offer valuable turning points and moments of decision which can lead to meaningful growth of one's 'existing and existence' (Kierkegaard 1992, p. 622, Webster 2004). This sort of growth, which is educational in nature, is characterised through one's capability to understand a greater number of possible ways of making sense of, and relating to, various phenomena. Consequently, such growth is accompanied by a greater appreciation for the long-term consequences of activities and why the pursuit of the public good is so important. In short, such continued growth can be likened to wisdom. This is important because, as Garrison has argued, educators ought to actually be growing personally through the relationships with which they are involved. This requires a frequent re-evaluation of one's agency, in particular, one's desires, ideals and *how* one relates to others, which ought to be an expression of devotion or even love. Dewey (1977b, p. 239) suggests that 'the three most powerful motives' enabling us to develop the desires we ought to desire, include a love for individuals and their educative growth, the improvement of society, and pursuit of the truth. Educators ought to see such motives reflected in their desires and the consequences of their activities if they are desiring what they ought to desire.

References

Alexander, T., 2013. *The human Eros*. New York: Fordham University Press.
Apple, M., 2004. *Ideology and curriculum. Third edition*. New York: RoutledgeFalmer.
Apple, M., 2013. *Can education change society?* New York: Routledge.
Ball, S., 2012. Performativity, commodification and commitment: An I-spy guide to the neoliberal university. *British Journal of Educational Studies*, 60 (1), 17–28.
Biesta, G., 2017. *The rediscovery of teaching*. New York: Routledge.
Caputo, J.D., 1987. *Radical hermeneutics*. Bloomington, IN: Indiana University Press.
Chomsky, N., 2017. *The responsibility of intellectuals*. New York: The New Press.
Dewey, J., 1929. *The quest for certainty*. New York: Minton, Balch & Co.
Dewey, J., 1977a. Religious education as conditioned by modern psychology and pedagogy. In: J.A. Boydston, ed. *John Dewey the middle works vol.3 1903–1906*. Carbondale/Edwardsville, IL: Southern Illinois University Press, 210–215.
Dewey, J., 1977b. Democracy in education. In: J.A. Boydston, ed. *John Dewey the middle works vol.3 1903–1906*. Carbondale/Edwardsville, IL: Southern Illinois University Press, 229–239.
Dewey, J., 1981. Experience and nature. In: J.A. Boydston, ed. *John Dewey the later works vol.1 1925*. Carbondale/Edwardsville, IL: Southern Illinois University Press, 1–326.
Dewey, J., 1989a. How we think. In: J.A. Boydston, ed. *John Dewey the later works vol.8 1933*. Carbondale/Edwardsville, IL: Southern Illinois University Press, 105–352.
Dewey, J., 1989b. Art as experience. In: J.A. Boydston, ed. *John Dewey the later works vol.10 1934*. Carbondale/Edwardsville, IL: Southern Illinois University Press, 1–352.
Dewey, J., 2008a. Freedom and culture. In: J.A. Boydston, ed. *John Dewey the later works vol.13 1938–1939*. Carbondale/Edwardsville, IL: Southern Illinois University Press, 63–188.
Dewey, J., 2008b. Theory of valuation. In: J.A. Boydston, ed. *John Dewey the later works vol.13 1938–1939*. Carbondale/Edwardsville, IL: Southern Illinois University Press, 189–251.
Dewey, J., 2008c. Ethics. In: J.A. Boydston, ed. *John Dewey the later works vol.7 1932*, vol. 7. Carbondale/Edwardsville, IL: Southern Illinois University Press, 1–462.
Garrison, J., 2010. *Dewey and Eros*. Charlotte, NC: Information Age Publishing.
Giroux, H., 2014. *Neoliberalism's war on higher education*. Chicago, IL: Haymarket Book.
Harvey, D., 2005. *A brief history of neoliberalism*. Oxford: Oxford University Press.
Kierkegaard, S., 1983. *Fear and trembling* and *repetition*. Princeton, NJ: Princeton University Press.
Kierkegaard, S., 1989. *The concept of irony*. Princeton, NJ: Princeton University Press.
Kierkegaard, S., 1990. *For self-examination and judge for yourself!* Princeton, NJ: Princeton University Press.
Kierkegaard, S., 1992. *Concluding unscientific postscript to philosophical fragments*, vol.1. Princeton, NJ: Princeton University Press.
Kierkegaard, S., 1993. *Upbuilding discourses in various spirits*. Princeton, NJ: Princeton University Press.

Nietzsche, F., 1996. *Human all too human*. Lincoln: University of Nebraska Press.
Peck, M.S., 1978. *The road less travelled*. London: Arrow.
Roberts, P. and Peters, M., 2008. *Neoliberalism, higher education and research*. Rotterdam: Sense.
Sennett, R., 1998. *The corrosion of character*. New York: Norton & Co.
Skourdoumbis, A., 2019. Theorizing teacher performance dispositions in an age of audit. *British Educational Research Journal*, 45 (1), 5–20.
Vygotsky, L., 1986. *Thought and language*. Cambridge, MA: MIT Press.
Webster, R.S., 2004. Changing pre-service teachers' purposes of education through existential crises. *Australian Journal of Education*, 48 (1), 82–94.
Webster, R.S., 2009. *Educating for meaningful lives*. Rotterdam: Sense.
Webster, R.S., 2017. Valuing and desiring purposes of education to transcend miseducative measurement practices. *Educational Philosophy and Theory*, 49 (4), 331–346.
Wolin, S., 2017. *Democracy Incorporated*. Princeton, NJ: Princeton University Press.

Chapter 3

Approaching education on its own terms

Joris Vlieghe and Piotr Zamojski

Rethinking education: phenomenology and immanence

This chapter deals with what we believe is the central issue in philosophy of education, the question raised by Arendt (1968): *what is the essence of education?* Or put differently: what exactly does it mean to educate and to be educated? We believe that exploring this question is inevitable today, because we are facing two mirroring phenomena that demand to take this question seriously, that is, the functionalization of education and the educationalization of societal problems. With the former we refer to the hegemony of a (meta)theoretical position that considers education as a means for particular political or economic aims. To such a stance, education is always conceived of in terms of what it is for (e.g. education is meant to support and realize democracy, sustainable development, and social justice, or it is expected to serve the job market, our knowledge economy, but also individual happiness and wellbeing). It is assumed that education is a means for a goal that comes from outside the sphere of education. This view has become dominant, and it seems almost inevitable not to try to justify education in view of the function it should play for the existing or the desired society.

On the other side there is the educationalization of societal problems (see: Smeyers and Depaepe 2008), which supports the currently dominant neoliberal ideology which sets economic prosperity as the chief goal of human endeavours. A good illustration of what we mean by this is Simons's and Masschelein's (2008) analysis of the governmentalization of learning. Societal, economic, and political problems are rendered in educational terms, and hence captured by the *learning apparatus*. For instance, unemployment becomes the responsibility of an individual who has to make sure she possesses the competencies necessary for her employability (p. 402). Hence, unemployment becomes an issue of education, that is, being un/employed depends on having the right kind of education. Similarly, other problems, like social inequality, hate speech or terrorism (Cf. Edyvane 2011) are rendered as problems that can be understood in educational (or quasi-educational) terms and need to be solved with the use of educational means.

These two mirroring tendencies suggest that education is predominantly defined in view of the society of which it is a part and in which it is intensely interwoven. It is believed that only through optimizing educational institutions can society reproduce and/or ameliorate itself. Paradoxically, seeing education as the master medium of the social fabric and therefore implying that education is omnipotent entails that education becomes a universal panacea. With this comes the risk of total inflation: education might finally disappear. It seems that within this view education is just a skeleton key that fits all the locks, but that doesn't have any meaning of its own.

We think, therefore, that we need more than ever to pose the question concerning the essence of education. We also believe that it is precisely *phenomenology* that can help us say something meaningful in this regard. In other words, we understand the inquiry into the question of the essence of education as involving an eidetic reduction, that is, carefully articulating the basic elements needed to describe what the phenomenon of education is all about (leaving out elements only superficially related to education).

But, there is another reason why phenomenology seems to be the most apt method: it fully respects the immanence of education, drawing from the transcendence–immanence opposition as introduced by Giorgio Agamben (1999). *Transcendence* refers to the felt need to have an explanation or a justification for domains of life/practices, the meaningfulness of which is *already* given in experience. That is, the meaning in question needs to be founded on (and governed by) something 'outside' of this experience, or on something that is structurally and/or temporarily 'prior' to this experience.

Such a strategy is widespread in the domain of education. A transcendent point of view is present whenever education is functionalized, as we analyzed earlier, that is, when education is seen as a means for goals that are not strictly speaking educational (e.g. sustainability, democracy or well-being). Here, education draws its meaning from a sociological, historical, political, moral, and/or psychological perspective. And, thanks to these perspectives education also gets its measure, as it becomes possible to assess education: does it, or does it not, contribute to these preset goals?

Over and above this, education could also be considered from an *immanent* point of view. This is, when we try to come to terms with a meaningful domain of life, there is no need to transgress that what is immediately given. This is because looking for an explanation or justification in terms of something external always replaces it with a diminished reality. Hence, we should try to elucidate it from the inside, and on its own terms. For the realm of education, this means that educating and being educated should be considered as practices that are valuable in and of themselves. They are practices that have their own specific logic that sets them apart from all other practices. Phenomenology seems to be the best method to investigate and express this intrinsic logic of education wholly from within.

It is worth mentioning that the idea of such an immanent approach towards education is already present in the history of educational thought. Here we would like to recall the tradition of the *Geisteswissenschaftliche Pädagogik* (Cf. Litt 1965, Biesta 2015). Essential to this approach is the idea that education is not governed by a principle outside, but that it has its 'Innere form' [inward form] (Nohl 1970, p. 141): this is not a normative principle that serves as an external gauge for education, but rather a principle of strength and growth, which constitutes education from the inside as a coherent and meaningful practice. This entails that we can only understand what it means to educate and to be educated, because – and in so far – we have been ourselves educated. The aim of educational theory, for this tradition, is not to assess education from the outside, but to offer a mirror by which this phenomenon can get a clearer picture of what it is about. This is, to look for words that may adequately bring to life that which has constituted us as educated beings – without stepping outside of the horizon of our own being-educated.

This 'inward form' of education is also called 'entelecheia', but it markedly differs from the classical Aristotelian conception in that it doesn't involve strong metaphysical assumptions – that is, that a form is impressed on formless matter *in view of* a further realization of this form that is set as an external goal. A better metaphor is that it regards a dynamic which works like a centrifugal force. There is a certain directedness that keeps everything together *without* referring to a point outside of the whole that is being kept together. Unity and coherence are entirely due to a constitutive logic that remains fully immanent (and that can never be fully intellectually grasped, although it can be experienced as such). In that sense education is conceived of like a reality of *life*, rather than in terms that point beyond life.

Interestingly, the tradition of *Geisteswissenschaftliche Pädagogik* stems from approaches that are close to the origin of phenomenology, such as hermeneutics and vitalism as, for instance, defended by Friedrich Schleiermacher (2000) and Wilhelm Dilthey (1967). We refer here to the early writings of Husserl in which the goal of phenomenological reduction is to start philosophy again from the position of 'absolute givenness' (see Marion 2002): the first stepstone to consider in any philosophical analysis is not the intentional relation between consciousness and world (as in the later work of Husserl), but the self-giving of phenomena, and hence the endeavour to be present to the highest degree possible to the fullness of meaning that is disclosed in the phenomena as they appear to us.

Geisteswissenschaftliche Pädagogik attempts to do exactly this: to stay true to our lived experience, and to formulate with great precision what makes education into a specific and unique dimension of all of our lives. This comes down to dealing with education as an existential practice. Now, the perspective of *Geisteswissenschaftliche Pädagogik* surprisingly dovetails with more recent developments in educational research, which stress the entanglement between social phenomena and the materiality of our lives: the relational, actor-network or socio-material approaches as defended by, for instance, Tara Fenwick *et al.* (2011).

Crucial to both approaches is that education should be thought of as a construction or composition entailing many diverse elements (i.e. actors). Whereas a socio-material approach has more eye for mundane stuff like blackboards or classroom windows that are equally important parts of the whole assemblage of education, *Geisteswissenschaftliche Pädagogik* approaches the educational in terms of gathering people (generations), things (pedagogical objects), and the life of a culture in which people and things are embedded. Nevertheless, in both cases, what is at stake is that education is a kind of piecing together of an assembly that is not to be judged – transcendentally – in view of criteria that remain external to it, but that is to be approached from the inside out as well or bad constructed (Fenwick *et al.* 2011), or in the more vitalist terminology of *Geisteswissenschaftliche Pädagogik*: as strongly or weakly composed.

The essence of education

We take from the *Geisteswissenschaftliche* tradition the insight that the sense of educating can only be elucidated by starting from something we have all experienced ourselves (although often forgotten), that is, that we can live through experiences of fundamental change, individually and collectively, and in relation to a world of meanings. Being cast out of our immediate life-world and sphere of interests, we experience that there is something in the world that really matters, so that we can see the world with new eyes and start anew with the world: *this* experience of a profound self-transformation is what education is all about.

This happens when people are led out (*e-ducere*) from their closest 'environment' which consists of a particular assemblage of objects, meanings, uses, schemes of action, and ways of ordering things. They are driven out of what they are accustomed to and fully immersed in, so as to be exposed to a world of new objects and meanings, and its immanent potentiality of new uses, ways of acting and ways of ordering things. Being introduced to the diverse domains of the world in a way that allows its exploration as something primarily unknown to oneself, one encounters the opportunity to undergo an experience of profound self-transformation.

Obviously, this only happens occasionally, but when people are asked to point out the intrinsic value of education, most likely they call attention to an experience of seeing the world with new eyes, seeing it in ways it was not experienced before, etc. What we want to stress in this chapter is that for those who have lived through such an experience it is utterly senseless to ask whether what happened was good or not. Asking for a justification is felt as completely redundant. When approached from the perspective of a lived experience, education is good in itself: it is intrinsically worthwhile to educate and to be educated.

If this sounds abstract, we are actually talking here about the most concrete of things. Consider that when people are asked about their own formation process, in spite of all the inevitable painful memories that come to mind, many can easily recall particular moments in which they experienced that – often thanks to a teacher that drew their attention to a particular subject matter the value and beauty of which they had never seen before – there is something in the world that (suddenly) comes to appear as worth the effort of being studied. At that moment, it starts to make sense for their own life, and it makes an enormous difference whether they engage with it or not. From now on, they will care for it and devote (part of) their lives to it. This happens for instance when one, all of a sudden, comes to see why it is important to proof a mathematical theorem, that rigorousness is of the highest importance, and that there is an irresistible beauty to the stringency of such a proof. Or, when one comes to sense, probably after a long period of exercise, that the preparation of a dish is a matter of carefully studying and handling ingredients, and mixing and preparing them in an order and in a way that is demanded by the art of cooking.

Those experiences are intrinsically meaningful. Hence, it is wrongheaded to start and ask for an explanation as to why this is (or should be) the case. The meaning is given in the experience *itself*. That one undergoes a significant transformation is fully sufficient. So, what we need to do is exactly staying true to this experience and phenomenologically elucidate what is at stake in it. Trying to come to terms with educational reality from a psychological, societal, political, ethical, etc. perspective inevitably pushes under the carpet what is at stake in the intrinsically educational experiences just described. They subject education to another logic and make us forget about what is properly educational about education, to use here an expression by Gert Biesta (2014).

But, what would it mean to follow these essential experiences and try to speak out education from within? In the remaining part of this chapter, we will try to give a more substantial account by focusing on three concrete educational issues: the meaning of schooling, how to conceive of freedom in education, and lastly, what it means to be a teacher.

Schooling, freedom, and love for the world

Ever since the vast criticisms that were raised in the 1960s and 1970s, the *school* has been under attack by educationalists for being an inefficient institution. Effective learning takes place outside of classrooms, the school is an oppressive milieu which surreptitiously prepares youngsters to function well (and without displaying a critical attitude) in a capitalist society, the only thing we learn at school is that we need to go to school to make it in life (instead of relying on our own resources and the wisdom already available in our communities), etc. This is defended with a particular fierceness by Ivan Illich (1972) in *Deschooling Society*.

Interestingly, Illich bases his argument on what he calls himself a *phenomenology of school*. It consists mainly of exposing and criticizing assumptions which do not necessarily correspond with most people's prejudices. For instance, it is often taken for granted (at least in the West) that childhood is a separate period in our lives, with its own characteristics, and that it has existed always and everywhere. Over and above this, Illich shows that this is a dangerous error: it is because people first invented schools that we have come to believe that a group of people within a particular age range need to be locked up between the walls of the classroom. Childhood is an invention of the school, not vice versa. Or, people take for granted that teachers, thanks to their professional knowledge, aura, and authority, are the cause of learning. However, if we would stay true to our experiences, we know that most of the valuable things we learn are acquired *in spite of* rather than thanks to attending compulsory education (1972, p. 14).

It could be questioned whether what Illich offers here is a compelling phenomenological analysis. What he actually does is reduce school to a particular sociological institution with specific functions and interests. First, he assumes that educational institutions should serve particular societal goals – such as fostering learning, supporting full human development, and generating more equality. The school falters miserably at all this. It is a highly dysfunctional institute in that regard. Second, being a critical pedagogue, he also assumes that there is an ideological interest behind this very institute: it hinders us in becoming truly developed and critical human beings. The recourse on experiences is then meant to back up these claims.

In their highly discussed *In Defense of the School*, Masschelein and Simons (2013) hold the opposite view that the school is not an institution that is established in order to serve particular social aims – or at least that in our world the school has become institutionalized, and hence functionalized and deformed. However, the school could also be approached from a *morphological* point of view. This means, first, taking the school on its own terms, that is, as a particular manner of bringing together in space and time the older and the new generation around a thing of common concern. And, second, concentrating on how the school, seen as a particular arrangement of time and space, bodies and things, *works*.

What we want to suggest here is that Masschelein and Simon's approach is fundamentally a phenomenological one. Leaving aside the question as to the external purposes of the school (and whether it fulfils this role efficiently), they try to conceive of the school from the inside out: they take it as a particular arrangement that allows for particular things to happen and to be experienced. Their morphological exercise could be seen as an answer to the question 'what is the essence of schooling?', and more precisely as an exercise in eidetic reduction. By way of illustration, we can go back one last time to Illich (1972):

> Classroom attendance removes children from the everyday world of Western culture and plunges them into an environment far more primitive, magical, and deadly serious. School could not create such an enclave within which the rules of ordinary reality are suspended, unless it physically

> incarcerated the young during many successive years on sacred territory. The attendance rule makes it possible for the schoolroom to serve as a magic womb, from which the child is delivered periodically at the school days and school year's completion until he is finally expelled into adult life. Neither universal extended childhood nor the smothering atmosphere of the classroom could exist without schools.
>
> (pp. 15–16)

What Illich describes here might be slightly exaggerated, although it is a fairly adequate description of school life. Now, Illich, interpreting these observations through a purely sociological and critical lens, concludes from this that schools are oppressive institutions and hence must disappear. However, the same observations could *also* be rendered in terms of morphological conditions that make particular educational experiences possible. The school, because of its unique characteristics, grants the possibility of full attention and devotion to a thing of study (a subject matter), but without *any* concern for the uses and applications it has in 'the real world' outside the walls of the classroom. This opens up a particular experiential realm where the possibility of educational transformation, as sketched here, is being granted.

The second illustration of how a phenomenological approach can articulate essential elements of education is *the issue of how education can bring about freedom*. More often than not freedom is conceived of as an important goal, if not as *the* most important aim of education. This is certainly the case since Critical Theory has set the parameters of how to think about education since the Second World War, thanks to a growing awareness of how educational institutions themselves have contributed to an oppressive status quo, critical pedagogues have warned time and again that education should not introduce the new generation into an existing world (as this inevitably comes with violence), but that only emancipation should be the goal of education (Freire 2005, Giroux 1983). Critical educators should make people conscious of the fact that they are oppressed (e.g. because we are prisoners of false consciousness) – or for that matter that most of their colleagues, that is, traditional educators, are a cause of oppression themselves (because the majority of teachers are attached to bourgeois, Eurocentric, heteronormative, etc. values). Criticism and emancipation go hand and hand, and constitute a never ending educational task (Cf. Adorno 2004).

Praiseworthy as this ideal might sound, it could be argued that such a rendering of education is at odds with the experience of the essence of education. The main assumption behind a critical approach is that we are *always and already* victim to some form of power outside of ourselves that oppresses us, and/or makes us lacking in self-awareness and the possibility of a correct and unbiased understanding of the world. Being slaves of Plato's cave is our inescapable condition, and it is in view of this that education gets its ground and measure: education, to a critical perspective, has to emancipate us from the darkness that holds us captive and lead us to the true world outside of the cave. It could be argued that this testifies to a fundamentally un-educational stance, in that it puts students in a particular, fixated position: they are those who are helpless and ignorant, and who need a master to come to true insight about themselves and their place in the world. Without a master who enlightens them, no emancipation will occur (Cf. Rancière 1991, 2003).

In that sense it could be asked whether true transformation takes place. Moreover, a critical approach renders everything that happens in education subservient to a goal that is purely political – that is, the realization of a dream of a better/a perfect world. As such the critical approach should be called transcendent in that the meaning of educating is drawn from an outside perspective – in this case a goal (justice, equity, respect, transparency, etc.) that is through and through political, and that sets limits to what good/desirable education is. For instance: the study of mathematics for the sake of mathematics is objectionable *on grounds of* its contribution to the status quo: the world needs people who use mathematics to change the world, not people who prove theorems for the sake of proving theorems. And the master-chef would be better concerned with making sure that the dishes she asks her students to prepare don't pass the hidden message that European cuisine is superior.

All this is not to say that freedom would not be an important educational issue. But, we hold that freedom in education could be conceived of from a purely immanent perspective too. This entails a particular reversal: starting from the idea that weakness is not on the part of people oppressed by the world we live in, but on the contrary, that the world itself is weak and that it might wither away if we don't care for it. We draw this idea from Hans Jonas (1984) and Georg Picht (1969, 1998), who have developed similar thoughts in a different context – a phenomenological ontology of responsibility. But, we do believe that what they say applies to education too, and that it offers precise words for articulating phenomenologically the experience of freedom in education. For Picht and Jonas, responsibility is not a juridical or ethical category (e.g. a duty), but a fundamental relationship everyone can experience to have with the world. Very briefly put, in this relationship particular things (*Sache*) of the world appear as intrinsically good. The measure of their worth, however, is that we are committed not to destroy these things, but to care for, to attend to them, to make effort. Things appear as vulnerable, meaning that we know and experience that we *can* do something that might foster *or* destroy them. We are able to intervene with the potentiality of these things. Hence, contrary to the perspective of emancipation, the starting point is not the diagnosis that we are slaves to an oppressive order, but that there is a sphere of free action in relation to things of this world. People experience to be *free* to care for intrinsically good things – for the sake of these things themselves, to the same extent that they are *free* to let them perish. Therefore, what is at stake is not regaining our freedom through education (emancipation), but making good use of our ability to act. And this assumes that we acknowledge that it is within our power to destroy or to sustain things, and that we need to decide what to do with this freedom (i.e. take up responsibility).

So far we have been concentrating on what it means to be educated. But, the phenomenological approach we propose in this chapter also has consequences for the related question: *what does it means to educate*? Indeed, in our analysis we have actually presupposed, but not yet wholly articulated, that the figure of the educator plays an absolutely crucial role in educational transformation – albeit not in the way of the critical educator who brings enlightenment to the victims of deception and slavery. Nonetheless, education is predicated upon teachers who make the effort to show others that there is good in the world. In other words: teaching is about making others *attentive* for something that all can appreciate as meaningful, rather than emancipating others by raising critical consciousness on the basis of a profound inequality between liberator and oppressed.

What we have in mind is also at odds with the way in which the teacher is conceived of in the mainstream educational discourse today. Very briefly, the teaching profession has become reduced to a technical issue (the art of instruction): becoming a teacher is a matter of training people towards the necessary knowledge and skill to efficiently support learning in students and to guarantee optimal learning outcomes (Biesta 2014). To such a view, teaching is not a valuable endeavour in and of itself. It is a practice that receives its ground and measure from something outside: effective learning results in students.

Opposed to this, it is also possible to explore teaching from a phenomenological angle, that is, as a practice that has its own meaning, to be disclosed from an internal point of view, from the perspective of those who experience teaching as a worthwhile and enjoyable activity. Hence, we need to go beyond the idea of teaching as a (merely) technical skill, and paint the portrait of a teacher who teaches *out of love for the world*. This is to regard teaching not as a matter of expertise, but as a matter of care. The notion of love might suggest many different connotations that are out of place – for example, that teachers *should be* overtly passionate and enthusiastic about their subject matter or that they *must* be conservative; after all, one must defend the things one is deeply attached to. However, we do not hint at any of this. Instead, we refer here to Max Scheler (1973), who describes love and hate as the *two fundamental attitudes* one can take towards the world, so that the world appears to us in a particular way: in a manner of opening-up or narrowing-down, respectively.

Phenomenologically speaking it makes sense to say that love is a stance one takes towards the world which allows for things of value to appear. The world is disclosed in a way that invites further exploration. It is opened and expanded, and comes into sight as something we want to study. Hate, on the contrary, is a relation vis-à-vis the world which narrows it down and which makes us, eventually, blind for what is valuable. In order to teach one must start from affirming that there is something valuable in the world, and that it is so valuable that one has to pass it on to the next generation. Hence, there is no space for hate in education. It could be argued that hate precisely defines the sphere of politics (or that politics is always driven by a combination of love *and* hate: there must always *first* be an indignation about something fundamentally wrong with the world which demands political deliberation and action (Cf. Vlieghe and Zamojski 2019)).

This implies that the meaning of teaching draws from the way in which a teacher constitutes herself and gives shape to her own life in relation to a particular object of care – her subject matter. This is, the teacher could be seen as someone who at a particular moment of her life fell in love with something (e.g. mathematics, cooking) and who has no choice but to profess about this love: to show to the new generation why it matters. Teaching is a matter of internal necessity. By displaying this love, she makes this generation attentive for a subject matter and shows why it is worth putting effort into it. She puts her love and devotion at stake: while teaching she puts it publicly to the test whether or not it makes sense to care about the thing she is attached to. Moreover, the new generation can also refuse to accept the gift, and to go further with the object of love. More generally, what is presented to the new generation is an opening, not a command. The teacher must present the world in such a way that newcomers are in the fullest sense of the word respected as new, that is, they can go on with the world in new and unprecedented ways (Cf. Vlieghe and Zamojski 2019).

The three issues we discussed, how to conceive of the school, freedom, and teaching, are illustrations of the idea that taking a phenomenological approach allows for shedding a fresh light on fundamental educational issues. What is at stake here is to stay true to experiences we have with education, and to try and articulate from within this experiential sphere what education is all about. Such an immanent approach is a highly relevant one today, as education is increasingly understood in terms that have nothing to do with education *per se*, that is, as a means that serves the societal order. This comes down to a highly problematic reduction of the rich phenomenon which education is, and as we argued throughout this chapter, a betrayal of the essence of education.

References

Adorno, T.W., 2004. *Negative dialectics*. Translated by E.B. Ashton. London/New York: Routledge.
Agamben, G., 1999. *Potentialities. Collected essays in philosophy*. Translated by D. Heller-Roazen. Stanford: Stanford University Press.
Arendt, H., 1968. *Between past and future: Eight exercises in political thought*. New York: Penguin.
Biesta, G.J.J., 2014. *The beautiful risk of education*. Boulder/London: Paradigm Publishers.
Biesta, G.J.J., 2015. Teaching, teacher education and the humanities: Reconsidering education as a 'Geisteswissenschaft.' *Educational Theory*, 65 (6), 665–679. Available from: https://doi.org/10.1111/edth.12141
Dilthey, W., 1967. *Über die Möglichkeit einer allgemeingültigen pädagogischen Wissenschaft*. Berlin: Weinheim.

Edyvane, D., 2011. Britishness, belonging, and the ideology of conflict: Lessons from the polis. *Journal of Philosophy of Education*, 45 (1), 75–93. Available from: https://doi.org/10.1111/j.1467-9752.2010.00779.x

Fenwick, T., Edwards, R. and Sawchuck, P., 2011. *Emerging approaches to educational research: Tracing the socio-material*. London: Routledge.

Freire, P., 2005. *Education for critical consciousness*. New York/London: Continuum.

Giroux, H.A., 1983. *Theory and resistance in education. A pedagogy for the opposition*. South Hadley, MA: Bergin & Garvey.

Illich, I., 1972. *Deschooling society*. New York: Harrow Books.

Jonas, H., 1984. *The imperative of responsibility. In search of an ethics for the technological age*. Translated by H. Jonas and D. Herr. Chicago/London: The University of Chicago Press.

Litt, T., 1965. *Pädagogik und Kultur*. Bad Heilbrunn: J. Klinkhardt.

Marion, J.L., 2002. *Being given: Toward a phenomenology of givenness*. Stanford: Stanford University Press.

Masschelein, J. and Simons, M., 2013. *In defense of the school. A public issue*. Leuven: Education, Culture & Society Publishers.

Nohl, H., 1970. *Charakter und Schiksal. Eine Pädagogische Menschenkunde*. Frankfurt: Schulte-Bulmke.

Picht, G., 1969. Der Begriff der Verantwortung. In: *Warheit, vernuft, verantwortung. Philosophische studien*. Stuttgart: Klett-Cotta.

Picht, G., 1998. The concept of responsibility. Translated by W. Davis. *Religion*, 28 (2), 185–203. doi:10.1006/reli.1997.0096

Rancière, J., 1991. *The ignorant schoolmaster. Five lessons in intellectual emancipation*. Translated by K. Ross. Stanford, CA: Stanford University Press.

Rancière, J., 2003. *The philosopher and his poor*. Translated by J. Drury, C. Oster and A. Parker. Durham/London: Duke University Press.

Scheler, M., 1973. *Formalism in ethics and non-formal ethics of values. A new attempt toward the foundation of an ethical personalism*. Translated by M.S. Frings and R.L. Funk. Evanston, IL: Northwestern University Press.

Schleiermacher, F., 2000. *Texte zur pädagogik. Kommentierte Studienausgabe*. Herausgegeben von M. Winkler und J. Brachmann. Frankfurt am Main: Suhrkamp.

Simons, M. and Masschelein, J., 2008. The governmentalisation of learning and the assemblage of a learning apparatus. *Educational Theory*, 58 (4), 391–415. Available from: https://doi.org/10.1111/j.1741-5446.2008.00296.x

Smeyers, P. and Depaepe, M., eds., 2008. *Educational research: The educationalization of social problems*. Springer: Dordrecht.

Vlieghe, J. and Zamojski, P., 2019. *Towards an ontology of teaching. Affirmation, love for the world and thing-centered pedagogy*. Cham: Springer. Available from: https://doi.org/10.1007/978-3-030-16003-6

Chapter 4

Pedagogical practice

Andrew Foran

Introduction

Time, when used reflectively can give us perspective, and understanding my pedagogical practice has come over 25 years, as a middle school and senior high school teacher, an outdoor educator, and a university teacher educator. I have seen education develop into a broad sweep of mandated policies that have become controlling practices for public-school teachers. The result has been an eroding shift in professional attitudes in what it means to be a teacher, leaving many educators to wither in frustration, as politicians define teaching though imposed, legislated, and forced contracts, mimicking *collective agreements*. I have also witnessed teachers continuously demonstrating tenacious resistance to government imposed controls on their practice. For some teachers, government centralization, curricular dominance, policy-practice control, has led to an ultimate resentment towards their ministries of education. Unfortunately, I have seen many invested public-school teachers become demoralized as they patiently ride out storms of governmental change. Seemingly, this turmoil was generated by slow yet powerful growth of neoliberal tendencies. Despite the educative-capitalistic impacts during this time, I have also observed a common element: teachers dedicated to the lives of their students. Thus I am confident that the sheer grit of teachers will be enough to provide hope for pedagogical practice in Canada.

Neoliberalism and pedagogical practice

Decades of *institutionalized education* have solidified a global hold on how children and young people are schooled. This comparative and competitive educative process, in principle, has evolved into a quasi-democratic-social equality learning model that is supposedly to empower all students to become self-actualized learners. Despite the numerous educational orientations motivated by social, religious, corporate, and political directives, many educators continue to struggle to practice a relationally responsive education for young people – the very reason *that called* adults to teaching (van Manen 2012). Questions in the minds of many teachers confronting a neoliberal agenda is: what constitutes a quality education and is education, in its current form, still an important right-of-passage for youth? This discussion explores what many teachers will claim as essential in the educational exchange – pedagogy. Yet, despite the value of relationality between teachers and pupils, teacher education in Canada, and elsewhere, has tended to ignore developing pedagogical practices in teacher preparation in favor of government initiatives that promote the value of testing scores and central-government controlled curricula.

The teacher's world is undeniably absorbed by *everydayness* in competing tensions and pressures of standardization. An institutionalized education comes with inherent inequities that highlight power through policy, marking, testing, rules, management, and procedures. School is not much of a place for children, or an environment that allows a child to be a child (Biesta 2012). For the last 20 years, teacher-education programs in Canada have shifted from preparing teachers to build a practice based on the relational encounter with pupils to one of being an information manager implementing and directing learning services. Teacher education programs largely ignore, or take for granted, the personal and non-professional significance implied in this use of the term *pedagogy*. A phenomenological orientation encourages educators to understand pedagogy anew in both its challenging complexity and unspecialized simplicity.

The relationship between adult and child forms the interpretive frame for understanding various educational practices. The pedagogical tradition still considers as indispensable, the human bond between the younger and the older generations; an unavoidable part of intergenerational interaction. The orientation of a pedagogical practice is based on the following premise: a relationship that does not exist for the sake of the adult, but comes into being for the benefit of the child. I am hopeful that *pedagogy in practice* will challenge an outcomes-based and assessment driven education that is not oriented to an open future for the child, and forecloses on multiple possibilities by insisting on pre-established criteria, percentiles, and performance norms. To this is added a biologistic conception of cognitive performance and cognitive deficits, tempting some in education to reduce the child to a "diagnosis" or a "dysfunction" (Foran and Robinson 2017). In this context, both the teacher's and the child's humanity are jeopardized.

By reviving pedagogical practice in teacher education, and exploring the lived space of schooling, beyond institutional learning, phenomenology can position attendant pedagogical priorities over *neoliberalized* norms and outcomes. The task of the teacher is to foster an educational practice that crosses divides: the personal-domestic private life of students, to the institutional-professional demand that confronts students in school. Many teachers are forced to default to the mounting pressure to reduce children to behaviors and managed growth, rendering children via academic scores and performance indicators. Children become metrics and government data. The result has forced teachers to rely on neoliberal reflections: professionally steeped in lesson plan efficiencies to improve technical-instructional delivery, *not* relational encounters. Giroux (2010) problematized this mindset as the pedagogical of neoliberalism, teachers becoming advocates for and gatekeepers of the system. Thus teachers are swept along a frantic reporting cycle to complete report cards that demonstrate achievement through assessment rankings comparing students-to-students, classes-to-classes, and schools-to-schools, districts-to-districts, regions-to-regions, and as a whole, countries-to-countries, and to that end, the comparisons are aimed at controlling education, and teachers. Thus objectifying the child through scores, ultimately dismissing the child entirely.

A teacher's practice

Merleau-Ponty (2010) attests that this layer of institutional practice is a barrier because "children have not yet acquired equal footing in their relations with adults" (p. 374) and in such an environment how can they be recognized for who they are and want to be. What does this mean for being and becoming a child? Have teachers lost the art of pedagogical practice due to pressures of neoliberal instruction? Hence, a struggle in teacher education: how do we shift a teachers' practice back from a technical-rational orientation to a pedagogical one? These questions are raised in response to neoliberal, globalized education agendas that have had profound implications in the lives of teachers and students. School is about standardization, the allowance and promotion of academic competition, a narrow curricula of predetermined learning outcomes and objectives, in pursuit of higher test scores, resulting in greater public accountability, heavily regulated classrooms that restrict teacher autonomy, and an institutional model that shapes the classroom experience.

Another orientation for education is to explore phenomenological contributions. This vision presents existential–philosophical positions that contradict neoliberal education, revitalizing school as experiential, relational, profoundly personal, intentional, and a moral-humanistic experience. Teaching accounts in this orientation are pedagogical, a lived experience (van Manen 2014), and illustrates unique moments in response to "why phenomenology matters to education." This offers a rich and ignored dimension of education that allows pedagogy, the relational practice in education to be at the center. By doing so, contemporary socio-political educational change, if problematized, offers an alternative vision for education by engaging with lived experiences. The voices motivating this discussion raise important moments that lead to more questions in ways that bring the practical, every-day world of educators and students into recognizable focus that offers an alternative to neoliberal, instrumental perspectives on education. Phenomenology shows another possibility for teachers and students: how adults and children can be together in educational settings, reclaiming something increasingly forgotten: pedagogy.

Situating pedagogy

Sharing pedagogical moments, as lived experience, can challenge programs dedicated to preparing future teachers. Teacher educators, and teachers, are encouraged to ask: What does it mean to be a teacher in the contemporary times? Considering the level of government interference and budgetary control, at the school and classroom level, this question draws attention to all involved in education to take into account the pervasive influence of neoliberal ideas and the impact this has on teaching practices. Teacher educators cannot dismiss teacher experiences that are emerging as a direct response to the consequences and pervasiveness of neoliberal influences.

The teacher accounts offered here can be interpreted as political and an effort to preserve what is left of their practice, pedagogically speaking. Many in teacher education could argue these lived experiences reveal that there has been an erosion of a deeper and more complex understanding in the area of pedagogical practice (Biesta 2011, 2012). These lived experiences reveal a dilemma: teachers controlled by government uniformity determined by centralized educational policy and practices limited to testing scores, denying what is of value for many teachers: teacher–student relationships (van Manen 2012). When teachers' lived experiences are examined they can offer a poignant counter narrative to position pedagogy as a practice based on intersubjectivity (van Manen 2014, 2015) in neoliberal times.

The anecdotes in this discussion offer a pedagogical resistance from teachers revealing the subtle control that has gripped the nature of their professional duties, controlled by bureaucratic forces, pressuring them to imposed standards of professional accountability (Nova Scotia Teaching Standards (NSTS) 2017), and increased governmental demand for "teacher performance" as outlined in imposed Bachelor of Education Program Standards (Inter-University Committee on Teacher Education 2018), under the guise of professional competencies that governments proclaim are reflections of public-societal demands (Inter-University Committee on Teacher Education 2017). I have seen the rise of political intentions in an effort to control teachers and the result has been a slow and constant erosion of pedagogical practice. The consequence in preparing teachers now ignores relationality in educational discourse and practice in Canada. However, when I am engaged in collegial conversations with teachers (at all career stages), I sense the pedagogical is not forgotten, it is there, almost secret, a subversive practice that comes alive when sharing their encounters with young people.

The term pedagogy is overused, even abused or misused, as a catch-all phrase to qualify instructional efforts or scholastic endeavors. Paramount to "getting back to education itself" must occur through practice, allowing for relational qualities between teachers and children (Saevi 2007, Foran and Olson 2008, Foran and Saevi 2012, van Manen 1991, 2015) as they grow and mature. Teachers sharing relational practices is an important step and this requires a heuristic exploration of encounters with children and young people, not limited to administrative tasks, recording student performance indicators via regulation government mandated documentation, that allows oversight of the increased testing, evaluation, and curricular inspection. Allowing teachers to draw on everyday language, offering a phenomenological showing of existential possibilities (van Manen 1997, 2014) offered opportunities for them to consider the relational aspects of their practices in education; suspending the technical thrust upon teachers allowed them to see again the pedagogical. When this aspect of teaching is focused on, the relationality surfaces as a rediscovered, a taken-for-granted in teacher reflections, an adult that is *fully there* for the child (van Manen 1991). These reflections counter the neoliberal narrative by presenting a sensitive relationship of a teacher that is thoughtfully focused on a child's growth. This is a relationship that is morally concerned with the growth of children and young people as they become a person (see Mollenhauer 2014, Foran and Robinson 2017).

A pedagogical relationship is different from one based on established teaching standards (Inter-University Committee on Teacher Education 2017, 2018). A phenomenological understanding of what it means to be human is taking us back to the relational capacity of a teacher to "enter into the world of a child," based on thoughtfulness and tact (van Manen 2002, p. 3), based on an encounter that has intention (Langeveld 1975): "[the] ability to actively distinguish what is appropriate from what is less appropriate for children or young people" (van Manen 2002, p. 8). Considering the external pressures confronting teachers, many are challenged to maintain pedagogical thoughtfulness in light of professionalization steeped in standardization, allowing neoliberalism to push aside pedagogical tact: "a caring attentiveness to the unique: the uniqueness of children, the uniqueness of every situation, and the uniqueness of individual lives" (van Manen 2002, p. 8). Hence, in the following conversations, I draw on the term pedagogy, as it was intended: the relational bond inherent in the teacher–student relationships, that are *practiced* not scored or measured. Pedagogy as practice, is phenomenologically shown by lived experience descriptions. Hermeneutic interpretation offers a rich possibility in the act of teaching by cultivating the relational.

Reclaiming pedagogy

The act of reclaiming a pedagogical practice, allowing teachers to "get back to education," starts with conversations that explore relationality. Many teachers identified these conversations as missing elements in their respective practices, despite recognizing relationships as central for teaching, acknowledging this is what brought them to teaching in the first place. Many teachers have also shared pupil connections were often sidelined in favor of more pressing neoliberal concerns. Teachers were clear, they felt relationality has given way to technical qualities and to teaching standards. Many of these teachers commented that when their reflections focused on children, not teaching performance indicators and standards, they came to realize their practice needed to change. Pedagogical reflection provided a different way of being with children and young people, capturing complexity and ambiguity in lived experience descriptions.

Lived experience descriptions, offer a counterpoint the current technical drive in impacting teachers, restoring their practice by drawing on unspecialized language (Galvin and Todres 2007) and for educators, these anecdotes allow for questioning and exploration of being human. The relationship between adult and child forms the interpretive frame that is difficult to understand using a neoliberal lens. The phenomenological orientation presents a realization for teachers that this relationship is deeply intertwined in everyday moral language, ethical actions, and relationality that is interested in the child. Phenomenology shows through lived experience (van Manen 2014) that a teachers' practice is more than competencies and technical information delivery.

Pedagogy in practice

Teachers reflecting on just pedagogical dimensions revealed concrete moments showing the relational, counter to what neoliberalism would lead many to believe is the act of teaching. By reflecting on pedagogical moments, these three teachers can reclaim the relational as practice and allow this to inform their identities and "get back to education" not mired in the rational-technical model. The phenomenological showing (van Manen 1997, p. 130) will blend the teachers' anecdotes, surpassing the neoliberal enterprise, with pedagogical insights as relational knowing. Phenomenology articulates the poignant teachers' insights, pedagogical moments revealing the meanings of human enterprise. These accounts isolated a pre-reflective moment and capture what teachers are experiencing, revealing what was distinct and significant about their everydayness in schools. Each anecdote offers a unique element form a teacher's practice, and with hermeneutical reflection, the intent is to make connections with a "practical pedagogic orientation to children" (van Manen 1988, p. 411) and to gain insight into relationality.

Heidegger (1962) reminds us that the concrete in these anecdotal moments represent the taken-for-granted, *the things* of our every-day world. Husserl (1970) posited that the lifeworld was a "world of immediate experience," a "world as already there," a "pregiven world," and a world that people experience in a "natural primordial attitude," simply for teachers, a pedagogical world. The examination of the teachers' lifeworld involves stories of their experiences that focus on the pre-reflective moment that captures the relational significance for teachers with children. The lived experience can bypass the neoliberal debate in education and allows for a more open investigation of teaching

Pedagogical practice 51

that is liberated from agendas. The interpretations of these shared pedagogical moments are essential for "getting back to education itself."

Exploring the centrality of teachers in pedagogical practice by making connections can revive the value and importance of personal and non-professional significance implied in this use of the term "*pedagogy*." The following anecdotes guard against "abstract theoretical thought" (see van Manen 1997, p. 119) that is reflective of neoliberal practices in school. The uniqueness, distinctiveness, and inevitable vagueness of each story becomes a part of the thematic structure that organizes the theme of this chapter – relationality as pedagogy. The following anecdotes are shared by John, a veteran high school teacher, Margaret, an itinerant mid-career support teacher, and Blair, a beginning middle school teacher.

A knock at the door

John has witnessed firsthand the numerous provincial government education policy changes over his career. These changes are often communicated in staff meetings. John is clear when he states: "Staff meetings are a professional interference." This position is based on numerous administrative controls connected to these information sessions. John states: "These are not staff meetings, this is the bi-weekly review of the rule book. And the problem is there are always new rules to the game – we never can figure out how this game is played." In my conversations with John, he revealed his resentment:

> These staff meetings are a joke, we attend so we can be told how to do our jobs. We never have opportunity to add items to the agenda, we can ask questions, but we never get to discuss the items, and there is never staff action – there is no vote on how we are to proceed as a school. This is information done to us and I have come to hate staying after school.

I sensed there was a nostalgic loss because John was active in leading an after-school explorers club for science students and this was discontinued due to budget cuts that resulted in his school no longer offering after-hour bussing. John summarizes staff meetings as regulatory: how to assess students, how to track behavior, how to report infractions, how to design our lessons, how to determine the direction for and participate in school improvement and accreditation.

> I marched, a frustrated walk, to the staff room because there was no agenda sent in advance, and that could only mean one thing: another info session! The meeting started and I was sort of listening, hearing the voices at the front, but listening to my own voice inside my head, and it was me droning on and on. . . . I was seething because this was about attendance concerns and our exam format again! I was worked up, knots in my stomach, there

> was a sweat forming. Why was I here? I did not sign up for this, I just want to be left alone to teach not meet. Sitting at the back table, I heard the four little knocks on the door and this stopped me – the tap tap tap tap cut right into my head. A colleague got up to answer, I could see it was a student and saw them whispering. And I thought: "what kid would dare interrupt the meeting . . . the audacity! When my colleague stepped aside his motion indicated it was for me and he stepped aside. I was boiling, the rudeness to interrupt, this kid needed to be taught their place. I stomped toward the door. I was going to let this student have it. I was . . . she started backing away into the hallway . . . it was the look on her face. I stopped at the doorway, looked at the front of the room, my admin did not looked pleased with the interruption. I looked back to my student. She was in the middle of the hallway, keeping her distance. I closed the door and it all dropped away, fell out of me somehow. I knew by the way she saw me that I had become the very thing I hate – rigid authority.

John realized in that moment the knock was not an interruption, but a disruption. The student reminded John that he was needed and she was not some form of measurement: an absenteeism statistic or an exam score. This was a child seeking his support. "You always hear about being saved by the bell, but I was saved by the knock. I saw the bitter man I had become when I saw her reaction; I was not a teacher at that door, I was frustration and a lost sense of self." John explained that in the hallway the student was asking for permission to borrow the field kits for her group. They wanted to complete the last activity from class and her mother would be picking them up after work. John realized through his student, that he did not like what he saw in himself: "I let them change me" and he lost his "sense of teaching." The meetings did come to control him, but not in the intended ways. John acknowledged that the mandates will come and go, but in that moment, his response to his student was the decisive factor and this aspect of relationality was in his entire control; the department could not take that away from him.

Miss

Margaret recalled an extra help session in the learning center at one of her schools. Due to school board restructuring, she had to travel to three schools, on different days of the week, to support identified students with learning challenges. Because her time was "not scheduled like a regular class," Margaret was expected to document each session. These reports were then scanned and emailed to her supervisor.

> I was running late and I wanted to finish the current batch of reports that were due at the end of the week. I was focused because I still had two more schools to visit and I was carrying a full caseload of students. I saw Mark shuffle in, I looked up gave him a smile and indicated that he sit. I shuffled

the files looking for his – I am not sure how much time passed. I was reading, trying to sort out the follow-up topics and I must have been reading out loud. I think I was muttering and I heard this soft little voice, "Why don't you just ask me Miss, I know what I am supposed to do." I stopped, I was so embarrassed; ashamed I think. I closed the file, and looked up smiling, but you know the smile is forced – fake. I started to apologize claiming so many students and that it's hard to keep it all straight, hard to remember everyone. And he said, "No worries Miss, happens all the time." I sat there empty.

The pressure to document and report outcome achievement is a real burden to many teachers; providing evidence of academic growth. But for Margaret, at what price? She explained that her emptiness was due to a sudden realization that she did not really know any of these students on her caseload – they were file folders full of checklists and work samples and testing results and her formative notes. There was nothing there that showed her the person and the "happens all the time" comment revealed her deficiency as a teacher. She was a reporter, not a teacher, and in her diligence to attend to her files, she came to realize that she really did not know the student in front of her, or any of her students. The comment haunted her, leaving her to question if this young boy thought all adults did not remember him. Margaret now believes the effort to support students in this academic model creates efficiency, but personal distance. Margaret explains: "I am able to complete tasks, but unlike my first years in teaching, I have not been able to get to know these young people." Margaret concluded our conversation with the following statement: "I need to get back to those early days in my teaching – that mattered, the check lists don't."

No more questions?

Blair entered teaching with aspirations that many of us share: to make a difference. Blair has completed the third year teaching grade 8 and grade 9 and is now deciding if there is a fourth year. "I know I should be grateful for a full-time contract, I have benefits and job security, and my own classroom, but this is not what I believed teaching to be." The disillusionment emerged when Blair realized that the department head was scrutinizing the planned lessons and tests. "I had to submit copies and we would discuss my plans and quizzes, including the tests to ensure a common exam. . . . But I know he was cornering me into teaching to the exam." Blair expressed frustration when discussing student interests and the impossibility to explore these developments with a particular child. "I know I have to teach the curriculum, I never had an opposing thought in this regard. But over my first couple of years, I have realized this is not about students as much as it's about coverage and results."

I was wrapping up the lesson and from a delivery stance it went fine. The students seemed interested and asked some good questions – that's always a good sign. But I became rattled during the group reports. Becka said, "We understand that education is a provincial control, but what about the little communities, like us, where were trying to keep our language and culture." And she asked: "Is this not more important?" I thanked them for the review and closing comment, but I knew I would not address this issue for Becka. Opening up this can of worms would derail the unit and we just did not have the time to explore this question – it was a powder keg in this part of the world. Yet, I know this is about her identity, her community, her family, her friends, and herself. But these answers were not going to be on the test and I was not going to be afforded the time to explore this with her or the class, but I wanted to. Like a good teacher, I acknowledged her summary and I know I was acknowledging a truth – I am teaching to the test. This inability to respond to her forced me to confront what I knew all along, this is not teaching. I moved on to the next group and a little voice repeated: "no more questions, just give me the group summary!"

Blair informed me that the confrontation was about accepting her place as a teacher: "I did not have the confidence or the courage to challenge my department head. I just towed the party line – deliver the units, quiz, and test." Blair was facing a truth, the reason for becoming a teacher was not living up to the practice that was being cultivated daily. "I think I came to fear the hands [going up] because they would ask for more and I was not going to go there. There was no room for me to explore the issues of their day because I have a curriculum to cover." A teacher's responsibility is to plan lessons according to curriculum guides, target learning outcomes, grade student work, assess for performative measure, provide constructive feedback, and guide students in their learning. For Blair this has become strictly academic and as a result, Blair questions the likelihood of a career that limits the pedagogical possibility that will allow young people to come into their own. "I always thought this was my purpose, to be there for them as they connect themselves to their worlds – that's learning! But that's not what I do and I now am reconsidering what it means to teach – this is not what I want to be doing."

Learned lessons

Mollenhauer (2014) posed the following paradox: academic achievement and motivation preserving a child's vitality; Mollenhauer is clear society wants and values achievement. The challenge for teachers is that striving for reliable results often curtails the desire to learn and teach. Teacher educators must ask: "How can we balance results without compromising the child in favor of predetermined learning outcomes?" Teacher education programs have become dedicated to a coordinated and government regulated approach to teacher training. Governments have ensured that teachers are credentialed professionals, licensed, and specialized to deliver a standardized program of evidence-based teaching connected to centralized curricular outcomes. This standardization is an ongoing effort to reform teacher practice to conform to Nova Scotia governmental influence (see NSTS 2017, Inter-University Committee on Teacher Education 2017, 2018). Neoliberalism would position these government directives as accountability measures, transforming the teaching profession, and ultimately teacher education programs to being transparent and responsive to public demands. Therefore, teacher expectations focus on managerial tasks, behavior management, and discipline policy enforcers as lived by John, Margaret, and Blair. Neoliberalism would see teachers following a *pathway of instruction* resulting in improved teacher effectiveness.

When we reconsider the typical teacher education program structure, I sense this pathway is causing teachers at all stages of their careers to drift away from teaching as a relational experience. The path is leading a teacher's practice to an over-simplified limitation and this leaves me with questions that disturb pedagogical practice: have teachers become learning managers and mediators in behavior and disciplinary classroom management practices? Have teachers become mere technicians implementing learning theories and mere presenters of knowledge? And is the teacher a classroom technician utilizing the latest tactics in subject matter specialization armed with assessment strategies that claim accurate measures in student growth further objectifying our children? John, Margaret, and Blair have resisted teaching to such a simplistic view of practice, they would not overlook the moral-relational complexities experienced in the everyday teacher–student encounter. Therefore, we could wonder if these imposed *pathways of instruction* over time have done damage to the profession by dictating pedagogical restrictions. If this is the case, the lived experiences described earlier call out to a teacher's sensibility to preserve the uniqueness of each child (Foran and Saevi 2012).

Imposed government standards

The NSTS (2017) leaves pedagogical practice vulnerable, leaving me to wonder how to contribute to this type of educational model as a teacher educator. Absent in the NSTS is a declaration, or at least a reference, for teachers to take their place relationally alongside children. Teacher education programs across Canada typically attempt to cover growth of children as a pedagogical practice as a stand-alone course topic. The disturbing feature of NSTS (2017) overview is that it confines the child to standardized development timelines according to human-development theories – the child is not a theory. John, Margaret, and Blair provided an alternative for what it means to be a professional and pedagogical. But is there room for both in current educational practice in neoliberal times? To be professional is to be accountable to imposed government standards (NSTS 2017), to be skilled in utilizing assessment tools, to adhere to an outcomes-based education, to be well versed using instructional strategies, to be an effective classroom manager controlling student behavior, to be informed and competent in educational law, to be compliant in school board policies, to foster inclusion models, and to be a diagnostician for special education. These topics are essential to teaching in Canada, but to teach requires more, because there is a moral pedagogical obligation to see each child as unique and not as a curricular outcome or imposed government standard.

Many would argue that a teacher education program, intent on developing future teachers to be committed to a strong program aims to incorporate content – subject specific knowledge, literacy, numeracy, social justice, reflective practice, and constructivist theory as it applies to lesson planning and integrated units of study. And there is no doubt that government officials would value this linear single-layered approach of professional competencies. However, the many adults who have spent time with children, and young people, know if they are unable to relate to youth on a human level, they will have difficulty in leading their growth. Therefore, a pathway for practicing teacher educators would cultivate pedagogical sensitivities as they steer professional growth.

The last decade

Pedagogy has become a low priority over the last decade, in the daily role of practicing teachers. Encounters with a number of Nova Scotian teachers allowed for collegial conversations, where I discovered a common theme: teaching is becoming a shallow and pressured practice. These introspective accounts as lived experiences reclaim the core element of a teachers' practice – the child. These lived experience descriptions contextualize teaching as pedagogical not technical, relational not managerial, hopeful not dismal, yes governmentally controlled, but somehow still rebellious. Those invested in neoliberalism approaches cannot understand how to control what it means to teach beyond the academic elements of coursework. The anecdotes reclaim the pedagogical, and these can guide our insights into what it means to teach in neoliberal times. I read resistance in each anecdote and have determined that subtly teachers are "taking back education." Each account places the relational as foundational countering the instructional demands common to many teachers across Canada. Pedagogy could serve as critical for teachers who have become immersed in a rational-technical approach due to neoliberalism, offering a humanistic direction guiding children to grow and mature.

Teachers cannot escape the predominant reality that curriculum, in its broadest sense, means restriction and an instructional recipe that is not necessarily geared toward helping a young person grow. A neoliberal curriculum determines the relationship between adult and child as institutionally mediated. The teacher will be acting in a professional capacity enforcing policy, rules, guidelines, reports, and codes of conduct. Children do not seek relationships with this in mind! Neoliberalism continues to guide and impact teacher–student relationship, but what it is unable to do is eradicate the pedagogical.

This remains special and foreign to neoliberal sensitivities, for pedagogical relationships lie outside the neoliberal agenda. Teachers need to relearn to listen to the call (Foran and Hultgren 2012) and allow their practice to return to *the things* themselves (Heidegger 1962).

References

Biesta, G.J.J., 2011. Disciplines and theory in the academic study of education: A comparative analysis of the Anglo-American and Continental construction of the field. *Pedagogy, Culture and Society*, 19 (2), 175–192.

Biesta, G.J.J., 2012. Giving teaching back to education: Responding to the disappearance of the teacher. *Phenomenology & Practice*, 6 (2), 35–49.

Foran, A. and Hultgren, F., 2012. Editorial: The pedagogical call. *Special Issue: Phenomenology & Practice*, 6 (2), 1–7.

Foran, A. and Olson, M., 2008. Seeking pedagogical places. *Phenomenology & Practice*, 1 (2), 24–48.

Foran, A. and Robinson, D.B., 2017. Mollenhauer's representation: The role of preservice teachers in the practices of upbringing. *Education*, 23 (2), 3–24.

Foran, A. and Saevi, T., 2012. Seeing pedagogically, telling phenomenologically: Addressing the profound complexity of education. *Phenomenology & Practice*, 6 (2), 50–64. (C)

Galvin, K. and Todres, L., 2007. The creativity of 'unspecialization:' A contemplative direction for integrative scholarly practice. *Phenomenology & Practice*, 1 (1), 31–46.

Giroux, H., 2010. Neoliberalism as public pedagogy. *In*: J. Sandlin, B. Schultz, and J. Burdick, eds. *Handbook of public pedagogy*. New York: Taylor & Francis Group, 486–500.

Heidegger, M., 1962. The worldhood of the world. *In*: J. MacQuarrie and E. Robinson, Trans. *Being and time*. New York: Harper & Row, 91–145.

Husserl, E., 1970. *The crises of European sciences and transcendental phenomenology*. Evanston, IL: Northwestern University Press.

Inter-University Committee on Teacher Education, 2017. *Accreditation timeline and approach*. Halifax, Canada: Author.

Inter-University Committee on Teacher Education, 2018. *ICTE final draft accreditation with 11 GCOs chart*. Halifax, Canada: Author.

Langeveld, M.J., 1975. *Personal help for children growing up*. The W.B. Curry Lecture. University of Exeter.

Merleau-Ponty, M., 2010. *Child psychology and pedagogy: The Sorbonne lectures 1949–1952*. Evanston, IL: Northwestern University Press.

Mollenhauer, K., 2014. *Forgotten connections. On culture and upbringing*. Translated by N. Friesen. New York: Routledge.

Nova Scotia Department of Education and Early Childhood Development, 2017. *Nova Scotia teaching standards: Excellence in teaching and learning*. Halifax, Canada: Author.

Saevi, T., 2007. Den pedagogiske relasjonen – en relasjon annerledes enn andre relasjoner [The pedagogical relation – a relation different from other relations]. *In*: O.H. Kaldestad, E. Reigstad, J. Sæther, and J. Sæthre, eds. *Grunnverdier og pedagogikk* [Basic values and education]. Bergen, Norway: Fagbokforlaget, 107–131.

van Manen, M., 1988. The relation between research and pedagogy. *In*: W. Pinar, ed. *Contemporary curriculum discourses*. Scottsdale: AZ: Gorsuch Scarisbride, 437–452.

van Manen, M., 1991. *The tact of teaching: The meaning of pedagogical thoughtfulness*. New York: State University of New York Press.

van Manen, M., 1997. *Researching lived experience. Researching lived experience human science for an action sensitive pedagogy*. 2nd ed. London, Ontario: Althouse Press.
van Manen, M., 2002. *The tone of teaching*. London/Ontario: Althouse Press.
van Manen, M., 2012. The call of pedagogy as the call of contact. *Phenomenology & Practice*, 6 (2), 8–34.
van Manen, M., 2014. *Phenomenology of practice*. New York: Routledge.
van Manen, M., 2015. *Pedagogical tact*. Walnut Creek, CA: Left Coast Press.

Part 2

Children, adults, voice and agency

On the problem of seeing education from children's perspective

Tone Saevi

Part 2 of this volume addresses the meaning of being a child, or young person, in contemporary society. Being a child or young person in our Western world includes taking part in daily education for at least ten years of your life. Education traditionally is considered the responsibility that any society has towards the next generation. Education as such, is a task that needs children and young persons to be relevant, in as much as children and young people need education to become *human* human beings, or at least we believe they do. Everybody wants something from children and young people; teach them, influence them, get their attention, interest, time, or energy. What is so important to teach them that an educational task of this amount is required? The term 'task' can be understood as any kind of job, commission or even transaction, but here we suggest that education is a particular task, an 'oppgave' in Norwegian, or 'Aufgabe' in German, a word meaning something that might be hard to do, but regardless it is my responsibility. The second part of the word, 'gave' or 'gabe' literally means gift. A task understood as an 'oppgave' might be understood as a difficult gift that might even be hard for the child or young person to receive, but which adults and society are responsible for giving to them. However, if education is considered an 'oppgave' it should be given to children and young people unconditionally; without expectation of a commission or a return of service, and definitely not as a transaction that demands an outcome, an acquired competence or even gratitude.

The intention that education should be meaningful and have qualities that address children is obvious, we might think. But herein lies the paradox. According to Lippitz (1986) we as adults and adult society cannot simply relate to children, because we do not know who the child is. We were children once, but over time the past experience of the child I once was, has become present remembrance of experiences that no longer are. My childhood is lost and even if I relate to children – in memory of the child within me as a kind of guiding star – the experience I get is not of the real child that I encounter, the child before me and with me but of my own image of what it is like to be a child. My halting memory of my own childhood experience lingers always in the past present. Thus the child in education cannot *not* be seen from an adult or societal perspective as being the object or project of education. The adult project is to educate the child and young person towards that which the adult world considers human humanity and good citizenship. The questions remain, however. How do we as adults balance the child's and the society's needs of what we consider educational qualities? Whose agency, voice and action are legitimate to form, influence, and create education? How do I as a researcher enter the field of education without increasing 'my original outsider quality by applying inappropriate categories and models of interpretation of my research activity?' (p. 62). Lippitz suggests that before we can understand something we must know it well, and in order to know something well we must be part of it somehow without rational intentions and attempts to control. Being familiar with something so to say happens 'behind the researcher's back' (p. 64), In this part of the book children and young people are present experientially, existentially and educationally, although often via adult voices. The educational relationship is the lived entity between children and adults, and the relationship is not simply a formal or informal encounter between child and adult, but as Løgstrup says, there is an existential relation present before the actual encounter takes place. We cannot simply look at the child or stop in front of the child to observe her. Rather we need to be invited into children's lives, be immersed in their activities, experiences, worries and imaginings. This I think, is only partially possible, and only if we as adults are trusted and invited by the children and young people.

A radical rethinking of educational means and aims actualizes a renewed interest in how to encounter the young generation in the complexity of their lived presence; rather than in their potential to increase the outcomes of education. In this section we promote the Rancierian idea that emancipation is about being able to speak and act – that children and adults already speak and act – without an overruling authority having to translate their speaking and acting to an acceptable language. We believe that the unique human voice and agency are sufficient for education to be educational, and suggest that school should be the place where the single vulnerable and open voice is heard and respected.

The second part of this edited book opens with Peter Roberts' chapter. We live in an educational world increasingly dominated by the language of measurement. This is evident at an international level (e.g., in the PISA rankings), within countries (e.g., via 'national standards' in schools), and within institutions (e.g., in systems of performance measurement and review). There is a heavy reliance on 'big data' in structuring educational decisions. Concomitant with this has been an appeal to the supposed 'science' of learning in determining policy priorities for education. Roberts critiques these trends, arguing that they rest on weak ontological, epistemological and ethical foundations and ignore what it means to exist as a human being. Drawing on the work of

Søren Kierkegaard, he suggests that the quest for certainty currently prevalent in education is misguided, dehumanizing in ways that silence voice and agency and is life-denying. Built on the idea that much of what is most important in education and human existence is immeasurable, unpredictable and uncertain, Roberts explores the implications for a theory of the concept and experience of pedagogical agency.

Walter Omar Kohan deals with the political implications of the relationship between education, philosophy and life, for contemporary education. What is under attack is the very possibility of dialogical critique towards a political-educational regime that separates cognition and experience, school and life. Kohan argues that philosophy as thinking and acting is a way of life. There is no such thing as a *life-free* thinking or a *thinking-free* life. He asserts that educators like Socrates, Simon Rodriguez, also called the 'Socrates of Caracas', and Paulo Freire, are attacked by the sustainers of the political order due to their deep reading of the world's educational and existential concerns. Freire does not only propose change in theory and thinking, but speaks to and lives up to a praxis where words are spoken and written to change the world. Freire's life, voice, and agency threaten neoliberal ideology because learning, insight and care are not meant to serve only those on the inside of rich and competing societies; but also the world of the outsiders, the lives of the marginalized, the poor, and those who suffer injustices are our responsibility and thus are what educational dialogue should address.

Western cultures and education systems are marked by a 'chirographic bias': literacy is seen as an unquestioned good, which needs to be brought to all human cultures, where it is disseminated into the minds of children through the process of education. Literacy, however, is not a natural phenomenon, but a textual technology that was invented and refined over the millennia. It has a profound impact on consciousness, memory, embodiment and cultural practices and discourses. Eva Simms, in her chapter, approaches the phenomenon of literacy by examining literacy as a technology which is inserted into the processes of human consciousness. Inserting textual technology into developing human minds by teaching them how to read and write restructures human perception and shapes cognitive practices, and hence the voice and agency of the young. It alters the child's existential field and relationships with others, places, things and time. Literacy brings great gains to cultures, but it also brings great psychological losses: indigenous cultures and non-textual voices and practices are devalued and eventually extinguished in the progressive march of textual colonialism; for literate minds, the immediacy and fullness of the sensory world begins to diminish and many adults feel alienated from nature and the body. The printed book is a forerunner of the contemporary information and communication technologies (ICTs) and understanding the virtual practice of reading as technology can help us understand the consequences of increasing virtuality, which our children encounter in the media landscapes they increasingly inhabit today.

In the final chapter of Part 2 Tone Saevi explores the phenomenological meaning of subjectivity, naivety and the possibility of freedom in school settings. She reflects on two educational events from a novel and from the classroom, respectively, and tries out – or reality-tests – their educational qualities. The theoretical idea of personal subjectivity – the student's as well as the teacher's own spontaneous response to that which comes from outside of themselves – is addressed to see which, if any, educational insights a phenomenological analysis might bring about.

Reference

Lippitz, W., 1986. Understanding children, communicating with children: Approaches to the child within us, before us and with us. *Pedagogy + Phenomenology*, 4 (2), 56–65.

Chapter 5

More than measurement
Education, uncertainty and existence

Peter Roberts

An obsession with measurement

In many countries of the Western world the logic of measurement exercises a pervasive influence over everyday life. We measure GDP, changes in interest rates, and movements in the stock exchange. International organisations such as the OECD produce elaborate diagrams and tables comparing nations on measures of economic, cultural and social performance. Websites and YouTube channels count and display hits, subscribers and likes. Individuals with Facebook sites can now measure their popularity and worth by the number of 'friends' they have, sometimes numbering in the thousands. Even happiness is now seen as something that can be measured, both within individuals and across countries. Almost from the moment we are born, we are subject to systems of measurement, some subtle, others more intrusive. We rate and rank ourselves and others almost constantly, and as technologies evolve, we frequently find new ways to do so. Measurement is not simply something 'out there', an external influence to which we become subject when we interact with the world. It is also 'within' us, both in our bodies (e.g., with medical devices that monitor the heart and other organs) and in our minds (e.g., in the way we understand ourselves through incessant comparisons with others). Measurement provides a platform on which to make judgements, to evaluate, to discern. It structures decision-making and assists in the process of predicting future outcomes. Measurement is, for the most part, portrayed as a good thing: as something that improves human lives.

The dominance of measurement as a ubiquitous presence in our lives is also evident in prevailing conceptions and practices of education. Measurement, of one form or another, plays a significant role in determining educational priorities and commitments. It allows those who distribute public funds to feel more confident that money invested in educational institutions and organisations is being well spent. Measurement in education is frequently associated with assessment, and assessment has, for many decades, been seen as sufficiently important to demand a small army of specialists devoted to it. There are assessment advisors in government departments, academics appointed to university positions in this area, and thousands of research studies on the subject. Assessment is regarded as a vital part of the education system, and in some cases, starts from the moment a child begins his or her formal schooling. In many countries, there has been a particularly heavy emphasis on assessment in the senior secondary school, but the trend internationally is to push the age at which children become 'measurable' lower and lower. Pressures to perform, and to be prepared adequately for this, are becoming ever greater as countries seek to improve their rankings in the PISA process. The early childhood education sector is now no longer free from the obsession with measurement and performance, and it is not uncommon for children as young as three or four to be given special tutoring to enable them to 'get ahead' of their classmates when they start school.

Measurement is ever present in the tertiary sector as well, reflecting the broad shift over the last three decades or more to a broadly neoliberal *modus operandi*. In countries such as England, Canada, Australia and New Zealand, universities and other tertiary education institutions have been reconstructed along managerialist lines, with forms of accountability, monitoring and marketing modelled on the corporate world. Students, now treated as customers or consumers, are counted, courted and counselled. Millions of dollars are spent on advertising campaigns, all designed to improve performance relative to other institutions of higher education, nationally and internationally. 'Performance' itself is construed in predominantly quantitative terms, with references, for example, to student numbers, funding and endowments, and rankings in league tables such as those produced by QS and Times Higher. Performance within institutions is also measured, via regular reviews, both of people and of courses and programmes. Judgements about teaching quality are often heavily reliant on student surveys, with ratings on Likert scales under various headings (organisation, content, attitude, interest generated, and so on) contributing to an overall measure of 'teaching effectiveness'. Research too is subject to the same obsession with measurement, with the value of research – and researchers – frequently being reduced to dollars generated in external grants, indices based on citation counts, and scores generated by performance-based research funding schemes. Journals are ranked on the basis of their 'impact factors' and in some contexts (e.g., the REF exercise undertaken in the UK) academics themselves are assessed, in part, on the basis of the demonstrable impact of their work beyond the academy.

In this measurement-driven world, knowledge has been reconfigured, sometimes to the point of appearing increasingly irrelevant in determining the value of teaching and research. Those evaluated through performance-based research schemes are not required to demonstrate that they know anything; what counts is measured performance. Indeed, the trend over the last two decades of educational reform has been to progressively separate the knower from the known; to create the means for generating knowledge, or information, without the presence of a knowing subject. The increasing use of 'big

More than measurement 65

data' in making key decisions, in education and in other areas of social policy, provides a contemporary illustration of this point. Data generated by powerful algorithms that sift through millions of pieces of information, often within seconds or micro-seconds, are sometimes presented as if they 'speak for themselves'. Human beings are, at times, several steps removed from the calculative process, with 'artificial intelligence' taking over functions that would hitherto have been the preserve of flesh and blood employees. The status and authority of claims is supposedly enhanced by the sheer scale of the enterprise. Those reading the figures can easily feel powerless in their presence, ill-equipped to comprehend, let alone contest, calculations undertaken with such massive data sets. Access to and control over information confers enormous advantages in shaping how people think and what they want. 'The numbers don't lie', we are led to believe, and thus the march of measurement as a defining theme of our epoch continues.

Needless to say, these trends have not escaped criticism in the international academic community. Scholars have problematised the dominant focus on measurement (Roberts 1997, Biesta 2009, Mack 2014, 2014, Webster 2017), the language and logic of performativity (Roberts 2007, 2013, Locke 2015), the interpretation and application of PISA results (Murphy 2014), 'what works' discourses (Smeyers and Depaepe 2006, Biesta 2007, Webster 2018), and developments in the use of big data (Argenton 2017, Ben-Porath and Shahar 2017, Prinsloo 2017). There are several important lines of critique open to those who have misgivings about these trends. We might find fault with some technical aspect of a measurement process. We can point to shortcomings in the way findings are interpreted or applied. We may object to the stress caused by endless assessment in schools, or to the way in which it shapes pedagogy and the curriculum. Such arguments can often be countered, for example, by offering a different approach to working with numbers, or with some concessions to reduce the time spent on measurement and assessment, or with an adjustment in the way a system works to better suit a range of learning styles. But debates over these matters, while sometimes helpful, can distract us from raising deeper concerns. Regardless of whether we understand how measurement systems work, how rankings and ratings are produced, or how algorithms are developed and applied in the world of 'big data', the question of why we appear to be so obsessed with measurement – and with attaining greater certainty – remains.

Why should this bother us? One answer to this question, to be fleshed out in this chapter, is that in constantly measuring ourselves – in becoming obsessed with numbers, and with rankings and ratings and likes and hits – we, as it were, 'forget' ourselves. Building on the work of Søren Kierkegaard, I argue that in seeking to understand the meaning and significance of education, our starting point should not be performance, productivity or prosperity but rather the existing human individual. Kierkegaard maintains that '[a]ll essential knowing concerns existence' (2009, p. 166). This proposition will be extended in this chapter to suggest that education too should be centrally concerned with the question of existence, with what it means to be a human being. A focus on the question of existence helps us to see that attempts to turn education into a 'science' with predictable and measurable outcomes are misguided. We need to acknowledge – and, indeed, celebrate – the fundamental uncertainties that structure educational lives. It is, I shall suggest, the very qualities that resist easy measurement that make education important and worthwhile.

Education, truth and existence: Kierkegaard's inwardness

Kierkegaard is widely regarded as one of the key figures in existentialist thought. Born in 1813, he was a prolific writer, producing an extensive body of published work in his short life. He devoted considerable intellectual energy to his exploration of three different modes of existence: the aesthetic, the ethical and the religious (Kierkegaard 1987). Themes such as anxiety, fear and death feature prominently in his writings (Kierkegaard 1980, 1985, 1989), but he is also known for his inspirational and 'upbuilding' discourses (Kierkegaard 1988, 1998, Wivestad 2011). Since his death in 1855, he has enjoyed a mixed reception in the philosophical community. Among analytic philosophers, his work has been largely ignored. Within what might broadly be conceived as the Continental tradition, however, he has exerted considerable influence, leaving his mark on thinkers such as Unamuno, Sartre, Camus, Derrida and many others. Over the years, his ideas have attracted considerable attention from educationists, who have found his work helpful in addressing ontological, epistemological, ethical, political and aesthetic questions (see, for example, Hill 1966, Kwak 2001, McPherson 2001, McKnight 2004, 2010, Reindal 2013, Roberts 2016, Saeverot 2013, Tubbs 2005, Webster 2009, Wivestad 2011). Kierkegaard was a master of irony and indirect communication, adopting various pseudonyms in his books, each with their own philosophical and religious orientations.

A key work in Kierkegaard's corpus is his *Concluding Unscientific Postscript* (Kierkegaard 2009). Kierkegaard assigns the authorship of this work to 'Johannes Climacus', a doubting presence among his pseudonyms. Climacus emphasises the development of what he refers to as 'inwardness'. This notion has clear relevance for education, with its emphasis on the formation of the self. Kierkegaard draws a contrast between 'objective' and 'subjective' paths to understanding and development, favouring the latter but not uncritically so. His central claim, that truth is subjectivity, has been much debated (Schacht 1973, McLane 1977, Hughes 1995, Hamilton 1998, Jacoby 2002, Evans 2008). Climacus argues that objective reflection 'makes the subject accidental, and existence thereby into something indifferent, vanishing'; if 'the subject fails to become wholly indifferent to himself, this only shows that his objective striving is not sufficiently objective' (Kierkegaard 2009, pp. 162–163). At its most extreme, the subjective path can lead to insanity, with madness and truth becoming indistinguishable. Cervantes' (2005) character Don Quixote is the prototype here, with his passionate, tragic/comic embrace of a single fixed idea, of no interest to anyone else. But a lack of inwardness is also madness, and of a more deeply worrying kind: 'although the something which the blissful individual knows is indeed the truth, the truth that concerns the entire human race, it does not concern the much-respected rattler in the least. This is a more inhuman kind of madness than the other' (Kierkegaard 2009, pp. 164–165). We can try to think ourselves away from existence, yet it is through existence that we have thinking at all. Existence is seen as an irrelevance or an impediment, yet it is the central problem to be faced by each individual; it is, for each individual, a distinctive and demanding task. We tend to think that 'existing is nothing . . . after all we all exist'; but to truly exist, 'that is, to permeate one's existence with consciousness, at once eternal as though far beyond it and yet present in it, and nevertheless in the course of becoming – that is truly difficult' (p. 258).

What are the implications of these ideas for education? Kierkegaard might seem a world away from our current concerns, yet his prompting to ponder the question of existence remains as relevant today as it was in his time. This is, he would insist, not merely an abstract problem but an intensely practical question. The task of existing is very much an educational endeavour; one that involves coming to know the self but also learning how to act and interact with others and the world. To 'exist' is not simply to be alive; it is to *live*. It implies a mode of being, an orientation to knowing, and a form of moral commitment. Existing, as Kierkegaard conceives of it, is a distinctively human task. We are not merely 'given' our existence as human subjects; we must *take responsibility* for existing. We must also constantly seek to reaffirm and 'remake' ourselves as existing individual subjects. In living in the truth of our subjectivity, we form ourselves as human beings, always in a process of becoming. This is what makes existence educational, in the sense intended by the German notion of *bildung*: education as a process of formation or development.

In the contemporary world, we neglect the problem of existence. At first glance, this claim might seem problematic. With the rise of social media, there is more of a focus on the 'self' than ever before. Many who use Facebook and other social media platforms communicate incessantly about themselves and their lives. They take regular 'selfies' (photographs of themselves), document their every move when on vacation, inform viewers of what they eat when dining out, and keep subscribers up to date with what is happening in their jobs and families. Platforms such as Twitter provide ample opportunity for users to voice their opinions on almost any imaginable topic. Far from fleeing from their existence, social media devotees seem to be fixated on it, expressing their thoughts and feelings freely and openly, making the personal visible, for all the world – or at least all online 'friends' – to see.

Yet, the concern with the self that is characteristic of our age is, in many respects, the polar opposite of the searching examination of existence that Kierkegaard had in mind. While Facebook, Instagram and Twitter can be employed in a multitude of different ways, the emphasis across these social media platforms is on surfaces, on appearances and what is projected outwardly rather than investigated inwardly. For Kierkegaard, the problem of existence demands serious, lifelong consideration. In the social media universe, there is often a tendency to focus on what is shallow, fleeting and entertaining. These tendencies are reinforced by the settings prescribed for users, with, for example, character limits in Twitter that prohibit lengthy, in-depth exploration of complex questions and issues. Individuality appears to be heavily promoted, yet there is also a sense of uniformity that prevails. Ideas can be conveyed, images can be displayed, and emotions can be captured – but only within the parameters set by the multinational corporations that oversee these sites. Not only that: individuals in the digital age often seem to want to be like other constructions of what it means to be an individual. Individuality, like almost everything else in a neoliberal world, is marketed and sold, creating endless 'copycat' individuals who are thus, in a sense, no longer individuals at all. Kierkegaard did not conform to any model prescribed for him by someone else. His individuality carried a heavy price, with social isolation, loneliness and derision from others for his dress, his manner and his ideas. He was very much an 'outsider' (Allen 1983). Individualism is alive and well in the twenty-first century, but the kind of courage exhibited by Kierkegaard in making inwardness his life's work is rare.

We should likewise be careful not to align Kierkegaard with the view, commonly expressed by young students today, that 'truth is relative' or that 'everything is subjective'. The related contemporary phenomenon of 'fake news' is a more extreme manifestation of similar thinking. In a so-called 'post-truth' world, news items that are demonstrably false can, with the aid of social media, be widely and quickly circulated – and believed, by thousands of people. A common example cited when discussing these trends is Donald Trump, who, in both his election campaign and his subsequent tenure as president of the United States, has demonstrated a blatant disregard for truth. Under the Trump administration, a new term, 'alternative facts', has come into being as a part of the political lexicon. The term was used by a member of the president's team in explaining differences between competing accounts of the numbers present at Trump's inauguration. An 'alternative fact' is a lie, or, at the very least, a form of wilful political blindness. Ironically, having been aided by 'fake news' in gaining the presidency, Trump now routinely turns the label back on the media, using it as a weapon to attack stories he does not like. In this environment, 'truth' can be whatever someone wants it to be. This is not the way Kierkegaard saw it.

Kierkegaard is, as Jan Evans points out, no relativist. There is an important difference between the notion that 'truth is subjective' and Climacus's claim that 'truth is subjectivity'. Climacus's main concern is not with the existence of 'multiple truths' but with 'the relevance of truth to the exister' (Evans 2008, p. 405). In Gert Biesta's words, '[t]his is about *how* the individual relates to the truth, . . . rather than *what* the individual relates to' (Biesta 2013, p. 458).

In distinguishing objective truth from subjective truth, Climacus is drawing a distinction 'between the theoretical and the existential, that is, between what is true and *what matters*' (p. 458). Kierkegaard's philosophical contemporaries held that the gaining of knowledge requires objectivity, and if an appropriately objective approach is to be taken, personality must be suppressed and individuality transcended. Striving to attain objectivity of this sort, for Kierkegaard, constituted a kind of 'self-annihilation' (Schacht 1973, p. 299). Truth as Climacus conceives of it is not something to be pursued abstractly; indeed, the ideal of becoming a 'completely rational, objective, impersonal knower' is an impossibility (pp. 301–302).

Results obtained from big data analytics, the PISA process, performance-based research assessment exercises, and teaching surveys are all premised on the assumption that gaining greater objectivity is desirable. But what counts as being objective can change over time (Biesta 2013, p. 458); being subjective, however, remains a permanent task. 'Objectivity' provides a kind of refuge; an escape from the demanding and potentially harrowing task of inward examination. To measure is, in some fashion, to *manage*. Confronted with a world that can be overwhelming, we immediately search for ways to impose order. Numbers provide a sense of security, but this can be misleading. We long for certainty, but education creates further *un*certainty (Roberts 2005). Education prompts us to question, to probe further, to keep investigating. Education makes us not smug and settled but restless and uncomfortable. At times it can leave us feeling 'on edge', as if we are standing on a cliff where we could fall at any moment. Existence refuses to be easily 'contained'; there is an unpredictable and unruly aspect to it. To exist, we must learn to live with unknowns – with events, situations and circumstances we cannot predict and cannot control. It is not only our encounter with what is external to us that remains unpredictable; it is also the inner spaces we enter, the emotions we experience and the thoughts that arise.

Measurement always seeks to constrain; to keep the object of investigation under sufficient control to count it or weigh it or assess it some other way. Measurement, if it is to work effectively, relies upon a certain standardisation, such that assessments made at one time can be compared meaningfully with those made at another time. If Climacus's 'truth is subjectivity' thesis is accepted, however, we find much that is beyond our control and we are seeking the very opposite of standardisation. Education with a focus on existence is concerned not with ensuring consistency for the purposes of counting but with allowing someone to become and be an individual. From an existential perspective, every pedagogical encounter is 'unique, unrepeatable and called into being by the present persons, for a purpose, and within a context' (Saevi 2011, p. 457). We must attend, as Climacus says, and as others such as Simone Weil (1997, 2001) and Iris Murdoch (2001) have argued, to *particular* human beings, not abstractions. For a teacher, it is the being in front of us now, at this moment, under these circumstances, with whom an educational encounter takes place. There is no yardstick against which existence can be universally measured; to exist is to be constantly 'in the making', always dealing with that which is different from what has gone before. Such differences may be evident in only the most minute of ways, but they are nonetheless important in giving each pedagogical situation its distinctive set of problems and possibilities (see further, Roberts 2011, Roberts and Freeman-Moir 2013).

If learning to exist is regarded a central purpose of education, almost everything that comes to matter will resist the logic of measurement. Existence does not proceed in a logical, linear, ordered manner. It need not be seen as chaotic, but even where there is coherence – even where the decisions made and the actions taken seem to make sense, viewed as part of a 'bigger picture' – the path taken is seldom smooth sailing. We develop in fits and starts, with 'successes' and 'failures', wrong turns and dead ends. This messy territory is exactly where education takes place. It is the very things that make life complex and difficult that are, potentially at least, most important for us in what and how we learn. Everyone who is educated exists, and in living, we make existence ever present as the potential object of our reflection. Yet we seldom take up the implied invitation to pursue such matters further. This may, as Kierkegaard teaches us, be because the very 'everydayness' of existence lulls us into a kind of sleep, where we act on the basis of habit and routine rather than thought. Or, it may be a resigned dismissal: what is the point of addressing such questions, when even the most learned philosophers cannot agree on the answers? Or, we may fear the consequences of inner investigation of this kind, having observed the angst they have prompted in others. But what remains unexamined does not disappear, and, as Schopenhauer (1966) observed, problems left alone in one context or at one time will often arise in other ways at other times.

To exist is to desire, to feel, to think, to be. We may experience love, anger, frustration, anxiety, and joy, all of which cannot, in any meaningful way, be 'measured'. We have commitments to others, and seek to better their lives as well as our own. We have hopes, fears and dreams. These immeasurable elements of our existence are not incidental or insignificant in a human life; *they are the very heart of it*. Yet they are often downplayed, if not ignored altogether, in educational discourse and practice. The relentless desire to measure and to manage is a kind of defensive mechanism in the face of uncertainty and fear. We can never know, fully and definitively, why we are here and what we are supposed to do with our lives. This is, in many ways, the basis for the whole body of existentialist thought from Kierkegaard onwards (cf. Cooper 1999, Flynn 2009, Webster 2009). Taking these questions seriously, as an educational task, is full of dangers. To commit to education involves accepting the risk of doubts, difficulties and even despair (Jardine 1992, McKnight 2010, Roberts 2013). Education involves agony and struggle (Kuhlman 1994). This does not mean we should lose hope, or that we need to lapse into a kind of ethical or pedagogical paralysis. We can still speak meaningfully of human agency and hope in the face of uncertainty, unpredictability and unhappiness (Roberts 2016). Agency does not have to be associated with aggression, assertiveness or power. It can instead proceed from a starting point of fragility – of contingency and ambiguity in human decisions and actions (Beauvoir 1948).

In *Concluding Unscientific Postscript* it is noted that the problem of existence is difficult, in part, because existence is a form of motion; we are always changing, always in a process of becoming. This means that the task of existing, as Climacus understands it, is lifelong; it is something to which we must always be committed. The same is true of education. 'The' problem or question of existence is really multiple questions: What *is* existence? *Why* do we exist? *How* should we exist? With *whom* or *what* do we exist? And in the educational sphere, other more specific questions arise: How do we *learn* how, why and with whom to exist? Who might play a role in *teaching* us about these things? What can the process of existing teach *us*? There are, it might be objected, no quick, easy, clear, or definite answers these questions. *That is precisely the point.* We often seek the easiest, fastest, most efficient ways of doing things, but education with a focus on the problem of existence is slow, demanding, *in*efficient. It does not provide 'solutions' but instead fosters a continual return, across a lifespan, to perennial problems. In refusing to comply with the dictates of measurement, education conceived in these terms poses a threat, albeit a 'quiet' one, to the established educational order. But this is exactly what education should be: a 'subversive' process that encourages people to ask questions, probe further, and dig deeper. Education should enable us to examine our most cherished assumptions about ourselves and the world in which we live. It should prompt us to examine afresh the very foundations on which contemporary social and economic institutions stand.

Conclusion

There is nothing inherently 'wrong' with measurement. Robust systems of measurement are essential if bridges are to serve their function well, if planes are not to fall from the sky, and if the automobiles we drive are to avoid crashing. Measurement can be informative and inspirational. It can be helpful in allowing us to assess progress, and in motivating us to achieve our goals. It is not measurement *per se* that is worrying but rather the *obsession* with it, in education as in many other spheres of contemporary life. The drive to measure – to rate, rank and compare – is relentless and much of value has been lost in the process. We have tried to make even the most 'unscientific' aspects of human life scientific. We try to convince ourselves that if we have a 'science' of happiness, for instance, such an approach will somehow produce a more accurate, trustworthy, 'objective' picture of what makes us happy and of how happiness can be attained. Education, as noted at the beginning of this chapter, has fallen prey to the same type of thinking, with appeals to the so-called 'science' of learning and an increasing reliance on 'big data' in making pedagogical decisions.

Yet, as Kierkegaard shows, the more objective we strive to become, the further we move away from ourselves. We become so awash with numbers that we cannot see the human beings that are meant to be at the heart of the process of education. We forget that we are, first and foremost, beings who *exist*. The obsession with measuring almost every aspect of human life – with reducing so much of what we do to a numbers game – has created its own blindness and education has a key role to play in restoring the sight that has been lost in this madness. Education is concerned with much more than measurement. Much of what matters most in education, this chapter has argued, is immeasurable, uncertain and unpredictable. The uncertainties and contingencies that characterise human existence need not be seen as deterrents in 'getting things done'; to the contrary, they can enhance rather than reduce the prospects for meaningful agency. Realising the possibilities in education, aware of the dangers we face in doing so, affirms our existence as unique, complex beings and allows us to see that some puzzles are not meant to ever be fully and finally solved.

References

Allen, D., 1983. *Three outsiders: Pascal, Kierkegaard, Simone Weil*. Eugene, OR: Wipf & Stock.

Argenton, G., 2017. Mind the gaps: Controversies about algorithms, learning and trendy knowledge. *E-Learning and Digital Media*, 14 (3), 183–197.

Beauvoir, S. de, 1948. *The ethics of ambiguity*. Translated by B. Frechtman. New York: Citadel Press.

Ben-Porath, S. and Shahar, T.H.B., 2017. Big data and education: Ethical and moral challenges. *Theory and Research in Education*, 15 (3), 243–248.

Biesta, G., 2007. Why 'what works' won't work: Evidence-based practice and the democratic deficit in educational research. *Educational Theory*, 57 (1), 1–22.

Biesta, G., 2009. Good education in an age of measurement: On the need to reconnect with the question of purpose in education. *Educational Assessment, Evaluation and Accountability*, 21 (1), 33–46.

Biesta, G., 2013. Receiving the gift of teaching: From 'learning from' to 'being taught by'. *Studies in Philosophy and Education*, 32, 449–461.

Cervantes, M. de, 2005. *Don Quixote*. Translated by E. Grossman. London: Vintage.

Cooper, D.E., 1999. *Existentialism: A reconstruction*. 2nd ed. Oxford: Blackwell.

Descartes, R., 1911. Discourse on method. In: *The philosophical works of Descartes*, vol. 1. Translated by E.S. Haldane and G.R.T. Ross. Cambridge: Cambridge University Press.

Evans, J.E., 2008. Miguel de Unamuno's reception and use of the Kierkegaardian claim that "truth is subjectivity." *Revista Portuguesa de Filosofia*, 64, 1113–1126.

Flynn, T., 2009. *Existentialism: A brief insight*. New York: Sterling.

Hamilton, C., 1998. Kierkegaard on truth as subjectivity: Christianity, ethics and asceticism. *Religious Studies*, 34 (1), 61–79.

Hill, B.V., 1966. Soren Kierkegaard and educational theory. *Educational Theory*, 16 (4), 344–353.

Hughes, E.J., 1995. How subjectivity is truth in the *Concluding Unscientific Postscript*. *Religious Studies*, 31 (2), 197–208.

Jacoby, M.G., 2002. Kierkegaard on truth. *Religious Studies*, 38 (1), 27–44.

Jardine, D.W., 1992. Reflections on education, hermeneutics, and ambiguity: Hermeneutics as a restoring of life to its original difficulty. In: W.F. Pinar and W.M. Reynolds, eds. *Understanding curriculum as phenomenological and deconstructed text*. New York: Teachers College Press, 116–127.

Kierkegaard, S., 1980. *The concept of anxiety*. Translated by R. Thomte and A.B. Anderson. Princeton, NJ: Princeton University Press.
Kierkegaard, S., 1985. *Fear and trembling*. Translated by A. Hannay. London: Penguin.
Kierkegaard, S., 1987. *Either/or*, 2 vols. Translated by H.V. Hong and E.H. Hong. Princeton, NJ, Princeton University Press.
Kierkegaard, S., 1988. *Stages on life's way*. Translated by H.V. Hong and E.H. Hong. Princeton, NJ: Princeton University Press.
Kierkegaard, S., 1989. *The sickness unto death*. Translated by A. Hannay. London: Penguin.
Kierkegaard, S., 1998. *Works of love*. Translated by H.V. Hong and E.H. Hong. Princeton, NJ: Princeton University Press.
Kierkegaard, S., 2009. *Concluding unscientific postscript*. Translated by A. Hannay. Cambridge: Cambridge University Press.
Kuhlman, E.L., 1994. *Agony in education: The importance of struggle in the process of learning*. Westport, CT: Bergin & Garvey.
Kwak, D.-J., 2001. A new formulation of the ethical self through Kierkegaard's notion of subjectivity: In search of a new moral education. *Asia Pacific Education Review*, 2 (1).
Locke, K., 2015. Performativity, performance and education. *Educational Philosophy and Theory*, 49 (3), 247–259.
Mack, M., 2014. *Philosophy and literature in times of crisis: Challenging our infatuation with numbers*. New York: Bloomsbury.
McKnight, D., 2004. Kierkegaard and the despair of the aesthetic existence in teaching. *Journal of Curriculum Theorizing*, 20 (1), 59–80.
McKnight, D., 2010. Critical pedagogy and despair: A move toward Kierkegaard's passionate inwardness. *In*: E. Malewski, ed. *Curriculum studies handbook: The next moment*. New York: Routledge, 500–516.
McLane, E., 1977. Kierkegaard and subjectivity. *International Journal for Philosophy of Religion*, 8 (4), 211–232.
McPherson, I., 2001. Kierkegaard as an educational thinker: Communication through and across ways of being. *Journal of Philosophy of Education*, 35 (2), 157–174.
Murdoch, I., 2001. *The sovereignty of good*. London/New York: Routledge.
Murphy, D., 2014. Issues with PISA's use of its data in the context of international education policy convergence. *Policy Futures in Education*, 12 (7), 893–916.
Prinsloo, P., 2017. Fleeing from Frankenstein's monster and meeting Kafka on the way: Algorithmic decision-making in higher education. *E-Learning and Digital Media*, 14 (3), 138–163.
Reindal, S.M., 2013. *Bildung*, the Bologna process and Kierkegaard's concept of subjective thinking. *Studies in Philosophy and Education*, 32, 533–549.
Roberts, P., 1997. A critique of the NZQA policy reforms. *In*: M. Olssen and K. Morris Matthews, eds. *Education policy in New Zealand: The 1990s and beyond*. Palmerston North: Dunmore Press, 162–189.
Roberts, P., 2005. Freire and Dostoevsky: Uncertainty, dialogue and transformation. *Journal of Transformative Education*, 3 (1), 126–139.
Roberts, P., 2006. Performativity, measurement and research: A critique of performance-based research funding in New Zealand. *In*: J. Ozga, T. Popkewitz, and T. Seddon, eds. *World yearbook of education 2006: Education research and policy*. London: Routledge, 185–199.
Roberts, P., 2007. Neoliberalism, performativity and research. *International Review of Education*, 53 (4), 349–365.

Roberts, P., 2011. Attention, asceticism and grace: Simone Weil and higher education. *Arts and Humanities in Higher Education*, 10 (3), 315–328.
Roberts, P., 2013. Happiness, despair and education. *Studies in Philosophy and Education*, 32 (5), 463–475.
Roberts, P., 2016. *Happiness, hope, and despair: Rethinking the role of education*. New York: Peter Lang.
Roberts, P. and Freeman-Moir, J., 2013. *Better worlds: Education, art, and utopia*. Lanham, MD: Lexington Books.
Saeverot, H., 2013. Irony, deception and subjective truth: Principles for existential teaching. *Studies in Philosophy and Education*, 32, 503–513.
Saevi, T., 2011. Lived relationality as fulcrum for pedagogical-ethical practice. *Studies in Philosophy and Education*, 30 (5), 455–461.
Schacht, R., 1973. Kierkegaard on 'truth is subjectivity' and 'the leap of faith'. *Canadian Journal of Philosophy*, 2 (3), 297–313.
Schopenhauer, A., 1966. *The world as will and representation*, 2 vols. Translated by E.F. Payne. New York: Dover.
Smeyers, P. and Depaepe, M., eds., 2006. *Educational research: Why 'what works' doesn't work*. Dordrecht: Springer.
Tubbs, N., 2005. Kierkegaard. *Journal of Philosophy of Education*, 39 (2), 387–409.
Webster, R.S., 2009. *Educating for meaningful lives through existential spirituality*. Rotterdam: Sense Publishers.
Webster, R.S., 2017. Valuing and desiring purposes of education to transcend miseducative measurement practices. *Educational Philosophy and Theory*, 49 (4), 331–346.
Webster, R.S., 2018. Being trustworthy: Going beyond evidence to desiring. *Educational Philosophy and Theory*, 50 (2), 152–162.
Weil, S., 1997. *Gravity and grace*. Translated by A. Wills. Lincoln: Bison Books.
Weil, S., 2001. *Waiting for God*. Translated by E. Craufurd. New York: Perennial Classics.
Wivestad, S.M., 2011. Conditions for 'upbuilding': A reply to Nigel Tubbs' reading of Kierkegaard. *Journal of Philosophy of Education*, 45 (4), 613–625.

Chapter 6

Paulo Freire and living a non-neoliberal life in education

Walter Omar Kohan

Introduction

This chapter deals with the political implications of the relationship between education, philosophy, and life. More specifically, it will focus on the figure of the well-known Brazilian educator Paulo Freire. Although the bibliographical references focus almost exclusively on Freire's nearly mythical book, *Pedagogy of the Oppressed*, he has a vast opera composed of more than 20 books (both classical and what he calls "spoken" ones). Freire is read widely not merely in the specific field of education, but also in other very diverse fields such as anthropology, religious sciences, theater, psychology, communication, nursing, social work, cultural studies, literature, and journalism among others. And it is not only about his books. Our hunch is that they would hardly be read as much as they are if it was not the extraordinary force of his life which involves a pilgrimage mainly around the third world. He is a universally well-known and respected figure, everywhere.

Nevertheless, today he is under attack in his native country, Brazil. His fortune has to do with the Labor Party he helped to create in 1980 when he returned from exile. In 2012 President Dilma, who followed Lula, both members of the Labor Party, sanctioned a law that declared Paulo Freire Patron of Brazilian Education. But in 2016 Dilma's government fell. Under attack from the media, the congress and the Judicial Party, the name of Paulo Freire appeared in public demonstrations against Dilma´s government as a symbol of "Marxist ideology" in Brazilian schools. Movements like "School Without Party" accused him of negating the role of the teachers and being responsible for the crisis in Brazilian education. Attacks against Paulo Freire were appropriately confronted but the situation became more delicate in October 2018 when J. Bolsonaro was elected president with an educational platform that proposed 'to purge the ideology of Paulo Freire from Brazilian education" (Bolsonaro 2018).

The personal and aggressive tone of Bolsonaro should not mislead us; the dispute is not only or mainly about a name, Freire, but educational policy. Bolsonaro is trying to impose a neoliberal educational structure that is on the antipodes of Paulo Freire's political ideas. Instead of policies in favor of the excluded, a meritocracy is proposed; instead of reinforcing the public system, privatization is proposed; instead of fostering solidarity and cooperation, entrepreneurialism is proposed. Never as it is today has it been so clear what is being disputed in the polemic between Paulo Freire and his detractors: to live or not to live a neoliberal educational life.

In this chapter, I give a philosophical framework to situate the work and life of Paulo Freire by connecting his philosophy and life to a tradition that might help us understand why he has been situated in this delicate position. We'll see how his life echoes other lives that fall under similar attack. It seems that something structural concerning the political dimension of an educational philosophy is at stake.

Let's set a broader conceptual framework for our writing. In a larger sense we are dealing with an enormous issue involving the history of the relationship between education and philosophy. This would require much more than what this chapter might accomplish. In this respect, in a previous correspondence with Jan Masschelein (Masschelein and Kohan 2015), I have argued how at least starting with the figure of Socrates there is a tradition in which the philosopher and the educator are not easy to separate from each other. In other words, the task of the philosopher has an unavoidable pedagogical dimension. Is Socrates an educational philosopher? A teacher in philosophy? A philosophical educator? The difficulty in responding to, and even in differentiating these questions shows their complexity.

This tradition of philosophy as education has been recreated in Latin American popular education by Simón Rodríguez, the master of Simón Bolívar who named him, not by chance, the "Socrates of Caracas" (Kohan 2015). Rodríguez reinvented a philosophical and educational life as lived by Socrates: one irreverent, hospitalarian, contestable and worth living because of its questioning dimension (Kohan 2015). In this chapter, I will focus these questions in the figure of someone who can be placed in this same tradition: Paulo Freire, who is one of the most prominent educators of our time (West 1993) and at the same time, has been under severe attack in Brazil in the last few years. Coincidentally, these three figures – Socrates, Rodríguez, and Freire – were attacked by the sustainers of the political order. This chapter throws light through conceptual analysis on the reasons for those political attacks, especially in the case of Paulo Freire, and helps us understand the nature of the current dispute in the politics of education in the age of neoliberalism.

Let us begin by focusing on how the figure of Paulo Freire is usually studied by academics. In the literature on Paulo Freire, there are dozens of books showing Paulo Freire's theoretical references. It is considered that he has been influenced by a range of schools of thought as different as Existentialism, Marxism, Phenomenology, Personalism, Pragmatism. For example, Irwin (2012) shows how Paulo Freire has been influenced by the existentialist notion of "fear of freedom" by Eric Fromm, Marx (his conception of philosophy, history, dialectics) and Marxism (in many of its aspects, for example, Franz Fanon and his analysis of cultural action for freedom in Third World countries). Elias (1994) highlights five most striking influences: political and educational progressivism (Liberalism), existentialism, phenomenology, Catholic theology, and revolutionary Marxist humanism. Mayo (1999) emphasizes the proximity and importance of Gramsci's work in the perspective of adult education. Saviani (1987) highlights Mounier's personalism and the existentialism of Marcel and Jaspers as the most significant brands and calls Freire's philosophy dialectic and idealistic. Gadotti (2001) shows similarities a very large set of personalities of the twentieth century. And the list can continue. Without denying the importance of these approaches, in this chapter I take a different approach. Inspired by Foucault (2011) and his distinction between two traditions in the history of philosophy (philosophy as theory, i.e., as an intellectual or cognitive activity and philosophy as wisdom, i.e., as a way of life), we'll inscribe Paulo Freire in this specific tradition where what matters is not only or not mainly what a philosopher produces as theory or system but how he or she lives a philosophical life, for example, how he or she contributes to the question and philosophical problem of how we should live our lives. This philosophical tradition is minor, underestimated, and unconsidered, and overshadowed by the big History of Philosophical Ideas and Philosophy with capital letters. Philosophy as a way of life begins with Socrates, the Athenian. He problematized the unexamined way of living as have other philosophers down through time.

I will show how Paulo Freire can be meaningfully considered one of the philosophers of this tradition that started with Socrates and the Cynics. The main contribution of Paulo Freire to this tradition is the manner in which his life shows the educational, philosophical, and political poverty of living what I will call "a neoliberal way of life." Freire offers us a way to problematize not only neoliberal lives but, more specifically, the neoliberalism pervading educators' lives today. If we are interested in this issue it is not only as a philosophical question, but because of the educational implications it has. This analysis might help us not only to enlarge the field of philosophy of education or, more broadly, educational foundations, but also broaden the aim and scope of education. Also, through this analysis we may come to understand why the figure of Paulo Freire, as others like Socrates and Rodriguez before him, is under severe attack by the defenders of a "new" educational reform.

Paulo Freire, philosophy and life

Is Paulo Freire an educational philosopher? Is he a philosopher of education? Is he a philosophical educator? In academic philosophy, there is a dominant form that makes philosophy a set of ideas, doctrines, and theoretical systems on certain themes or problems. In this academic philosophical tradition of thought, there is a sub-discipline commonly called philosophy of education. Even though many scholars do not strictly consider Paulo Freire a philosopher – especially in Brazil, from fairly narrow conceptions, doctrines or techniques of philosophy – he is commonly studied in this field, particularly outside Brazil. Many studies have highlighted Paulo Freire's philosophical sources and inscribed him in certain traditions of thought. That is, while discussing whether he is a philosopher, numerous studies in Brazil, but especially abroad, seek to identify "the philosophy of Paulo Freire," meaning the philosophical assumptions that situate his ideas in a given current of thought.

A variety of thinkers and traditions of the most consecrated in so-called Western philosophy are usually shown as influential in his thinking. There is practically no philosophical tradition that, to some degree, is not related to the educator from Pernambuco. Paulo Freire was an inveterate reader, dedicated, interested and open to different traditions of thought that would help him to think the problems of his time he was passionate about. It is also necessary to remember his declared and constant Christian faith, which he never abandoned, and which made him try to reconcile with the various philosophical currents; even some that, like Marxism, are in frank tension with it.

Other traditions for philosophy: Marx and the requirement of transformation

In this text I explore and at the same time do not explore this possibility of connecting him to other thinkers. We will do so in the sense that we consider that there are two philosophical traditions that have a special significance in thinking about Paulo Freire's relationship with philosophy. But what is common in these two traditions is that philosophy is understood more by its effects in relation to the outside of philosophy than as a content or theory itself. So that these two traditions point to a path that somehow dissolves the interest in his philosophical influences and transfers the accent from an intellectual tradition in a specific discipline to the broader field of human life and, as we'll see, to the nature and role of education in it.

One of these traditions comes from the late Marx with his critique of speculative philosophy. The most obvious reference is Marx's Thesis 11 on Feuerbach: "So far, philosophers have interpreted the world. The point is to transform it." This revival has already been quite prominent in scholars studying Paulo Freire (for example, by West [1993]), showing how the educator from Pernambuco is very sensitive to this Marxian critique of the more speculative philosophical tradition and always bets on the power of a problematizing or philosophical education, not only to change the modes of thought but above all the prevailing forms of life. As it is often underlined, the Marxian notion of praxis is of particular importance in Freire's work.

Moreover, Paulo Freire considers himself as part of this tradition that conceives philosophy as directly committed to the transformation of the state of things. For example, in an interview with the Institute of Cultural Action in Geneva in 1973, he criticizes the various dualistic forms of subjectivist and objectivist views and proposes to understand philosophy as praxis, action, and reflection, the dialectical unity of subject–object, theory–practice (Freire 1988). For Freire, philosophy involves a dimension of reflection and another of action and both are necessarily transforming the world when proposing a conscious, deep, "scientific" reading. That is why the reading of the words presupposes the reading of the world, understood as a transforming praxis in the world. In *Cultural Action for Freedom*, he affirms that, contrary to what he proposes, it is characteristic of a political illiterate to have the idea that philosophy has only the role of "explanation of the world and instrument for its acceptance" (Freire 1988).

So, for Paulo Freire, philosophy is not only a tool to understand reality or the position of the human being in the world, as in almost all philosophical traditions mentioned earlier. It is true that, particularly in its first period, the idea of "conscientization" densely influenced by the phenomenological tradition is of particular importance. However, it is conceived as an inseparable awareness of an effective transformation of the living conditions of the oppressed. If a philosophical education allowed the oppressed only the theoretical awareness of its condition but did not change its material conditions of life, it would not be properly liberating. For Paulo Freire, life is, in a way, inseparable from thought.

So there is a certain indissoluble tension when the work of Paulo Freire is compared with those traditions that understand philosophy as interpretation while Paulo Freire explicitly shows the limits of it. If it is true that they certainly influenced him, as he himself admits, it is no less true that his understanding of philosophy is very different from the understanding of those same traditions. Paulo Freire himself criticizes "very good" Marxists who have never set foot in a favela or in the home of a worker (Freire and Shor 1986, p. 86). They may be theoretically and conceptually very knowledgeable in Marxist theory, experts in Marx's ideas, but, in fact, they are not Marxists because Marx is to them only a set of texts studied, but completely removed from concrete life; for them Marx is concepts and theory without life. What is the problem of being a Marxist and not setting foot in a favela? "Being a Marxist" here stands for having a given theoretical position, in this case, one in favor of the transformation of society; "setting a foot in a favela" stands for actually trying to do something to transform society in favor of the oppressed, the excluded, the voice-less. So that you can theoretically be in favor of the transformation of society but actually not do anything for that. More, you can be theoretically Marxist and actually live a very neoliberal way of life. This is unacceptable for Paulo Freire. It is not just about one tradition. What would Paulo Freire say about phenomenologists who do not give life to phenomenology? Or about existentialists who do not give life to existentialism?

In any case, Paulo Freire is clearly Marxian in this sense of affirming a philosophy that not only contemplates or understands the problems of education but also tries to transform educational practices. Even though he might have lost at least part of his faith in social transformation, Paulo Freire affirms a philosopher as a figure that needs to be an educator (which means an engine of transformation), not only or mainly of ideas but of practice, i.e. of *praxis* to be more precise. From the coup of 1964 in Brazil he realized more and more clearly the limits of the transformative effects of education (Freire and Shor 1986, p. 26ff) and defended a more cautious stance, a critical optimism, between a "naive optimism" (i.e. the school can be the lever of "social transformation") and a "terrible pessimism" (i.e. to think that it only reproduces the dominant ideology, Freire and Shor 1986, p. 82).

In a text from 1992, after going through the tough test of chairing the educational department of the city of São Paulo, he still affirms of the role of education: "that, not being a maker of everything, is a fundamental factor in the reinvention of the world" (Freire 2001, p. 10). He repeated this statement in many interventions at this time (Freire 2001, p. 28). In a speech in Jamaica he states that "if education, cannot everything, it can something" (Freire 2001, p. 20). In one of the letters that compose the book *Teacher Yes, Auntie, No* written in 1993, he phrases what would become almost a motto in his last years: "It is true that education is not the lever of social transformation, but without it this transformation does not happen" (Freire 2000, p. 39). Still in his final and less optimistic works, Freire considers that "changing the world is as difficult as possible" (Freire 2000).

In short, Freire never gave up considering that the transforming power of a theory or thought lies in its capacity to modify the oppressed lives. He would subscribe to Marx's criticism of all Western previous traditions of thought, including some of those that marked his own thinking because they had remained on a purely speculative dimension. For him, a philosopher cannot but be a liberator of the oppressed lives, that is, a philosopher cannot be just an intellectual light that postulates a liberated life but an actual liberating educator of the oppressed lives.

Another tradition: Michel Foucault and life as a problem for philosophy

The relation of Paulo Freire to the second tradition is more controversial and less explored. It is closely related to the first, in as much as Foucault was a reader, attentive, sensitive, and critical of Marx's philosophy of praxis. At the same time, Foucault also criticizes this Marxian tradition in a way (Foucault 2011) that perhaps Paulo Freire himself, particularly in his last years, would not disagree with. So that by inscribing Paulo Freire in this tradition, we are introducing some tension in the framework that we are offering.

This second tradition makes it possible to relate the figure of Paulo Freire to figures somewhat more remote and unexpected. This is what matters: encounters with less explored intercessors, almost unrelated if we think of the more orthodox readings of the intellectual of Pernambuco. M. Foucault dedicated his last seminars at the *Collège de France*, to the notion of *parrhesia* (true speech). In them he proposes a philosophy of the history of philosophy which, in a way, recreates Marx's critique to speculative philosophy according to other categories. According to Foucault, differently from Marx, the history of philosophy is not just a speculative tradition. This tradition certainly exists, but in addition to it, Foucault finds another: the "history of philosophical life as a philosophical problem, but also as a form of being and at the same time as a form of ethics and heroism" (Foucault 2011, p. 196). This tradition, according to Foucault, was underestimated not only by the Prussian philosopher but by the dominant names of this tradition to whom Marx himself belonged. This is precisely what Foucault is looking for in these last seminars: a history of ethico-philosophical heroes, not because of the supposed brilliance of his doctrines or ideas, but because of the ethical-heroic character of his ways of life, that is, not because of what they thought or wrote but because of the explosive, militant, and revolutionary power of their forms of life; because of the force they have to register, critically and devastatingly, in the tradition of how a philosophical life must be lived and even of what is done, in one's life, in the name of philosophy.

According to Foucault, Socrates and the ancient Cynics are the initial heroes of a philosophical tradition of life that can be reconstructed to the present days. It is a minor tradition, overshadowed by the dominant philosophy, but it is no less philosophy. In modernity, Foucault considers that the history of a philosophical life could be reconstructed, for example, from figures such as Montaigne and Spinoza (Foucault 2011, p. 248). That is to say, it is not Foucault who inaugurates this tradition, as seems to be Marx's pretension ("hitherto, philosophers . . ."). On the contrary, this one is an old tradition. But it has been erased, disregarded, neglected by the history of triumphant philosophy. The differences between Marx's and Foucault's approach to the history of philosophy seem clear: Marx seeks to interrupt a tradition and generate a new beginning for it; on the contrary, Foucault seeks to help to perceive a tradition that already exists but cannot be perceived.

Let's consider the case of Socrates. He also does speculative philosophy, as theory or knowledge. In fact, if we take into account Plato's dialogues, with all the hermeneutic difficulties of the case, the two conceptions of philosophy previously opposed are difficult to separate: philosophy as knowledge, intellectual activity, what Foucault calls a "metaphysics of the soul," and philosophy as a form of life or wisdom, what Foucault calls an "aesthetics of existence."

Foucault (2011) shows how the relations between the two are complex, flexible, variable. In *Alcibiades I*, Socrates understands philosophy as the knowledge of oneself; philosophy is presupposed as a metaphysics of the soul: Socrates tries to help Alcibiades to understand his real conditions to dedicate his life to politics; he argues that to be a good politician he should have been educated to take care of others; and only someone who knows how to take care of himself can take care of others. In its turn, to take care of oneself demands to know oneself and particularly the most important part of oneself, considered as the soul. So, in this dialogue Socrates seems to affirm a view of philosophy in which it is associated with a certain intellectual knowledge or activity: self-knowledge.

Foucault contrasts the view offered in the *Laques*, in which, Nicias, one of Socrates' interlocutors, realizes that any conversation with Socrates no matter what subject it begins with, will always end with Socrates' interlocutor being forced by Socrates to give the reason of his way of life, that is, of why he lives the way he lives. That is, what matters to philosophy in this dialogue is not an intellectual activity but a way of life. It is philosophy as style, aesthetics of existence.

It is worth noting that in both dialogues, the main question that lies at the heart of Socrates' conversations with his interlocutors is how to educate Athenian youth, how to deal with what is perceived as an educational crisis, in order to give importance to what is needed in the education of the new generations of Athenians. Thus, Foucault highlights, from these two Socratic beginnings, philosophy as a problematization of life.

The two beginnings are born interspersed, crossed, and often confused. But philosophy gradually emerges as a cognitive activity, according to which it concerns above all the intellectual exercise generated from the examination of the questions sought to be understood. It is the history of philosophy that won in the academic world, particularly from the period Foucault calls the "Cartesian moment," European modernity. It is that tradition that classifies philosophers, according to their doctrines, into existentialists, pragmatists, personalists, Marxists, phenomenologists, postmoderns. It is the philosophy that Marx considers merely speculative.

Foucault builds a genealogy of philosophy as a way of life, beginning with Socrates and continuing it with the Cynics. Ethics and heroism are intensified in the body of the Cynics because in them there is even less theory, doctrine, body of thought than in Socrates. In the Cynics, the philosophical life is the very body of the philosopher; his life expresses in a direct, profound, coherent, and radical way his philosophy.

Thus, in Foucault's reading, cynicism deepens the relation that Socrates himself establishes between truth and life, as he presents it to his accusers in Plato's *Apology*, so much so that several Cynics were also judged and condemned for irreligion in the same way as Socrates. Cynicism is a school of life, characterized much more by the practice of a form of life than by having developed a sophisticated theoretical framework (Foucault 2011).

One important aspect of this philosophy that is born with Socrates and the Cynics, is that a philosophical life is at the same time an educational life. In this tradition, philosophy is a form of education and without it completely loses its meaning and sense. The philosophical hero is an educational hero who educates with his own example, with his own life. The educational value of such a life is not an accessory, but its main characteristic: without this educational projection this life is nothing: it loses all meaning. A philosophical life cannot be lived other than in a way that inspires other lives: it can only be lived if it inspires other lives. This is why Socrates says in the *Apology* that he wouldn't accept an absolution of the accusation against him if that would imply a life with no philosophizing: without the impact on others, without the educational effects of it his life would have no political effect, he couldn't accomplish the mission given by Apollo and then it would be not worth living.

So another dimension of this philosophical life is that it is necessarily political. The philosophical and educative life needs to be political because any life without affecting the lives in the polis itself is meaningless. This is for example what Socrates argues with Crito when he wants to persuade Socrates to escape from prison: not only would it not be fair to escape – why it would be to deny a whole way of living in the polis – but above all it would not make sense because there would be no meaningful life outside the polis.

Paulo Freire and the history of life as a philosophical problem

Paulo Freire can be inscribed in this tradition of a philosophically educative, political, ethical and heroic life that Foucault begins with Socrates and the Cynics and continues in our era with the Christian ascetics. Because Paulo Freire is a confessed Christian, let's look at this Foucauldian recovery of the ascetics of Christ. For Foucault, Christianity is an example of a metaphysics of the soul that has been relatively stable for centuries, giving rise at the same time to very diverse aesthetics of existence. In this tradition, Christian ascetics are inspired by the Cynics to wage a kind of spiritual combat against the impurities of the world. Among the various forms taken by Christian ascetics, one seems particularly interesting in relation to Paulo Freire: the figure of the militant, who criticizes real life and the behavior of human beings in a battle that should lead to the complete transformation of the world (Foucault 2011).

However, it is no less certain that there are at least two aspects of Christian asceticism that seem to be almost opposed to the thinking of Paulo Freire. On the one hand a world beyond this world (for the Christian ascetics) was much more significant than making this world a different world; on the other hand, the principle of obedience (to the Lord, to the law, to the god) for the ascetics is a founding principle of their way of life. These aspects are in tension with the life of Paulo Freire.

In this sense, the analogy with Socrates and the Cynics gains even more force if we remember the way Freire describes, in close proximity to the Athenian and the Cynics, his life as a kind of sacred mission. Both Socrates and Paulo Freire describe themselves as heroes, prophets in pastoral mission. They say it explicitly, for example, in his last statements: Socrates, when he recounts the well-known anecdote of the oracle of Delphi in his defense (Plato, *Apology* 20 ff.); Paulo Freire in his last interview (Freire 1997), making history of his beginnings in the literacy of young people and adults in poor areas of Pernambuco.

Paulo Freire perceives himself like Socrates as a Shepherd, a prophet in an educative mission. He describes his mission in quite Socratic terms: human beings are unfinished beings and his mission is to awaken in others, with a pedagogy of the question, a feeling of search: equally inconclusive, they do not recognize themselves as such (Freire 1997). This is the value of the unknown viable, the epistemological vocation of human beings for "being more." Freire is very close to Socratic philosophy in that for both it is not a noun, a theory, but a verb, a certain relation to knowledge that is exercised. There is, in Socratic and Freirean terms, an anthropology, an epistemology and an ontology with strong common traits: a way of being, knowing, and inhabiting the world based on question, curiosity, incompleteness, and life as a way of accepting and at the same time "critically" confronting this condition. The Socratic dictum: "a life without examination does not deserve to be lived by a human being" (*Apology* 38a) would make a lot of sense for the life of Paulo Freire, so much that if the Pernambuco had inhabited Athens a few centuries before Christ there is high probability that he would have been one of those "who philosophize" with whom Socrates identifies as the true target of the accusations against him.

Of course, when it comes to specifying the concrete ways in which each of them perceives this mission, there are clear and notorious differences characteristic of historical, social, political, and cultural contexts, so markedly different. I will specify just a few: Freire perceives and presents himself as a pastor of the poor and excluded in the name of Christ (Freire 1997). We might say, inspired by Foucault, that if, in elitist and slave-owning Athens, Socrates calls on other citizens to take care of what they do not care for, with no basis other than a radical trust in the power to questioning and submitting life to examination, and without no specific worry about those who were literally outside this minority adult men, citizens of Athens, Paulo Freire, in a peripheral region of a peripheral country like Brazil, seeks to take care of the oppressed that nobody seems to care of in this same society, with his Christian religious faith and the Marxist scientific faith as the way of understanding social and political relations. The Socratic questioning is political and addresses those who engage in politics in Athens; Paulo Freire's questioning is also political in this sense but in an even more radical sense: he questions the bases of the social order that sustains the oppression it faces. As for the ways of conceiving philosophy, there are also clear differences. If Socrates does not present any theory that sustains his philosophical life, Paulo Freire relies on dialectical materialism to support his educating life that will seek to realize Christian ideas on earth. In other words, Pastor Freire relies on a Marxist conception of class struggle and historical dialectics, within the capitalist system, through a revolutionary educational practice, infusing Christian values and class consciousness of the oppressed into their lives.

There is a close religious background in both stories. Socrates has his knowledge legitimized by the god Apollo, the supreme divinity of the Athenians. Paulo Freire presents himself as a comrade of Christ in the Christian Brazil

"The more I read Marx, the more I found a certain objective reasoning to remain a comrade of Christ," says Paulo Freire (1997). This is his impressive docility, theoretical, intellectual, and vital malleability. Only someone who is open to the tensions and challenges of the real and of an antagonistic philosophy and religion can see in Marxism a foundation for realizing Christian ideals when, in so many respects, these two metaphysics of the soul contradict each other.

As an intellectual committed to Christianity, Freire nourishes his mission from the values of a Christian ethic, such as hope, faith, solidarity, compassion, humility, tolerance, heroism and, at the same time, with the social theory of dialectical materialism humanist and non-doctrinal (Greene 1999, p. 155), which Freire never abandoned in his life. A Socratic and materialist Christian, a Christian and Socratic Marxist, a Christian Socratic and Marxist, all these somewhat strange figures fit the thinking and life of this utopian hero of the liberation of the oppressed.

It is in this specific sense that Paulo Freire has been a philosopher: not so much for theories or systems that might have influenced him, not even for the philosophical quality of his theories or thought, but for the way in which he made his life a philosophical questioning path, that is, for the way he understood philosophy as education and living a philosophical life as living an educational life that would liberate others from oppression.

Just as Socrates devoted his life to trying to wake the Athenians from what he considered a life without self-examination, Paulo Freire devoted his life to trying, through a pedagogy of the question, to liberate the oppressed from their condition, while at the same time liberating their oppressors.

It is also in this dimension that Paulo Freire inspires our present, when education and philosophy seem both to be, in our Neoliberal dominant times, dissociated from a concern for the lives on the outside (Biesta 2015) and this is the main reason why his name is under attack nowadays in Brazil. To say it like Paulo Freire, in educational institutions (i.e. schools) and in philosophy as a school of thought and life, there is a growing dissociation between the reading of words and the reading of the world (Freire and Shor 1986, p. 85): words that are read in school are words that no longer tell the world, are separated from the world lived by those who live in school. In an age of learnification, students learn for the usefulness of what they learn and not to know the reasons why things are the way they are in the world, as Freire would consider. The double consequence of this is that they learn to read a school world that is functional to reproduce the outside world and does not enable them to put this world into question.

This neoliberal ideology is what is being fostered by the actual detractors of Paulo Freire in Brazil. The accusation against him of ideologization covers a reduction of the role of the teacher to a technical transmission of contents so that none of the reasons why things are the way they are in Brazilian society could enter inside the classrooms; the pretension to forbid teachers to refer to ethico-political problems like abortion, gender, and race issues, have all the same consequence: to strengthen institutions like family and church and weaken public educational institutions. In other words, they confront what Paulo Freire aims schools should be: places where teachers and students through dialogue can put into question their common social world and think together about the kind of social world they would like to build together.

Maybe this is why the figure of Paulo Freire might receive some renewed attention in our days. The core of his thinking is exactly in opposition to the kind of neoliberal politics of education that is on the agenda of the new Brazilian government (and also the politics that is spreading all over Latin America with some few exceptions): an education interested in teaching just the words citizens-consumers need to reproduce the world as it is and not even to consider questioning the forms of life dominantly lived in our times. Neoliberal policies aim to foster neoliberal forms of life against which Paulo Freire's opera and mainly Paulo Freire's life are a strong testimony. Maybe the reading of Paulo Freire, of his philosophy of education but mainly of his philosophical and educational life teaches us not only the possibilities of another philosophy but also of another educational life, inside and outside schools. Maybe this is why the study of Paulo Freire's opera and life is more meaningful than ever.

References

Biesta, G., 2015. Freeing teaching from learning: Opening up existential possibilities in educational relationships. *Studies in Philosophy and Education*, 34 (3), 229–243. doi:10.1007/s11217-014-9454-z

Bolsonaro, Jair. O caminho da prosperidade. Proposta de Plano de Governo, 2018. Disponível em: https://flaviobolsonaro.com/PLANO_DE_GOVERNO_JAIR_BOLSONARO_2018.pdf [Accessed 12 Feb 2019].

Elias, J., 1994. *Paulo Freire: Pedagogue of liberation*. Malabar, FL: Krieger Publishing Company.

Foucault, M., 2011. *The courage of truth: The government of self and others II*. New York: Palgrave Macmillan.

Freire, P., 1988. *Cultural action for freedom*. Cambridge: Harvard University Review.

Freire, P., 1997. Última entrevista. (PUC São Paulo, São Paulo, 17/4/97). Available from: www.paulofreire.ufpb.br/paulofreire/Controle?op=detalheandtipo=Videoandid=622 [Accessed 11 Oct 2017].

Freire, P., 2000. *Pedagogia da indignação*. Cartas Pedagógicas e outros escritos. São Paulo: UNESP.

Freire, P., 2001. *Política e educação*. São Paulo: Cortez.

Freire, P. and Shor, I., 1986. *Medo e ousadia. O cotidiano do professor*. São Paulo: Paz e Terra.

Gadotti, M., 2001. *Paulo Freire. Uma biobibliografia*. São Paulo: Cortez.

Greene, M., 1999. Reflexões sobre a *Pedagogia do Oprimido* de Paulo Freire. In: Ana M. A. Freire, ed. *A pedagogia da libertação em Paulo Freire*. São Paulo: UNESP, 155–156.

Irwin, J., 2012. *Paulo Freire's philosophy of education: Origins, developments, impacts and legacies*. London: Continuum.

Kohan, W., 2015. *The inventive schoolmaster*. Rotterdam: Sense.

Masschelein, J. and Kohan, W., 2015. The pedagogue and/or the philosopher? An exercise in thinking together: A dialogue with Jan Masschelein. *In*: W. Kohan, ed. *Childhood, education and philosophy. New Ideas for an old relationship.* New York: Routledge, 90–113.
Mayo, P., 1999. *Gramsci, Freire and adult education. Possibilities for transformative action.* London: Zed Books.
Saviani, D., 1987. *Escola e democracia.* São Paulo: Cortez Editora e Autores Associados.
West, C., 1993. Preface. *In*: P. Leonard and P. McLaren, eds. *Paulo Freire: A critical encounter.* New York: Routledge, xiii.

Chapter 7

A phenomenology of reading
Textual technology and virtual worlds

Eva-Maria Simms

Introduction

One of our most fundamental, cherished, and taken for granted intellectual tools is the written text, and we go through great pains to produce the psychological ability to decode it in our children. In educational circles, literacy is rarely questioned as the foundational event of Western education, and its practice is taken for granted. In three earlier essays I have tried to tackle the phenomenology and history of literacy (Simms 2008a, 2008b, 2010) in order to understand how reading and "bookishness", to use Illich's term (1996), alter human consciousness in Western history, but also in the life of every child who learns to read. I want to return to this topic and think through textuality as an event that is not natural but technological. My goal is to highlight the implicit technological essence of textuality and show that it creates virtual worlds, which are then intensified and developed by contemporary information and communication technologies. My argument will be that the book itself is already a virtual technology that brings with it fundamental changes in human consciousness and human existence in general, and if we understand the book's virtuality we might be in a better position to analyze the psychological and political effects of the contemporary electronic media landscape as it intersects with the education process.

How technology works

The word "technology" is generally defined as the application of tools and methods, particularly the study, development, and application of devices, machines, and techniques for manufacturing and productive processes. On the surface technology might be the application of scientific findings to the creation of sophisticated tools that make life better for human beings (which is the claim of most creators of technological inventions), but on a deeper level technology reveals itself to be a socio-psychological process that has profound consequences for the structure of the human life-world. In a lecture at Duquesne University, the social critic Ivan Illich described briefly the way technology works, and I have come to call his very useful, elegant, and simple hermeneutic device the "Illich Principle". The Illich Principle has four steps:

1   Technologies *extract the essences* out of human abilities
2   Technologies *instrumentalize* essential human abilities through technological devices
3   Technologies *reduce or eliminate the original lived context* of these human abilities
4   Technologies have far-reaching *unintended consequences*

Illich used the example of the invention of the automobile to illustrate this process. The essence of human locomotion is extracted and intensified through the technology of the car (speed and duration of forward movement increase exponentially), which in turn reduces the lived and embodied context of human motility: when we sit in the speeding car, our senses are insulated from the heat, smell, and touch of the places we pass, and we do not notice their details anymore. The adoption of automobile technology in turn has required changes in infrastructure, which have deeply altered the landscapes and social fabric of American cities. According to Illich, when human experience becomes technologized, a double process of *intensification* of some experiential elements and the *de-contextualization and reduction* of others can be observed. The *unintended consequences* often cannot be observed immediately, but manifest over time. I have found the Illich Principle of identifying the intensifications, looking for what is lost in de-contextualization, and searching for unintended consequences very helpful in analyzing the impact technologies have on human experience, and it will guide our discussion of textual technologies in the following sections.

It is not customary to think of the written text as a technological implement, but literacy is actually a technological practice which intensifies and de-contextualizes particular aspects of perceptual consciousness. Illich and Sanders (1988) have argued that alphabetization, that is, the translation of the phonetic sound system into visual alphabetic notation, is an epistemological practice with far-reaching impact on mind and culture. Illich (1996, p. 5) has traced the creation of the "bookish" mind to the monastic reading and writing tradition of the twelfth century, which built the foundation for new thinking practices, the founding of schools and universities, and the dissemination of ideas through the printing press in the following centuries. The invention of pervasive literacy, as Postman (1994) has argued, has changed what people think about (the stuff in books), talk about (ideas that are removed from the present situation), how they think (in linear, logical ways) and what they value (education). In literate cultures those who cannot read and write cannot participate in the cultural commerce of their culture – and that is true of its children. Illiterate children are set aside from adult life in educational reservations where their consciousnesses are restructured by intensive literacy training until they "graduate" and are allowed to share in adult activities. Reading and writing are part of a textual technology that changes the structure of human consciousness. Textuality is a *consciousness technology*: it alters the very way we perceive, think, and believe in what is real.

On the cultural level, the introduction of reading and writing and the cultural practices and ideologies that come with it are not always greeted with enthusiasm. Introducing literacy into non-literate cultures has had profound effects on indigenous cultural practices (McCluhan 1962, Goody 1968, Eisenstein 1979, Ong 1982) and native peoples often recognize that textuality is not innocuous. Some of the Pueblo peoples of New Mexico, have refused to allow their languages to be written and taught in schools as recently as the 1990s. They argue that written language is sacrilegious, gives indiscriminate access to esoteric religious practice, and is an imperialist tool that undermines the cultural identity and political sovereignty of Pueblo peoples (Martinez 2000, Webster 2006). This echoes Ong's statement that "writing is a particularly pre-emptive and imperialist activity that tends to assimilate other things to itself" (1982, p. 12).

In the following, the term "textuality" will be used in its traditional definition from the *Oxford Dictionary of English* (Stevenson 2010): "The quality or use of language characteristic of written works as opposed to spoken usage", and not in the wider structuralist and post-structuralist sense which understands textuality as the larger open field of social and cultural contexts of interpretation and the working of signification in general (Hanks 1989). The reason for returning to the pre-structuralist definition of textuality is that post-structuralist engagement with textuality takes the written work as the given, while this chapter attempts to put into question the very production of written texts from the production of oral events. Reading texts leads to an existential shift in individual and cultural life with far-reaching consequences. I will use the word "reading" to stand in for "reading and writing" as an experiential practice of engagement with written material, and I understand *reading* to be the situated, embodied, psychological practice of engagement with texts. Investigating the experience of reading allows us to enter into the phenomenology of *lived textuality* and discover how texts intersect with and restructure human consciousness. A phenomenology of reading in children leads us to the genesis of textuality in the human mind and reveals how texts intersect with bodies, the perceptual environment, social relations, and the structure of reality at large.

The phenomenology of reading

The magic of synesthesia

In his phenomenological analysis of alphabetization as a perceptual phenomenon, Abram (1996) shows how perception changes in the transition from oral to textual engagement with the world in non-literate, indigenous cultures. His analysis, however, also applies to the restructuring child consciousness undergoes in the transition from orality to literacy. Prior to the immersion into textuality, the creative, synesthetic interplay of the senses with the perceived world creates a sense of magical envelopment. The earth is experienced as alive and meaningful and full of messages to the perceiver: "Direct, prereflective perception is inherently synesthetic, participatory, and animistic, disclosing the things as elements that surround us not as inert objects but as expressive subjects, entities, powers, potencies" (p. 130). Abram's analysis of indigenous nature experience parallels Piaget's description of preschoolers' animistic and participatory consciousness and style of thinking (Piaget 1929/51). Merleau-Ponty's re-interpretation of this semblance allows us to see the similarity not as a denigration of indigenous experience and knowledge as childlike, but that there is a plurality of possibilities in each infant, whether indigenous or acculturated in the Western tradition, and that different cultures inhibit or choose to emphasize and develop different perceptual and epistemological abilities (Merleau-Ponty 2010). The insertion of textual technology into the developmental process is one of the prime ways of altering the perceptual and epistemological structure of children's consciousness.

One of the key elements of perception is *synesthesia*, which is the ability of the senses to constitute each other. Synesthesia works by bringing all the senses into play in the act of perception (Merleau-Ponty 1962). We see something and know at the same time what sound it will make if we knock on it, how its texture will feel if we touch it, or how heavy it will be if we pick it up. Even very young infants have this ability of cross-modal, synesthetic perception (Meltzoff and Borton 1979, Stern 1985). When one sensory mode is evoked, the others come into play as well. In reading, synesthesia is a key feature, as Abram (1996) has pointed out:

> In learning to read we must break the spontaneous participation of our eyes and our ears in the surrounding terrain (where they had ceaselessly converged in the synesthetic encounter with animals, plants, and streams) in order to recouple those senses upon the flat surface of the page. As a Zuni elder focuses her eyes upon a cactus and hears the cactus begin to speak, so we focus our eyes on these printed marks and immediately hear voices. We hear spoken words, witness strange scenes or visions, even experience other lives.
>
> (p. 131)

Abram's analysis of the relationship between alphabetization and perception makes clear that the magical synesthesia, the evocation of all the senses, is relocated from the world to the text. When the eye perceives something, the other senses participate, even if they do not perceive directly. *This is the virtual, imaginary dimension of perception* (Merleau-Ponty 1962), where the body acts as if it encounters a full sensory field, even though only one sense is directly activated. As the eyes read through the signs on the page, the mind brings all the senses into play to create a whole virtual world complete with sensory resonances. The magical power of books has its roots in the phenomenon of synesthesia: as we read, the world of the book is as compelling and sometimes more real to us than the actual world of the senses. "As nonhuman animals, plants, and even 'inanimate' rivers once spoke to our tribal ancestors, so the 'inert' letters on the page now speak to us! This is a form of animism that we take for granted, but it is animism none the less – as mysterious as a talking stone" (p. 131). And Abram is correct: we are animists when it comes to textual signification. We give ourselves over to the mysterious voices and beings that arise through the letters on the page and take them seriously – and among literate people we take the world of texts more seriously than the world of the senses: most children spend more time in the text centered symbolic discourse of school than in exploring and talking about the world they directly perceive; most adults spend the majority of their time dealing with textual matters such as e-mails, books, social media, blogs, websites, and so on which all co-opt the natural synesthesia of the body and eliminate attention to the world of the senses.

The introduction of literacy changes children's relationship to the world because it shifts their attention from the animated, meaningful context of their perceived worlds toward the purely virtual and *unperceived* dimension of the text's virtual world. Abram argues that the magic of full, synesthetic perception, the spell that it casts upon us and the force with which it draws us into a connection with the world, changes its direction when we enter a literate world. Literacy is a technology that distances us from the life world and dulls our ability to attend to and "read" fully the expressions of the world of minerals, plants, animals and the elements: "it is only when a culture shifts its participation to these printed letters that the stones fall silent" (Abram 1996).

Here we recognize the structural intensifications and context reductions which are hallmarks of the Illich Principle: textual technology *reduces* the body's perceptual engagement with a plentiful, signifying, sensory environment and *intensifies* the virtual/symbolic dimension of language through manipulating synesthesia.

The loss of the embodied situation

In order to be a reader and to be transported into the world of the text, children have to let go of the lived context of the perceived world. Vygotsky (1986) noted that the young child's entry into literacy introduces an abstract process that is removed from the child's actual situation. Attention must focus through the visual process of decoding to the world of meaning the text transmits. This world of the text has no relationship to the child's here and now. The lived context for the conversation between speakers has to be eliminated: the room must be forgotten, other children must be blocked out, and the only one speaking is the text. Other bodies – and even the child's own body – are intrusions and must be restrained to a chair behind a table so that they don't occupy the space in social and disruptive ways. This is a change in the situatedness of language. Postman puts it succinctly:

> But with the printed book another tradition began: the isolated reader and his private eye. Orality became muted, and the reader and his response became separated from a social context. The reader retired within his own mind, and from the sixteenth century to the present what most readers have required of others is their absence, or, if not that, their silence. In reading, both the writer and reader enter into a conspiracy of sorts against social presence and consciousness. Reading is, in a phrase, an asocial act.
> (Postman 1994, p. 27)

When we teach reading to children, we also teach them to repress their senses and the presence of embodied others. Most children love to talk to each other and they draw each other forward into the world of ideas that they talk about. Reading as an "asocial act" requires the child to engage with a speaker, the author, who is disembodied and unresponsive and does not create openings for the child's own introjections into the web of language and thought. The conversation, from the child's perspective, is passive and receptive, and the reader has no power to shape and alter the course of the conversation. The child moves from the dialogue of oral exchange to the monologue of the text (Vygotsky 1986). This is especially difficult for beginning readers, who cannot yet reconstitute the symbolic world behind the letters on the page, and have not yet tasted the pleasure that a good text evokes. Even though reading requires an active mind, this activity is virtual, solitary, and disembodied. The very power of texts comes from the *reduction of the actual, social, and embodied dimensions of language* experience. The loss of the immediate social context opens the reader to the new context that the text offers. From a lived sociality the child moves into a virtual sociality that promises encounters with fictional characters. These encounters are powerful, disembodied, and invisible to others, which *intensifies the reader's sense of privacy and interiority*.

According to the Illich Principle, the reduction of the immediate social context leads to an intensification of virtual sociality with disembodied people who exist in fiction only. An unintended consequence is the overdetermination of interiority, privacy, and inner monologue, which are hallmarks of the Western self.

Entering a text

In his phenomenological analysis of the literary work of art, Ingarden (1973) points out that out of the component parts of textuality (phonemes, words, sentences, and the textual unfolding as a whole) a particular *world* arises, and it is this world (which transcends the author's intended meaning) which the reader finds compelling – or not. The reader has to be able to "climb aboard" and "accept the given perspectives" (Iser 1972), while at the same time be willing to collaborate with the text to allow it to come to fruition in the imagination:

> The literary text activates our own faculties, enabling us to recreate the world it represents. The product of this creative activity is what we might call the virtual dimension of the text, which endows it with its reality. The virtual dimension is not the text itself, nor is it the imagination of the reader: it is the coming together of text and imagination.
>
> (p. 284)

The reader's imagination fills the gaps in the text, supplies what is not there. The text, on the other hand, allows the reader to live and experience worlds that could never come to his or her immediate, embodied senses. The virtual dimension, as Iser points out, lies in the engagement between mind and text and is created through the interaction between consciousness and chirographic material.

Virtuality, as we saw before, is an essential constituent of synesthesia: we see a red dress, but we also virtually assume the softness of its texture or the weight of its fabric without ever touching it. Perception itself has a virtual dimension which weaves sense perceptions into a coherent whole and which functions as a present absence. The virtual dimension of textual technology *intensifies* this sense of present absence and drags consciousness along in its wake by promising it a coherent, satisfying world. But it is a world that leaves our senses behind. The absent becomes more real than the present.

A book takes on its full existence only in its readers (Poulet 1969). If it receives their full participation it allows them to absorb new experiences.

> As soon as I replace my direct perception by the words of a book, I deliver myself, bound hand and foot to the omnipotence of fiction. I say farewell to what is, in order to feign belief in what is not. I surround myself with fictitious beings; I become the prey of language. There is no escaping this take-over. Language surrounds me with its unreality.
>
> (p. 55)

The reader's thoughts and feelings are occupied by the thoughts of the author, and these in their turn draw new boundaries in our personality. The consciousness of the reader "behaves as though it were the consciousness of another" and "on loan to another" who feels, suffers, and thinks in it (pp. 56–57). Reading requires the sustained immersion in the fictional world created by an author. The silence of the reader and the temporal structure of the continuous, uninterrupted voice of the author preclude the reader from interjecting and changing the direction of the language exchange. The world of the book worms its way into the consciousness of the reader. All a reader can do is close the book and refuse participation in the symbolic world the text promises.

Here we have another intensification and reduction of language practice according to the Illich Principle: the possibility of thinking according to others (when we listen to them) is intensified in the exposure to the text's voice, and in the reduction of the reader's own speech. The unintended consequence is that the truth that the text proclaims seems to have persuasive and ultimate reality status ("it is written") and supersedes the truth that I see with my own eyes. When I cannot look the speaker in the eye and verify the veracity of her story by understanding our shared context and her ethos within our social field, the truth becomes relative and has no grounding in personal verification. In the virtual world, truth and reality are determined by other textual endorsements and the persuasive voices that grab the available public textual platforms.

Virtuality and the reproduction of culture

In oral conversations, children take up each other's thoughts and weave a shared web of mind processes. In textuality, however, others' thought processes, memories, and images are recapitulated and accomplished in the child's mind without the child's direct, embodied response. Silencing the back and forth of embodied conversations intensifies the reader's exposure to the author's thoughts, images, and feelings. The most significant change that literacy introduces is the amplification of virtual realities in the minds of children.

The virtual reality displayed by the text refers to Merleau-Ponty's idea of the "organism of words", which creates a new dimension of experience alongside the perceptual world:

> The greatest benefit of expression is not to consign to paper ideas which might otherwise be forgotten: authors seldom reread their own texts, and great works install in us at first reading all that we will later draw out of them. The operation of expression, when it is successful, does not simply serve as a memory aid for the reader or for the writer himself; on the contrary, the expression makes the signification exist as a thing, at the very heart of the text. The expression gives life to the signification in an organism of words, it establishes the signification in the writer or reader as a new sense organ, and it opens our experience to a new field or a new dimension.
>
> (Merleau-Ponty 1962, p. 182)

The virtual space between the reader and the text requires a different way of perceiving and what Merleau-Ponty calls "a new sense-organ" for the phenomena of the virtual world. It catapults readers into a new reality in which they have to understand *mental* landscapes and navigate complex discursive terrains which were established by other texts before a particular text was created. The "new field" or "new dimension" is the reality of cultural discourses which transcend the exchange of situated, embodied, social speech that individuals engage in on a daily basis. This new virtual field is real to the people who have been initiated into it.

As soon as children cross over the threshold of alphabetic decoding, they enter a compelling wonderland of ideas and experiences *which are not their own*, but which powerfully shape the mind. Literate cultures know that they need this virtual world and that they have to colonize it. I call the reality which is created by textuality *the virtual field* with reference to Merleau-Ponty. By replicating the virtual field in the minds of children, literate cultures reproduce themselves on a massive scale over generations by establishing canons of texts that have to be read and internalized by children. Cultural memory is transmitted by texts. We call this process "education". From the perspective of Abram's oral, animist cultures who engage with the sensory world and are conversant with the signs of a full perceptual spectrum, Western culture, through its promotion of the textual virtual field, is engaged in a massive repression and restructuring of embodied perception in order to make each person a citizen of the particular virtual world the culture claims as its reality.

We can get a better view of the significance of the virtual order when we look at it from a cultural-historical perspective. Literate cultures have commerce in the realities that are created by texts: books hold knowledge and cultural memory. Virtual media, which includes books as well as electronic media today, are a storehouse for memories of all sorts – records of legal transactions, historical events, philosophical argument, poetry, scientific inventions and ideas, religious texts and commentaries, maps and calendars, political polemics. Historically, book content is the cultural currency that is transferred in the conversations of literate people and determines the intellectual and moral climate. Mumford argues that the invention of the printing press and the ensuing spread of writing technology led to a radical transformation of Western culture.

> More than any other device, the printed book released people from the domination of the immediate and the local. . . . print made a greater impression than the actual events. . . . To exist was to exist in print: the rest of the world tended gradually to become more shadowy. Learning became book learning.
>
> (Mumford 1934, p. 136)

Print technology multiplies the audience for texts, as well as the number of authors who want to occupy the reader's mind. In turn, the dissemination of ideas in print, as Mumford indicates, inserts itself into everyday life practices and changes them radically. The invention of the automobile, the telephone, and electronic media were possible because their inventors could acquire the sedimented knowledge of previous generations through reading. In turn, these inventions changed where and how people lived, how they attended to and perceived their environment, and what they talked about with their neighbors.

Books do not merely contain information, but they structure the way we think about reality. Literacy makes it possible to erect a conceptual scaffold above our everyday experience, which then is disseminated and transmitted through the authority of media and the formal processes of systemic and compulsory education. The virtual reality of texts becomes believable and compelling, even if it contradicts our senses: *to exist is to exist in print*. The immediate and local experience has been sacrificed to the virtual dimension of texts.

In terms of the Illich Principle, the unintended consequences of literacy gradually become apparent. Literacy is not merely the acquisition of the ability to read, but the introduction into a different level of cultural discourse which is no longer fully connected to the embodied, perceived environment. When the virtual field becomes more "real" than the corporeal field, we lose the "sense-organs" that perceive the variety and signification of a complicated and shifting natural world: "the stones fall silent", as Abram (1996) put it so eloquently.

Conclusion

The intensification of the virtual field and the reduction of people's embodied context are deeply entangled with the practice of literacy itself. The printed book is the first intensification and relocation of the virtual field, followed by further reiterations and relocations of the virtual dimension through our contemporary use of information and communication of technologies (ICTs). Their growing use in education increasingly intensifies the virtual capacity of human beings and sacrifices the lived, perceptual, embodied context of the learning situation. Literacy itself carries within it the seeds of alienation from nature and social life, and the field of education is especially prone to its excesses. From a structural perspective, schooling as an institution is deeply entangled with literacy – and also with the problems of literacy. For example, the insistence on "written", "documented" testing as a measure for educational achievement intensifies learning of facts and measurable skills while reducing the full context of children's and teachers' motivation for learning and the diversity of their abilities. It proposes a virtual, average child and a virtual average teacher without body and social relationships. The unintended consequences of the testing and measurements practices in education has been the commodification and manipulation of test-scores in order to get government funding, and a general loss of enthusiasm and motivation in teachers and students. As Mumford (1934) put it: "to exist was to exist in print", and what does not exist in print tends gradually to become more shadowy and devalued.

The phenomenology of reading has made me more critical and aware of what we do to children when we initiate them into textual practices and the virtual field. What we ask our children to give up is the ability to hear, see, smell, touch, and live in a full natural, sensory, embodied environment. With the intensification of the information and communication technology landscape, the disconnect between human consciousness and the natural world becomes even greater, and the divide is normalized: children are not allowed to live their lives outside, playing freely (and sometimes dangerously) with other children, unsurveilled by adults – a practice that was the norm in Western cultures until a quarter century ago. Parents think that their children are less vulnerable sitting inside, alone, before their devices – but that is an illusion. The dangers might not be to their bodies, but to their minds and to their hearts and to their long-term emotional wellbeing. And once more we glimpse the unfolding of the unintended consequences of technological innovation . . .

More than ever, the virtual worlds of educational ICTs that we expose our children to need to be balanced by a conscious cultivation of bodily learning-engagement with the natural world and a renewed valuation of the social relationship between teachers and students. From the perspective of child development, more virtuality calls for *more nature play and more direct conversation with others* in order to safeguard the emotional and physical wellbeing of children.

One final note: the irony of deconstructing textuality and the process of reading by writing a text has probably not escaped the reader. But how else can we grasp what literacy does to the human mind and to human existence but by holding onto it as we are swimming in it?

> Nowhere, Beloved, will be world but within.
> Life passes in transformation. And, ever diminishing,
> the outside vanishes. Where once an enduring house was,
> a conceptual structure suggests itself, askance and completely
> belonging to thinking as if it still stood in the brain.
> The Zeitgeist creates great reservoirs of power, formless
> like the tense urge it extracts from everything.
> It does not know temples anymore.
>
> Rainer Maria Rilke (2019), *Duino Elegies*

References

Abram, D., 1996. *The spell of the sensuous*. New York: Vintage Books.
Eisenstein, E., 1979. *The printing press as an agent of change: Communications and cultural transformations in early-modern Europe*. New York: Cambridge University Press.
Goody, J., 1968. *Literacy in traditional societies*. Cambridge: Cambridge University Press.
Hanks, W.F., 1989. Text and textuality. *Annual Review of Anthropology*, 18, 95–127.
Illich, I., 1996. *In the vineyard of the text: A commentary to Hugh's Didascalicon*. Chicago, IL: University of Chicago Press.
Illich, I. and Sanders, B., 1988. *ABC: The alphabetization of the popular mind*. San Francisco: North Point Press.
Ingarden, R., 1973. *The literary work of art*. Evanston, IL: Northwestern University Press.

Iser, W., 1972. The reading process: a phenomenological approach. *New Literary History*, 3, 279–299.
Martinez, R.B., 2000. Languages and tribal sovereignty: Whose language is it anyway? *Theory into Practice*, 39, 211–220.
McCluhan, M., 1962. *The Gutenberg galaxy.* Toronto: University of Toronto Press.
Meltzoff, A.N. and Borton, W., 1979. Intermodal matching by neonates. *Nature*, 282, 403–404.
Merleau-Ponty, M., 1962. *Phenomenology of perception.* London: Routledge & Kegan Paul Ltd.
Merleau-Ponty, M., 2010. *Child psychology and pedagogy: The Sorbonne Lectures 1949–1952.* Evanston, IL: Northwestern University Press.
Mumford, L., 1934. *Technics and civilization.* New York: Harcourt, Brace & Co.
Ong, W., 1982. *Orality and literacy: the technologizing of the word.* London/New York: Routledge.
Piaget, J., 1929/51. *The child's conception of the world.* Savage, MD: Littlefield Adams.
Postman, N., 1994. *The disappearance of childhood.* New York: Vintage Books.
Poulet, G., 1969. Phenomenology of reading. *New Literary History*, 1, 53–68.
Rilke, R.M., 2019. *Duino Elegies.* Unpublished translation, E.-M. Simms.
Simms, E.-M., 2008a. *The child in the world: Embodiment, time, and language in early childhood.* Detroit: Wayne State University Press.
Simms, E.-M., 2008b. Literacy and the appearance of childhood. *Janus Head*, 10, 445–459.
Simms, E.-M., 2010. Questioning the value of literacy: A phenomenology of speaking and reading in children. *In*: K. Coats, ed. *Handbook of children's and young adult literature.* London/New York: Routledge, chapter 2, 20–31.
Stern, D.N., 1985. *The interpersonal world of the infant: A view from psychoanalysis and developmental psychology.* New York: Basic Books, Inc.
Stevenson, A., 2010. *Oxford dictionary of English.* Oxford: Oxford University Press.
Vygotsky, L.S., 1986. *Thought and language.* Cambridge, MA: MIT Press.
Webster, A., 2006. Keeping the word: On orality and literacy (with a sideways glance at Navajo). *Oral Tradition*, 21, 295–324.

Chapter 8

Reality-testing subjectivity, naivety, and freedom – or on the possibility of educational moments

Tone Saevi

Introduction

In this text I try out two concerns I have in my teaching and in my reflections about teaching. By doing so, I put at stake my own pedagogical insight and sensitivity. I start where Gert Biesta ends in his little book *The Rediscovery of Teaching* (Biesta 2017) by trying to put into educational practice the idea of reality-testing what it means to appeal to young people's' subject-ness[1] (Biesta 2015) – the latent potential of human subjectivity (Saevi 2014) that in the German tradition has been called "Bildsamkeit". I try to reality-test the idea that educational teaching – teaching that has the required qualities to deserve the name of teaching – intends to appeal to the young person to open up to a more difficult freedom (Levinas 1990), than a freedom of choice or a freedom to realize oneself. Then, I explore an insight that I have continuously pursued indirectly for many years. Fourteen years ago, I suggested, "The challenge of teaching is to know when to see and when to pass over seeing something (and thereby bringing it to notice)" (Saevi 2005, p. 167). And I ask, how would teaching be, if teaching was exercised with a certain naivety and blindness to conventional practices and professional regulations? My two concerns might blend together by addressing, in different ways, aspects of the complex question of what educational freedom might be like. I intend to work from a phenomenological perspective including examples, and the reflection on examples that this method requires. The concrete descriptions of pedagogical relationships and the sources deriving from practice and theory are related *to* and *via* the experiential examples.

Education and educational questions are given to us as practices where the older generation encounter the younger with a certain purpose. However, as no one actually owns education, education is not something we can offer the young for a charge. We cannot really expect anything in return from those we educate; no thanks, no provision or results. The one-sidedness of education, the fact that we (society, teachers, parents) give it (although we do not possess it) or perhaps better, we pass on something that we have been given ourselves once and try to adjust and renew it for the next generation. Because education – again basically – is an existential practice that cannot solve any problems or take care of issues on a permanent basis; educational moments actually are events (Romano 2014) that address possibilities more than factualities; the possibility of subjective acts and thoughts of young people. An event, similar to time, is provisional, and like time, an event cannot be posed in a "timeless manner" (p. 1). Events cannot be repeated and will lose their quality of events if we make them into routines and best practices. Romano sees events as "openings to the present" but "an event is not first present (as fact), to be deferred later (as event); rather. . . it precedes itself, is prospective, opens a future and receives itself from this future that it opens, from which and through which it appears . . . as originally time" (p. 128). Romano even says that an event is "more future than itself" (p. 135).

This might mean that in education encounters between teacher and student are always events – acts that impact (through the present) the future, and here in particular the future of the student.

Opening of possibilities

Pelle Sandstrak has written a documentary novel entitled *Mr. Tourette and I* (Sandstrak 2014), where he in a straightforward way describes momentous events in his life as a child and young boy with Tourette syndrome. The book has a phenomenological flavor in that it includes experiential descriptions dripping from subjectively sensed details of sound, smell, taste, words, sensations – so crisp that I – without Tourette, get a sense of how life with this condition might be like for the young boy. Sandstrak describes an episode in grade 8 with one of his teachers, Anton:

> We have carpentry. Anton bends down to show me how to use the file. The wallet in his back pocket lights up to me like Apollo 3. It is black and worn and smells good. "Shake my stomach", and now his wallet is in my hand. And what does Anton do? He does nothing. He stands, looks at me, at the wallet, at me, and still does nothing. I'm thinking: shouldn't he grab my left arm, walk the ninety-eight steps up to the school's most fragrant lurid sofa, listening to yet another two-minute humanity monologue? Shouldn't he, shouldn't he? But he doesn't. He just stands still and looks me in the eye. My brain doesn't get what it expects at all. A little tiring silence is needed, as if it is my turn to act, do something unexpected, "shock, start, now". I get a look that is becoming more and more like a shy labradors, while Anton continues to look me straight in the eye, serious and angry, determined and direct. A sort of gurgling, loud sound breaks the weary silence – it is Anton who lets go of the licorice candy he has probably hidden under his tongue in the last few minutes. It continues to roll around in his mouth, calm and provocative at the same time.
>
> Anton does something no one else has done before – he does nothing. And inside of it, he goes on with it. For all of a sudden, he says, sour,

direct, serious, and completely unexpected: "Put the wallet on the floor and count down from forty to zero, like Wayne Gretzky. As you count, I go into the warehouse and pick up two planks". He goes into the warehouse.

I really can't think or analyze what he does. The obvious in his behavior, makes me with wide open mouth and eyes big as plates put the wallet on the floor in front of my feet and start counting down from forty to zero, like Wayne Gretzky: Forty, thirty nine, thirty eight . . . twenty two, twenty one, twenty, nineteen, eighteen . . . Anton enters the room again. Now he has two boards with him, about a meter long. He gives me one of the boards and, says: "The planks are hockey sticks, the wallet is the puck. Here you have your stick, this is mine. Now you are Wayne Grezky and I am the goalkeeper of the national team. We shoot five shots each. Whoever wins the shoot-out decides what to do in the next twenty-five minutes after the shoot out".

(Sandstrak 2014, pp. 158–160, my translation)

Anton acts differently from what Pelle expects. He does nothing, Pelle says. And he continues doing nothing. To the young boy, what the teacher actually does counts for nothing, perhaps because what he does is not – as Pelle from experience expected – a typical educational return-act in shape of a "just" consequence for his tendency to grabbing things. Pelle cannot figure out what is going on and why, as the usual pattern of his action and the teacher's response, is broken.

Where does the sudden impulse to touch a thing like a wallet come from? Perhaps it is a whole lot of things. Pelle says that to him the need to touch something comes suddenly, calms him, and satisfies a boredom that comes from worries, repetitions and routine (p. 158). He does not plan to do it in the very moment when it happens. It just happens. He does not understand why he takes the wallet out of the teacher's pocket, however, he at least partly, explains the act as a result of his disability. But educationally, should we simply rely on neuro-biological or psychological explanations? Where would that lead our pedagogical attention? We might think (like Pelle was used to) that a consequence is required, and accuse him of unlawful possession of a wallet and – to break what is considered a bad habit – bring him to the principal's office. Or we might excuse the act, due to his disability, and give no penalty. Practice offers several solutions and ways of executing what we consider "wrong" actions. A crucial pedagogical point however, is whose perspective the event is seen from. This event is described by Pelle Sandstrak, now a grown man, then a young boy of 13. From a young person's perspective fundamental events happen all the time, and small moments might change one's life. But life does not necessarily change for the adult or teacher, who might even be unaware of what the moment meant to the young. The event might be one of many for a teacher. In the case that the moment is recognized, a teacher might believe that young people forget, and anyway, it is adults' responsibility to check and teach them to behave correctly and obey the rules. Still, for a particular student the direction of his life might be altered. Witte-Townsend says,

> Certain memories seem to ride along just beneath the surface of our lives where everyday awareness might find them . . . they are our connection with ourselves, and our knowledge of the past. Because we have these memories, we know that we are legitimately and solidly a part of the story of our own life.
>
> (2002, p. 171)

Pelle remembers this event while he writes his memoirs. Anton has become a significant person in the story of Pelle's life. He obviously must have altered Pelle's present and past connection with himself in a positive way. How so? If we listen to the pedagogical possibility of the event we might be addressed as teachers and adults. I believe that Pelle's experience is not just an occasional episode in school, and the person inhabiting it is not only a boy with Tourette requiring extraordinary pedagogical treatment from his teacher. All children and young persons are extraordinary as well as existentially unavailable – an aporetic quality of education that we too often seem to forget. Being a subject – whether a teacher or a student – is to allow the other to interrupt my self-sufficient and ego-logical way of life, and to be attentive to the otherness that addresses me from the outside world. Anton practices this pedagogical attentiveness to interrupt and be interrupted, and his sour and closed personality does not prevent him from being addressed by Pelle's typical behavioral tendency as something other, something that should be met as existentially different. Biesta suggests that the moment when I am addressed by the other and this other asks for something that only I can do, might be the decisive educational moment (2017, p. 11). Pelle's adoration for the Canadian all-time top hockey player Wayne Gretzky was familiar to Anton. But even though he knows Pelle quite well, what he does during the event somehow seems to free the young boy from his past (his Tourette diagnosis, his history, his behavioral problems), and is able to approach him in new and unimagined ways. Anton does not tie, hold to that which is – the acquisition of a wallet – and by that places the burden of education on the young boy. Rather, he takes the responsibility for placing the burden on education and on his own pedagogical imagination to find out how to teach. Løgstrup (1971) claims that it is my relational responsibility to put a stronger focus on imagination than on dependency. I am urged to dare to use my senses and imagination to find out what the other needs rather than asking him or her, and by this asking making myself a servant for the other. By taking responsibility for his responsibility Anton interrupts the immanent self – both the boy's and his own – and reveals to them both the deep and risky relationality we are bound to live under.

Contradictory to the inside-out way of thinking of freedom (that freedom is a feeling or something you obtain if you do this or that), Anton brings to life the experience that a student's subject-ness is "an ongoing 'state of dialogue' with what and who is other, with what and who speaks to us, addresses us, calls us, and thus calls us forth" (Biesta 2017, p. 3). When I look at the wallet event, teaching gains new significance as an address from the outside, a pointer or a suggestion for a particular attentive orientation. "Teaching becomes concerned with opening up existential possibilities for students . . . possibilities *in* and *through* which students can explore what it might mean to exist as subjects in and with the world" (p. 3). Anton lets himself be addressed by Pelle's acquisition of his wallet, and without evidence that the boy is capable of acting in another manner in order to fulfill particular expectations, he believes in the boy, and by this opens up existential possibilities. Teaching along these lines is the opposite of control and of treating students as objects by expecting them to conform and meet preset criteria (Saevi forthcoming). The educational task, as I see it, is to teach the young (and ourselves) a way of being receptive (in contrast to intentional) and passive (in contrast to active) toward the world, and by this, allow the world to have "its own integrity", as Biesta says (2017, p. 33).

We really don't know[2] . . .

Educational practice and thinking as existential is "a first-hand moral interest for the adult . . . to be attentive to the existential meaning held within a particular educational situation and in particular how the situation is experienced by the child" (Saevi 2015, p. 344). What we can do as teachers and grown-ups actually is to appeal to the young person's will and willingness to take the risk on us, to trust us and relate to us. Biesta (2017) presents worldly existence for young people as well as adults, as a sustained and durable dialogue, "a way of being together that seeks to do justice to all partners involved" (p. 14). This existential dialogue never ends and is the opposite of the burst of energy performed in competition or the introvert energy that orients solely to ourselves. Existential dialogue is "sustained energy, attention and commitment" (p. 15) toward what is other, and therefore it requires interest and exploration of the difficult situations, questions and relationships of the real world. Real existence is only possible in this dialogue with that which is outside of ourselves, where the self "encounters limits, interruptions, responses" (p. 15) which all have the quality of disrupting and confusing my intents and questioning my ego-logical orientation (Levinas 1969). This is the difficult freedom, different from good emotions and wellbeing. This kind of freedom is the only freedom that has to do with what only I can do, Biesta with Levinas, assert (2017, p. 5). The issues I encounter and become involved in, are issues that I somehow become aware of, issues that address me. This makes me a subject among the other subjects of the world. The moments when I am a subject to myself and the world are the moments when I stay in the middle ground (Biesta 2015) – in this ongoing dialogue of existence – where existence is ex-istence – meaning that I, as first person – the one being addressed – is oriented to the world *outside* myself. The teacherly educational responsibility is to try to "arouse such a desire in another human being" (p. 15), a student, a young person whose behavior, language, habits and ways of being and acting might not be of my liking. But how do we do this? What does it mean to appeal to young people to relate to that which is other and comes from the outside of them?

The following event took place in a secondary high school in Norway:

> *This morning fifteen young boys of 17 and I meet for the first time in their classroom at the Department of Machine & Mechanics. They seem uninterested, some even hostile. As a relatively new teacher I sense we are not at the same wavelength. We will be spending three lessons every week on Norwegian language and literature, and I am discouraged by what I see. Some of the young boys walk around, some are talking to each other or fiddling with cartoons or car magazines. None of them attend to me by the teacher's desk. The first thing I can think of is to offer them a pedagogical deal. I say: "We have three lessons every week dedicated to Norwegian language and literature. How should we make the best out of them? If one of the lessons is for something that you would like to do, something relevant for our subject, the two remaining lessons are for the curriculum." Silence. I could hear myself breathe. "You read aloud for us," a boy wearing a grey coverall to my left, says after the silence. Some nod affirmatively. One lesson of reading aloud is much. But if that is a deal that brings us forth, I think I could. "Which book?" Silence. "You tell us," a boy says. He throws an empty bottle in the air and catches it. Okay. It strikes me that I might be exploited now. But what then. "What kind of books do you like then?" Now many voices raise. "Something exciting, a thriller or something." Okay. I try to think of books I know that might be exciting for 17 years old boys. "Have you read 'The murder on the Askøy ferry'?" I ask. No one has. And no one has heard of Gunnar Staalesen, the author. But yes, that sounds like a book they might like, and they were willing to give it a try.*
>
> *After having picked up the book from the library I sat on the teacher's desk every Tuesday morning reading for them. They sit, lay, hang, sprawl at or by their desks, eating something or drinking coke, silent, listening, laughing and commenting. The latter not so often. The boys were captivated. We read five books by the same author that school year. Thrillers from a Bergen perspective. Local humor. Saucy language. Recognizable for me and them. The books were speckled with daring, sometimes indecent descriptions, which they clearly enjoyed. I had to read every word, as even the slightest hesitation or attempt to rephrase, were discovered and someone corrected me. So, I gave in and read every word just as the author expressed it.*

How do we teach ourselves and the young of our responsibility to listen, be receptive, open themselves up, so that other than what comes from the inside can address them? The previous example depicts teaching as a non-transactive act – where the teacher's teaching and the student's responses – listening, doing nothing, being confused, hesitant, frustrated, expectant, learning, not learning, indifferent, interested, bored, or any other response or reaction – are not direct causes of the teaching. Rather teaching and learning (or other responses) are related, but not one being the cause of the other. Teaching – if that is what the teacher is doing while reading aloud for the class – is a "uncompensated" event (Biesta 2017, p. 28), free for the students to take or not. Additionally, I suggest that although adults and teachers have a great deal of insight, knowledge, power and responsibilities these qualities are highly questionable because they can mean all kinds of different things depending on how they are practiced and how they are received. In other words, educational qualities – for example, teaching practices – depend on how they are practiced rather than what their results are. Educational responsibility is "a responsibility for the unique child [or young person] and in the same breath a responsibility for one's own adult responsibility" (Saevi 2014, p. 42). Biesta (2015) asserts that human existence only is possible in the middle ground between the extremes, because only here can our self-expression encounter limits, interruptions and responses, and thus become a responsible existence. Only here can what I do matter for someone, and only here might my irreplaceable subject be at stake with others. Only here do I encounter the responsibility that calls me to action and only here am I interdependent of others in the real reality where we both exist as subjects.

The young boys in secondary high are not first of all *learners* or *educational projects*, but simply young people growing up in the world. What they should have done, been or obtained are different from what *is* as experienced in the present event. The difference between an orientation to the event in itself and to a prescribed future outcome, denotes a difference between existential education and a psychological foundation for education (Saevi 2014). Existential events are "open to experiential insight, rather than being educationally effectuated, explained or resolved" (p. 42). The teacher lets herself be addressed by how the students' subjectivity might be pedagogically nurtured – as she realizes that subjectivity cannot be forced but should meet something present in the young person that is ready for that which is given without expectation of receiving anything in return from the teacher.

What the example is an example of, is above all an educational attempt that could easily have gone "wrong", for the teacher as well as for the students. Moments during my reading aloud might have not worked out or been meaningless for one or some of the students. I did not know then, and do not know now. The consequences of the action initiated could go wrong or disappoint one or some of us, or fail for many reasons that were, and are out of the teacher's or any of the students' hands. Despite of inventive and positive scholarly or professional intentions and actions education is never predictable to the full extent. Or, to be more precise, education *should* not be fully predictable if it at the same time should be educational. Educational limitations prevent that.

The reading aloud event is an example of education that does not happen steady and even, but more often is interrupted and problematic, even painful for one or both parts. Here, as elsewhere in school, teaching often confronts teachers and students with disruptions in terms of problems with understanding or explaining, lack of time and space to elaborate or finish actions or intentions, confrontation of wills, frustration, disagreement (and at other times bullying, and more serious issues like illness, accidents and death). If we work from the assumption that teaching is going to make a student more competent, we think of teaching as concurrence – agreement, consent – rather than as dissensus, and thus work perfectly within the educational modes of qualification and socialization but miss attempts to support a possible subjectification. The student will learn, develop and require skills and knowledge but remains an object and will not be a subject in his or her life. Unlike knowledge and skills, subject-ness is not something that a person can possess but is an event that may or may not occur. Biesta refers to Levinas, who writes that this is not about a capability although far beyond capacity, but "the possibility of a command, a 'you must' which takes no account of what 'you can'" (Hand 1989, p. 205 in Biesta 2017, p. 90). Masschelein (1997) calls for "disarmament" instead of empowerment, as subject-ness is not the result of a trajectory of learning, but "an event that breaks through all this, irrespective of whether the child – or anyone of any age, for that matter – is ready for it or not", Biesta says, (2017, p. 91). To bring about subject-ness in another person then calls for trust in that person – a trust without reason or evidence – a trust that "puts their subject-ness at stake" (p. 92), strikingly similar to the trust Jean Valjean experienced in the bishop's unconditional trust in him in *Les Miserable* (Saevi and Eikeland 2012).

Concluding comments

There is a chance that Anton's blindness to Pelle's behavioral problem, and my own naivety to the possibility that the class might want to take advantage of their new teacher could be of educational value. Perhaps the teachers' lack of a common teacherly response might open a possibility for freedom for the students to act, think and feel differently. Existential experiential events in a sense are moments that have the educational quality to open for unforeseen things to happen, things that might disorient and disrupt but anyway be of educational value. What the seemingly successful examples might show us is that sometimes education can turn out to be good despite the risk taken. Or, of course, this is not really the whole truth, because we do not know if the descriptions are descriptions of good education or not. Education is not just about the present and not just about one or a particular perspective or achievement. Every educational moment is about the present *and* the future – the open and unforeseen and unpredictable future where "everything" can happen with what has happened already in the present or even the past. Each of the students in the class leads his or her life and a "successful" event in the classroom when they were 17 might turn out to mean little or much to them, to be good or bad, to be of significance or not. My point here is that we do not know. We really do not know what a teacher and his or her teaching will come to mean to the other – the student. This is why education by nature is and has to be risky, and why this is a beautiful quality in education (Biesta 2013). Education, whether in neoliberal times or not, experiences these moments of possibility to address subjectivity – the student's as well as the teacher's. The moments come and leave, and our responsibility as teachers is to be aware of them, seize them if we take the risk, care and have imagination, and then we should leave the effects to lead their own life – if any – *in* and *with* the students.

Education basically does not consist of success-stories but is about uncertainty, doubtfulness, not knowing what is right or not right. This "happens to such an extent", Bollnow (1989, p. 22) says, "that any success of education can be called into question". The need for educational theory emerges from teachers' reflection on how to understand their experienced problems in order to find better ways to act next time. "It [educational theory] arises from the needs of the practice, because the emerging difficulties force the educator to reflect, and to reflect in the original sense of the word," Bollnow continues (p. 23). Education is a practice as well as a human science with multiple answers and alternative solutions. A quality of education that comes in play here is precisely this risky nature that belongs to its basics. Whatever we do in education, there is a risk that it would not be the right, the best or the most pedagogical. Despite good intentions, like those intended in the previous examples, the outcome of the action might fail immediately, later or in the future. My responsibility as a teacher, however, still is to give what is *other*, the alterity and integrity *in* and *with* the world a place in my life – or not, if I decide so (Saevi 2015). The other though, is not the same as me, or my product, interpretation or construction. The other, the student (alike with the teacher) is other – the one addressed by me and the one that addresses me. This is a decentering of my ego, and my consciousness "loses its first place", Biesta says (2017, p. 32). The other calls me, addresses me, speaks to me, and I can respond or not – herein lies my freedom, and the freedom of Pelle and of each of the 17-year-olds. This means that communication and relationships in education are not exchanges of opinions or views, but responsible events coming from the outside addressing the ego – the teacher's as well as the student's – and perhaps most important, education is anchored in real life experiences of a common reality.

Notes

1 The word "subject-ness" could be understood as "being a subject" which a person actually is in the encounter with others in life. See Biesta (2015, p. 196, footnote 103).
2 This phrase is from an interview with Jan Masschelein performed by Trond Sandvik in June 2018. See Sandvik, T. 2019. *Frihet: hva er frihet og hva er pedagogisk frihet? Utforskning av de to fenomenene med utgangspunkt i et utvalg pedagogisk-filosofisk litteratur, beskrivelser fra egen praksis og intervju med Jan Masschelein*. Bergen: NLA University College.

References

Biesta, G.J.J., 2013. *The beautiful risk of education*. Boulder: Paradigm Publisher.
Biesta, G.J.J., 2015. Hva er en pedagogisk oppgave? Om å gjøre voksen eksistens mulig. *In*: P.O. Brunstad, S.M. Reindal, and H. Saeverot, eds. *Eksistens og pedagogikk*. Oslo: Universitetsforlaget, 194–208.

Biesta, G.J.J., 2017. *The rediscovery of teaching*. New York: Routledge.
Bollnow, O.F., 1989. Theory and practice in education. *Teaching and Learning* (5), 20–32.
Hand, S., ed., 1989. *The Levinas reader*. Oxford, UK & Cambridge, MA: Blackwell Publisher.
Levinas, E., 1969. *Totality and infinity*. Pittsburgh: Duquesne University.
Levinas, E., 1990. *Difficult freedom. Essays on Judaism*. Baltimore, MD: The John Hopkins University Press.
Løgstrup, K.E., 1971. *The ethical demand*. Philadelphia: Fortress Press. doi:10.1023/A: 1009920122725
Masschelein, J., 1997. In defence of education as problematisation. Some preliminary notes on a strategy of disarmament. *In*: D. Wildemeersch, M. Finger, and T. Jansen, eds. *Adult education and social responsibility: Reconciling the irreconcilable?* Frankfurt/Bern: Peter Lang, 133–149.
Romano, C., 2014. *Event and time*. New York: Fordham University Press.
Saevi, T., 2005. *Seeing disability pedagogically*. Bergen: University of Bergen. Doctoral dissertation [Unpublished].
Saevi, T., 2014. Mollenhauer and the pedagogical relation: A general pedagogic from the margins. *Phenomenology & Practice*, 8 (2), 39–44.
Saevi, T., 2015. Learning in pedagogical relations. *In*: D. Scott and E. Hargreaves, eds. *The Sage handbook of learning*. London: Sage, 242–252.
Saevi, T., forthcoming. How does Gert Biesta's book The *Rediscovery of Teaching* matter to education? *Phenomenology & Practice*.
Saevi, T. and Eikeland, T., 2012. From where does trust come and why is "from where" significant? *Phenomenology & Practice*, 6 (1), 89–95.
Sandstrak, P., 2014. *Mr. Tourette og jeg*. Oslo: Cappelen Damm.
Witte-Townsend, D., 2002. Remembering the childhood loss of a mother. *In*: M. Van Manen, ed. *Writing in the dark. Phenomenological studies in interpretive inquiry*. Ontario: The Althouse Press, 168–178.

Part 3

The existentials – lived time, body, space, and relations

Andrew Foran

In Part 3, the phenomenon of education as understood through the universal themes of lived experience, the four existentials, offers a heuristic guide allowing us the opportunity to more deeply understand the educational lifeworld. Here, the contributors explore themes connected to spatiality (lived space), corporeality (lived body), temporality (lived time), and relationality (lived relation) that challenge the neoliberal narrative that has come to dominate the educational landscape. Lived time, lived body, lived space, and lived relations create the fundamental lifeworld themes through which we can come closer to what is experienced in education, and the existentials challenge us to not take for granted these lived moments. Neoliberal worldview sees education as something less than a humanistic endeavor. In this section, the authors, in their unique ways, explore the educational lifeworld and question the multiple meanings that run counter to the instrumental and the standardized.

Navigating the vastness of the phenomenon of education, of "learning places" and all those involved in the complex process is no simple task. At every angle there is yet again another challenge to what it means to teach: from politicians, the public, parents, and students who question the value of this thing called "an education." Some may argue that neoliberalism has effectively obscured the way forward for those dedicated to *bringing up* children into this world. In this part of the book, the authors focus on getting *back to education itself* through the heuristic of the existentials. For example, we have come to expect how time and movement will be organized in children's lives in schools. The regulation of children's relationships, and how children and adults are together in a classroom, and more recently, how technology structures the bodies and experiences of the learners are most often taken for granted. Therefore, they become subjects of rich theoretical and phenomenological inquiry. Central to a phenomenological approach, and the search for lived meaning in people's experiences is the realization that relationality is at the core of human experience. Arendt, who spoke adamantly of a crisis in education (a precursor to our times?) reminds us that education is predicated on a web of relations.

The phenomenon of time is core to human existence, and imbues our being, doing, speaking, and thinking. Time "as experience" is different from clock time, although both are present in school and other educational settings. In fact, time is not only present, but at the very center of education and upbringing. Phenomenology takes up the responsibility of not just describing the lives of those engaged in education, but to interpret and reveal what may be concealed by political structures and the analyses of cultural theory. The existential theme of the lived body can focus our reflection on the corporeality and how schools, classrooms, and institutions are experienced and perceived. In this section, theorists and phenomenologists explore the common, and sometimes uncommon spaces in education, the experience of living in the presence of others in a shared space, and the notion of difference as interpreted through the four universal existentials to say something more about the life worlds of teachers and students.

Malte Brinkmann explores lived body, time, space and democratic education by providing an overview of the four existentials in a historical, systematic and pedagogical perspective from the perspective of phenomenological educational studies. The anthropological foundations of a phenomenology of the lifeworld are systematically presented as pedagogical experiences in educating as the embodied experience that is circumscribed by the concept of *negativity*, which is based on withdrawal and passive or pathic experiences. The concept of negativity refers to the experience of dependence, vulnerability, and interweaving with others. Education from a phenomenological and existential perspective is profound in that the relationship to oneself and the world changes. The educational process is dynamic with dimensions of embodiment, spatiality, and sociality interwoven in response to the existential experience of others. Brinkmann reveals learning as experience driven by negativity and relearning in the context of an intergenerational questioning as part of a *counseling* community.

Herner Saeverot and Glenn-Egil Torgersen present time, individuality, and interaction as pedagogical factors that impact teaching. Saeverot and Torgersen note that there are many different forms of time, from the everyday perception of time to biological time, to concepts of time in quantum mechanics, and that different kinds of time are often related to each other. Saeverot and Torgersen investigate the importance of time in educational settings and argue that to only talk about time as if there is one true or real time is a mistake, especially in teacher–student relationships, in an educational situation. They provide a basis for addressing questions about quality in relation to education, and seeing time as choice. These authors state that time has been altered due to neoliberal influences in education. When education is steeped in neoliberal practice, time becomes chronological and mechanistic. Time turns into an instrument of control. However, time as a lived phenomenon, can be exploited positively, in favor of both communication and learning. For this to be achieved, teachers must teach with an ongoing or proceeding perspective, in which a mechanistic understanding of time is given less emphasis whilst focusing on the here-and-now.

Eva Alerby delves into an intertwined relationship of the school building and the people who inhabit it. Drawing on the French philosophers Gaston Bachelard, Maurice Merleau-Ponty, and the Swedish philosopher and educator Jan Bengtsson, Alerby presents a grounded intertwined and reciprocal relationship between humans and the physical world – specifically the place of learning – the building itself. The relationship between the school space and the people who inhabit it is problematized. Alerby explores places/spaces beyond the physical school building – when the horizon of the classroom is unlimited, and the boundaries of the room become infinite. In addition, the horizon of the classroom is discussed, as well as the spaces beyond the room. On an ontological level, rooms and spaces, which are both shaped by humans and provided by nature, are discussed. Alongside this, how the space/room sometimes arouses memories and feelings that may affect the human body are explored. Alerby takes into account how educational sites during the current era of neoliberalism have been altered to become marketplaces.

David Seamon presents phenomenology, lifeworlds, and design in an effort to understand the lived dimensions of human experience as a pedagogy of self-conscious place making. Seamon considers the significance of the four lifeworld existentials for architectural and environmental design in education. Seamon challenges the reader to question how a phenomenological sensitivity to the lifeworld may contribute to envisioning pedagogical possibilities in architectural and environmental design. Seamon wonders if the unself-conscious place making of the past may be regenerated self-consciously in our hyper-modern world, through a phenomenologically grounded education characterized by knowledgeable planning, equitable policy, and creative design? Seamon explores this question, but more poignantly, he offers a phenomenological perspective countering much of everyday life and challenging everyday educational places that often go unnoticed, as an automatic unfolding.

Stephen Smith untangles the neoliberal bind that ensnares active and interactive bodies by discussing educators' concerns for the physical wellbeing of children and youth due to declining levels of activity among children and youth. Smith notes the contributory effects of sedentary modes of digitized interactivity are largely overlooked in the widespread embrace of instructional modalities of an on-line and socially mediated world. He positions the following: students sit in elementary, secondary, and tertiary classrooms, increasingly hard-wired and hyper-mediatized to interactions requiring seemingly minimal corporeal minds. The neoliberal response has been to insist on incorporating self-regulatory and social-emotional learning interventions to address the disconnection between agentic activity and communal interactivity. Yet Smith calls for educators to take up the potential of interacting synchronously and harmoniously with others in full-bodied ways. It is then, he asserts, that there arise shared, communal feelings of the powers of life expression. The implications for educational practice point to ways in which educators can best foster the joyful spontaneity of movement expression.

Erika Goble brings us directly back into the lived time of education reminding us that time is central to education. Goble states the lived time of education is about our experience of ourselves: of who we understand ourselves to be based on the past, and who we imagine ourselves becoming because of the future possibilities. Central to Goble's discussion is the pedagogical relation. The parent to child or teacher to student relationship is time-bound. Our formal educational systems, moreover, are divided into set time periods, the most common of which is the "school year," a 12-month period punctuated at regular intervals by weekends and holidays. But, Goble asks, is this the lived time of education? Goble shows us how time is experienced by teachers, students, parents, and children as a rhythm of the school year, which is often distinct to schools and grades as the rhythm and feel of a true moment of teaching and learning, where time seems to stand still but also pass far too quickly. Goble opens the reader up to kairotic moments when we realize once again we are learning something important.

In the final chapter of this part of the book, Marcus Morse and Sean Blenkinsop explore the experiences in which teaching towards the phenomenological attitude might also provide a relationally focused way of responding to the ecological and social crises of our time. The authors examine possibilities of teaching towards a phenomenological attitude with students outdoors. The authors show the importance of understanding the lives of others and relational ways of being. They believe developing teacher abilities and pedagogical insights may be directly beneficial in the lives of students. Blenkinsop and Morse provide descriptive examples and offer pedagogical aids as their discussion explores the lived experience offered to children by natural places. The natural locations seem to fulfill the child and allow them to engage with school in different yet productive ways.

Chapter 9

Bildung and embodiment
Learning, practicing, space and democratic education

Malte Brinkmann

Embodied experiences in practicing and learning

> *When I recently practiced cycling with my three-and-a-half-year-old son, he was already able to do a lot, because he had trained to keep his balance with his balance bike (a small bike without pedals). The first time on the bike he did quite well. He was very proud to have taken another step towards more independence. With the bicycle he was able to extend his circle of action with a new experience of speed and space, although he was not able to fully control what was happening. For example, he could not brake yet, so that he often involuntarily went off the bike, simply fell over or drove against obstacles. But the pain didn't stop him from climbing up again and keep on practicing. However, these experiences of disappointment and failure left obvious traces – scratches and abrasions, tears and rage. By now he can ride a bicycle as good or as bad as most children of his age.*
>
> (Brinkmann 2012, p. 16)

This example shows some aspects of experience and negativity that I would like to work out first: The phenomenological ontology of the lived body makes clear that we can see the lived body in this example of practicing as an "expressing body" (Hua IV p. 247) that articulates itself in movements as well in gestures and mimics (cf. Hua X pp. 13 f.). In his late work, Husserl describes this phenomenon with the term "movement-sensations", which express themselves in the mode of "I can" (Hua XI pp. 13 f.). Merleau-Ponty follows Husserl, but not his solipsism, in determining the kinaesthetic unity of the lived body in an inter-corporal way. "The conscience in its original sense is not an 'I think to . . .', but an 'I can'" (Merleau-Ponty 1974, p. 166). Knowledge is first incorporated and implicit knowledge in the body schema, not intellectual or cognitive knowledge. By repeatedly mastering situation-specific requirements and tasks, forms of knowledge, skills and behavior – through which the world and others come to us in a familiar way – become sedimented. As a bodily acquisition of certain meanings, the body schema manifests itself as an "I can do again and again" and is, as a system of lived habits, involved in the foundation of meaning. It responds in a habitualized way to the appeals of things and the behaviors of others. In this way, it gains its "Gestalt" (Merleau-Ponty 1974, p. 132 f.). Through the repeated interaction with things and others, we form a certain structure of behavior, perception and judgment, which Merleau-Ponty and, following this, Bourdieu call style: a typical way of perceiving the social world and of behaving and acting in it (ibid., p. 378).

So we can say, experience is structured in a twofold way: Through repetition, experience can result in routines, automatisms and dogmatisms. Experience is thus conventionalized, habitualized and sedimented and manifests itself in certain types (Schütz and Luckmann 2003) and habits. The pedagogical practice that enables these sedimentations and habitualizations is practicing (Brinkmann 2012). Practicing is a specific form of learning. It takes place when we perform the same action which we actually want to practice, as Aristotle said. Within practicing and by practicing, skills and abilities are cultivated and perfected. We are practicing something to be able to perform this specific activity in a more cultivated, aesthetic or elegant way. The path toward it is repetitive practicing. Within practicing, implicit knowledge as practical ability is primary, verbally explicit and formalized knowledge on the other hand secondary. In addition to this, practicing is a form of learning which aims at continuity and permanence. It is characterized by repetition. In the same moment of practicing we experience a break. That's why we only practice when we are not already able to perform the action we are aiming at, when we are disappointed and irritated, when we fail and try anew – like the boy in the example. The experience of not-knowing-how means that the experience process is interrupted. It is not just the failure of a task, but the experience process itself is in its temporal structure to disposition. The anticipation of being able to ride a bicycle is disappointed at the moment of the negative experience.

Buck (2019) describes this structure as involving cycles of experiential anticipation and fulfilment – or alternatively, disappointment or *negation*. "Anticipation means precisely the openness to new experiences that belong to said experience" as "preceding interpretation" and "understanding in advance" (Buck 2019, p. 69). The disappointment of anticipation in the negativity of experience "does not manifest itself in the fact that a deception is simply seen through and a correction or deletion takes place" (ibid., p. 69). While a fulfilled anticipation explicates the horizon (not reinforcing it), a non-fulfilment or contradiction leads to a change in the horizon of experience and new anticipations. This negation brings a moment of discontinuity into the continuity of experience. By undergoing a "negative" experience that is in this sense a determinate negation or a specific disappointment of anticipations, we not only experience something, but we also experience ourselves reflexively. As our horizon is changed in an experience, future anticipations change, as do experiences from the past.

The horizon of experience is changing, which also means that the structure of sedimentation and habitualization is changing. They are not deleted but provided with a new "index" (Husserl). In other words: The little boy who practices does not merely perform an action and practices a skill. The boy who is practicing also changes his horizon. Self-relation and his self-image are challenged by the failure, the non-abilities and the new efforts that go along with practicing. He is therefore also practicing himself. He experiences *something* but also himself: the horizon of experience is changed due to the boy changing his relation to himself and to the world. Learning and practicing from experience can then be seen as learning and practicing *as* experience (Meyer-Drawe 2008). *Negative* experiences enable us to change previous knowledge and experience; and at the same time they open us to new experiences. By undergoing negative experiences, we are able to become aware of latent attitudes and habits. Learning itself is a reflective moment within the process of experience. By using hermeneutic methods of understanding, we can explicate the latent structures of the meaning of experiences of learning.

The resistive and passive aspects are negotiated in newer theories of learning and Bildung under this label. Negative experiences are regarded as constitutive moments of processes of Bildung and learning. Negativity is here not to be understood in a common sense as something bad, annoying or dangerous. Irritations, disappointments, misunderstandings, failures and mistakes stimulate searching, questioning, trying or research (cf. Benner 2005). Negative experiences are therefore important occasions for learning and re-learning (Meyer-Drawe 2008, Brinkmann 2012, Rödel 2018). An unsolved problem, an unanswered question, an irritated wonder and amazement can challenge the already existing "positive" knowledge and skills. As experiences of crisis, they are also an important element in biographical processes of Bildung in which self and world relations are transformed (cf. Koller 2011). This ontological experience level of learning will be specified in the following section on the spatial experience.[1]

Space and spatiality

In our example, the boy also changes his spatial orientation and entanglement. In a phenomenological perspective, the lived body is seen as the "starting point of all orientation" (Hua IV, p. 158). It lets all orientations and movements of the "space register" arise from the lived body (Waldenfels 1999, p. 206): Directions of space like right and left, above and below, where from and where to, inside and outside, open and closed as well as the spatial divisions such as fullness and emptiness or near and far (ibid., p. 202 ff.).

Phenomenology distances itself from the Eurocentric, geometric model of space, which is dominated by the scheme of empty space (spatium). In this schematism, objects are collected one above the other in measurable distances (cf. Brinkmann and Westphal 2015, p. 8). Kant defines space formally as a "necessary idea" and as an a priori of "absolute first formal reason of the world of senses" (Kant 1974, p. 72 f.). Following Kant (1974), Piaget (1969) also determined space as a cognitivist and intellectualist construction within the framework of his cognitivist schematism and thought of it as more important than perception. In contrast, phenomenological concepts and theories of space focus on the corporal, sensory-aesthetic, social and emotional qualities of the experience of space. Space is to be determined from activity or movement as well as from the situation. Like in the example of practicing cycling, the space is experienced as a space of orientation and movement. The spatial is determined by the space, the surrounding by the giver and that what is given as well as the things in it by their "readiness-to-hand" or by the lack of it (Heidegger 2001). The things in space – like the bike – can thus also be seen, in their "challenging character" (cf. Waldenfels 1999, p. 222), as gestalt psychologists suggest.

Spatiality of orientation

In *Being and Time*, Heidegger presents an ontological analysis of space as spatial orientation (cf. Heidegger 2001, pp. 101–113). Space is understood "in recourse to the world" as "being-in-the-world." as the "basic constitution of existence" (ibid., p. 113). The handling of things in the "spatiality of existence" has a caring character, be it in the construction of houses, in the furnishing of a room, in the giving of space as shaping of the "environment" or in the use of tools, to which the "handy" bodily movement corresponds (ibid., p. 109). Tools are primarily "used for the body" (ibid., p. 108). According to Heidegger, the "spatialization of existence" has its basis in a "corporeality (Leiblichkeit)" (ibid., p. 108).

The meaning of things only becomes apparent in their practical use: the hammer in hammering, the bike in cycling. The readiness-to-hand-structure of existence in the use of environmental things is at first unexpressive or pre-reflexive. The relation of man to the world, his worldliness of the world, becomes clear when this structure is disturbed, that is, when the pencil is broken off (ibid., p. 73) or the boy falls off the bike, when – so one can add – the use becomes "difficult". Heidegger thus takes up the important topic of phenomenology: that of negativity. This perspective focuses on experiences in the execution of practice and therein on moments of irritation, on resistances and "disturbances". According to Heidegger, it is a "break in the ontically experienceable context of reference" in which the "world" (ibid., p. 75) appears (cf. Brinkmann 2012, p. 180). Here, existential and ontological experiences become possible. The human being existentially experiences his spatiality and through it his care for orientation and for the need to care for his existence.

Spatiality of situation

Merleau-Ponty continues the phenomenological analysis of space using the term "body scheme". The "acquisition of a world" (ibid., p. 184) happens in a concrete situation. While the mere body or the mere objects possess a "spatiality of position", a living body has a "spatiality of situation" (ibid., p. 125). As shown earlier, according to Merleau-Ponty, the body schema arises in repeated practice. As bodily-intentional acts, motoric movements themselves are already embedded in the world's space of meaning. For this reason, movement is the central medium for experiences of a situational spatiality that is structured kinesthetically, socially and existentially. Against this background, the handling of things is based on a spatial-kinaesthetic "complicity" (Meyer-Drawe 1999, p. 330). Things themselves have their own challenging character (cf. Stieve 2008). Children in particular are encouraged by things to do something – like the ball rolling across the street or a scarf lying around asking them to play and dress up. The character of these "demands" corresponds to the requesting character of the things – for example, in dressing, bandaging or in dealing with artefacts such as pens or the bicycle. The demands made by things show that their meaning is only revealed to us in the context of the situation.

Spatiality of resonance and responsiveness

From the perspective of the lived body and the response to the demands of the things, the perspective shifts. Not only other things and other people in space, but also the foreign and the demands of the foreign become recognizable (cf. Lippitz 2007). Following the phenomenological approach, Bernhard Waldenfels (1997) developed a topography of the foreign. The experience of the foreign disturbs existing orders. It leads beyond them into an atopia or heterotopia, where there is no distinct place, but only an "in-between" (ibid., p. 8). According to Waldenfels, however, foreign spaces elude social, discursive and symbolic orders. Existential events can only occur in the experience of foreignness. Thus, a singularity only becomes recognizable from the point of view of the foreign, that is, an event that cannot be classified as an individual case in individual cases or classified as an event to further events. In this "a different way of seeing and acting" is enabled (ibid., p. 121).

The topography of the foreign appears as a space of resonance and response to life-worldly and bodily experiences that lead out of existing discursive and symbolic orders. The answers to the demands of the foreign make themselves perceivable as experiences. With Waldenfels, therefore, there is a social-theoretical determination of negativity. Waldenfels focuses on the passive, unavailable and social aspects on the basis of a philosophy of the lived body. Responsivity here means the crossover (chiasmus) of strangeness and peculiarity in the social communicative experience.

Negativity has so far been presented as a dimension of experience in learning (Buck 2019), as a dimension of experience in space, and as a dimension of the crossing of foreignness and otherness in the mode of responsiveness (Waldenfels 2007). In the following, it is supposed to be related to a theory of education. In German-speaking countries, this reference is made in different approaches – but it is always emphasized that negativity as an individual, social and communicative dimension of experience determines processes of Bildung (cf. Brinkmann 2016). There is a debate that critically refers to Humboldt's theory of Bildung. In the following, from the perspective of embodiment, I will try to explain the role of the lived body in the process of Bildung more precisely.

Bildung and embodiment

According to Humboldt, Bildung is the "highest and most proportional" development of all human powers (Humboldt 1960a, p. 64) under the condition that a "linking of the self to the world to achieve the most general, most animated, and most unrestrained interplay" takes place (Humboldt 1960b, p. 235 f.). Interplay is the basic category of Humboldt's dynamic view of man and the world. Human spontaneity interplays with receptivity. Here, the world cannot be a material of human arbitrariness, but is itself something active, something original (ursprünglich), that is the uncatchable foundation of all human knowledge. "Man is also dependent on a world beyond himself" like other living beings (ibid., p. 233). For this purpose, man should strengthen all his powers (Kräfte). According to Humboldt, Bildung is therefore also the formation of powers with the aim of strengthening all powers. Powers are man's mental, physical and emotional faculties, such as reason, imagination, the power of imagination, judgment, physical-practical power and the power to perform actions. Thus, Bildung can only be determined formally; contents and materials cannot be goals, only means of Bildung. Man must therefore seek the goal and meaning of his life for himself. He can take on these tasks because he is ductile (bildsam, he has the ability of Bildung), that is, he can give himself goals and appropriate the world, in other words: give himself a form (sich bilden). Bildung is thus in principle inconclusive and open, teleologically indeterminate (cf. Benner 2005).

Criterion of an interplay as an instance of Bildung is the concept of alienation. Because man's "nature drives him to reach beyond himself to the external objects", he runs the risk of losing "himself in this alienation" (Humboldt 1960b, p. 64 f.). Bildung is therefore determined negatively. It is necessary alienation in and through the world and at the same time a way back from alienation. However, this way back from alienation is not the fundamental abolition of alienation. For only something that is foreign and unknown, uncertain and unavailable, something that leads the human being out of himself, can have an effect of Bildung. In mere identity with himself, man could not give himself a form (sich bilden), man could not ask for his own purpose. In pure identity with the world, no experiences could be made (cf. Benner 2003, p. 104). Bildung is thus a new experience through appropriation of the world and at the same time progressive alienation into the world. Bildung in this sense aims at a change and transformation of the relationship to oneself and to the world (cf. Koller 2011). According to Humboldt, this relationship is primarily structured through language as a language ability, the possibility of expression in and with languages (Humboldt 1963).

Humboldt's theory of language is condensed in the introduction to his work on the Kawi, one of Java's high-level languages, under the title *On the Diversity of Human Language Construction and its Influence on the Mental Development of the Human Species* (Humboldt 1963, pp. 368–756). There he writes that Bildung of language means the learning of "a foreign language as the acquisition of a new point of view in the previous world view" (ibid., p. 434) and thus the transformation of the relationship between self and world. In this way, man not only learns a new material (the foreign language in the sense mentioned earlier), but he also gains a new way of accessing the world and himself. Each language contains "a peculiar view of the world" (ibid., pp. 433 f.). The intersubjective dimension of language as a formative (bildend) medium and expression of a worldview comes to bear when Humboldt relates his philosophy of language to empirical reality.

> In appearance, however, language develops only socially, and man understands himself only by testing the comprehensibility of his words to other people. For objectivity is increased when the own word resounds from a foreign mouth.
>
> (ibid., p. 429)

The objectification of subjective imagination does not only succeed by the subject expressing it. It also succeeds above all by the fact that the idea of one is expressed by another and through it returns to the subject. Self-understanding and understanding the foreign/alien are thus interdependent. The alienation of subjective objectification occurs in foreign understanding. Precisely because everyone speaks their own language and articulates their own worldview, "all understanding . . . is always at the same time a non-understanding" (ibid., p. 439). Thus, the non-understanding is the fundament of the possibility of understanding (cf. Koller 2003, p. 524). Self-understanding thus becomes possible only through the detour of foreign understanding. The basis of the possibility of understanding other people is therefore difference, that is, non-identity and not-understanding. Foreignness and otherness as alienation and estrangement are thus seen as the premises for processes of Bildung and transformation becoming possible.

With Humboldt, imagination has its premise of possibility not in reason, but in language. In language, an elementary corporal reflexivity takes place: "Language is the formative organ of thought. . . . The activity of the senses must synthetically connect with the inner action of the mind. . . . For this, however, language is indispensable. For as the spiritual aspiration breaks its way through the gaps in it, its product returns to its own ear. The imagination is thus transferred into real objectivity without being withdrawn from subjectivity. Only language is capable of doing this" (ibid., pp. 428 f.).

In speech a connection between the corporeal and the spiritual occurs. This "synthesis" comes about based on the specific corporal structure in speech, that the spoken is being heard at the same time. The "mental", which is expressed in the spoken in the medium of symbols and based on ideas, becomes empirical in language, that is, it enters experience, space and time. Speaking establishes an elementary reflexivity between subjectivity and objectivity: from the mouth to the ear and back to the self. The "resounding" of language is thus not only social and intersubjective, but as a structure already bodily arranged. It is based on an interplay between expression and internalization. The alienation of which we were previously talking also determines both the possibility of intersubjective understanding and the possibility of human reflexivity. In other words, without speaking there can be no thinking. Both are closely connected due to the bodily-spiritual interplay.

To summarize, the corporal-empirical constitution of the human being is the precondition of the possibility first of all for speaking, second, for thinking and third, for Bildung, insofar as the corporal "mediation" between mouth and ear or between hand and eye is at the same time a "mediation" between sensuality and mentality, which requires a reflexive self-relationship. This self-relationship is in turn a prerequisite for the human being to be able to give himself a form (sich bilden) in the interplay between expression and internalization and to change or transform himself in it. However, Humboldt only hints at the idea of the connection between mentality and corporeality and refers only to language or speech. He lacks a theory of embodiment. For a contemporary theory of Bildung, however, the corporal and aesthetic, that is, non-linguistic and social dimensions of the relationship between world and self are important. There is broad agreement in the discourse of theory and philosophy of Bildung (cf. Brinkmann 2016), that traditional theories of Bildung cannot adequately grasp the social and societal foundations. Thus, a shift is currently taking place in education studies from an individual-theoretical to a social-theoretical orientation. It is assumed that something is not only learned from each other or from others, but also in front of each other – even if these others are only imaginarily present (cf. Bedorf 2010). Power, recognition, subjectivation and otherness become important terms in the discourse of the current theory of Bildung (cf. Brinkmann 2016). The dimensions of experience mentioned here are taken up by Eugen Fink in a philosophy of education.

Democratic education in the community of counselling ("Beratungsgemeinschaft")

Following Husserl and Heidegger, Eugen Fink developed a social phenomenology, a co-existential anthropology and a systematic philosophy of education. Fink describes fundamental human phenomena in a phenomenological-praxeological analysis (cf. Brinkmann 2018a). He differentiates five fundamental phenomena and practices of human *Dasein* (Fink 2018): play, power, work, love and death. He then adds a sixth one: education (Fink 1970). They are seen as social, co-existential and embodied practices in time and space of society and as an expression of care about *Dasein*. They allow humans to stay in a productive openness toward the world, the foreign and the other.

Fink describes the practice of meaning making and finding a solution to the existential questions as counselling (cf. also Burchardt 2001, p. 188 ff., Meyer-Wolters 1992, pp. 159 ff., 223 ff.) in a situation in which there are no general, authoritative concepts of meaning and values. With Nietzsche, Fink calls this situation nihilism. Councelling is the answer to this historical situation in pedagogy (Fink 1970).

Counselling as a co-existential practice cannot be understood as an authoritative and knowledge-based procedure, like drug counselling, tax counselling or career counselling. There can be no expert in the co-existential counselling, because all are equally affected by the existential situation of plight, all are in the equal situation of aporia, of pathlessness and aimlessness. Only the relative advantage in time and life experience can justify the "assumption of a certain leadership and authority" (ibid., p. 181) by the educator. Counselling takes place under conditions of social institutions, in family, school, university. The power of the discourse and the space of power of society are as much a part of the counselling situation as are the different levels of knowledge and skills of the participants. Counselling is thus a pedagogical-political practice. Not equality, but difference of the participants stands in the foreground. Counselling is a controversy of interpretations and styles as a controversy of the subjects in the socio-political area. This is precisely where it proves to be democratic education (cf. Brinkmann 2018b).

Counselling aims at the future and actively reverses the concrete existential plight (cf. Meyer-Wolters 1992, p. 166 f.). It is therefore an expression of communality and caring, a productive and projective negotiation in the mode of practical reason (phronesis), an educational solution for the described plight. It is directed at a particular situation, at a particular plight, which can only be averted if one thinks beyond the present situation. Fink calls the educational form of the community of counselling a community of questioning ("Fragegemeinschaft"). Since it is no longer possible to rely on answers that are authoritative in terms of knowledge and facts, education becomes "the mediation of a common search" (Fink 1970, p. 147). Learning together as a practice of questioning and researching becomes important. At the beginning of an understanding about the mutual experience of the aporetic situation stands the exposition of the thing *as* thing, the question *as* question, the problem *as* problem. The community of questioning thus discusses and radicalizes the problem and the phenomenon of education itself as a "question of the interpretation of the world to be learned and taught" (Meyer-Wolters 1992, p. 229).

In contrast to the community of counselling, the relationship between generations is explicitly and reflexively emphasized in the community of questioning. Educators and children are equal in the previously mentioned sense, they can learn something from each other. The difference between the generations is not equalized but explicitly emphasized: "Child and adult learn different things from each other. Because we are accustomed to interpret 'learning' only as learning about the world of adults, we all too easily overlook the experiences that flow to the human teacher from the didactic attention to the child, – we overlook how much the child also gives by taking" (ibid., p. 206). We can add: If the adult experiences the memory of his own childhood, then the child can experience the experiences of the physical being-in-the-world of the adult as well as the experiences of aging. Here it can be seen that learning experiences in this sense always remain experiences of foreignness. The generational difference manifests itself in the community of questioning in the different "state of development of the respective freedoms" (Fink 1970, p. 214). From this perspective, the child has more possibilities than the adult and at the same time less experience of the finiteness of human freedom. The child is still about to face failure from experiencing the resistance and obstinacy of things and others.

Intergenerational learning in the community of questioning and counselling can be described as anthropologically disclosed, worldly-bodily learning in the difference of age with the aim of a caring and providing, democratic understanding of meaning. In a democratic theory perspective, both Fink and Nancy extend the concept of democracy to the community, to being-present. Politics is placed under the conditions of the communal and thus its scope and "violence" is limited (Nancy 2012, p. 88). In a post-industrial democracy, educational goals cannot be derived from the – in their own rights legitimate – claims of other social practices and systems (economy, art, media, religions, politics) (Fink 1970). Rather, Bildung and pedagogy must be distinguished from other areas of social practice and knowledge as independent areas of practice and knowledge. Bildung and school cannot and must not be turned into an applied part of politics or economics by normative setting of teaching goals from the political, economic, aesthetic or religious spheres (Benner 2001). Rather, Fink emphasizes the inherent logic of pedagogical thought and action by asking about the specific pedagogical practice of being-together. The democratic education and the formation of democracy therefore cannot be legitimized in relation to a form of government or to knowledge about political contexts, nor to a form of life (Dewey 2009), the smallest unit of which would be the school (the so-called "Embryonic Society" following Dewey). Rather, democracy as a way of co-existence lies ontologically prior to all communications, all social institutions and practices by allowing both the existential and the social to emerge from a difference. This calls conventional promises of pedagogy (Schäfer 2012) into question, which hope for a "reconciliation" of individual and community, for the "mediation" of cultural knowledge, social norms and social identity or for the "preparation" of the learner for an uncertain and contingent future in the protective space of education. To see the pedagogical as part of the social and to see in it the constitution of subjectivity as a broken and fragile relationship to oneself in the face and in response to others and the other – this makes a new perspective on processes of subjectivation possible that neither merge into submission nor into liberation and reflection, that is, on the relations of these constitutional processes within the social.

Finally, I would like to refer to the conclusions for a theory of education. Education from a phenomenological and existential perspective is an eventful experience in which the relationship to oneself and to the world is changed (cf. Brinkmann 2018a). First, this change is an experience in which the whole person changes (Buck 2019). Theories of Bildung must reflect that the self can find neither its foundations in an all-encompassing, logocentric reason nor in a humanistic tradition or its Eurocentric history. Emancipation and autonomy become "formulas of pathos" (Rieger-Ladich 2002), autonomy becomes an illusion (cf. Meyer-Drawe 1990). Bildung must therefore neither colonize others and strangers nor one's own plural and different parts of the self under the guise of an identifying reason (cf. Reichenbach 2001, p. 443). In this perspective, the educational process is dimensioned bodily, spatially and socially. In each of these dimensions, a relationship to oneself and to others is established in a special way by responding to existential experiences of the body, the time of space and to others. It is precisely these experiences that are negative experiences of deprivation and strangeness. They can thus become productive moments in an educational experience.

Note

1 On the temporal dimension of experience in learning as relearning and re-practicing see Brinkmann 2012.

References

Bedorf, T., 2010. Der Dritte als Scharnierfigur. Die Funktion des Dritten in sozialphilosophischer und ethischer Perspektive. *In*: E. Esslinger, ed. *Die Figur des Dritten. Ein kulturwissenschaftliches Paradigma.* 1st ed. Frankfurt am Main: Suhrkamp, 125–136.
Benner, D., 2001. Bildung und Demokratie. *In*: J. Oelkers, ed. *Zukunftsfragen der bildung.* 43. Beiheft der Zeitschrift für Pädagogik. Weinheim: Beltz, 46–65.
Benner, D., 2003. *Wilhelm von Humboldts Bildungstheorie: Eine problemgeschichtliche Studie zum Begründungszusammenhang neuzeitlicher Bildungsreform.* 3rd ed. Weinheim: Juventa.
Benner, D., 2005. Einleitung. Über pädagogisch relevante und erziehungswissenschaftlich fruchtbare Aspekte der Negativität menschlicher Erfahrung. *In*: D. Benner, ed. *Erziehung, Bildung, Negativität. Theoretische Annäherungen, Analysen zum Verhältnis von Macht und Negativität, exemplarische Studien.* Zeitschrift für Pädagogik 51 (49). Weinheim: Beltz, 7–21.
Brinkmann, M., 2012. *Pädagogische Übung. Praxis und Theorie einer elementaren Lernform.* Paderborn: Schöningh.
Brinkmann, M., 2016. Allgemeine Erziehungswissenschaft als Erfahrungswissenschaft. Versuch einer sozialtheoretischen Bestimmung als theoretisch-empirische Teildisziplin. *Vierteljahresschrift für wissenschaftliche Pädagogik,* 92 (2), 215–231.
Brinkmann, M., 2018a. *Phänomenologische Erziehungswissenschaft von Ihren Anfängen bis heute. Eine Anthologie.* Band 4 der Reihe "Phänomenologische Erziehungswissenschaft". (M. Brinkmann, W. Lippitz, and U. Stenger, eds.). Wiesbaden: Springer VS.
Brinkmann, M., 2018b. Bildung, Sprache, Demokratie im (Fremdsprachen-)Unterricht. Sozial- und demokratietheoretische Überlegungen mit Humboldt und Nancy. *Fremdsprachen Lehren und Lernen (FLuL),* 47 (1), 88–104.

Brinkmann, M. and Westphal, K., 2015. *Grenzerfahrungen. Phänomenologie und Anthropologie pädagogischer Räume.* Weinheim: Beltz Juventa.

Buck, G., 2019. *Lernen und Erfahrung. Epagoge, Beispiel und Analogie in der pädagogischen Erfahrung.* Band 5 der Reihe "Phänomenologische Erziehungswissenschaft". (M. Brinkmann, ed.). Wiesbaden: Springer VS.

Burchardt, M., 2001. *Erziehung im Weltbezug. Zur pädagogischen Anthropologie Eugen Finks.* Würzburg: Königshausen und Neumann.

Dewey, J., 2009. *Democracy and education.* Radford: Wilder Publications.

Fink, E., 1970. *Erziehungswissenschaft und Lebenslehre.* Freiburg im Breisgau: Rombach.

Fink, E., 2018. *Existenz und Coexistenz.* München: Karl Alber.

Heidegger, M., 2001. *Sein und Zeit.* 18th ed. Tübingen: Niemeyer.

Humboldt, W. von, 1960a/1792. Ideen zu einem Versuch, die Gränzen der Wirksamkeit des Staates zu bestimmen. In: A. Flitner and K. Giel, eds. *Werke I: Schriften zu Anthropologie und Geschichte.* Darmstadt: WBG, 56–233.

Humboldt, W. von, 1960b/1792. Theorie der Bildung des Menschen. In: A. Flitner and K. Giel, eds. *Werke I: Schriften zu Anthropologie und Geschichte.* Darmstadt: WBG, 234–240.

Humboldt, W. von, 1963. Schriften zur Sprachphilosophie. In: A. Flitner and K. Giel, eds. *Werke IV.* Darmstadt: WBG.

Husserl, E., 1950. *Husserliana: Gesammelte Werke.* Den Haag: Martinus Nijhoff. Quoted as HUA.

Kant, I., 1974. Kritik der reinen Vernunft. In: W. Weischedel, ed. *Werkausgabe Band III/IV.* Frankfurt am Main: Suhrkamp

Koller, H.-C., 2003. "Alles Verstehen ist dabei immer zugleich ein Nicht-Verstehen". Wilhelm von Humboldts Beitrag zur Hermeneutik und seine Bedeutung für eine Theorie interkultureller Bildung. *Zeitschrift für Erziehungswissenschaft*, 6 (4), 515–531.

Koller, H.-C., 2011. *Bildung anders denken. Eine Einführung in die Theorie transformatorischer Bildungsprozesse.* Stuttgart: Kohlhammer.

Lippitz, W., 2007. Foreignness and otherness in pedagogical contexts. *Phenomenology & Practice* [online], 1 (1). Available from: https://journals.library.ualberta.ca/pandpr/index.php/pandpr/article/view/19806 [Accessed 26 Oct 2019].

Merleau-Ponty, M., 1974. *Phänomenologie der Wahrnehmung.* Berlin: De Gruyter.

Meyer-Drawe, K., 1990. *Illusionen von Autonomie. Diesseits von Ohnmacht und Allmacht des Ich.* München: Kirchheim.

Meyer-Drawe, K., 1999. Herausforderung durch die Dinge. Das Andere im Bildungsprozeß. *Zeitschrift für Pädagogik*, 45 (3), 329–336.

Meyer-Drawe, K., 2008. *Diskurse des Lernens.* München: Fink.

Meyer-Wolters, H., 1992. *Koexistenz und Freiheit. Eugen Finks Anthropologie und Bildungstheorie.* Würzburg: Köningshausen & Neumann.

Nancy, J.-L., 2012. Begrenzte und unendliche Demokratie. In: G. Agamben, A. Badiou, S. Žižek, J. Rancière, J.-L. Nancy, W. Brown, D. Bensaïd, and K. Ross, eds. *Demokratie? Eine Debatte.* Berlin: Suhrkamp, 72–89.

Piaget, J., 1969. *Das Erwachen der Intelligenz beim Kinde.* München: Klett-Cotta.

Reichenbach, R., 2001. *Demokratisches Selbst und dilettantisches Subjekt. Demokratische Erziehung und Bildung in der Spätmoderne.* Münster: Waxmann.

Rieger-Ladich, M., 2002. *Mündigkeit als Pathosformel: Beobachtungen zur pädagogischen Semantik.* Konstanz: UVK.

Rödel, S., 2018. *Negative Erfahrung und Scheitern im schulischen Lernen. Phänomenologische und videographische Perspektiven.* Wiesbaden: Springer VS.

Schäfer, A., 2012. *Das Pädagogische und die Pädagogik. Annäherung an eine Differenz*. Paderborn: Schöningh.
Schütz, A. and Luckmann, T., 2003. *Strukturen der Lebenswelt*. Konstanz: UVK, UTB Sozialwissenschaften.
Stieve, C., 2008. *Von den Dingen lernen: Die Gegenstände unserer Kindheit*. Paderborn: Fink.
Straus, E., 1956. *Vom Sinn der Sinne. Ein Beitrag zur Grundlegung der Psychologie*. 2nd ed. Berlin, Heidelberg: Springer.
Waldenfels, B., 1997. *Topographie des Fremden. Studien zur Phänomenologie des Fremden*. Frankfurt am Main: Suhrkamp.
Waldenfels, B., 1999. *Sinnesschwellen. Studien zur Phänomenologie des Fremden*. Frankfurt am Main: Suhrkamp.
Waldenfels, B., 2007. *Antwortregister*. Frankfurt am Main: Suhrkamp.

Chapter 10

Time, individuality, and interaction
A case study

Herner Saeverot and Glenn-Egil Torgersen

Introduction

Time is a very complicated concept for many to grasp or explain as a lived experience. To discuss time as one time is not possible. There are many different types or forms of time, that often stand in relationship to each other, from our everyday perception of time to biological time as embodied, to a quantum mechanical perspective of time that is abstract and in some applications highly theoretical. Even though there is more than one time, our everyday lives are often ruled by so-called clock time – mechanistic time – chronological time. By using a clock, time can be followed by its divisions: hours, minutes, and seconds. Both day and night are ordered chronologically: 1 to 12, representing a.m. and then from 13 to 24, representing p.m. In a contemporary sense, this is only one way to order time, it is in many ways necessary to make and keep appointments, as we need to know when we are going to school, to work, to the doctor, and all the ever-day-ness associated in life (Rovelli 2018). Still, clock time is not really time (Bergson 1990); rather it is a human-made device that shows "time," as a way to gain control of everyday life (Saeverot 2013).

Similarly, the calendar is a tool for understanding and controlling seasonality throughout the world. Such organization became a natural part of the Roman Empire's rule. In fact, it was the Roman Emperor Julius Caesar who introduced the calendar to the Western world, the so-called Julian calendar, in 46 BC. This calendar, like clock time, is formed chronologically. Thus Caesar could control the people and the society. The Julian calendar was used for over 1600 years, but was eventually adjusted, corrected, and simplified by Pope Gregor XIII in 1582. This was the so-called Gregorian calendar, which is also formed chronologically, from January to February to March and so on. The Gregorian calendar is still being used in many parts of the world. Hence, we are more strongly influenced by the Romans' time orientation than we might think. In any case, the basic ideas of the Julian calendar are still applicable and spread throughout much of the world. Thus, this chronological categorization, and order of time, characterize much of society's perception of time.

Such understanding of time has been part of the so-called neoliberal education. Neoliberalism emerged as a political idea in the 1930s, challenging both

American capitalist liberalism and communist-based economy (Strobelt 2018). In recent times, the term has resurfaced with a different meaning, referring to market liberalism. This has had major consequences for schools, education policies, and curricula in Norway, which are increasingly organized and operated according to market economy principles (ibid.). The neoliberal influence in schools and teacher training is evident by an increasing focus on testing and education programs which are based on management by objectives (Torgersen 2015) within a prescribed time frame to meet academically imposed standards. The goals of education then, which are subject to a calculated and chronological idea of time, steer the teaching not pedagogically by the teacher, but by governments to control the daily operations in the classroom.

Time and Dewey

John Dewey offers a critique of neoliberal education and its imposed mechanistic concept of time. In particular, we turn to *Time and Individuality* (1998), in which Dewey discusses problems that may arise when time is perceived as homogeneous and chronological, similar to the clock or calendar arrangement discussed earlier. According to Dewey (1998, p. 219), such understanding of time leads to a problem when viewed in light of education that has a purpose to individualize and free the students. The chronological structure of the homogenous time forces us to perceive reality in a predetermined manner, often by expanding something in a particular order. We end up with a mechanical structure, which lacks prerequisites for freedom. The reason being that the individual will be trapped in a pattern characterized by routines and habits. Dewey, on the other hand, makes a case for "genuine time," which is connected to individuality and freedom. Dewey states:

> Genuine time, if it exists as anything else except the measure of motions in space, is all one with the existence of individuals as individuals, with the creative, with the occurrence of unpredictable novelties. Everything that can be said contrary to this conclusion is but a reminder that an individual may lose his individuality, for individuals become imprisoned in routine and fall to the level of mechanisms. Genuine time then ceases to be an integral element in their being. Our behaviour becomes predictable because it is but an external rearrangement of what went before.
> (Dewey 1998, p. 225)

Genuine time is connected to contingency, novelty, and unpredictability, opposing the neoliberal's chronological conception of time. According to Dewey, it is the contingent and unpredictable that individualizes us as humans: "Individuality conceived as a temporal development involves uncertainty, indeterminacy, or contingency. Individuality is the source of whatever is unpredictable in the world" (ibid., p. 224).

Instead of being guided by conventions, habits, and routines, Dewey wants to provide room for artistic creation and artistic activities, that is, abilities connected with individuality. To achieve this through educational processes, a contingent concept of time is required, first and foremost because such a concept of time will open the future, rather than blocking it by way of predetermination. Dewey offers the following:

> To regiment artists, to make them servants of some particular cause does violence to the very springs of artistic creation, but it does more than that. It betrays the very cause of a better future it would serve, for in its subjection of the individuality of the artist it annihilates the source of that which is genuinely new.
>
> (ibid., p. 226)

Dewey argues for a concept of time that can create space for that which is genuinely new, including unforeseen events, which in turn can make room for individuality where each individual can stand forth as creative and original, both in thought and action. As a concrete example, Dewey points to Abraham Lincoln and how "genuine time" shaped him into a distinctive and individual person, quite different from everyone else (ibid., p. 224).

In other works by Dewey, specifically *Democracy and Education* (1966), individuality is an advantage for the education of each and every individual. And it also functions as an opening for unreserved interaction with others – in a common development and learning process, while the actions occur and the experiences are being built up. Not least, for Dewey (1966), interaction, based on communication, was the foundation of his criticism of an individual-oriented philosophy, or, Cartesian subjectivity (*Cogito, ergo sum/* I think, therefore I am) (see Biesta 2006, p. 36). Like Dewey (1966, 1998), we connect both individuality and interaction in the practice of education.

Whilst Dewey emphasizes the art of teaching the students to be free and unique individuals, schools which are influenced by neoliberalism are characterized by instrumental and mechanistic thinking, efficiency, and quantifiable results, such as national and international tests. Behind the neoliberal ideology we find a chronological and mechanistic conception of time. As educators create space for both individuality and interaction, they create space for a form of freedom that will be elaborated in the following sections.

Description of the observation "object" and a typical school situation

In the extension of this perspective of freedom, we want to concretize and contextualize Dewey's theoretisized thoughts about time, with direct relation to current educational practice. Therefore, in the following, we will present key extracts from a case study of "John," a ninth grade student. The purpose of the case is to clarify what the meaning of the concept of time, based on Dewey's understanding, can have for practical teaching today. It is important for us to convince practicing educators that educational philosophy not only represents theoretical knowledge, created by theoreticians, but that this domain of education actually has tangible value in the demanding everyday life of practicing teachers and educators. Thus, the case "John" is used, both as a starting point for our analysis and as an educational tool, with the aim of clarifying our theoretical findings, related to the meaning of time in teaching.

John is not the student type on which the Norwegian state curriculum (*Knowledge Promotion*) in primary and secondary education and training is based, that is, a streamlined and learning-willing student. John is rather a reluctant student who opposes most of the school's academic tasks. As a backdrop to our main question – how is it possible to meet John in such a way that "genuine time" becomes an integral element in his being – we wish to provide a description of John and how he behaves in a typical school situation, and not the least how he is met by his teacher and teacher assistant.

John is a weak student academically, and his results (aka scores), in the vast majority of the school subjects are low when compared to students within a set metric. There is no particular difference in the theoretical and practical subjects in this way, and he shows little noticeable interest in anything but computer games. The only visible ambition John expresses during the observed school hours is the ever-repeated effort of perfecting his skills to make the least out of a school day. Any situation where he risks learning he turns away, something he seems to be quite good at. In some subjects, John is provided academic support, a special education program where he is in a group of other academically challenged students. But here, too, he manages to hide from the learning and escape the tasks prescribed by the teacher.

A day in the life of John

How does a typical school hour look like for John? As the hour begins, John is one of the last of the students to find his place in the classroom. The teacher initiates the teaching by introducing and elaborating on the theme of the school hour. When the time has come for the students to conduct their tasks, John utters that he has not received any information of what he is supposed to do. However, he does not express this before the teacher has discovered that he is not doing anything related to the lesson. The teacher approaches John to describe the contents of the assignment. After the explanation, the teacher walks away from John and resumes class-wide attention to the rest of the youth. John, on his part, clearly demonstrates that he is not bothering to read the text that is connected to the assignment. As explained by the teacher, he will require other materials, form of books or classroom resources, in order to perform the assignment. However, John spends a very long time trying to find this supplemental material. In addition, the task requires a specific format, assignment information is to be filled out in certain ways, but again, he spends a very long time on what he says: "I am thinking what to do." However, it is often difficult to perceive the results of this "thinking process." One reason for that is that he often wanders around the classroom, whilst, for example, searching in his rather chaotic shelf, before emptying his school bag with all its contents on the floor, whereas disturbing his classmates on his way back to his seat. At best, he finds some of what he needs, but often he does not anything useful. Either way, he is often found seated without doing what he is supposed to do. In fact, he seems quite happy doing nothing, while chatting to one of his classmates, who consequently is distracted from doing their own assignment.

Eventually, the teacher discovers that John is not doing what is expected academically. The teacher then walks over to John. Most often, the teacher struggles to gain John's attention. In one case, a train passes by the school. Instead of talking to the teacher, John prefers to count the train wagons. The teacher, on his part, really makes an effort to draw John's attention away from the train, when at long last, they can concentrate on the task. Whenever the tasks contain written information, the teacher must read this out loud, as John himself does not make an effort to read. And as soon as the turmoil increases in the classroom, John gets very excited and pays all his attention to these upheavals. John never raises his hand to ask for something, nor does he ever contribute verbally in the classroom in any way. He only answers direct inquiries from the teacher, often in a mumbling fashion and with obvious discomfort. As such, the school hours continue, until it is time to finish and clear the desk before the end of the hour. In these moments he is both very fast and efficient, usually being the first student to leave the classroom.

How was John met by the teacher and the teacher's assistant?

One of the reasons for this is, in our opinion, the neoliberal education's tendency to standardize, meaning that all students are supposed to achieve the same goals within a set-standardized time. Thus John academically isolates himself, creating an ego existence, in which "genuine time" is blocked. Hence, the individuality that Dewey (1998) is talking about is suppressed. Due to this isolation, there is also no interaction with either the teacher or his fellow students; unless in disruption. The school has made many attempts to break John from this dysfunctional learning pattern, but so far the professionals have not succeeded. Regardless, it is important to note how the teacher, and the teacher's assistant (TA), meet John on his terms within the class time.

At one particular time, in the classroom, John sat by his personal computer. He was supposed to work with a photo editing task of his own photographs. The assignment, which was first communicated in writing and then orally for the whole class, was to be filled with personal content and each of the students had to take responsibility for their own progression. Overall, the task implied self-motivating and well-functioning students. Not least, the task was arranged for those students who could easily submit to certain frameworks, guidelines, and defined patterns that pointed to predetermined solutions and correct answers. One problem with such a task is that it does not make room for what Dewey categorizes as "genuine time," neither for John nor the other students in the class. Due to these circumstances, the possibilities for providing a good experience for John were almost nonexistent. Nothing in the task is concerned about his inadequate skills. As for John, he spent his time in a typical fashion, apparently working on the PC. But his real activity was to shoot down enemies in a war game he had found online.

Since the teacher had his hands full with a rather large group of students, it took some time before he discovered this game diversion. When he eventually observed John's diversion, he shouted out in pure irritation, "Start working and do what you're supposed to do!" From our vantage point we determine the teacher seems to be influenced by a neoliberal language, in which all the students are brought into a pattern controlled by the mechanistic clock time. This commanding call did not make the task either more understandable or more tempting for John. One reason being that there was no unpredictability, for this was predictable for many frustrated teachers. The teacher's admonition in which genuine time could come to life for John, but this outburst does not act as an incentive for further engagement on John's part.

Such absence of unpredictability in an educational situation will, according to Dewey (1998, p. 225), hinder students from acting independently, which in turn will suppress the individual's individuality. John, on his part, continued his war game on the computer, which he actually did understand on a gaming-interest level. Through direct pedagogy, where time is chronologically ordered similar to the time of a clock (Saeverot 2013), the teacher had attempted to awaken his student, who not only avoided doing what he was expected to do, but even did something the students were not allowed to do. Perhaps this competitive interest in spending time playing games versus doing academics, along with the fact that the teacher's directive lacked clarifying information and was steeped in frustration, contributed to the reasons why a hopeless situation did not change.

In time, the TA tried to lure John into activity by offering herself as a model for his task, with the ugliest grimaces she managed to make. Through humor, she tried to draw him out of his state of learning resistance, and at the same time, "make him" interested in the assignment. The humor was surprising in its form of a more indirect approach, as opposed to the teacher's direct approach. The advantage of "indirect pedagogy" is that it can give life to certain aspects that characterize "genuine time," as offered by Dewey (dates), be it surprise, unpredictability and contingency (see Saeverot 2013, for an elaboration of the concept of indirect pedagogy). Regardless, we observed the TA's rather unorthodox approach at best created a slightly better mood. We also found that the TA's form of indirect pedagogy by way of humor lacked a thoughtful, thorough, and pedagogical plan. The humor was more an impulsive act, here and now, and all the teacher assistant seemed to achieve was that time went by for John. In short, the TA created a diversion to distract John from the gaming world, but in the end, John was not anymore focused or productive academically.

For John, it was more tempting to shoot enemies than to be "seduced" by the TA's enticing attempt to get him out of his chair so as to find a photo camera. John now had total control of how much time was left of the school hour, and argued very well that he did not have time to do anything before the end of the hour. John managed to maintain this discussion for so long that his point turned out to be right – he ran out of time. From a neoliberal stance, his learning shift was over. Clearly annoyed, the teacher replied that he at least had to make sure he had a photo to work with for the next time. Then the school bell was ringing and the reluctant student left the classroom. The teacher's realization was it was going to be an entire week until the next one-hour session would be dedicated to this particular task. Thus we observed that it is quite obvious that such a lack of continuity in the work did not give much hope of John finishing the assigned task.

How may "genuine time" become an integral element in John's being?

In the previous section we have seen that the teacher, along with the TA, tried many ways to penetrate John's academic learning defenses. The teacher was direct in his approaches, and he spent time talking to John face-to-face, while the TA used indirect approaches; nothing succeeded. Certainly, there is no formula for struggling students like John, whose individuality and interaction with others are suppressed. So, if the teacher really wants to make a difference in John's life, he must find ways of breaking up the routines that govern John's way of life and, not least, create spaces so that "genuine time" can become an integral element in John's being. And this is not a simple task in the highly regulated classrooms of today. When such time becomes part of being the individual's individuality can come to life, which in turn can lead to interaction with others. Said differently, "genuine time" connects the individual to life itself, in which freedom can unfold. All this will require risk, both from the teacher and the student (see Biesta 2014, for an elaboration of the concept of risk in educational situations). Not least, there should be room for "genuine time," both in addition to, and in combination with, the learning goals, which in themselves are based on the chronological principles of the so-called clock time.

Now, to teach in such a way that "genuine time" may become an integral element in John's life is a highly demanding matter. The teacher cannot go half way into the situation; rather, an unreserved effort will be required from the teacher who may risk failing (Bollnow 1959). For example, the teacher may risk losing his authority, as well as his belief in his own ability to help and support others. The whole thing may even make the teacher discouraged in relation to other, similar situations (ibid.). Nonetheless, the teacher has no other choice than to spend all his effort on this situation, sacrificing time spent with the other children in the class; hence the teacher is outnumbered in the neoliberal classroom. How can John's teacher afford this amount of dedicated time to ensure John meets the established learning outcomes? Among other things, the teacher must be able to seize the (coming) time or the "moment" (Saeverot and Torgersen 2015), that is, every possible thing that resists the typical defense of John. This is very demanding because such moments cannot be predicted, the reason being that "genuine time" can never be foreseen or calculated, as opposed to clock time.

In this context, Torgersen and Saeverot (2015) speak of "concurrent learning," which "is a deliberate and continuously functional and interacting learning process among actors that occurs simultaneously with the interaction" (Steiro and Torgersen 2018, p. 253). Concurrent learning

> involves not only being familiar with one's own competence, but also learning so that individuals can connect to their own expertise and thus develop this further with the others to create something new. This learning process takes time – it needs to take time, and the process must be deliberate and organized.
>
> (ibid.)

Essential here is to take advantage of the productive moment, grasp the situation and use the moment, finding solutions "here and now," on the student's premises, without being guided by the school hour's defined learning goals.

This must take its (metric) time. It is important that it is the process that controls the duration, neither clock time nor any other instrumental idea (including predefined goals). In this process, where "genuine time" comes into practice, and concurrent learning arises, unforeseen situations will and must be grasped. The unexpected arises as a result of a free interaction between the teacher and the student, without any external correctives or guiding frameworks. The dialogue and the student are in the center; however, the teacher (as organizer) plays an important role in this process. The teacher must make sure that surprising and seemingly unimportant words and opinions of the student are actually grasped and followed up. In practice, this represents the unforeseen. However, the teacher's follow-up or response, should not be subject to specific goals, but rather function as assistance in such a way that statements and actions are elaborated, and possibly corrected by the student himself. The indirect pedagogy can be of help in this situation (Saeverot 2013, 2019). For example, the teacher may ask questions as a way of responding to the student. Another indirect strategy may be to mirror the statements, repeat what the student says, to force the student to reflect and articulate on how his statements and opinions should be understood. In situations where chronological time functions as a framework for the dialogue and interaction between teacher and student, such learning processes will not occur.

The unforeseen represents an unopened source of learning, ready to be "uncovered" and used, here and now, in the moment. When the unforeseen is brought into education in this way, we are dealing with a non-chronological and coming time perspective (Saeverot and Torgersen 2015). The ongoing-based situation will then steer the teacher's choices and actions, which are focused on the "present," with less attention to the predetermined learning goals. The emerging situation will contain a lot of information, which will thus serve as the basis for the teacher's reflections and actions. But to detect this information diversity that appears in the present, the teacher must make every effort to identify and process this in an open and unreserved manner. By no means should the teacher ignore the unforeseen; rather, he must actively work to ensure that the unforeseen can come to light and unfold as graspable information (Torgersen and Saeverot 2015).

The point is not to replace the typical structure and chronology of teaching with the unforeseen. It is rather a matter of breaking up a one-sided pattern in the state and politically controlled education, which in many ways are farfrom Dewey's thoughts on "genuine time" and individuality. The state-controlled education, which is influenced by neoliberalism, thinks that the school education is not good enough and therefore needs constant quality control by way of national and international tests and rankings. A consequence of that is that many schools and teacher education programs in the Western world focus too little on improvisation and teacher creativity, which are essential characteristics of an education for the unforeseen (Torgersen 2015). Instead, schools and teacher education programs are based on management by objectives (ibid.), often part of neoliberal agendas to control education systems. This is exactly what Dewey (1998, p. 226) warns us against; namely, that teaching turns into routines and mechanical patterns, predictable and controllable by external authorities, most often at the expense of a teacher's time and the pedagogical possibilities that would emerge as a natural part of the day. Nevertheless, the focus on learning goals, which have the order of clock time, can be combined with the unforeseen, whose foundation is formed by "genuine time." Such a combination does require that the teacher seizes both direct and indirect signals and hints from the students, here and now, while using this as the basis for pedagogical choices, communication, and practical facilitations. However, interaction requires active involvement from all parties, not just from the teacher's side.

John must also be open for something to happen, and he must, independently, choose to accept the teacher's gift. But as many know, not all students wish, or are ready to receive the teacher's gifts. So, it is certainly not a small task that the teacher must try to accomplish. What's at risk is that the student will, perhaps in a disrespectful manner, say no to his gift. But this must not stop the teacher from making new attempts that can create space for "genuine time," in which John can let go of his defense and be open for the gift. The teacher cannot simply wait passively for John to open up. The teacher's task is to work actively for certain moments to occur, so that "genuine time" can be part of the life of John. However, such moments always happen surprisingly, if at all. Thus the teacher must constantly seek new approaches, perhaps searching for interests that can touch John, and then use these interests as means in order to come closer to John's world (see also Werler 2015). By seductively inciting John's curiosity, going beyond traditional teaching methods, the teacher can "deceive" John to open up, before he starts resisting. This is an indirect approach, a backdoor, and with luck it may sow a tiny seed of curiosity and interest on John's behalf (see Saeverot 2019).

But to receive the teacher's gift is far from a simple matter seen from the perspective of the reluctant student struggling academically. Such a reception will probably be very demanding for John, who faces a risk where his world ends in disaster. But like the teacher, John cannot go half way into the situation, even though success is never a guarantee in matters like these. As the situation looks like now, he seems pretty sure he will not succeed. We can therefore assume that he has chosen a safer way of existing where it is, for him, easier and more comfortable not trying. It may be easier to live with the world conception and self-deception he leans on, than risking to choose a new worldview where individuality and interaction are involved, that is, a worldview which not only requires a lot of effort, but also requires that he lets go of his safe and highly controlled way of existing in the world. It is therefore possible that John, unlike the teacher, has no desire to change the situation. For his way of existing in the world works perfectly well, from his perspective. In such a background it is quite likely that John says no to the teacher's gift, after which the teacher may be forced to make use of drastic means in his teaching. For example, the teacher may try to draw John away from his escaping from both himself and the world, by way of unexpected disruptions and interferences, which do not allow John to continue to exist in an almost undisturbed and self-imposed drowsiness (see Saeverot 2013, 2019). If, however, John still does not want to receive the teacher's gift, there is nothing the teacher can do about it, other than trying again, with new perspectives and strategies.

There is a lot at stake here, not only in relation to the teacher's professional development, but also in relation to the pedagogical through interpersonal relationships and interaction. In addition to teaching in such a way so as to create space for "genuine time" and individuality, teachers also need to strive for a democratic and social aspect, just as Dewey (1966) assumes. Furthermore, teachers must be aware that their communication and requests must not be perceived by the students as a personal and superficial act. And they must invite trust and involvement during the communication (Torgersen and Saeverot 2015). There are two perspectives involved in this process. First, the realization of individuality is good for each and every student. Second, the realization of individuality is good for the others (the class, the students, the teacher, and the community). Teachers should therefore strive to make the students understand their important role in the community and that they do have a place in the world, which is the prerequisite for interaction.

Conclusion

If John never experiences a life-changing meeting, both he and the teacher will fail (Bollnow 1959). The teacher may experience this as a personal loss, while John may be eternally and existentially injured. Both parties risk losing, but they may also gain something in the form of freedom, such as individuality and interaction, and that is why such a risk can be regarded as "beautiful" (see Biesta 2014). What we have tried to highlight is that it is important that teachers, in their lesson planning, place less emphasis on management by objectives, which is based on a chronological and highly predicted understanding of time. In addition, they should plan teaching in such a manner that it is possible to exploit unforeseen events in teaching situations, along the way. Thus, "genuine time" can become an integral element in the students' being.

Utilizing unpredictable moments and situations should be perceived as part of the natural interaction processes in the classroom and should be emphasized more in the planning of teaching. This, however, requires a pervasive reorganization of the school day for both teachers and students. For example, a lesson must not necessarily be guided by clock-time; rather, it can be adapted to the learning processes. This requires a political governance of the school and education sector which is based on education as a discipline, instead of the neoliberal control and management regime. This will in turn make room for genuine time, which goes hand in hand with the unforeseen, having no cause, but may itself be the cause of something else (for example, an experience or an insight). The neoliberal education, on the other hand, presupposes the foreseen, making it virtually impossible to create space for freedom, unique individuality, and novelty. Thus the immense paradox: How to make room for freedom, novelty and innovation in school, when the boat is moored both in the front and back (Løvlie 2015, p. 269).

References

Bergson, H., 1990. *Time and free will: An Essay on the immediate data of consciousness*. Translated by F.L. Pogson. Montana: Kessinger.

Biesta, G.J.J., 2006. *Beyond learning. Democratic education for a human future*. Boulder, CO: Paradigm Publishers.

Biesta, G.J.J., 2014. *The beautiful risk of education*. Boulder, CO: Paradigm Publishers.

Bollnow, O.F., 1959. *Existenzphilosophie und pädagogik* [Existential Philosophy and Pedagogy]. Stuttgart: Kohlhammer.

Dewey, J., 1966. *Democracy and education*. New York: Free Press.

Dewey, J., 1998. Time and individuality. *In*: L.A. Hickman and T.M. Alexander, eds. *The essential Dewey, volume 1. Pragmatism, education, democracy*. Bloomington/Indianapolis: Indiana University Press, 217–227.

Løvlie, L., 2015. Det uforutsettes pedagogikk [The Pedagogy of the Unforeseen]. In: G.-E. Torgersen, ed. *Pedagogikk for det uforutsette [Pedagogy for the Unforeseen]*. Oslo/Bergen: Fagbokforlaget, 267–272.

Rovelli, C., 2018. *The order of time*. New York: Riverhead Books.

Saeverot, H., 2019. Indirect teaching. In: R. Hickman, ed. *International encyclopedia of art and design education, volume 1: Philosophies and histories of art & design education*. Oxford: John Wiley & Sons, Inc., 1–13.

Saeverot, H. and Torgersen, G.-E., 2015. Tid, kunnskap og didaktikk i lys av det uforutsette [*Time, Knowledge and Didactics in light of the Unforeseen*]. In: G.-E. Torgersen, ed. *Pedagogikk for det uforutsette [Pedagogy for the Unforeseen]*. Oslo/Bergen: Fagbokforlaget, 310–317.

Saeverot, J., 2013. *Indirect pedagogy. Some lessons in existential education*. Boston/Rotterdam: Sense Publishers.

Steiro, J.T. and Torgersen, G.E.,2018. Samhandling under risk: Applying concurrent learning to prepare for and meet the unforeseen. In: G.E. Torgersen, ed. *Interaction: 'Samhandling' under risk. A step ahead of the unforeseen*. Oslo: Cappelen Damm Akademisk/NOASP, 251–265. Available from: https://doi.org/10.23865/noas.

Strobelt, M., 2018. Kritisk pedagogikk – svar på dagens kunstpedagogiske utfordringer? [Critical pedagogy – An answer to today's challenges in Art Education?] *Journal for Research in Art and Sports Education*, 2 (2), 5–19.

Torgersen, G.E., ed., 2015. *Pedagogikk for det uforutsette [Pedagogy for the unforeseen]*. Oslo/Bergen: Fagbokforlaget.

Torgersen, G.-E. and Saeverot, H., 2015. Strategisk didaktisk modell for det uforutsette [*Strategic didactic model for the unforeseen*]. In: G.-E. Torgersen, ed. *Pedagogikk for det uforutsette [Pedagogy for the unforeseen]*. Oslo/Bergen: Fagbokforlaget, 317–339.

Werler, T., 2015. Refleksiv improvisasjon. Undervisning og det uforutsette [Reflective improvisation. Teaching and the unforeseen]. In: G.-E. Torgersen, ed. *Pedagogikk for det uforutsette [Pedagogy for the unforeseen]*. Oslo/Bergen: Fagbokforlaget, 283–296.

Chapter 11

The school building and the human

An intertwined relationship

Eva Alerby

Introduction

In this chapter,[1] I intend to explore, reflect on and discuss the relationship between humans and educational places and spaces using the phenomenology of the life-world as a theoretical foundation. The discussion will be based mainly on the writings of the French philosophers Gaston Bachelard and Maurice Merleau-Ponty and the Swedish philosopher and educator Jan Bengtsson. This discussion is grounded in the intertwined and reciprocal relationships between humans in the physical world in which they exist. The building itself, the place, the space, the room will be discussed in terms of their physical and actual existence and also, as in Bachelard (1994), metaphorically. The relationship between the school space and the people who inhabit it will be highlighted and problematised. In addition, the horizon of the classroom will be discussed, as well as the spaces beyond the room. On an ontological level, rooms and spaces, which are both shaped by humans and provided by nature, will be discussed: two aspects of space that, according to Bengtsson (1998a), exist in the philosophical investigations of the lived space carried out by Husserl early in the twentieth century and which have current relevance for how the school space/room may be understood and explained. Alongside this, how the space/room sometimes arouses memories and feelings that may affect the human body will be explored.

Accordingly, this chapter should be viewed as a theoretical contribution to the discussion of the relationship between humans and places – more specifically, school buildings and their intertwined relationships with students and teachers. The discussion will also take into account how educational sites – schools – during the current era of neoliberalism have been altered to become marketplaces.

Schools and their buildings are not only places in which people are educated. Instead, they are sites for training and teaching and the formation and transformation of ideas and relationships, where good citizens and good society can be formed. Notwithstanding, they have taken many different forms throughout history. From education mostly taking place at home, where the educators were often priests, representatives from the church or governesses, to education taking place at different buildings and educational sites, all with the noble goal of educating people. In today's society, however, schools are no longer solely sites for education. Instead, the marketisation and privatisation of education have transformed schools into marketplaces for education, where teaching and learning are considered goods that can be sold and purchased (Ball 2007, Ball and Youdell 2008, Burch 2009). Different companies and business leaders are free to be the owners of, and to run, schools, and students are considered clientele and an important target group for increased profit. This trend of market reform towards a market-oriented system is a global phenomenon (Dahlstedt and Fejes 2019) that is having a profound effect on both the form and the content of the school, and above all, on the everyday lives of the students and teachers in schools.

School buildings – both create and are given significance

A fundamental goal for education is to create democratic citizens with good knowledge and skills who are ready to build tomorrow's society. This happens today primarily, as mentioned earlier in special buildings, even though the spatial formation of these varies. A school may therefore be considered an architectonic and material structure, but it is so much more. Bengtsson (2004a) claimed:

> From one point of view school architecture is nothing more and nothing else than material buildings. But if we were limiting our understanding in this way, it would be difficult to understand why certain schools are inviting and other repellent. Actually, it would be hard to find the school at all.
> (p. 2)

For a building to become a school, it must be filled with people – students and teachers. Only when pedagogical acts take place in the building does it become a school. It is also highly likely that students and teachers experience the spatial formation of the school and the activities which take place therein in different ways. Thus, complex and intertwined relationships emerge between the spaces and the people who spend time there. The spatial formation of the school creates expectations and opportunities and appears inspiring and inviting for certain activities. However, the opposite is also true, where the space may seem limiting and may sometimes even be experienced as intimidating and unsafe.

School buildings and spaces for education play a crucial role for the persons in the spaces, regardless if the person is a student or a teacher. According to Bengtsson (2004b), school spaces both create and are given significance, and these significances concern us. They have an influence on people – the teachers and the students who work and study there – not just in the present, but in the future, too. A school building therefore has different temporal dimensions. It would, for example, have been designed, constructed and prepared before the teachers and students took up occupancy and, irrespective if it has been well or badly prepared, it will have an impact for a long period of time, sometimes as much as a century or longer. It follows that many of the school buildings in use today were built under the visions and ideals of the past.

Bachelard (1994) stressed precisely this relationship between the different temporal dimensions of a building in the following way: "Past, present and future give the house different dynamisms, which often interfere, at times opposing, at others, stimulating one another" (p. 6). Merleau-Ponty (2002) also talked about temporal dimensions linking the past, the present and the future in what he calls the *intentional arc*. By bringing together the intentional arc and the school building, it may be said that the past of the school building, its history, is linked with what is happening in the present, which in turn will have an impact on the future lives of students and teachers within it.

In the current time, and especially in the era of neoliberalism, it is essential to be attentive and aware of how market forces may have influences on the design and architecture of education. An issue to consider is whether the formation of the architecture of education is, for example, a way to exert control over students or if the design of the building opens up the dynamics of education (Biesta 2006). If education is altered to be more of a marketplace for different business leaders and entrepreneurs, the goals of the school transform from educational goals to economic goals. When market forces enter education, the views of the same change. Dahlstedt and Fejes (2019) raised pertinent questions – not only what is education and what it is for, but also what should it be? With regard to the question "what is education for?" Biesta (2010, 2018) distinguished between three domains of educational purpose: qualification, socialisation and subjectification. Even though these domains can be differentiated, they cannot, according to Biesta, be separated. They are all of significance in the design of education, and the architecture of education should take these domains into consideration – to actually create spaces for qualification, socialisation and subjectification (Biesta 2018).

Given this, students and teachers in school buildings are affected by their spaces/rooms. Nonetheless, they can also themselves have an effect on the spaces/rooms. People and the world are thereby intertwined, and according to Bengtsson (2004b), all parts of a school refer to each other and to the people who work there, who together make up a specific world of pedagogical significance which bestows meaning on the various parts. The school, or perhaps more specifically, the classroom is a place where many different activities and encounters take place on a daily basis, but as Merleau-Ponty (2002) expressed it: "Space is not the setting (real or logical) in which things are arranged, but the means whereby the position of things becomes possible" (p. 284). The classroom is hopefully a place where "things" become possible for the students and the teachers within it.

How the room is used depends, however, not only on its design and formation, but also on how the size, the social context, the colours, the atmosphere and so forth are experienced and lived by those existing in it (Alerby *et al.* 2014). On a normal school day, the classroom space is filled with both teachers and students who most likely experience the space and its possibilities and limitations in different ways depending on their different experiences, as well as on what status and influence each person has in the room. Langeveld (1983) maintained that the room is experienced in very different ways depending on whether it is experienced by a child or an adult, a student or a teacher, and further on what role or power position an individual has in this context. In the interaction between the human and the room, there are always aspects of power. Merleau-Ponty (see e.g. 1964, 1982, 2000) stated that power relationships are clear in those situations and places where the control of people is important – such as in a school – which in turn means that mutual relationships are laid to one side and people become objects in the eyes of their beholders. According to Merleau-Ponty (2002), in situations such as this where people are objectified, actions and utterances are not: "taken up or understood, but observed as if they were an insect's . . . the objectification of each by the other's gaze is felt unbearable only because it takes the place of possible communication" (p. 420).

When discussing the formation of the classroom, it can be of interest to look at the boundaries or horizon of the room and to contemplate where the classroom space begins and where it ends. Since Husserl (1995), phenomenologists have taken an interest in and investigated spatiality, where the concept of the horizon in particular is an expression of humans existing in space. From this, it follows that the concept of horizon attains a fundamental significance in the understanding of human spatial existence (Bengtsson 1998a).

The horizon of the classroom

One way of understanding the horizon of the classroom is to say that it begins and ends with its walls, even if there are classrooms and educational spaces that do not have walls at all. Regardless of whether the classroom has walls or not, it is the task of the teacher to see that the students are in the place where, for that period of time, they should be. Educational activities are thus often strictly determined based on time and space. However, a teacher may in most cases only control the physical presence of the students in the room/space, not where they are mentally. Even if the students are physically in the classroom, they may, for example, look out the window and mentally flee from the space, especially if the teacher is not successful in filling the space and in engaging the students with his or her teaching (Bengtsson 1998b).

The windows (and doors) of the room serve as the dividing line between the inner and outer, and windows have the effect of making the horizon of the classroom infinite. If students use the windows to mentally flee the room, the windows may be seen as competing with the teacher. One way of avoiding this is to cover the windows with curtains, but shadows that appear behind the curtains may awaken the students' imaginations even more, such that the students rather than mentally fleeing out through the window, flee into an imaginary world.

The fact that the horizon of the classroom is extended to infinity by means of windows and that the students look through them does not necessarily have to be seen as a mental escape from the teaching situation, but rather as a way for the students to reflect and mull over what has just been said or done. Bachelard (1994) argued that contemplation and daydreams transport the person from the immediate world out to a world of infiniteness.

As mentioned earlier, the classroom comprises a kind of framework for the actions of students and teachers. The walls, floor and ceiling of the room serve not only to delimit, but also to protect. Both teachers and students are to a certain extent bound to the room, not only physically (they can leave the room) and mentally (they can think about other things), but also beyond the physical and mental by being in and using the room (Alerby et al. 2014).

Humans and rooms are in a constant interplay, though in different ways depending on which room and which people are in that space. In certain cases, the teaching is removed to outside the actual school building, for example, to an outdoor area. These outdoor areas are examples of spaces which go beyond the boundaries of the physical room created by humans to where the space/room is extended to the infinite. These places are often located in nature, perhaps in the shade under a tree. The place, or the room, is thus to a great extent provided by nature itself, even if the purpose created by humans contributes to the formation of the place. To take a group of students and go outside is not, however, especially common in today's public education, but there is, according to Foran (2005), something unique and often overlooked in "the simple act of passing through the doorway, from the inside to the outside world" (p. 2). Passing through the doorway and relocating the education to an outdoor place can also be seen as an attempt to "add green to an otherwise very un-green system" (Blenkinsop et al. 2019, p. 490).

Even though, in some cases, lessons take place outdoors – in a space without walls, a floor or a ceiling – the space is not without boundaries. Even if the boundaries do not comprise physical walls, the boundaries of the space instead consist of power dimensions and explicit rules, as well as material guidelines. The teacher frames the space by establishing both mental and physical boundaries with the aim of both controlling the students and looking after their safety. The students who spend time in this space are, for example, not allowed to leave it to simply stroll around in the surrounding countryside – a kind of mental boundary is established to ensure the students' safety and also to maintain order. The students might sit on mats during the lesson, which then form a kind of material boundary. The branches and foliage of the tree also function as a kind of material boundary. Not only do the branches and leaves provide protection from the weather, but this protection also creates a feeling of fellowship and an existential territory – a lived space.

To let a lesson take place in an outdoor space, beyond the boundaries of the ordinary physical classroom, not only affects the relationship between the humans and the space, but also the relationship between the teacher and the students. Foran (2008) suggested that "the responsibility associated with teaching in the outdoors imposes a greater emphasis on the relational aspect of teaching" (p. 4). These relational aspects are of significance for the educational situation and the students' experiences of school, and according to Foran, the outdoor space is often a forgotten space that can enrich these experiences. However, to go outside with the students instead of containing learning within indoor places may bring the students (and teachers) "closer to the natural world and enable them to feel the power of a world that is not technological but is something much more" (Foran 2008, p. 7). In an outdoor educational space, the lack of physical boundaries in the form of walls facilitates the extension of the horizon of the space since the students and the teacher can gaze out towards the horizon unhindered.

Another type of classroom horizon extension is what happens in relation to other types of distance and web-based education – or what is sometimes dubbed online learning. Here, the teaching stretches out via the ether to completely different places and spaces from the ordinary physical classroom. In this way, it may be said that the classroom horizon is extended to infinity and learning takes place where the person in question happens to be at that moment. In these kinds of virtual spaces, face-to-face meetings have been replaced with online meetings, and interpersonal relationships between the teacher and the students and between the students themselves are challenged and transformed (Kostenius and Alerby 2020). In web-based education, there is a distance not only between the teacher and the students located in different geographical places, but also between the persons and the technique, and it is thus essential to consider how these circumstances affect the interpersonal relationships. In this regard, Adams (2014) asked the question: "Who is the 'who' with whom we correspond online?" (p. 61). In addition, pedagogical approaches and teaching methods are challenged and transformed by web-based education; van Manen and Adams (2009) explored whether writing by the old technology using paper and pen differs significantly from writing online. The way students (and teachers) communicate and experience writing has changed due to online writing, something which in turn has increased during the twenty-first century (van Manen and Adams 2009).

Independently, if the teaching is taking place in a classroom with walls or in an outdoor space, it may be worth considering opportunities to move the horizon of the room by giving the students and the teacher the option of looking out through a window or over the horizon of the landscape from a place or a space where there are no walls to obscure the view. Rather than seeing these outward gazes as a threat or competition to the teacher and the activities taking place, they could be seen as stimulating and creative possibilities for thought and reflection. Other kinds of extension of the horizon take place, as discussed earlier, by means of online learning, where the boundaries of the classroom are blurred or extended and learning happens in a completely different place rather than within traditional classroom walls.

By opening up the boundaries of the classroom, it is possible, according to Alerby *et al.* (2014), to transcend the subject–object boundary. Thus, the possibility arises for an intertwining relationship between the human and the room, or to quote Merleau-Ponty (1995):

> The extraordinary harmony of external and internal is possible only through the mediation of a *positive infinite* or . . . an infinite infinite. . . . If at the center and so to speak in kernel of Being, there is an infinite infinite, every partial being directly or indirectly presupposes it, and is in return really or eminently contained in it.
>
> (pp. 148–149)

As humans, we need places and spaces: we are always positioned somewhere in time and space (Bollnow 1994). Being in a place brings various mindsets, regardless of how far the horizon of the room extends. As humans, we can feel closest to, or distant from, the place or the room; we can feel in harmony or alienated from it, and we can establish ourselves there (Bollnow 1994). Tuan (2001) stated that, due to humans' intimate experiences with both their own bodies and those of other humans, we organise space in conformance to, among other things, social relations. He also emphasised that experiences are composed of thoughts and feelings, and these feelings are memories and anticipations that can give sensory effects to a changing stream of experience.

Memories, the lived body and a sense of belonging

Whether the human in a place or a room, be it a teacher or a student, feels in harmony or alienated from the same, it in turn has an influence on the memories which arise in the place/room. It is, according to Casey (2004), in an intersubjective nexus, which is both social and collective, as well as cultural and public, where the primary locus of memory can be found. This in turn means that the memory cannot be reduced to being only in the body nor only in the mind.

For Bachelard (1994) the building – the house – is a metaphor for the human. It is thanks to the building (or human) itself that many of our memories are housed there, in the body of the building (or the person) with all its rooms and spaces: "Of course, thanks to the house, a great many of our memories are housed" (p. 8). Memories are however not only housed or contained in the rooms/spaces of the building, but they also originate there. There are previous experiences that create the actual foundation for the memories. The experiences of the person, and therefore his or her memories, emanate from all the dimensions of life, but with school and education being key for a very large number of people. A student in a previous study about significant places in school, while sitting at an outdoor place in school, expressed this: "This place is important to me because it is where I have spent time over seven years. I've got lots of memories from my time spent under the wattle tree" (Alerby 2019b, p. 535).

It is, however, not only the education itself that leaves memories. Other forms of experience related to school spaces/rooms leave memories which perhaps never fade, or as Bachelard (1994) posits: "All our lives we come back to them in our daydreams" (p. 8). It is perhaps not only in daydreams that memories are recalled. Certain places and spaces/rooms in school – moments of education which are not limited to classrooms – are strongly connected with previous experiences, which in turn bring memories to mind (Foran and Olson 2008). Previous experiences, memories and the feelings awakened in connection with the spatial formation of a school building can even be so strong that they affect the human body and produce physical symptoms, for example, in the form of anxiety and palpitations, but also in the form of stillness and a feeling of belonging.

Tuan (2001) viewed the body as an "it", and he emphasised that "it [the body] is in space or takes up space" (p. 34). It is through our bodies that we experience – and have experience of – the world, and the lived body is, according to Merleau-Ponty (2002), humans anchoring in the world: "To understand is to experience the harmony between what we aim at and what is given, between the intention and the performance – and the body is our anchorage in a world" (p. 167). In other words: as humans, we are in our bodies; we can never place ourselves outside of them. Our bodies are always with us. Thus, the body is both a condition for, and a part of, the experiences humans have in the world, as well as what memories and feelings are evoked.

Bachelard (1994) stated that every space that is truly inhabited holds the actual spirit, the essence of the concept of home – a place where we belong. We do not always find ourselves in spaces where we feel a sense of belonging or, as Bollnow (1961) puts it: "the space where a man finds himself at the moment may not be the space to which he belongs" (p. 32). The question is whether the rooms and spaces in a school are truly inhabited and thus include in the contents of the concept of home – "a space to which one belongs". Perhaps more important to consider is what an inhabited space is. Bachelard (1994) himself maintained that inhabited space transcends geometric space. Linked to the school building and rooms, Bengtsson (2004b) also pointed out that the school cannot be understood and explained only as an architectonic and material building. The phenomenon of school transcends the building itself.

Some closing words

School buildings and pedagogical sites are (or should be) relational places for educative activities, sites for training and teaching and the formation and transformation of ideas and relationships, where good citizens and good society can be formed. Accordingly, they cannot be reduced to marketplaces; instead, they are – and always become – something more than just places for economic profit. One of the goals of this text was to challenge the views and understandings of the physical, mental and conceptual boundaries of the school building, or rather the educational place, and to provoke diverse ways of understanding these educational places and spaces; places and spaces that in turn are constantly shifting, expanding and evolving. Educational places and spaces can thus be seen as vital and energising influences on educational openings and directions. These places are never neutral and thereby of significance in terms of the experiences of the place – both materially and relationally. Rather, an educational place is always complicated and value laden (Alerby *et al.* 2019), and depending on which openings and directions are present (or not present) in the place/space, the experience and the traces of memories they leave will differ.

Based on the ideas of Gaston Bachelard, Maurice Merleau-Ponty and Jan Bengtsson, I have argued that there is a mutual interplay and intertwined relationship between humans and spaces. Spaces affect people and people affect spaces in a reciprocal interaction. Life-world philosophical ontology thus includes a pluralistic and integrative view of reality. The world and life affect each other mutually in the sense that life is always worldly, and the world is always lived (Bengtsson 1999). The world and life are intertwined in this way. Or as Merleau-Ponty (2002) puts it: "the world is not what I think but what I live through" (p. xviii). Another argument is that education must be embodied in the building and its space in order for a building to be a school and for a room to be a classroom – students and teachers must fill or rather *inhabit* the place and space.

Places and spaces – rooms – can, however, be moulded in different ways: created by humans or given by nature. Regardless of which, I have discussed the value of considering what a room can be and how it may be viewed. The question of whether a room is only a room if it has four walls, a floor and a ceiling has been asked in opposition to rooms whose horizons may be extended to infinity. Based on the life-world approach, the space may be understood as *lived space* which is neither purely matter or the physical nor wholly an idea or a cognition; rather, it is concrete experienced reality in all its complexity. Places and rooms concern us as they are our living spaces.

Finally, it should be stressed that the life-world approach, with its openness and humbleness, may be used as a fruitful way of theoretically conceptualising and empirically investigating various educational issues and, more specifically, the relationship between humans and educational spaces/places. In this way, various dimensions of human–space relationships may (hopefully) be brought to light and understood.

Note

1 Parts of this chapter are a translated and adapted version of Alerby, E. 2019a. Skolans rum: fyllda av minnen, känslor och pedagogiska betydelser. [The school room: filled with memories, feelings and educational significance], in I. Berndtsson, A. Lilja, and I. Rinne 2019 eds). Fenomenologiska sammanflätningar [Phenomenological intertwinings]. Göteborg: Daidalos.

References

Adams, C., 2014. What's in a name? The experience of the other in online classrooms. *Phenomenology & Practice*, 1 (1), 51–67.

Alerby, E., 2019a. Skolans rum: fyllda av minnen, känslor och pedagogiska betydelser. [The school room: filled with memories, feelings and educational significance]. *In*: I. Berndtsson, A. Lilja, and I. Rinne, eds. *Fenomenologiska sammanflätningar [Phenomenological intertwinings*]. Gothenburg: Daidalos.

Alerby, E., 2019b. Places for silence and stillness in schools of today: A matter for educational policy. *Policy Futures in Education*, 17 (4), 530–540.

Alerby, E., Arndt, S., and Westman, S., 2019. Philosophical reimaginings of educational places and policy: Through the metaphor of a wardrobe. *Policy Futures in Education*, 17 (4), 460–473.

Alerby, E., Hagström, E., and Westman, S., 2014. The embodied classroom – a phenomenological discussion of the body and the room. *Journal of Pedagogy*, 5 (1), 11–23.

Bachelard, G., 1994. *The poetics of space: The classic look at how we experience intimate places*. Boston: Beacon Press.

Ball, S.J., 2007. *Education plc: Understanding private sector participation in public sector education*. London: Routledge.

Ball, S.J. and Youdell, D., 2008. *Hidden Privatisation*. Brussels: Education International.

Bengtsson, J., 1998a. *Fenomenologiska utflykter. Människa och vetenskap ur ett livsvärldsperspektiv*. [Phenomenological outings. Human and science from a life-world perspective]. Gothenburg: Daidalos.

Bengtsson, J., 1998b. Rumsgestaltning och tidsreglering i klassrummet, [Room formation and time management in the classroom]. *Pedagogiska Magasinet*, 3, 34–39.

Bengtsson, J., 1999. *Med livsvärlden som grund*. [With the life-world as a foundation]. Lund: Studentlitteratur.

Bengtsson, J., 2004a. *What is a school?* Symposium paper presented at the 32nd NERA-conference in Reykjavik 10–13 Mar 2004.

Bengtsson, J., 2004b. *Pedagogiska betydelser i skolbyggnader*. [Educational significations in school buildings]. Paper presented at the symposium *Pedagogical significations in school-buildings* at the 32nd NERA-conference in Reykjavik 10–13 Mar 2004.

Biesta, G., 2006. *Beyond learning: Democratic education for a human future*. Boulder, CO: Paradigm Publishers.

Biesta, G., 2010. *Good education in an age of measurement: Ethics, politics, democracy*. Boulder, CO: Paradigm Publishers.

Biesta, G., 2018. Creating spaces for learning or making room for education? New parameters for the architecture of education. *In*: H.M. Tse, H. Daniels, A. Stables, and S. Cox, eds. *Designing buildings for the future of schooling: Contemporary visions for education*. London/New York: Routledge, 27–40.

Blenkinsop, S., Maitland, C., and MacQuarrie, J., 2019. In search of policy that supports educational innovation: Perspective of a place- and community based elementary school. *Policy Futures in Education*, 17 (4), 489–502.

Bollnow, O.F., 1961. Lived-space. *Philosophy Today*, 5, 31–39.

Bollnow, O.F., 1994. Vara-i-rum och ha-rum. [Being-in-space and having-space]. *Nordisk Arkitekturforskning*, 7 (1), 111–119.

Burch, P., 2009. *Hidden Markets. The new education privatization*. London: Routledge.

Casey, E., 2004. Public memory in place and time. *In*: K. Phillips, ed. *Public memory*. Alabama: Alabama University Press.

Dahlstedt, M. and Fejes, A., ed., 2019. *Neoliberalism and market forces in education: Lessons from Sweden*. London: Routledge, 1–12.

Foran, A., 2005. The experience of pedagogical intensity in outdoor education. *Journal of Experiential Education*, 28 (2), 147–163.

Foran, A., 2008. An outside place for social studies. *Canadian Social Studies*, 41 (1) Fall.

Foran, A. and Olson, M., 2008. Seeking pedagogical places. *Phenomenology & Practice*, 2 (1), 24–48.

Husserl, E., 1995. *Fenomenologins idé*. [Original title: Die Idee der Phänomenologie. Translated J. Bengtsson]. Göteborg: Daidalos.

Kostenius, C. and Alerby, E., 2020. Room for interpersonal relationships in online educational spaces – a philosophical discussion. *International Journal of Qualitative Studies in Health & Well-being*.

Langeveld, M.J., 1983. The stillness of the secret place. *Phenomenology + Pedagogy*, 1 (1), 11–17.

Merleau-Ponty, M., 1964. *The primacy of perception*. Chicago, IL: Northwestern University Press.

Merleau-Ponty, M., 1982. *Sense and non-sense*. Evanston, IL: Northwestern University Press.

Merleau-Ponty, M., 1995. *Signs*. Evanston, IL: Northwestern University Press

Merleau-Ponty, M., 2000. *Humanism and terror: The communist problem*. New Brunswick, NJ: Transaction.

Merleau-Ponty, M., 2002. *Phenomenology of perception*. London: Routledge.

Tuan, Y.-F., 2001. *Space and place. The perspective of experience*. Minneapolis: University of Minnesota Press.

Van Manen, M. and Adams, C., 2009. The phenomenology of space in writing online. *Educational Philosophy and Theory*, 41 (1), 10–21.

Chapter 12

Active and interactive bodies

Stephen J. Smith

Introduction

Current concerns for the physical wellbeing of children and youth can be understood within neoliberal educational agendas emphasizing individual responsibility for the health risks associated with deleterious lifestyle choices. Prescribed Health and Physical Education curricula appear motivated by the 'inactivity epidemic' afflicting the present generation of school children and youth (e.g. Active Health Kids Global Alliance 2018, Pan-Canadian Public Health Network 2013) where potential consequences have to do with obesity, type-2 diabetes, coronary artery disease, osteoporosis, particular cancers, depression and anxiety disorders (e.g. Heart and Stroke Foundation of Canada 2019). Physical wellbeing becomes a personal health matter for each of us, as presumably free-thinking and acting individuals, who must learn how to take care of ourselves in exercise-approved and diet-recommended ways. A consequence of this 'risk-preventing health promotion', however, is not only the undue stress placed on individual responsibility and culpability, but more specifically, the emphasis placed on particular practices of bodily care, often requiring commercially produced fitness and health-monitoring devices, that 'narrow the meanings we might make of our bodies' and 'our capacity to engage with the world' (Adams 2019, p. 112).

The inherent contradiction to this public concern for physical wellbeing becomes apparent in current preoccupations with 'twenty-first century, personalized learning' (e.g. British Columbia, Ministry of Education 2019) where sedentary, albeit customized and technologized modes of teaching and learning (Hallman 2018) are emphasized. Increasingly neglected, amidst technology pods, interactive whiteboards, personal computers, tablets and smartphones, are manifestly active bodies and their inherent capacities for deeply immersive, vibrant and vital interactions with other similarly animated bodies. In fact, while some attention is paid to the contribution of on-line connectivity and social media to sedentary lifestyles, the longer-term risks of physical inactivity seem largely overlooked in the widespread embrace of particular kinds of interactive instructional designs and digital communication tools in schools.

Students may not sit passively in rows any more, but they are still mostly *seated* in elementary, secondary and tertiary classrooms, hard-wired and hyper-mediatized for interactions requiring minimal movement capacities.

Interestingly, attending to the physiological activation possible in classroom environments can also be beset by the very limitations of the technological apparatuses used to monitor physical activity (Henrie et al. 2015, p. 47). Recesses, activity breaks, field trips, and even mandatory physical education classes appear, for the most part, insufficient to sustain a level of invigoration students' bodies need and the kinesthetic alertness necessarily for students to engage with different bodies of knowledge. The curricular and extracurricular dimensions of the school day seem increasingly to constrain rather than enable the active and interactive possibilities of a 'physical literacy' for life (Canadian Sport for Life 2019, PHE Canada 2019).

Closely coupled to this tension between the individually focused, risk-aversive promotion of physical activity and the stress on personalized learning technologies that determine the parameters of bodily conduct, is the incorporation in school classrooms of 'meta-cognitive' strategies of 'self-regulated learning' (Zimmerman and Schunk 2011) for the sake of having students learn to take care of themselves physically and emotionally. 'Social-emotional learning' (Durlak *et al*. 2015) and the educational goals of 'personal and social responsibility' (Martinek and Hellison 2016) are then added to government-sanctioned curricula otherwise focused exclusively on individualistic learning metrics. The result of this multi-faceted press toward individual responsiveness to social, economic and technological imperatives is that it is increasingly difficult to see beyond the 'subjugation of bodies' (Macdonald 2011, p. 28) to envision how inherently active and interactive bodies can themselves be the rightful locus of educational attention.

Phenomenological reprisals under the banner of *embodiment* challenge the pervasive neglect of full-bodied existence. Maurice Merleau-Ponty's (1962) insights are certainly worth keeping in mind regarding the 'motility' of the lived body and particularly in regard to the 'child's relations with others' (Merleau-Ponty 1964). Yet one has only to observe children, and especially the younger ones, outside classrooms, in school corridors, or on playgrounds (Smith 1997) to appreciate them as 'embodied beings who experience the world sensually, kinesthetically, and con-sensually' (Smith 2007, p. 49; also, Smith 1998). The long-standing phenomenological stress on embodiment points in an holistic educational direction, however lived and living bodies need to be appreciated in their motile possibilities, their individual ranges of motion and relational dynamics, such that educators may better understand possible curricular frameworks of movement exploration and take up more purposefully, more animatedly, more vitally the kinds of curricular designs and instructional strategies that can bring classrooms boldly and bodily to life.

The lived body requires articulation for educators in its present tense, or *living*, activity potentials. The long-held phenomenological axiom that I do not just have a body but am my body (see Smith and Lloyd 2006, pp. 253–255) needs to be taken seriously as requiring a mode of drawing reflectively upon the lived body in all its active possibilities (Smith and Lloyd 2019). The relational, interactional possibilities can then be drawn out of what Michel Henry terms the immanent 'auto-affectivity' intuited in the motile 'flesh' of not just 'incarnate subjectivity' (Merleau-Ponty 1962, 1968) but of the affectively 'saturated flesh' of intercorporeal engagement with others (Henry 2015; see also Marion 2002, pp. 82–103). In doing so, the lived, living, and living-with-others body can be described phenomenologically, from Husserl to Henry, as extending the reach of activity and interactivity from the 'I can' of intentional agency to the pathic receptivity of community life.

It is this arc of educative possibilities, from active to interactive bodies, with which I will be primarily concerned in this chapter. Tracing this arc, I shall critique the long-standing, phenomenological tenet of subjectivized intentionality that continues to confine educational outcomes to singularly motivated movement expressions. By calling upon a 'radical phenomenology' of movement impressionality (Henry 2008), I shall indicate the intersubjective realm of life feeling that gives rise to appearances of the self and others yet is affectively, relationally, motionally self-generative and essentially a donation of oneself to others. The celebration of 'incarnate subjectivity' as movement intentionality in, say, Husserl's, Merleau-Ponty's, and Maxine Sheets-Johnstone's embodiment phenomenologies, will be shown to manifest a more fundamental truth expressed in Michel Henry's 'life phenomenology' (cf. Smith 2016, Smith and Lloyd 2019) – that active bodies are inherently and impressionally interactive. That which any child or youth can do and thus show to others as proof of learning is but a surface manifestation of what are essentially and always potentially interactional affects and effects. In other words, assessed learning outcomes, and particularly those validated through high-stakes testing, are only meaningful in a truly inter-personalized learning context where these outcomes reflect the deep resonances of shared life feelings.

The active 'I can'

The most distinctive characteristic of the bodies we think we inhabit, exercise, exhaust, and very often neglect, is that they are experienced as motile, sensing, feeling bodies 'from within' (Behnke 2019). Training the body, sculpting the body, and getting pumped-up may well be comprised of actions ostensibly done to a musculoskeletal framework and a cardiorespiratory system, yet even amidst the regimes of fitness attainment there remains the experience of this body as still mine, and that it is I who am feeling good at times, or feeling tired, or feeling I cannot go on. I can be motivated at some more superficial level by admonitions to exercise for my health. I may even be shamed into getting off the couch and going for a walk or run with a Fitbit recording my steps. But these motivations pale in comparison to the feelings that infuse my motions and that create a shift of consciousness from having a body to the awareness of what I can actually do

My embodiment rests upon my inherent powers of motility and the movement amplitudes, tensions, speeds and durations of which I am capable. The lived body is actually a living, breathing, balancing, walking, running, jumping, leaping and landing body that remains as much a potential for activity as it is the result of the actions I have performed. It is in this regard for the motility of the animate, living body that Merleau-Ponty stressed 'motility as basic intentionality. Consciousness,' he wrote, 'is in the first place not a matter of "I think that" but of "I can"' (p. 137). The 'living body' can no longer be thought of as 'an exterior without interior' and 'subjectivity' no longer thought of as 'an interior without exterior' (p. 55). This living, moving body is a concatenation of forces which, 'as the potentiality of this of that part of the world, surges towards objects to be grasped and perceives them' (p. 106).

Maxine Sheets-Johnstone picks up this phenomenology of the living body as the 'I can' of animate consciousness. There is, for her, a primal animate consciousness (Sheets-Johnstone 2011, pp. 134–135) that undercuts any 'I can' expressions. Before I even have the self-possession of my movement, prior to any claim to subjectivity, there is 'primal animation and its spontaneously experienced existential realty' (Sheets-Johnstone 2009, pp. 249–250). Before I gain the sense that it is 'I' who am moving things and moving with others, my capacities for self-movement are really a certain range of effort qualities and intensities that overcome some degree of inertial resistance. My movement comes from a 'unity of powers' that constitutes the '"I can" of our original corporeity' (Henry 2015, p. 150). This self-realization of an inherent vitality is a far cry from the encapsulated bodies that figure in lists of behavioral learning outcomes stipulated in government-mandated curricula as fitness standards, skill progressions, and attitude formations. A movement repertoire that can be observed and measured tends to control physical activity outcomes and, at best, provides an inkling of the immeasurable upsurges of life that make particular actions appear so life-like. How shall we get due measure of this potentiality to living bodies when restricted to, say, the physiological metrics of fitness testing, the biomechanics of functional motor skill development, and the most superficial sociometrics of teamwork and fair play? What empirical indices of force, distance, time, frequency and quantity will assure us of a child's motivation to realize her inherent movement powers?

Michel Henry unpacks this more primal sense of 'I can' through a series of critiques of the phenomenologies of bodily intentionality. Beginning with *Philosophy and Phenomenology of the Body* (Henry 1975) through to *Incarnation* (Henry 2015), he consistently lays claim to a movement sensibility that is rooted in '*an invisible originary corporeity*' (p. 120, original emphasis). He means by this a body that is not to be experienced so much in its representational forms as it is in the nonrepresentational sensibility of 'flesh' as the very 'manner' in which the body becomes enlivened, animated and motivated (p. 120). Henry insists that it is, in fact, life itself in its self-generative, self-revelatory powers that is at the core of this flesh-filled corporeity. 'The flesh is precisely the manner in which life is made Life. No life without a flesh, but no flesh without Life' (p. 121).

The 'Life' to which Henry refers becomes sensible kinesthetically in particular forms of movement expression such as dance and martial and meditative arts where we are opened to 'the mysterious reality of movement' in which there need be no end, no purpose beyond the very expression of the powers and forces of life (Henry 2009, p. 44). Yet kinesthetic sensibility is still regarded as 'a marginal and secondary phenomenon' which 'comprises a totally relative interiority which has nothing to do with the interiority of subjective movement' (Henry 1975, pp. 89, 90). Henry draws heavily on the work of Maine de Biran to intuit a motion-sensing capacity that cuts deeper than kinesthetic consciousness and that really is at the epicenter of the motivation to move. This intuition of the life-generative power of human movement may seem obscure to those who have little inclination to move in meaningful, joyful ways. Yet to those who are accustomed to dance, run, swim, throw and kick balls, tackle and wrestle one another, climb rock faces, and race down ski hills, there is the distinct impression of being animated by life powers and forces. In meeting and overcoming resistances, and especially in those moments of seemingly effortless action, I come to '*feel* my effort . . . feel my bodily intention . . . feel *myself*' (Gaines 1990, p. 69). This Biranian coupling of effort and resistance via the powers of a 'subjective' or soul-filled body points, for Henry, to the very 'auto-affectivity of life' (Henry 2008, 2015).

We feel our movements in bursts, rushes, surges, swellings as well as in the ebbing and fading of these energies. We feel the emanations of a force of life arising from within. And when literally jumping into action, taking off for a run, or diving into a pool, the 'auto-affectivity of life' becomes self-evident. Active bodies sustain themselves within the power of life to know itself, as it were, within the resistances it meets and overcomes. Enjoyment increases as we become increasingly proficient at certain forms of activity. We say that there is skill development matched to activity demands as a practiced automaticity to our actions. Yet this tendency to assume an habitual 'I can' (Henry 2015, pp. 103, 186) remains rooted in an essentially life-affirming movement sensibility. This is the motivation celebrated in earlier school curricula where children were encouraged to explore a range of environments, structures, surfaces, shapes, and levels in ways that were not predetermined by certain skill development schemata (cf. Smith 2007, Smith and Lloyd 2006). Yet something of the spontaneity of movement expression has been lost amidst current concerns for the safety of children and for teaching them the movement skills of prudent self-management. While a kind of agency is still being stressed, it seems a far cry from the impressionality of movement exploration, and the joyfully infusive and effusive spontaneity, to which the radical phenomenology of Michel Henry points.

We can broach a more active register of motional possibilities expressing a 'sensible individuality' that is 'more primitive in us' and is 'the foundation for all other determinations and all other modalities in which this life will be able to express itself' (Henry 1975, pp. 105, 106). This body is my own, and though I am able to move it in certain ways and through different terrains and milieux that show what I can do, this individuality of movement expression belies the 'reality of the body' that 'has nothing to do with what we habitually represent to ourselves by this term' (Henry 2015, p. 149). Again, this is not the bodily encapsulation that is the object of personalized learning with respect to cognitive and metacognitive skills coupled to the competencies of self-regulation and social responsibility. While the blending of classroom instruction with on-line learning outside the classroom may create curricular space for students to be more actively engaged in what and how they learn, the vibrantly animated self-formation that is at the heart of education is of a deeper impressionable order. It draws upon an affectivity not of personal whims and fancies but from life's necessary generation of itself.

The clue to understanding this Henryean bodily reality, and the more tellingly interactive aspects to it, lies in the afore-mentioned insight of Maxine Sheets-Johnstone regarding 'primal animation and its *spontaneously* experienced existential reality' (Sheets-Johnstone 2009, pp. 249–250). Coupled to Henry's insights about the 'spontaneity of our sensible life' and that 'absolute subjectivity is a spontaneity' (Henry 2015 p. 106), the 'I can' that we experience in physical activity can also reveal interactive capacities and capabilities of which we may be self-consciously unaware. It is not, therefore, simply a matter of teaching self-regulatory, reflective practices to bring these interactive capacities and capabilities to light. As Froese and Fuchs (2012) have pointed out, the 'continuing affinity with the basic assumptions of classical cognitivism' (p. 207), and even the individualist, cognitively representational affinities of 'embodied social interaction' (p. 211), do not necessarily afford insight into the living experiences of moving with others, especially where 'our lived and living bodies can become extended such that they are essentially intertwined with those of others' and in a manner in which there need not be 'any conceptual or ontological reduction to the isolated individual bodies' (p. 214). We can learn how to engage with others through partnered, group, and team configurations to feel an interactive and communal togetherness. Personalized learning, as a matter of heightened sensory and kinesthetic awareness, can now be spoken of as the impressionable capacity of living bodies to be attuned to, or in sync with, other living bodies.

Interactive 'We-ness'

Active engagement with others can appear to be a mutual and synergistic coming together of otherwise active agents. Yet such appearance does little to challenge the prevailing, cognitively loaded conceptions of interactivity where there is assumed to be some representational medium of exchange whether it has simply to do with linguistic means or codified gestures, or with, say, some digitally enabling media (cf. Smuts 2009). Even if it is admitted that interactivity is 'something that necessarily involves bodies in space and time and can thus be examined in ways that elucidate the corporeal, temporal and moral dimensions of doing things together' (Barker *et al.* 2017, pp. 274–275), the very spontaneity of 'moving in concert with others' (Sheets-Johnstone 2014, p. 260) may remain an individualistic hopefulness rather than a bodily awakening to communal sensibility.

We can run with others, stride for stride, dance with a partner in sequenced, matching steps, or press our weighty bodies and pull with strength against one another in seemingly antagonistic movements that blur distance and distinctions between us. A reciprocally felt upwelling of life gives the impression of 'withness' (Shotter 2006) which is not so much an achievement of individual wills, which may well run, dance and play counter to any motional and emotional unity, as it is a willing realization that resistances, pressures, touches, and contacts are the very expressions of an already felt attunement (Smith 2014). Modeling, matching, and synchronizing our motions, we can reach deeply into an interactive we-ness.

As Henry (2015) wrote, 'the bodies of the universe are given originally only to the immanent powers of our corporeity' (p. 149). Each unfolding, enfolding action and reaction, each push and pull, each draw and release, each postural, positional, gestural and expressive interaction that is felt in its waxing and waning affectivity is essentially about bringing up life, moment-to-moment, in an unfolding, enfolding process of 'interaffectivity' (de Jaegher 2015) or what Henry (2008) termed 'transcendental affectivity' (p. 81). I clap hands with another in something reminiscent of the playground games of childhood where rhymes like 'Patty cake, patty cake, baker's man, bake me a cake as fast as you can' literally give expression to the feeling of our hands coming together. Conversely, I sit on the floor beside an autistic child, watching, waiting to take my movement cue from him. He gets up and moves randomly around the room. I follow. When he jumps, I jump too. I follow this child's lead and enter his kinesthetic awareness. He begins to twig to our matching movements. Now I am more deliberate in having the child interact with me, posing movement challenges that have him communicating gesturally with me. I jump in front of him. He dodges to the side and then leaps ahead of me. In this manner of mimicking, matching, provoking and responding, we are no longer encapsulated within our respective kinespheres (cf. Greenspan 2019).

Although Henry makes 'hardly any mention of relations to others, of knowledge of others, of the reciprocity of consciousness, or of subjectivity' (Racette 1969, p. 93), his later writings provide much insight into the 'hetero-affectivity' that is the constitutive force of our most enlivening bodily interactions (Henry 2008, pp. 101–134). This force of 'hetero-affectivity' is nothing other than the overpowering sense of 'bringing up life' in oneself as if in another when the other's actions are felt to enliven my own (Smith 2017, 2018b). The deep enjoyment of gesturally reciprocated motions, this shared kinesthetic conviviality, is 'experienced where living individuals are concretely in the process of living and interacting' (Gély 2012, p. 155) with one another. We are able 'to enter into a particular way of singularly experiencing a common power of life' (p. 157).

Partnered activities, for example, 'activate, in one or another, the originary power or life' (p. 157). We move in unison, harmony, and synchrony when we are each free to experience the 'original shareability of life' (p. 161). More than just a 'pairing', which is to say, more vitally felt than as just 'the representation of two bodies paired in the world' (Henry 2008, pp. 109–111), partnered activities bring up life in one another. Contractions and extensions, pushes and pulls, pressures and releases along with the activity-specific postures, stances, shapes, patterns and movement sequences can be taught as the functions and forms of an interactive liveliness. They are not so much individual skills, techniques and tactics as they are the mutual and reversible means of realizing a shared life.

Interactive bodies reveal the 'hetero-affectivity' of a communal sensibility waiting to be activated. There is what Henry terms 'the living and pathetic intersubjectivity in which I am with the other, intersubjectivity in the first person' (p. 113). Nowhere do I feel this more forcefully and more powerfully than when the interactions of the group with whom I run, or the team on which I play, afford a spontaneity of expression within the otherwise repetitious footfalls or the well-rehearsed patterns of play. It could be a surge of second wind on the running track or a deftly deflected pass on the soccer pitch. Something shifts profoundly in my motional sensibility to have me feel that, in relation to my running partners or teammates, 'every experience of the other in the sense of a real being with the other occurs in [me] as an affect' (p. 115).

This essential and fundamental 'pathos-with' others that I feel most strongly in moments or 'relational flow' (Smith and Lloyd 2019) is not confined just to the realms of human interaction. 'Pathic community' may well be revealed in interspecies interactions and in the feeling of kindred connectedness that Maine de Biran (Gaines 1990) described as 'a pre-intellectual feeling of unity, a feeling for a *community of feeling* that one living thing shares with others' (p. 72, original emphasis). And within this echoing, resonating, symbiotic affectivity shared with other creaturely lives (Smith 2017), might we not, in turn, come to interact pathically with supposedly inanimate lifeforms and where the most human of relational gestures find their most elemental forms (Smith 2006, 2020).

The communal sensibility being invoked runs counter to the 'rational community' so often assumed in educational circles (see Biesta 2004). Whether they be learning communities, communities of practice, neighborhood communities, or some abstract reference to 'on-line, virtual communities', these categorical designations gloss over the 'community of those who have nothing in common' (Lingis 1994) yet, for all that, are those who work and play together to realize, in fact, community as an ongoing process rather than an achievement. Communities are comprised essentially of life-animated bodies who each, in their particularities of life expression, come to realize an active and interactive conviviality (cf. Smith 2018a). Manifesting the upwelling of life, the communal sensibility that is felt in motional attunement with others carries within these very interactions the 'original phenomenological possibility' in which 'every conceivable community is born' (Henry 2015, p. 243). Stressing the agentic autonomy of 'personalized learning' through an emphasis on 'twenty-first-century skills' can thus be seen as sustaining a view of education that is contrary to the flourishing of life. Active bodies are not just interactively and communally animated; they are the living expression of what it means to move and play together and, furthermore, to teach and learn from one another.

Conclusion

This radical phenomenological meditation on active and interactive bodies allows us now to regard concerns about the inactivity of children and youth in a different light. Focusing on the deleterious short and long-term health effects of increasingly sedentary lifestyles not only has had little impact on activity participation rates, it has also reinforced a rather dour and lifeless promotion of the benefits of physical activity. Earlier on I asked: What comes of a fitness that is so single-mindedly self-absorbing? What are we to make of a 'physical literacy' premised on 'meta-cognitive, self-regulated learning'? What 'personal and social responsibility' is achievable when the mirror and the weight scale are the points of physical activity promotion? I suggested that 'we may be overlooking the physical experiences, indeed the embodied senses, of interactivity that held such promise in childhood' (Smith 2015, p. 6).

The case can now be made that we need not just look to childhood in nostalgia for the *lived* experiences of, presumably, once physically active lives. In fact, a concern for the *livingness* of active and interactive bodies means examining in the here and now the very conditions of life that motivate one to get up and move. This primary motivation is not an admonition or a plea. It is not a berating, shaming litany of ills. Nor is the 'twenty-first century skills' distraction of a digitally mediatized semblance of interactivity. On the contrary, Henryean life phenomenology shows physical activity promotion to be a matter of discerning the affective warp and woof of enlivening, sustaining, and mutually engaging movement practices. Active and interactive bodies need less to be made and more to be revealed as the very potency of the forces of life and the possibilities of life's manifold expressions.

How, then, might such bodies be taught? The phenomenological insights that interactivity is not simply a compounding of the singular experience of being physically active, and that partnerships and group affiliations are only fully realized as 'hetero-affectivity' and 'pathic community', provide telling guidance for our pedagogical relations with children and youth. We can come to see that it is not just the interactional affects and effects of introducing students to fitness practices, games and sports, dance, meditative and martial arts that matter, but the spontaneity of learning and participating together in these active and interactive forms of life that is key. Fundamentally, 'that which is alive as an animal has the capacity to move spontaneously' (Tanaka 2017, p. 143). This definitive criterion of 'relational flow' (Smith and Lloyd 2019), this characteristic of 'effortless action' (Slingerland 2014), that enjoins human beings in shared practices as well as reaches across inter-species divides, finds phenomenological articulation as the guiding principle of teaching children and youth how to be active and interactive for life.

Teaching is itself also an activity, a practice, and essentially an enactment of purposes composed literally and figuratively of postures, positions, gestures and expressions that influence the behaviors of others, yielding bodies of knowledge, and otherwise realizing corporeal affects. David Jardine asked suggestively in a conversation with David Abram: '[W]hat if we try to think of our human inheritances, cultural, disciplinary, textual . . . our mathematics, our buildings, our schools of art with their pulls of paints, the oddly named "language arts" found in schooling . . . as somehow *bodies of knowledge*?' (Abram and Jardine in Hocking *et al.* 2001, p. 316). We might then consider the range of gestures and their thrusts, pushes, and presses into even the supposedly cognitive disciplines and realms of non-bodily intelligences. Active and interactive bodies bring into this equation of teaching and curricula a still more probing, penetrating question: What if we regard the affects and effects of spontaneous pedagogical engagement within planned curricula as giving rise to living bodies of knowledge? The potential reach – the measure, stride, leap and dive – of intercorporeal, inter-active, hetero-affective liveliness may reveal to us how these very bodies of knowledge can pertain to our most meaningful actions and interactions with others across space and time and even interspecies lines.

References

Abram, D. and Jardine, D.W., 2001. All knowledge is carnal knowledge: A correspondence. *In*: B. Hocking, J. Haskell, and W, Linds, eds. *Unfolding bodymind: Exploring possibility through education*. Brandon, VT: Foundation for Educational Renewal, 315–323.

Active Healthy Kids Global Alliance, 2018. National physical activity report cards. Available from: www.activehealthykids.org/ [Accessed 17 Feb 2019].

Adams, M.L., 2019. Step-counting in the 'health society': Phenomenological reflections on walking in the era of the FITbit. *Social Theory and Health*, [Online] 17, 109–124. Available from: https://doi.org/10.1057/s41285-018-0071-8 [Accessed 28 Feb 2019].

Barker, D., Wallhead, T., and Quennerstedt, M., 2017. Student learning through interaction in physical education. *European Physical Education Review*, [Online] 23 (3), 273–278. doi:10.1177/1356336X16640235 [Accessed 24 May 2019].

Behnke, E., 2019. Edmund Husserl: Phenomenology of embodiment. *Internet Encyclopedia of Philosophy*. [Online] Available from: www.iep.utm.edu/husspemb/ [Accessed 20 Apr 2019].

Biesta, G., 2004. The community of those who have nothing in common: Education and the language of responsibility. *Interchange*, 35 (3), 307–324.

British Columbia Ministry of Education, 2019. Education for the 21st Century. [Online] Available from: https://curriculum.gov.bc.ca/curriculum/overview [Accessed 17 Feb 2019].

Canadian Sport for Life, 2019. *Physical literacy.* [Online] Available from: http://sportforlife.ca/wp-content/uploads/2016/06/Physical-Literacy.jpg [Accessed 17 Feb 2019].

De Jaegher, H., 2015. How we affect each other: Michel Henry's 'pathos-with' and the enactive approach to intersubjectivity. *Journal Consciousness Studies,* 2 (1–2), 112–132.

Durlak, J.A., Dimitrovich, D.E., Weissberg, R.P., and Gullotta, T.P., eds., 2015. *Handbook of social and emotional learning: Research and practice.* New York: The Guilford Press.

Froese, T. and Fuchs, T., 2012. The extended body: A case study in the neurophenomenology of social interaction. *Phenomenology and the Cognitive Sciences,* [Online] 11, 205–235. doi:10.1007/s11097-012-9254-2 [Accessed 24 May 2019].

Gaines, J.J., 1990. Maine de Biran and the body-subject. *Philosophy Today,* 34 (1), 67–79.

Gély, R., 2012. Towards a radical phenomenology of social life: Reflections from the work of Michel Henry. *In:* J. Hanson and M.R. Kelly, eds. *Michel Henry: The affects of thought.* London: Bloomsbury, 154–177.

Greenspan, S., 2019. *The Greenspan floortime approach.* Available from: www.stanleygreenspan.com/resources/about-floortime [Accessed 24 May 2019].

Hallman, H.L., 2018. Personalized learning through 1:1 technology initiatives: Implications for teachers and teaching in neoliberal times. [Online] *Teaching Education.* doi:10.1080/10476210.2018.1466874 [Accessed 24 May 2019].

Heart and Stroke Foundation of Canada, 2019. *Position statement: Physical activity, heart disease and heath.* Available from: www.heartandstroke.ca/-/media/pdf-files/canada/2017-position-statements/physicalactivity-ps-eng.ashx?la=en&hash=F643664372EAE482E864F0503FE387FE20C497AA [Accessed 24 May 2019].

Henrie, C.R., Halverson, H.R., and Graham, C.R., 2015. Measuring student engagement in technology-mediated learning: A review. [Online] *Computers & Education,* 90, 36–53. Available from: http://dx.doi.org/10.1016/j.compedu.2015.09.005 [Accessed 28 Feb 2019].

Henry, M., 1975. *Philosophy and phenomenology of the body.* Translated by G. Etzhorn. The Hague: Martinus Nijhoff. (Original published in 1965.)

Henry, M., 2008. *Material phenomenology.* Translated by S. Davidson. New York: Fordham University Press. (Original published in 1990.)

Henry, M., 2009. *Seeing the invisible: On Kandinsky.* Translated by S. Davidson. New York: Continuum. (Original published in 1988.)

Henry, M., 2015. *Incarnation: A philosophy of flesh.* Translated by K. Hefty. Evanston, IL: Northwestern University Press. (Original published in 2000.)

Lingis, A., 1994. *The community of those who have nothing in common.* Bloomington, IN: University Press.

Macdonald, D., 2011. Like a fish in water: Physical education policy in the era of neoliberal globalization. [Online] *Quest,* 1, 36–45. doi:10.1080/00336297.2011.10483661 [Accessed 24 May 2019].

Marion, J.-L., 2002. *In excess: Studies of saturated phenomena.* Translated by R. Horner and V. Berraud. New York: Fordham University Press. (Original published in 2001.)

Martinek, T. and Hellison, D., 2016. Teaching personal and social responsibility: Past, present, and future. [Online] *Journal of Physical Education, Recreation & Dance,* 87 (5), 9–13. doi:10.1080/07303084.2016.1157382 [Accessed 28 Feb 2019].

Merleau-Ponty, M., 1962. *Phenomenology of perception.* Translated by C. Smith. London: Routledge and Kegan Paul. (Original published in 1945.)

Merleau-Ponty, M., 1964. The child's relations with others. *In*: J.M. Edie, ed. *The primacy of perception, and other essays on phenomenological psychology, the philosophy of art, history and politics*. Evanston, IL: Northwestern University Press, 96–155.

Merleau-Ponty, M., 1968. *The visible and the invisible*. Translated by A. Lingis. Evanston, IL: Northwestern University Press.

Pan-Canadian Public Health Network, 2013. *Towards a healthier Canada – 2013 progress report on advancing the federal/provincial/territorial framework on healthy weights*. Available from: www.phnrsp.ca/indexeng.php [Accessed 17 Feb 2019].

Physical and Health Education (PHE) Canada, 2019. *Physical literacy*. Available from: https://phecanada.ca/activate/physical-literacy [Accessed 17 Feb 2019].

Racette, J., 1969. Michel Henry's philosophy of the body. *Philosophy Today*, 13 (2), 83–94.

Sheets-Johnstone, M., 2009. *The corporeal turn: An interdisciplinary reader*. Exeter: Imprint Academic.

Sheets-Johnstone, M., 2011. *The primacy of movement*. Expanded 2nd ed. Philadelphia: John Benjamins.

Sheets-Johnstone, M., 2014. Animation: Analyses, elaborations, and implications. *Husserl Studies*. [Online] 30, 247–268. doi:10.1007/s10743-014-9156-y [Accessed 31 May 2016].

Shotter, J., 2006. Understanding process from within: An argument for 'withness'-thinking, *Organization Studies*, 27 (4), 585–604.

Slingerland, E., 2014. *Trying not to try: Ancient China, modern science, and the power of spontaneity*. New York: Broadway Books.

Smith, S.J., 1997. Observing children on a school playground: The pedagogics of child-watching. *In*: A. Pollard, A. Flier, and D. Thiessen, eds. *Children and the curriculum: The perspectives of primary and elementary school pupils*. London: Falmer Press, 143–161.

Smith, S.J., 1998. *Risk and our pedagogical relation to children*. Albany: State University of New York Press.

Smith, S.J., 2006. Gestures, landscape and embrace: A phenomenological analysis of elemental motions. [Online] *The Indo-Pacific Journal of Phenomenology*, 6 (1), 1–10. Available from: www.ipjp.org [Accessed 31 May 2016].

Smith, S.J., 2007. The first rush of movement: A phenomenological preface to movement education. *Phenomenology & Practice*, 1 (1), 47–75.

Smith, S.J., 2014. A pedagogy of vital contact. *Journal of Dance and Somatic Practices*, 6 (2), 233–246.

Smith, S.J., 2015. Balls, barbells and sock poi: The progression of keeping fit. [Online] *PHEnex Journal*, 7 (2), 1–13. Available from: http://ojs.acadiau.ca/index.php/phenex/article/view/1589 [Accessed 18 Aug 2015].

Smith, S.J., 2016. Movement and place. *In*: M. Peters, ed. [Online] *Encyclopedia of educational theory and philosophy*. New York: Springer. doi:10.1007/978-981-287-532-7_92-1 [Accessed 4 Apr 2016].

Smith, S.J., 2017. The vitality of humanimality: From the perspective of life phenomenology. *Phenomenology & Practice*, 11 (1), 72–88.

Smith, S.J., 2018a. Vital powers: Cultivating a critter community. *Phenomenology & Practice*, 12 (2), 15–27.

Smith, S.J., 2018b. Bringing up life in horses. [Online] *Indo-Pacific Journal of Phenomenology*, 18 (2), 1–11. doi:10.I080/20797222.2018.I499266 [Accessed 2 June 2019].

Smith, S.J., 2020. Flow motions and kinetic responsiveness. *In*: I.L. Stefanovic, ed. *The wonder of water: Lived experience policy and practice*. Toronto: University of Toronto Press, 27–41.

Smith, S.J. and Lloyd, R.J., 2006. Promoting vitality in health and physical education. *Qualitative Health Research: An International, Interdisciplinary Journal*, 16 (2), 245–267.

Smith, S.J. and Lloyd, R.J., 2019. Life phenomenology and relational flow. [Online] *Qualitative Inquiry*, 1–6. doi:10.1177/1077800419829792 [Accessed 4 Mar 2019].

Smuts, A., 2009. What is interactivity? *The Journal of Aesthetic Education*, 53 (4), 53–73. [Accessed 15 Nov 2019].

Tanaka, S., 2017. Intercorporeality and *aida*: Developing an interaction theory of social cognition. *[Online] Theory & Psychology*, 27 (3), 337–351. doi:10.1177/0959354317702543 [Accessed 28 Feb 2019].

Zimmerman, B.J. and Schunk, D.H., eds., 2011. *Handbook of self-regulation of learning and performance*. London: Routledge.

Chapter 13

"Awakening to the world as phenomenon"

The value of phenomenology for a pedagogy of place and place making

David Seamon

Introduction

In this chapter, I illustrate how phenomenology can be useful pedagogically to understand the central importance of places in human life and for improving those places, particularly via architecture and environmental design. I begin by drawing on educator Max van Manen's (2014) five existentials of human life and my work on lived emplacement to illustrate how more focused phenomenological concepts provide a pedagogical means for locating and disclosing aspects of environmental and place experience typically out of sight. Next, I turn to the work of architect Christopher Alexander, particularly his method of "pattern language," which provides an invaluable pedagogical tool for envisioning architecture and environmental design as place making. Last, I discuss how a phenomenology of place contributes to a place-based education that incorporates active learning, community engagement, and environmental stewardship. I argue that a pedagogical focus on place is considerably different from the dominant neoliberal emphasis on standardized testing, curricula unrelated to locality, and an instrumentalist knowledge too often in the service of a global capitalism that undermines natural and human places.

Described most simply, phenomenology is a conceptual and methodological approach that aims for a careful description and interpretation of human experience and meaning.[1] First introduced by phenomenology founder Edmund Husserl, two central phenomenological concepts are *lifeworld* and *natural attitude*. The lifeworld is the taken-for-granted pattern and context of everyday life, normally unnoticed and thus hidden as a phenomenon (Finlay 2011, Jacobs 2013, Moran 2005, p. 9). The lifeworld is *simply present* and depicts life's latent, normally unexamined givenness that typically goes forward without self-conscious attention or reflection. Unless it changes in some significant way (for example, our community is disrupted by natural disaster), we are almost always, in our usual human lives, unaware of the lifeworld, which we assume is *the* way that life is and must be (Moran 2013). This typically unquestioned acceptance of the lifeworld was identified by Husserl as the *natural attitude*, because of which we habitually assume that the world as we know and experience it is the *only* world. We "accept the world and its forms of givenness as simply *there*, 'on hand' for us" (Moran 2005, p. 7). Husserl characterized the natural attitude as "naïve" because "we are normally unaware that what we are living in is precisely given to us as the result of a specific 'attitude'. Indeed, even to *recognize* and identify the natural attitude as such is in a sense to have moved beyond it" (Moran 2005, p. 55).

One important pedagogical question is "How one can awaken to the world as phenomenon instead of being directed at the things and events that appear within that world?" (Jacobs 2013, p. 353). To "awaken to the world as phenomenon" is difficult because, in the natural attitude, we unquestioningly accept the lifeworld that, normally, unfolds uneventfully with a minimum of self-conscious awareness or direction. Most of the time, lifeworlds *just happen* and natural attitudes *just are*. In working phenomenologically, one shifts from the natural attitude to a *phenomenological attitude*, whereby he or she aims to make the lifeworld and natural attitude a focus of research attention. One pedagogical value of phenomenology is its conceptual and methodological power to help students discover unnoticed, taken-for-granted aspects of everyday life and experience.

Van Manen's five existentials

Though there are many ways phenomenologically to delineate the lifeworld more precisely, one simple but illuminating depiction is offered by educator van Manen (2014, pp. 302–307), who identifies five "existentials" that describe integral lived dimensions of any lifeworld, regardless of the person or group's specific personal, social, cultural, or historical situation. Van Manen (2014) calls the first existential "lived others," or *relationality*, which refers to the lived connections we maintain with other human beings, including bodily co-presence and interpersonal encounter. The second existential is the "lived body," or *corporeality*, which relates to how lived qualities of human embodiment – for example, bilateral symmetry, upright posture, corporeal habituality, degree of ableness, and modes of sensuous encounter with the world – contribute to human experience. Van Manen's third existential is lived space, or *spatiality*, by which he means the ways that people experience and know the spaces and environments in which they find themselves. The fourth existential is "lived time," or *temporality*, which locates us time-wise personally, chronologically, and historically. Temporality relates to the various ways we experience time – for example, pleasant moments seem to pass more quickly than difficult or boring moments. Van Manen's last existential is "lived things," or *materiality*, which refers to the importance in human experience of things, which work in a wide range of ways to sustain, improve, or undermine situations and events. He emphasizes that things "represent themselves at different scales" (van Manen 2014, p. 307). In this sense, buildings, environments, landscapes, and places are things integral to human life at a wide range of spatial, environmental, and geographic scales.

In asking how these five lifeworld existentials have significance for a pedagogy of place and place making, one might argue that spatiality, corporeality, and materiality are most central, since their specific manifestations have much to do with environmental and architectural aspects of human life, especially as one considers larger-scale human movements and actions, whether habitual or intentional, ordinary or out-of-the-ordinary. If, however, these three existentials are important for understanding the lived role of environments and places in human life, temporality and relationality must also be considered, since any environment or place always incorporates time-related and interpersonal dimensions. For example, how do the regular time-space routines of individuals coalesce spatially to sustain a "sense of place," or how does the spatial configuration of pathways keep users apart or draw them together bodily and communally?[2]

In the pre-modern past, relational, temporal, and spatial aspects of human life largely involved physical and environmental co-presence with immediate others in the world at hand, whether of the household, neighborhood, or community. Because of the social media of today's digital world, relationality often bypasses spatiality, corporeality, materiality, and time-specific requirements and situations. A major question is what this lived circumvention means for place experiences and place making. Are materialized structures and places still important in human life, or will they be largely superseded by virtual environments, places, and realities? Questions like these are central for a pedagogy of place and place making, and van Manen's five existentials are a useful starting point for specifying lived aspects of lifeworld and for getting architecture and environmental-design students aware of the integral relationship between human experience and the material world in which that experience unfolds.

Phenomenologies of place

One pedagogical means to consolidate van Manen's five existentials is available in the considerable research literature on a phenomenology of place, which is recognized as an integral constituent of human life and experience.[3] As a phenomenon, *place* can be defined as any environmental locus in and through which individual or group actions, experiences, intentions, and meanings are drawn together spatially and temporally (Seamon 2018, p. 48). Places range from intimate to regional scale and include such environmental situations as a regularly used park bench, a cherished household, a favorite neighborhood, a city associated with childhood memories, or a geographical locale to which one vacations regularly. Phenomenologists are interested in the phenomenon of place because it is a primary contributor to the spatial, environmental, and temporal constitution of any lifeworld. As phenomenological philosopher Edward Casey (2001) explains:

> The relationship between self and place is not just one of reciprocal influence (that much any ecologically sensitive account would maintain) but also, more radically, of constitutive coingredience: each is essential to the being of the other. In effect, there is *no place without self and no self without place*. What is needed is a model wherein the abstract truth of this position . . . can be given concrete articulation without conflating place and self or maintaining the self as an inner citadel of unimplaced freedom.
>
> (p. 684)

As indicated by Casey's emphasis on lived inseparability and intertwinement – what he perspicaciously calls "constitutive coingredience" – place is not the physical environment distinct from the people associated with it. Rather, place is the indivisible, typically transparent phenomenon of person-or-group-experiencing-place. Place is a helpful concept in relation to van Manen's five existentials because it provides a framework for their integration via the claim that *human being is always human-being-in-place*. Place is not only the material and geographical environment distinct from human beings but also the indivisible, normally taken-for-granted phenomenon of person-or-people-experiencing-place. As Casey (2009, pp. 14–15) explains, "by virtue of its unencompassability by anything other than itself, place is at once the limit and the condition of all that exists. . . . To be is to be in place." This claim means that human being is intrinsically emplaced and any understanding of human life is intimately related to the quality of place in which that life happens.

A phenomenology of place-as-process

Phenomenologists recognize that places are dynamic, shifting, and encountered differently by different experiencers (Casey 2009, Relph 1976, Seamon 2018). The same physical place can invoke a wide range of place experiences and meanings, both supportive and positive or unsettling and negative. Over time, a person or group's experiences and understandings of a place may alter. In this sense, places are multivalent in their physical and lived structure and complex in their spatial and temporal dynamics. A major phenomenological question is how places change for better or worse. Are there underlying lived processes impelling ways that places are what they are and what they become? In my own work (Seamon 2018), I have identified six processes that provide at least a partial answer to these questions: place *interaction*, place *identity*, place *release*, place *realization*, place *intensification*, and place *creation*. Here, I describe each of these six place processes briefly and argue they are useful pedagogically because they provide an integrated structure for realizing how different aspects of place experience, meaning, and events play a role in fortifying or eroding specific real-world places.[4]

1 *Place interaction* refers to the typical goings-on in a place and summarizes the constellation of actions, situations, and events unfolding in that place. Some place interactions are routine and taken for granted, while others are occasional or one-in-a-lifetime. Yet again, some interactions are habitual and happen without any conscious intention or organization; other interactions are willfully directed and involve some degree of intentional motivation and plan. Place interactions are foundational to place experience and place making because they are the major engine whereby users conduct their everyday lives and a place gains in activity and a particular environmental ambience. Interactions undermine place when they become fewer, uncomfortable, stressful, or destructive, and pleasure in place becomes discomfort.

2 *Place identity* relates to people associated with place taking up that place as a significant part of their world. Place becomes integral to a personal and communal sense of self and self-worth. If people live their entire lives in one place, then place identity is an integral aspect of who people are as they are born into and live their lives in that place. Today, many people regularly change places, and strong place identity is less certain, since it requires time and continual, active involvement. Identity undermines place when people come to feel apart from place and are less comfortable with taking up that place as a matter-of-fact part of their world.

3 *Place release* refers to an environmental serendipity of happenstance encounters and events. Through unexpected engagements and situations in place, people are "released" more deeply into themselves. Partly because of the surprises offered by place, "life is good" as when one meets an old friend on the sidewalk or notices by chance a poster advertising a local coffeehouse performance of one's favorite musical group. Release unsettles place when serendipitous events transpire that are unpleasant, threatening, or inappropriate for the place – for example, one's apartment is burglarized.

4 *Place realization* relates to a distinctive environmental presence sustained by both effable and ineffable qualities of place, including ambience and atmosphere. The place evokes a unique consonance, feeling, and character that is as real *in itself* as the people who know and experience that place. One speaks, for example, of the "Vancouver-ness" of Vancouver or the "Tokyo-ness" of Tokyo. Realization undermines place when its taken-for-granted coherence, ambience, and character become negative in some way or non-existent.

5 *Place intensification* refers to the independent power of the material, designable environment to contribute actively to human wellbeing and place quality. Place-strengthening intensification relates to the power of appropriate plans, policies, and designs to bolster place. The negative variant of

place intensification involves inappropriate or destructive plans, policies, and designs that unsettle and even destroy place.

6   *Place creation* relates to how people, responsible for and committed to their place, envision and fabricate creative changes that make the place better. Individuals and groups associated with a place empathize with that place and generate designs, plans, policies, and actions that respect the place and make it more whole and vital. Creation undermines place when it produces inappropriate plans and constructions that misunderstand and squelch the life of the place.

The pedagogical value of the six place processes

In studying the six place processes, one realizes that place interaction and place identity are the generative foundation of place and place experience in that they relate to the everyday actions, meanings, and situations that presuppose and ground robust places. Via place interactions, users identify with place and accept it as an integral part of self. In turn, this lived dynamic between interaction and identity sets the stage for potential place release and place realization. The last two processes of intensification and creation relate more to what places might become via thoughtful understanding and envisioning (place creation) actualized via well-crafted improvements in the place (intensification).

It is important to realize that the six place processes are dynamically interconnected. On one hand, they interact to maintain and energize real-world places; on the other hand, they interact to undermine and cripple those places. In thriving places, the six processes mutually support and invigorate each other at a wide range of environmental scales and generative levels. No one process is more important than the others, though for specific places and historical moments, the dynamic may involve different generative combinations and contrasting gradations of quality, intensity, and duration. In synergistic fashion, one process activates and is activated by the others via a complex interplay of intricately intertwined elements, happenings, and relationships, typically in flux, sometimes evolving and sometimes devolving in their degree of relationship, resonance, and animation. These ever-shifting interrelationships suggest that, if we are to resuscitate and strengthen real-world places, all six processes must be present and active; they must be given deliberate attention and provided openings in which to happen continuously and exuberantly.

In using the six place processes pedagogically, a first useful exercise is to ask students to select two or three places important in their lives and to describe those places thoroughly, as they are physical environments and lifeworlds. Students then ponder the ways these places incorporate the six processes and their relative roles in effecting vigor or debility. Students can also consider interconnections among the six place processes. For example, in examining interaction and identity, one typically finds that, for many places, this relationship marks the pivotal place dynamic, since interactions provide the everyday situations and happenings through which place participants identify with place and feel attachment, fondness – even profound loyalty. Or if one considers the relationship between identity and creation, one recognizes that people-in-place are more likely to wish to improve their place if they understand place as an integral part of who they are. Strong place identity motivates individuals and groups to bolster their place (place intensification) and often triggers the inspiration for discovering what those improvements might be (place creation).

Particularly for architecture and environmental-design students, the two most professionally relevant place processes are place intensification and place creation, since they point toward the actions, processes, situations, and constructions by which place might be fortified and transformed, grounded in an empathetic understanding of how places work. Appropriate, effective interventions and fabrications are envisioned and made via inspired planning and design. One important thinker giving central attention to place intensification and place creation is architect Christopher Alexander, who has dedicated his professional career to studying and creating life-enhancing buildings and environments. Though he has never associated himself with phenomenology directly, one can argue that his work is implicitly phenomenological and is invaluable for a pedagogy of place and place making.

Christopher Alexander's pattern language

In all his writings and building designs, Alexander aims to understand how the parts of a designed thing – whether an elegant doorway, a gracious building, or an animated city plaza – belong together and have their proper place in the whole.[5] He asks how architectural and environmental wholeness comes into being and how an ever-deepening reciprocity between understanding and designing might allow for more and more wholeness to unfold. In relation to a phenomenology of place, Alexander's efforts are important because he seeks to understand the ways by which qualities of the designable environment contribute to invigorative place making. His work demonstrates how an inspired reciprocity between thinking and designing might lead to deeper understandings and to more livable buildings and places.

Alexander's work has significant pedagogic value because it provides an accessible, real-world picture of how environmental, place, and design qualities contribute to human life and can strengthen human wellbeing. One of his most useful pedagogical tools is *pattern language* – a heuristic method whereby designers and their clients identify and visualize the underlying elements and relationships in a built environment that facilitate a sense of place (Alexander *et al.* 1977). In his master volume, *A Pattern Language*, Alexander and colleagues identify 253 of these elements, or *patterns*, arranged from larger to smaller environmental scale and each given a number from 1 ("independent regions") to 253 ("things from your life"). A pattern is both interpretive and prescriptive:

first, it is a description of a specific element of the built environment that contributes to a sense of place – for example, "identifiable neighborhood" (no. 14), "degrees of publicness" (36), "main gateways" (53), "high places" (62), and "window place" (180). Second, a pattern is a practical instruction that suggests how to design the element effectively. In considering main gateways, for example, one is directed to "Mark every boundary in the city which has important human meaning – the boundary of a building cluster, a neighborhood, a precinct – by great gateways where the major entering paths cross the boundary" (Alexander *et al.* 1977, p. 278).

Pattern language is a helpful pedagogical tool for getting architecture students to envision an ensemble of designable elements that actualize environmental wholeness and effective place making. The approach provides a compilation of time-tested design elements that contribute to place activity, ambience, and vitality. In writing a pattern language for a particular design problem, students draw on existing patterns but also develop new patterns, since each design problem is unique and requires its own specific pattern language. Perhaps the most useful aspect of the pattern-language approach is the requirement that one identify the largest-scale patterns first so that he or she can then picture where smaller-scaled elements fit within the larger whole. In this way, all the parts of the design can be understood in relation to each other and fabricated in such a way as to contribute appropriately to a whole of integrated parts (Alexander 2002–2005, Coates and Seamon 1993).

The Meadowcreek studio as an example

Here, I illustrate the pedagogical value of Alexander's pattern language as used by ten advanced architecture students in an upper-level architecture studio co-taught at Kansas State University. The studio focus was the "Meadowcreek Project," an environmental education center in the Ozarks region of Arkansas. In preparing a master plan for the center's long-term development, our students sought to immerse themselves in the Meadowcreek experience: they visited the 1,500-acre site and thoroughly mapped its natural and human-made features; they interviewed students, staff, and the program's two directors; they studied the geography and history of the Ozarks – in short, they worked to establish an intimate familiarity with the project, personnel, and site.[6]

To master an accurate understanding of Meadowcreek's philosophical and ethical aims, my students wrote a series of six *meta-patterns* that included "stewardship ethic," "sustainability," "sense of place and regions," "community commitment," "place as process," and "connective education." As the studio proceeded, these meta-patterns were crucial in providing a sighting device for keeping the student's design work in touch with Meadowcreek's central purposes and needs. For example, "stewardship ethic" reminded students that the Meadowcreek property should always be treated as a natural and human community rather than an economic commodity. "Community commitment" emphasized that all new physical design should support and strengthen sociability and group solidarity.

Having a comprehensive understanding of clients and site, the students next generated a Meadowcreek pattern language, of which the 49 patterns are listed in Table 13.1. These patterns were then transformed into design elements, as illustrated in Figure 13.1, which describes the primary patterns used to guide design of the site as a whole. These site patterns aimed to preserve and enhance Meadowcreek's natural character by limiting and concentrating new development as well as identifying and refining the site's natural features such a slope, water, vegetation, and prominent views. The largest pattern, *degrees of human impact*, specified that new development should be concentrated around existing places and pathways. This pattern supported others such as *sacred sites* and *site repair*, which called for protecting the site's special natural and historic places and focusing new construction on portions of the site already occupied or less striking environmentally. Figure 13.2 illustrates the patterns and design for a path to Ripple Ridge, which offers panoramic views of the valley in which the Meadowcreek property is located.

Once the students had produced a broad pattern language for Meadowcreek, they broke into smaller groups to take on more focused design projects that

Table 13.1 Pattern Language written for Meadowcreek (originally published in Coates and Seamon 1993, p. 337; used with permission)

Meadowcreek's Pattern Language

1. Degrees of Human Impact*	18. Path Shape	34. Edible Landscape*
2. Sacred Sites	19. Path and Rest*	35. Outdoor Rooms
3. Site Repair	20. Looped Local Roads	36. Communal Eating
4. Activity Nodes	21. Green Streets	37. Small Parking Lots
5. Hierarchy of Paths*	22. Something Near the Middle	38. Garden Growing Wild
6. Identifiable Edges*		39. Tree Places
7. Degrees of Publicness*	23. Activity Pockets	40. Fruit Trees
8. Small Learning Groups	24. Shielded Parking	41. Meditation Places*
9. Circulation Realms	25. South Facing Outdoors	42. Master and Apprentices
10. Work Community	26. Main Building	
11. Self-Governing Groups	27. Positive Outdoor Space	43. Small Meeting Places
12. Main Gateways	28. Building Complex	44. Small Work Groups
13. Paths and Goals	29. Connection to Earth	45. Bulk Storage
14. Access to Water	30. Building Edge	46. Seat Spots
15. Pools and Streams	31. Main Entrance	47. Stair Seats
16. High Places	32. Quiet Back	48. Sitting Walls
17. Terraced Slopes	33. Entrance Transition	49. Garden Seats

* Not originally in *Pattern Language* (Alexander et al. 1977) and written especially for Meadowcreek.

"Awakening to the world as phenomenon" 173

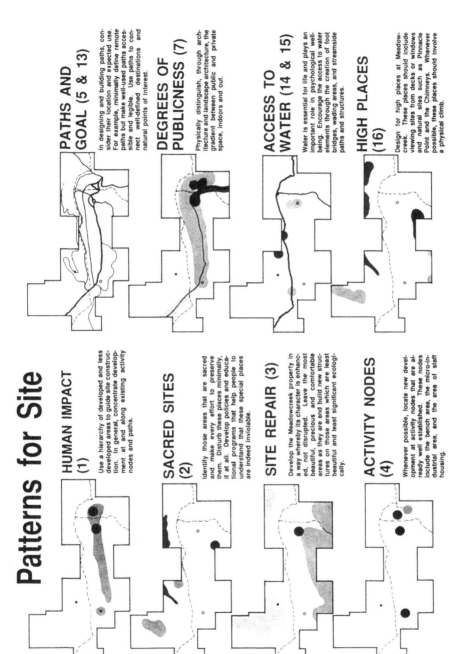

Figure 13.1 Key patterns for the Meadowcreek site design (originally published in Coates and Seamon 1993, p. 338; used with permission).

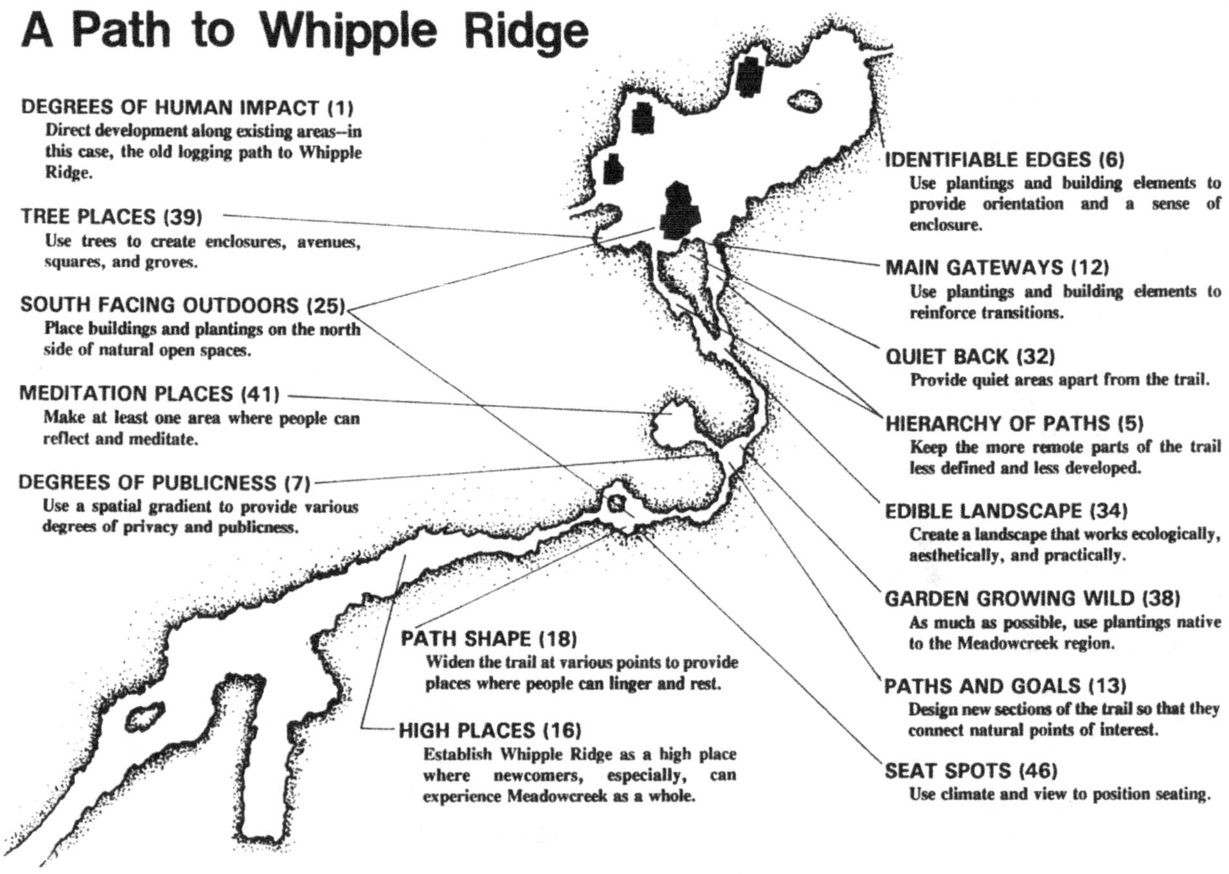

A Path to Whipple Ridge

DEGREES OF HUMAN IMPACT (1)
Direct development along existing areas—in this case, the old logging path to Whipple Ridge.

TREE PLACES (39)
Use trees to create enclosures, avenues, squares, and groves.

SOUTH FACING OUTDOORS (25)
Place buildings and plantings on the north side of natural open spaces.

MEDITATION PLACES (41)
Make at least one area where people can reflect and meditate.

DEGREES OF PUBLICNESS (7)
Use a spatial gradient to provide various degrees of privacy and publicness.

IDENTIFIABLE EDGES (6)
Use plantings and building elements to provide orientation and a sense of enclosure.

MAIN GATEWAYS (12)
Use plantings and building elements to reinforce transitions.

QUIET BACK (32)
Provide quiet areas apart from the trail.

HIERARCHY OF PATHS (5)
Keep the more remote parts of the trail less defined and less developed.

EDIBLE LANDSCAPE (34)
Create a landscape that works ecologically, aesthetically, and practically.

GARDEN GROWING WILD (38)
As much as possible, use plantings native to the Meadowcreek region.

PATHS AND GOALS (13)
Design new sections of the trail so that they connect natural points of interest.

SEAT SPOTS (46)
Use climate and view to position seating.

PATH SHAPE (18)
Widen the trail at various points to provide places where people can linger and rest.

HIGH PLACES (16)
Establish Whipple Ridge as a high place where newcomers, especially, can experience Meadowcreek as a whole.

Figure 13.2 Patterns used to design a path to Ripple Ridge (originally published in Coates and Seamon 1993, p. 340; used with permission).

included site design; staff and student housing; an educational and conference center; and a "micro-industrial area" for experiential learning related to farming, forestry, and regional crafts.[7] As the studio proceeded, the students continually returned to the 49 patterns and the six meta-patterns as an important means for keeping in sight how Meadowcreek as a place could be strengthened via appropriate design. I overview the Meadowcreek studio here because it demonstrates how Alexander's approach offers an organized conceptual means for translating a complex planning problem into effective design grounded in the needs of place and actualized as effective place making. Readily complementing a phenomenological perspective on place, Alexander's approach offers a design pedagogy to create environments that work practically and also evoke vibrancy, amity, and the pleasure of place.

Phenomenology and place-based education

Though my Meadowcreek example relates to architectural and environmental-design education, I emphasize that phenomenological insights relating to place and place making might contribute to pedagogical efforts more broadly, including the education of children, adolescents, and adults. In most conventional school programs today, regulated by neoliberal directives, learning is disconnected from the communities and places where the schools are located (Buxton 2010, Gruenwald and Offei Manteaw 2007, Hursh *et al.* 2015). Driven by standardized testing and measurable accountability, teachers follow a pre-set curriculum that emphasizes student regurgitation of pre-determined facts, principles, and points of view (Smith 2013). Since the early 2000s, some educators (Foran and Olson 2008) have sought to develop a *place-based pedagogy*, which works to "make the boundaries between schools and their environs more permeable by directing at least part of students' school experiences to local phenomena ranging from culture and politics to environmental concerns and economy" (Smith 2007, p. 190).[8] Place-based learning is considerably different from the standard neoliberal model in that teachers draw on natural, social, and cultural features of local place to focus instruction in science, social studies, and the language arts. Students learn from community members as well as from teachers and actively produce knowledge rather than passively accept it via pre-structured classroom instruction and standardized examinations. This pedagogy of engaging place via active involvement and learning may facilitate a deepening interest in and concern for one's home place, including its natural and ecological aspects. With this knowledge in hand, students may more likely contribute to making "social healthy and ecologically sustainable communities" (Smith 2013, p. 215). In this way, place-based education can be a valuable pedagogical and community counter to the homogenizing culture of global capitalism, too often responsible for the disintegration of places and the breakdown of terrestrial ecosystems (Relph 1976, 2015, Seamon 2018).

At this point in the development of place-based education, the potential contribution of phenomenology has been given only minimal attention.[9] Here, I suggest that, as well as bringing student awareness to particular places, place experiences, and place meanings, we need to realize that the existential structures of place and lived emplacement are an integral part of human beings and have a lived complexity that, once seen and understood, may offer an innovative, complementary point of view for thinking about specific places, place experiences, and modes of lived emplacement. To consider place experience in terms of van Manen's five existentials or my six place processes, for example, gets one thinking about aspects and patterns of place that he or she might miss otherwise, not typically alert to the always-already presence of place as an integral aspect of lifeworld.

In this sense, phenomenological concepts and principles offer unsuspected insights into a particular locality, just as real-world features of that locality assist in concretizing and clarifying broader phenomenological concepts and principles. As indicated by the six place processes highlighted earlier, "place" is as much a phenomenon-in-itself as it is a phenomenon involving the experiences, actions, and meanings of the individuals and groups associated with that place. The perceptions, situations, and experiences of every Londoner, for example, are unique and hugely various, whether for that Londoner as an individual or as she is part of some larger group identity. At the same time, however, London is a place-unto-itself with a singular environmental character and ambience. From a phenomenological perspective, place presupposes and incorporates all these many lived dimensions, each of which must be considered in a comprehensive place-based pedagogy.

"To Awaken to the World as Phenomenon"

In this chapter, I have emphasized phenomenological insights as they contribute to a pedagogy of place and place making. A central task of phenomenology is to disclose the taken-for-grantedness of human life, an integral part of which are the phenomena of lifeworld, natural attitude, and place. Van Manen's five existentials offer one helpful means to probe and clarify specific lifeworlds. In turn, I have sought to demonstrate that the phenomenon of place, interpreted phenomenologically, provides one way in which these five existentials can be consolidated into a larger conceptual structure that has pedagogic value for architecture and environmental design as place making.

Philosopher Hanne Jacobs (2013, p. 353) suggests that the broadest aim of phenomenology is "to awaken to the world as phenomenon" – in other words, to realize how a vast portion of human experience is typically matter of fact, taken for granted, and unnoticed as a phenomenon. Phenomenology offers a way to disclose the concealed givenness of human living and to realize that "the quotidian everydayness of daily life experiences is much less simple than we tend to think" (van Manen 2014, p. 42). If an efficacious pedagogy aims to facilitate deeper awareness and more comprehensive knowledge, one crucial starting place is realizing how much about human experience we don't know because we are almost always caught up in the natural attitude and lifeworld. Penetrating beneath this natural attitude and discovering the all-encompassing presence of lifeworld is the crux of phenomenological learning. One awakens to the world as phenomenon. In this chapter, I have sought to illustrate this awakening via a pedagogy of place and place making.

Notes

1. Useful introductions to phenomenology include Moran (2000), Finlay (2011), van Manen (2014).
2. On the first question see Hillier (1996), Seamon (2018, pp. 145–147); on the second question see Broadway *et al.* (2018), van Eck and Pijpers (2017).
3. Research relating to the phenomenology of place includes Casey (2009), Malpas (2018), Patterson and Williams (2005), Relph (1976, 2015), Seamon (2018), Stefanovic (2000).
4. See Seamon (2018), for a derivation and justification of these six place processes.
5. For introductions to his work, see Alexander (2002–2005), Alexander *et al.* (1977). For a recent overview of his work, see Pontikis and Rofè (2016).
6. For an extended discussion of the Meadowcreek studio, see Coates and Seamon (1993).
7. Designs for these projects are included in Coates and Seamon (1993).
8. Useful overviews of place-based education include: Greenwood (2013), Gruenewald (2003), Smith (2007, 2013).
9. One important exception is Foran and Olson (2008); also see Gruenewald (2003, pp. 621–628). On the relationship between education and phenomenology more broadly, see Friesen *et al.* (2012). On the relation between pedagogy, learning, and architectural design, see Darian-Smith and Willis (2017).

References

Alexander, C., 2002–2005. *The nature of order*, 4 vols. Berkeley, CA: Center for Environmental Structure.

Alexander, C., Ishikawa, S., and Silverstein, M., 1977. *A pattern language*. New York: Oxford University Press.

Broadway, M., Legg, R., and Broadway, J., 2018. Coffeehouses and the art of social engagement: An analysis of Portland coffeehouses. *Geographical Review*, 108 (3), 433–456.

Buxton, C.A., 2010. Social problem solving through science: An approach to critical, place-based science teaching and learning. *Equity and excellence in education*, 43 (1), 120–135.

Casey, E., 2001. Between geography and philosophy. *Annals, Association of American Geographers*, 91 (4), 683–693.

Casey, E., 2009. *Getting back into place*. 2nd ed. Bloomington, IN: Indiana University Press.

Coates, G.J. and Seamon, D., 1993. Promoting a foundational ecology practically through Christopher Alexander's pattern language: The example of Meadowcreek. *In*: D. Seamon, ed. *Dwelling, seeing, and designing: Toward a phenomenological ecology*. Albany, NY: State University of New York Press, 331–354.

Darian-Smith, K. and Willis, J., eds., 2017. *Designing schools: Space, place and pedagogy*. London: Routledge.

Finlay, L., 2011. *Phenomenology for therapists: Researching the lived world*. London: Wiley-Blackwell.

Foran, A. and Olson, M., 2008. Seeking pedagogical places. *Phenomenology & Practice*, 2 (1), 24–48.

Friesen, N., Saevi, T., and Henriksson, C., eds., 2012. *Hermeneutic Phenomenology in education: Method and practice*. Rotterdam: Sense Publishers.

Greenwood, D., 2013. A critical theory of place-conscious education. *In*: M. Brody, J.J. Dillon, R. Stevenson, and A. Wals, eds. *International handbook on environmental education research*. London: Routledge, 93–100.

Gruenewald, D., 2003. Foundations for place: A multidisciplinary framework for place-conscious education. *American Educational Research Journal*, 40 (3), 619–654.

Gruenewald, D. and Offei Manteaw, B., 2007. Oil and water still: How child left behind limits and distorts environmental education in US schools. *Environmental Education Research*, 13 (2), 171–188.

Hillier, B., 1996. *Space is the machine*. Cambridge: Cambridge University Press.

Hursh, D., Henderson, J., and Greenwood, D., 2015. Environmental education in a neoliberal climate. *Environmental Education Research*, 21 (3), 299–318.

Jacobs, H., 2013. Phenomenology as a way of life? Husserl on phenomenological reflection and self-transformation. *Continental Philosophical Review*, 46, 349–369.

Malpas, J., 2018. *Place and experience: A philosophical topography*. 2nd ed. London: Routledge.

Moran, D., 2000. *Introduction to phenomenology*. London: Routledge.

Moran, D., 2005. *Edmund Husserl: Founder of phenomenology*. Cambridge: Polity Press.

Moran, D., 2013. From the natural attitude to the life-world. *In*: L. Embree and T. Nenon, eds. *Husserl's Ideen*. Dordrecht: Springer, 105–124.

Patterson, M. and Williams, D., 2005. Maintaining research traditions on place. *Journal of Environmental Psychology*, 25, 361–80.

Pontikis, K. and Rofè, Y., eds., 2016. *In pursuit of a living architecture: Continuing Christopher Alexander's quest for a humane and sustainable building culture*. Champaign, IL: Common Ground.

Relph, E., 1976. *Place and placelessness*. London: Pion.

Relph, E., 2015. Place and connection. *In*: J. Malpas, ed. *The intelligence of place*. London: Bloomsbury, 177–204.

Seamon, D., 2018. *Life takes place: Phenomenology, lifeworlds, and place making*. London: Routledge.

Smith, G., 2007. Place-based education: Breaking through the constraining regularities of public school. *Environmental Education Research*, 13 (2), 189–207.

Smith, G., 2013. Place-based education. *In*: M. Brody, J. Dillon, R. Stevenson, and A. Wals, eds. *International handbook on environmental education research*. New York: Routledge, 213–220.

Stefanovic, I.L., 2000. *Safeguarding our common future: Rethinking sustainable development*. Albany, NY: State University of New York Press.

van Eck, D. and Pijpers, R., 2017. Encounters in place ballet: A phenomenological perspective on older people's walking routines in an urban park. *Area*, 49 (2), 166–173.

van Manen, M., 2014. *Phenomenology of practice*. New York: Routledge.

Chapter 14

From *kairos* to *chronos*

The lived experience of time in education

Erika Goble

The first day of school: The introduction

> *On my first day of school, I held my mother's hand nervously as she walked me into a large building, around a corner, and up to the door of a classroom. In the doorway stood a teacher. After greeting my mum and me, she suggests I find a seat, gesturing to the room full of unknown kids around my age. Before I can move, my mum gives me a quick hug and a 'have a good day,' and turns away. As I watch her walk back around the corner, I run after her, crying for her to stop. I catch her just before she reaches the front doors. Wrapping my arms around her, I plead, 'Don't go! I don't want to be here.' I can't stand the thought of being left here alone. A look of exasperation crosses her face. 'Don't be silly. You'll be fine. I have to get to work or I'll be late,' she explains, extracting herself from my arms. Then she walks out. Standing there, staring after my mum, I hear a bell ring throughout the halls. The busy hallways quickly empty as everyone but me moves into different rooms. I just stand there, alone by the doors, not sure what to do, until the teacher comes to find me.*

For adults looking back, the years spent in school may be remembered with fondness, dislike, or a combination of both. We may remember our childhood friends, our favorite teacher, the time we went to the dinosaur museum, or that year we were bullied. Rarely, however, do we stop to consider the experience of time in education, despite how long we live it. What is the experience of living through and in our school years? How do pupils experience time in the course of their formal and informal education? How do teachers? And how does the structure of time in our schools and the way we raise our children shape our experience and understanding of the world?

The first day of school, as recalled in the account above, can be a daunting experience for a child, and for many this marks the start of a new phase of life. Most often, children are brought to an unfamiliar building that is filled with strangers and introduced to a foreign set of rituals and practices that we call 'school.' For some, the very first step can be terrifying or strange (Lippitz and Levering 2002), and attending school for the first time may be our first experience of significant change. It may even seem as if we are pulled from the warm safety of our family's arms and left in a cold, alien environment. We may not know what is expected of us, nor how we should act. And yet, we will become intimately familiar with the rituals and practices of school for they will shape the structure of much of our lives for the next decade. By the time we finish our compulsory education, society will largely consider us to be 'adult' (or near enough), assigning to us new rights and responsibilities (e.g., marriage, voting, military service), including full self-determination under the law and the expectation that we become contributing members of society. The first day of school, then, may be thought of as the first step along this trajectory of educative time, marking the start of a child's slow and inexorable movement from operating solely within private familial life to becoming full members of the public.

Time, in many ways, is central to education. The pedagogical relation, whether that of parent to child or teacher to student, is time-bound and generational. Over time, children become adults, with education and our upbringing guiding and shaping this transformation. Our formal educational systems, moreover, embody and teach time. But the lived time of education is much more than the control and organization of bodies and activities that comprise schooling. It is how time is experienced by teachers, students, parents, and children. It is the rhythm of the school year, the feeling of a true moment of teaching and learning, and the endless time spent plodding through curricula we are expected to cover. Perhaps most importantly, the lived time of education is about our experience of ourselves: of who we understand ourselves to be, the past we tell ourselves, our anticipated future, and who we become because of the possibilities opened up by education.

This chapter considers the lived experience of time in education in light of the growing neoliberal model of education being adopted world-wide. While schooling practices have traditionally differed by country, region, and culture, under neoliberal policies and approaches, the school experiences of pupils and teachers are becoming increasingly controlled and homogenized (see: Foran and Robinson 2017). From one perspective, this may be seen as aligning diverse educational systems and ensuring evidence-based decisions, while from another, it may be considered a challenge to the very basis of what education is. Whereas other authors in this book have explored the nature of neoliberal educational models and the lived impacts of increased educational regulations and standardization, in this chapter I explore how the logic of the broader neoliberal system is manifest through how we structure, teach, and experience time within our schools. I also explore how this temporal structure of schooling is enacted by parents, teachers, and administrators *upon* children, re-shaping children's lived experiences of time and, ultimately, changing their way of being in the world. This chapter also explores how deeply meaningful educational encounters can still spontaneously erupt within this tightly managed environment, suggesting that the existential roots of education periodically supersede all attempts at control.

Starting school introduces us to *chronos* time

When one first starts school, a fundamental change of being is initiated, which is most acutely reflected in how we operate within and understand our world. It is the moment where we begin the transition from our childlike understanding to that of the adult world. Consider the previous account: the child being introduced to school does not understand why her mother needs to leave after bringing her to the classroom door. Frightened by the new environment, the child wants her mother to stay and provide comfort. The mother, however, recognizes that she is going to be late for work if she stays with her daughter. The child does not seem to comprehend why her mother is willing to leave. The mother, in turn, understands that her child is upset, but she also knows that her child will be safe in this new environment and, so, tries to reassure her daughter before taking her leave.

What is striking about this account is that the child and mother do not appear to be experiencing the moment in the same way. The mother recognizes the passing of 'clock time' and it drives her actions: her time is that of a worker. To the young child, however, this understanding of time is strange, foreign, and to a large degree, nonsensical. The child's experience appears bound to the immediacy and urgency of the moment – she needs her mother *now* because she is scared. Her mother's experience of the encounter, however, seems anticipatory: she will *become* late if further detained and her child *will be* fine after she leaves. One seems to be of the moment, the other of a potential future state for them both. Despite sharing in the encounter, child and adult appear to have radically different orientations. Indeed, they may be living in two different times.

This account demonstrates two fundamentally different experiences of time as lived: time as *kairos*, time that is of the moment and event-based, and time as *chronos*, chronological or sequential time (a.k.a., 'clock time'). While adults largely live time as *chronos*, time that is marked by a keen awareness of past, present, and future, a constant flow, young children appear to primarily live time as *kairos* – they occupy the ever present *now*. This is not to say that children do not experience sequential time. Rather that, before children start school, their lives seem oriented around moments in time: playtime, dinnertime, and bedtime, as well as the time when one visits the park or when one goes to visit grandpa. Children do know special times, such as Christmas, but these are experienced as emergent events. Playtime, dinnertime, even holidays are moments that arise amid the course of the rest of a child's lifeworld, only becoming apparent to them in the 'living now.' In the middle of playing, the child may suddenly discover, when called by her parent, that it is dinnertime or that it is time to go to bed.

Only rarely – such as when she is hungry or when cued by her parents that Saturday is a particularly special day, her birthday – may she come to experience time in a more chronological sense. And soon children learn that it is time to go to school.

The daily experience of school, however, firmly introduces children to chronological time. Their world becomes oriented to and driven by the clock, with one of the first steps being to teach children time. Marie recalls a memory from kindergarten:

> *I'm sitting in a circle with the other kids, looking up at Ms. Francis, excited. I know what comes next – it is the same each day, but every day she chooses someone new. 'There are seven days in a week. Sunday, Monday . . .' She starts slowly reciting the days of week while pointing to each word on the wall in large block letters. I bubble with excitement, waiting for her question, hoping she will call on me. Instead, she says 'What day is it today, Shawn?' We all glance over at Shawn, whose frown tells us he doesn't know. Why didn't she ask me? I know it is Wednesday. I asked Dad before he dropped me off. 'Sunday?' Shawn offers hesitantly. Ms. Francis replies, 'No, Shawn, it isn't Sunday. If yesterday was Tuesday, what is today?' Shawn stares at her blankly. Eventually, one of the other students can no long wait and answers for him. 'It is Wednesday!' she shouts. 'Yes, Jane, it is Wednesday,' Ms. Francis agrees. She continues with Shawn again. 'Sunday is on the weekend. We don't come to school on Sunday. Today is Wednesday.' She moves on. 'Now, who can tell me what month it is?' I glance at my classmates, not knowing, 'Marie?' Ashamed, I bow my head. 'April?' I guess one of the few names I can remember. 'No, it is October,' Ms. Francis corrects me. 'You see the leaves on the wall and outside?' she asks, pointing to the bright yellow, red, and brown paper leaves pinned around the classroom and then at the window. 'They mean it is fall and October is in the fall.' I think to myself 'it is October, I will remember that.'*

In school, children are taught the various units of chronological time. The lessons, much like the passage of the time itself, are cyclical, repeating on a regular basis until innately understood. For young children, the concept of time as taught by their teachers has little relation to how they directly experience their world. There is little noticeable difference in how they experience specific days of the week or even months. Names like 'Sunday', 'Wednesday,' 'April,' and 'October' seem interchanged for they are not directly lived. To teachers, however, these units of time have unique qualities that pupils need to learn to recognize. As such, teachers may coach comprehension by using questions, signs, and classroom decorations until students recognize the minutes and hours of the day, the days of the week, and the months and seasons of the year. What children are learning is time, not as they live it, every variant and of the moment, but time that is standardized to a collective and public understanding. It is learning that Wednesday follows Tuesday, and that we do not attend school on Sunday. It is learning that October is in the fall and that, when leaves change color and fall to the ground, it is fall. It is learning time as sequence. It is learning time as it is objectively understood and shared by others, an understanding that is essential knowledge for participating members of society.

For students, like Marie and Shawn, however, this specific information can seem irrelevant other than as a means to please their teacher. Units of time may even seem like riddles that, once solved, need to be remembered, something with its own internal logic, but which stands apart from the everyday. Indeed, young children's experiences of the world seem to resist the temporal structure imposed by adults. Even still, over time, most children will not only learn the various days and months, they also begin to intuitively identify its markers within their own lived experience.

Yet how does childhood time become the chronological reality of youth and adults? For Gaston Bachelard (1969), it is achieved through the process of recounting.

> The history of our childhood is not psychically dated. Dates are put back in afterwards; they come from other people, from elsewhere, from another time than the time lived. Dates come from precisely that time when one is recounting.
>
> (Bachelard 1969, p. 106)

Early school days may be the first instances when children, like Marie and Shawn, experience their life being retold through formalized 'clock time' on an ongoing basis. Their experience of being present each day may be reframed by the teacher in terms of units of time: the day, month, and year. The insertion of time's markers into what they are experiencing may be considered a form of inscribing children's experiences with chronological logic. Inscription is a form of marking – writing or engraving – on a lasting record (Merriam Webster 1994). We might then consider this common educational practice as a form of rewriting children's experience of endless, amorphous childhood time into the logical, chronological, order of adult time. This experience, when repeated in school and normalized by both teachers and parents alike, may become so routine that it becomes permanent: the child may begin automatically inserting these markers and dates into their own recollections when telling parents about their day. With enough repetition, the child may even cease to be able to articulate their experiences without them, coming to fully embody the chronology of the adult world.

School's structure as the structure of workers' time

School structures our experience of time beyond merely teaching chronological time and revising experiences with temporal logic. The very structure of schools seems to forcibly embody a particular experience of time as 'scheduled.'

Consider how schools operate. Each school day is divided into units of meaning and specific activities. First, we all wake up, dress, have breakfast, and travel to school. School officially begins when the first bell rings. We all move to our designated spots and study our first subject, whether that is practicing our reading, tending to our science experiments, or playing instruments in music class. At a prescribed time, the teacher calls for us to stop and take up our next activity. A bell rings to indicate recess, where we stop and go outside to play. Then another bell calls for an end to our games and return to our seats; classes resume. Stragglers, those unfortunate enough to not hear the bell or who choose to ignore it, are chastised by teachers, for they are not following the rules. Over the course of the day, a combination of bells and calls start and stop a whole series of actions undertaken by students and teachers alike. School, it seems, introduces children not only to the concept of time, but also the notion of common, collective practice *in time*. Indeed, this repeated collective action of bodies in motion may even be thought of as a kind of training.

Training is commonly considered the pejorative counterpart to learning.[1] Whereas learning involves the acquisition of knowledge through reflection, training is:

> To cause to grow as desired; to form by instruction, discipline, or drill; to make or become prepared for a test of skills; to aim or point at an object.
> (Merriam-Webster Dictionary 1994, p. 762)

Training is externally directed and eminently practical. It frequently involves repetition to achieve mastery but without the trainee obtaining the deep, critical understanding that is integral to 'learning.' Undoubtedly, school trains us in particularly useful skills, such as reading, writing, and teamwork. We will employ these throughout our lifetime, even if we do not critically reflect on why our ability to read is important or are unable to debate the various theories of teamwork. But while school trains us in certain skills, its overarching goal remains that of educating youth, to ensure we become members of our society with the knowledge, aptitude, and ability to thrive.

Perhaps, however, the common assumption that *learning* is more valuable than *training* too readily dismisses training's import. Teachers readily acknowledge that the curriculum they teach will be long out of date by the time their pupils graduate. Students, themselves, may also question the value of what they are learning ('when in life will I need conics?'). And while some curriculum will remain relevant, its content is more often viewed as a means of learning how to learn, to think critically, creatively, and rigorously. So, might the training our pupils receive have a similar underlying purpose beyond the skills obtained? The way students are trained to respond during a fire drill is incredibly valuable during an actual emergency. Moving calmly and collectively while following instructions saves lives when a quick evacuation is required. Might the training we experience through the structure of our school day similarly serve a social good?

If we stop and consider how pupils and teachers move through time and space in school, what we observe – 30-odd people collectively stopping one activity (like studying math) and suddenly starting another (like a heading to a gymnasium to play basketball) or 500 students suddenly stopping their studies to eat lunch – should seem strange, and does initially to many children. But in school, such collective action becomes routine and normalized. Indeed, the school experience is built around it. For those first starting school, shared actions as a trained response to the bell or a teacher's call at a particular time of day – both external markers of time's passage – may be another means by which 'clock time' in learned. 'Clock time,' then, not only reflects specific units of meaning, it is something that we collectively live and partake in. In school, the collective routine built around time's external markers may be a means of bodily learning the measure of time.

Yet, these collective practices tend to continue well past the age that children have learned to recognize and live in chronological time. Why? Consider how, although this collective movement stands in sharp contrast to the way children have previously lived their lives, it is very much how many people continue to live after they complete school, as they work as adults. In most workplaces, cohorts of employees start and stop at particular times of day. Employees have scheduled tasks and scheduled breaks. Just as a pupil's week is divided into school days and weekends, so too do employees have workdays and weekends. And just as pupils have homework, some employees must work overtime. School, it seems, manifests time as routine introduced, controlled, and normalized, a routine that they will continue to practice well beyond graduation. Might the enforced structure of the school day, then, be a means of preparing pupils for the time-managed requirements of their future employment? Just as enforcing standardized curriculum, assessments, and measures are designed to improve teacher performance and student outcomes, might the very rigidity of the school's day similarly serve the proposed outcome of neoliberal education: the increased employability of graduates by ensuring they already live the time of workers?

School makes time objective, external, and something to be used

Through being taught the units of time both directly (in lessons) and indirectly (through the school day routine), schools may do more than change children's lived experience of *kairos* time into a worker's experience of chronological time. It may, in fact, separate 'time' from experience. Consider how school not only teaches the arbitrary division of the day, the formalized routine built around external markers of time, and the concepts that make up chronological time, it also seems to teach the simultaneity of time. We all start class at the same time. We all take recess together. We all end school at the same time. We all take vacation at the same time. We all proceed, year after year, through the same routine, until we finally graduate. In its way, our formal educational system appears to manifest time as specific units of meaning on both the micro and macro levels. Our educational system, itself, is divided into set time periods, the most common of which is the 'school year,' a 12-month period punctuated at regular intervals by weekends and holidays. The school year is divided into semesters, which are divided into courses, within which are units, which are spread over days and taught in their respective periods within the school day. Within these various units of time, students and teachers move both literally and figuratively. While students, primarily grouped into age-based cohorts, will move through classes, grades, and the system, teachers tend to stay within a single grade, repeatedly cycling one full year. Through its imposed repeated routine, school seems to take emergent lived experiences and turns them into calendrical events. When our schooling is understood and experienced in linear form (even as a that line repeats), we may begin to expect that which comes next. For instance, a class despised is a class the student waits for to end, until it is replaced by the next class, one more enjoyable. It is the restless student watching the clock, waiting for recess. Even when school is wholly enjoyed, students may find themselves waiting for the end of the school day, for the weekend, for Christmas, for spring break, for summer vacation, for graduation – always waiting for that which comes after; an anticipation that we carry into the workforce and our constant striving toward achievement and acquisition. Education, it seems, manifests the lived experience of chronological time as constant anticipation, attending to the future over the now.

Our educational practices similarly promote our experience of time as reflection and recall. Parents ask: 'What did you do in school today?' Pupils are asked to reflect on past practices and activities. Classes build on one another, with concepts previously learned readily recalled in the next class, the next year. And pupils are taught history. In as much as we live in anticipation of the future, education manifests time as reflection upon the past. Might it be that through promoting both anticipation and reflection, education shifts us away from the living now? Young children have only a limited ability to conceive forward and back in time but this skill extends as we age. For a teacher, the beginning of June can already feel like the end of the school year, while next week can seem like the far distant future for a child. Might it be that, with age, we start to live more and more in the future (via anticipation) and the past (in reflection) than the present?

In his description of the lived experience of time, van den Berg (1972) writes, 'The past provides the conditions for what is going to happen in life, but the acts of life are rooted in the future' (p. 86). If, as adults, our experience of time always holds this dual trajectory, what happens to our sense of time when both past and future extend indefinitely? Might it be that, as we live time as that which was and that which is to come – neither of which we can directly experience – the present passes us by unnoticed? If we are rarely present in the now and have no ability to experience the time with which we are occupied, might time then come to seem external to us? Might time then appear to be a separate entity? Rather than something that we are always living in, our very adoption of chronological time may make time seem objective, external to us, and always passing us by from future to past.

As adults, we live in a world driven by the clock, but we do not directly live clock time. Rather, our actions are oriented to the clock: when we start work, when we take lunch, when we have our doctor's appointment. We worry about being late for work, or early for a date. We get through our week in order to enjoy our weekends. We get through work in order to retire. And this relationship to the clock is introduced in school. But our shift to clock time involves more than merely tracking the passage of our day; it also has meaning. We say that time *passes us by*. We call certain activities a *waste of time* and others *time well spent*. Objective, chronological time appears to have a value – *time is money* because labor and effort take time. Time for the adult worker seems to be a 'standing-reserve' (Heidegger 1977, p. 322). In learning and embodying chronological time, our school systems may not just be preparing us for our future work routines, they may also be instilling in us a conception of the world wherein the value of everything, including time and ourselves, is understood in terms of usefulness, potentiality, and exploitability even if it is yet untapped (see Maitra and Maitra 2014).

In being so very different from one another, the shift from childhood's time to the time of the adult world may be difficult. Bachelard (1969) describes how:

> Childhood knows unhappiness through men. In solicitude, it can relax its aches. When the human world leaves him in peace, the child feels like the son of the cosmos. And thus, in his solitude, from the moment he is master of his reveries, the child knows the happiness of dreaming which will later be the happiness of the poets.
>
> (Bachelard 1969, p. 99)

For Bachelard, there is a dissonance between the way a child wants to live and the way adults force a child to live, between the child's world of 'solitude' and imagination and 'the human world' of society and shared responsibility. Might part of this dissonance, this 'unhappiness' that is inflicted upon the child, be through how adults enforce a particular experience of time upon children? *Feeling like the son of the cosmos* resonates with the experience of *kairos* time, to be in and of the moment, in the living now. And yet, through the various upbringing and educational practices, we become adults who view time as a commodity.

Not all of adulthood is marked by this attitude, however. Bachelard tells how that the child's experience of time can be recaptured by adults, if only briefly. 'These times without a clock are still within us. Propitious and appearing, reverie gives them back to us' (Bachelard 1969, p. 130). They may be experienced in ecstatic moments, moments of silence, moments of reminiscence, and moments of true art – those rare moments where we seem to slip the confines of chronological time.

Lived time as identity maker

Beyond our educational experience teaching us a particular concept and experience of time, temporality of education also involves how time is experienced by teachers and students, parents and children in educational encounters, and how these experiences make us who we are. Don tells of one incident that occurred near the end of school:

> *It was a few days before graduation when I finally realized that school was really going to end. I'm sitting in French class, listening to the teacher drone on, and find myself looking around at my classmates thinking 'I may never see them again.' It is like I'm seeing them differently, like* really *seeing them. I look over at Jennifer, a bully of a girl, and feel a weird twinge of regret that I might never sit in another class with her. I have spent years trying to avoid her taunts, wishing she'd disappear, and now I might just miss her when we're done. I glance around at my other classmates. The thought of not being with them is weird. If I don't have this, what will I have after grad and exams and the summer? I know some of us are going to university, but it won't be all of us. It won't be like* this. *And I'm struck by the fact I don't know where I am going to be, who I am going to be with, come September. Everything is going to have changed. It's like my school days are at a close, but my future hasn't yet opened.*

As pupils pass through school, they increasingly live time chronologically. School's routine and repetition, while externally enforced, also provides structure, safety, and comfort, not in the least through forming who they are. By virtue of their time spent in school, children and youth are pupils and students. After 12 years, Don has come to firmly identify as a student in this particular class.

While knowing for some time that his schooling is coming to an end, Don seems to have not fully realized it until this moment. His uncertainty seem less about what he will do after school ends, than who he will become. When youth finish school, their existence as 'pupils' comes into question. Their identities change. High school graduation has long been identified as an exemplar of liminality: students are not yet graduates; youth are not yet adults; they are neither fully, but simultaneously both. Liminal moments are both chaotic and full of possibility. An unknown future may begin to manifest in the present without full articulation. Just as entering school was terrifying to the young child, so too may the end of school frighten the young adult.

Balancing time in a neoliberal system

While a pupil's identity is created through their time in school, so too is the teacher's, though in a different way. If a pupil is one who moves through the system, a teacher is one who never leaves, one who is time bound and endlessly working within the constraints of the school year. Kirstin tells how:

> *When I started teaching Grade 8, the principal said to me 'I shouldn't be telling you this, but you're not going to get through the curriculum. Just do as much as you can.' And he was right. There is no way I get through it. I feel bad about it, but there is too much to cover. I end up picking and choosing what I think is most important, and what they need to know for the tests. You are always balancing how much you focus on the content and how much time you spend making them better human beings.*

Under neoliberalism, how teachers spend their time is increasingly prescribed. Canadian teachers, like Kirstin, are routinely expected to cover more content than is possible to teach within the timeframe given. In addition to the required topics and outcomes, they must also complete checklists, activities, and assessments. These scripted items – seen as forming the crux of their 'jobs' – are considered comprehensive by the governments that mandate them. In reality, however, they do not account for what teachers face daily: that which is unscripted, cannot be prescribed, and emerges within the pupil–teacher interaction – what Aoki (2005) called the 'curriculum as lived.'

For all but the most novice teacher and administrator, failure to meet the system's expectations is known in advance. Whereas teachers and pupils alike are measured on tasks completed, demonstrable skills, and information retained, teachers are acutely aware that, at root, education is about making pupils 'better human beings.' Some, like Kirstin, find this failure difficult, forever considering the value of using their limited time with pupils for one activity against the necessity of the other.

Even still, expectations loom and can shape teachers' sense of accomplishment. Kirstin tells of a recent incident.

> *It was the end of the day and I felt like I had done nothing. I had covered nothing. I got nothing done. I hadn't taught them a single concept much less completed an assignment. And yet, there had been a moment with Jack* [a student in her class]. *It was the first time in the entire year that he looked up and made eye contact. I had to remind myself, that is what I accomplished today and that is more important than any literary concept.*

Even as they attempt to keep in mind their dual responsibilities to both pupil and system, teachers may internalize the neoliberal focus on performance. As adults, they live in a world where time is a scarce commodity. Class time spent should be reflected in a progression through the prescribed curriculum. On days when they have not made headway in their lesson plans, they may feel as if they have achieved *nothing*. And yet, *something* has happened. While it may not be trackable by the system, like Kirstin's encounter with Jack, what occurs in these moments is often incredibly important, even if it cannot be articulated. Such moments – whether an instance of first eye contact or a prolonged class discussion – make up the warp and weft of education as lived. It is the unrecognized structure upon which the formal curriculum is taught and assessments are made. And yet, it frequently goes unseen and uncounted. In an education system driven by neoliberal values, these moments exist outside of its logic and, therefore, tend to be missed, ignored, or devalued.

Pedagogical moments and *kairos* time

As many of the previous examples suggest, the lived experience of time in education is most evident in the direct interactions between adult and child, teacher and pupil. In a memoir of her early life, Tove Jansson (1968) describes a visit to a country home with her mother in the depths of winter. While her mother paints, young Tove plays games, many of which involve imagining the world being created by the snow, which is falling relentlessly outside. One morning, young Tove wakes early to find that the windows are actually covered by snow and is convinced the snow has covered the world. She sits by the fire and waits to tell her mother the terrible news. Jansson (1968) recounts:

> Mummy woke up and came in and said: look how funny it is with snow covering the windows, because she didn't understand how serious it all was. When I had told her what had really happened she became very thoughtful.
> In fact, she said after a while, we have gone into hibernation. Nobody can get in any longer and no one can get out!
> I looked carefully at her and understood that we were saved. At least we were absolutely safe and protected. This menacing snow had hidden us inside in the warmth for ever [sic] and we didn't have to worry a bit about what went on there outside.
>
> (Jansson 1968, p. 165)

Upon discovering the windows covered by snow, young Tove becomes scared. Her previous days' games, like imagining an avalanche, seem to have come true, leaving her, her mother, and the rest of the world buried beneath a cold, endless swath of snow. Her mother, although initially pointing out the wonder of the situation to her daughter, immediately recognizes that her child is experiencing it differently. Rather than arguing with her daughter that the world is not covered and they are not trapped, she provides an alternate, more cozy interpretation of the situation they find themselves in, one that both recognizes her daughter's understanding and makes it safe. Her mother demonstrates, in this moment, what van Manen (2015) calls pedagogical tact. It is the adult's fitting response to a call made by a child. As Jansson's story demonstrates, in moments of pedagogical tact, an adult's reaction can transform a child's terror into comfort and joy. But more than being a moment of pedagogical tact, this account is also what van Manen (2015) describes as a *kairos* moment. 'Kairos moments are pure, perfect, unpredictable, and uncontrollable moment that possess possibility' (p. 52). Van Manen notes that, in *kairos* moments, one doesn't have time for reflective action, one must act immediately or they will pass us by. They are moments marked by a need for a particular rejoinder – a time when one can and should respond. If one delays – whether it be an adult or child – one may miss the opening and, once passed, it cannot be retrieved. *Kairos* moments are pedagogical moments that must be responded to with immediacy and largely intuition.

Van Manen examines the power of *kairos* moments from the perspective of parents and teachers, but they can also occur to children and students. I have examined at length elsewhere the aesthetic impact of an experience I had in grade 12 (see: Goble 2017).[2] Considered in light of the temporarily of education and upbringing, however, it is further revelatory.

> When I was in Grade 12, one of my teachers showed a film about World War II. . . . As the video started and the teacher dimmed the lights, we were caught by the black and white documentary. Although I do not remember its title, I remember the film distinctly. I had never seen anything like it. . . . *All* is burned into my memory. I was stunned, caught, by those images. I couldn't look away despite how horrible it was to see evidence of how inhuman humans can be.
>
> . . . These images were indescribable and beyond reason. They were stupefying, unimaginable, and inconceivable. . . . The pictures were harrowing to look at it, to see, and to accept, but I would not have looked away from them, for they were images that demanded to be seen. And I saw and knew: we – the collective 'we' of humanity – did *that*.
>
> The teacher's timing was impeccable. The film ended just as the bell rang but no one moved.
>
> We just sat there.
>
> Silent.
>
> A normally loud, boisterous class of teenagers had been silenced and made still by images of war's aftermath.
>
> And in that silence we were waiting – I was waiting – for something. I'm not sure what. Perhaps a word to explain those images, explain them away or justify man's barbarism, or maybe just permission to return to what now seemed like a vacuous existence.
>
> After a few minutes, I heard the teacher's voice from the back of the room, a little confused, maybe even a little shaken, say 'you can go now.'

We all stood, quietly picked up our books, and shuffled out into what now seemed like a too loud hallway.

(Goble 2017, p. 156)

Like Jansson's experience, this anecdote reveals how teachers may demonstrate pedagogical tact in unexpected *kairos* moments; in this case, by not responding or providing a solution to the difficult knowledge the students have just learned. This experience, however, also reveals how *kairos* moments of education can be experienced by students. They may be moments that seem to break through school life and override the students' everyday concerns. *Kairos* moments may even supersede the subject they are studying and the internal logic of school. They can be moments so full of meaning that they far surpass any curricular outcomes set for the class. But more than challenging what is to be learned, these moments also challenge the how. In a *kairos* moment, getting up to leave at the bell – something ingrained in students for years – suddenly becomes recognizably *meaningless* compared to the demands of that moment to sit, stay, and contemplate what has just been revealed. The *kairos* moment can even override and makes negligible the taught urgency of chronological time. *Kairos* moments in education are moments that demand we *make time* to address them *now* rather than simply fit them into their respective class period.

Kairos moments in education appear to be *events* as described by Jean Luc Marion (2002). He describes events as unique phenomena.

In happening, it [the event] attests to an unforeseeable origin, rising up from causes often unknown, even absent, at least not assignable, that one would not therefore any longer reproduce, because its constitution would not have any meaning.

(Marion 2002, p. 31)

Kairos moments cannot be anticipated, planned, or reproduced. They must be addressed as they manifest. Marion (2002) explains, the event:

gives *itself* as much as it shows *itself*, but only insofar as the manifestation happens in it in the mode of an arrival, which falls as a *fait accompli* upon my gaze, where it is accommodated.

(Marion 2002, p. 40)

The event *happens to* us, known only after the fact, singular and irreproducible.

Events as *kairos* moments in education can be powerful and are often memorable. Twenty years on, I remember very little of my high school life, but I do remember seeing this particular film. One may even suggest that events such as these may be true moments of education: instances where the import of the experience is immediately recognized, even if we may not be able to articulate or even fathom what we have learned right after it has happened.

And yet, these powerful moments, so strong and meaningful, so spontaneously emergent within the classroom, continue to be shackled by contemporary schooling practices. While the moment sat with the students and stopped our daily routine, the teacher did call it to an end. His assertion 'you can go now,' perhaps meant kindly or simply offered out of his own confusion, also reasserted the structure and logic of school time. It ended the *kairos* moment. Under neoliberalism, *kairos* moments may take place but only if they do not inconvenience the educational system's operating structure.

The latency of education

While some profound educational experiences are immediately recognizable, others only reveal their import over time. They may be small, almost incidental encounters that have long lasting consequences for the pupil or child. Sheppard tells of a book she was given as a child.

> *My mother had laid the artbook on a table that I was responsible for dusting. From the first moment that I picked it up, that book became mine. I looked at it for hours, staring at one picture then the next, feeling wonderment at knowing that there is something else, something more to life. I remember sitting in the quiet of the afternoon, my mom in the kitchen and I snuggled in a chair, looking at the paintings, thinking, 'Who did these? Who thinks like this? What does this mean? And how does this fit in the world because this is not at all similar to the world that I am living in?' The images were so unusual, their colors so vivid, such a stark contrast to my white, Christian, middle class, small town life where nothing much happened. Those pictures were otherwise to life as I knew it: they were exciting, strange, and different. And they made me want to find out more. I realized that there had to be other books and pictures like that, so I started looking in the local library for more things that were different like that. I went in search of them, of this 'something else,' of a different kind of life. What those pictures revealed became part of the future story I had about my life. That 'something' was going to be my life.*

For Sheppard, it is only retrospectively that she can recognize the pivotal role that book and her mother gifting it to her played in her life. She sees it as starting her young self along a different trajectory by opening up as possibility an entirely new way of being. This way of being, she realizes years later, stood in stark contrast to the only life she had known up until that point. But in the moment of receiving that book, it is unlikely that young Sheppard recognized its full significance. She likely only found it a very intriguing book that quickly became her favorite. No, it is only as an adult that Sheppard can articulate its importance in her life.

It seems there are moments in education and upbringing that appear almost the inverse of *kairos* moments. Rather than a moment of potentiality that demands a reaction, these are subtle moments that carry hidden meaning,

meaning which slowly emerges over time. They are a form of *retroactive kairos moments*, moments that we recognize as meaningful only long after the fact. But how does one reconcile these two perspectives? How can something gain meaning over time? Van den Berg (1972) explains:

> The past is not possession of a past time. To recollect is not to return to the anchorage of correctly or incorrectly fixed *engrammata*. The past is *what was, as it is appear now*.
>
> (van den Berg 1972, p. 82)

Past moments, previously thought innocuous, may become highly meaningful over time. For Sheppard, looking back, the book marks the moment she began to discover who she would become as an adult. It may be through the stories we tell of our past that we discover the most meaningful moments of our upbringing.

Does this mean that teachers and parents will never know the full impact of each educational encounter? To a degree, yes. Despite our lesson plans, tests, routines, pedagogical approaches, and child-rearing practices, despite our attempts to attend to the full humanity of the child before us, the long-term impacts of education and upbringing are always unknown. While many of our actions are immediate responses to the needs of the young person before us, they are also future-oriented. We hope that they do more than merely immediately alleviate fear, address a concern, or recognize a particular engagement. The ultimate consequence of what we have done or not done, however, may be unknown for years. Moreover, what we may initially assume to be a small, inconsequential encounter may have significant impacts on the child as they age, while larger gestures may not even be remembered. This is the paradox of education: while our educational encounters can only happen in the now, driven by responses to *kairos* moments or our set chronological activities, their ultimate impacts may only be known long after they have passed.

At the end of the day: A conclusion

In human lives, the lived experience of time carries deep meaning. It is an existential element to all that we experience, every moment of every day, and both reflects and shapes understanding. How we structure our experiences within time, then, is not neutral. To change how we experience time is to change our way of being in the world and, ultimately, who we are. Our current educational system – through how it structures its activities, teaches time, approaches interruptions, manages bodies, and assigns identities – re-shapes children's experience of time from being of the living now to the chronological, clock-time of workers. Its practices, whether explicit or unintended, serve the neoliberal social agenda of creating *productive citizens*. And yet, despite the system's organization, standardization, and control, contemporary education as it is lived by teachers and pupils remains a strange amalgamation of neoliberal practices and existential events, *chronos* time and *kairos* moments. Whereas the former are controlled, implemented, and enforced, the latter are chaotic, spontaneous, and full of possibility. As the accounts explored here reveal, even within the most neoliberal of schooling systems, education cannot be denied its existential basis: it erupts inconveniently and indifferent to our plans. While proponents of the current model will argue for system efficiency, teacher effectiveness, and ultimately the success of children when they become adults, what is put at risk are adults' ability to recognize truly educative moments, foster their emergence through thoughtful engagement, and respond humanely and with pedagogical sensitivity to the unique and very human needs of the young.

While it would be ideal if the educational system – parents, teachers, administrators, and governments alike – collectively recognized the flaws of the neoliberal model and adopted a different approach, such a fundamental shift is unlikely to occur. What, then, may be our recourse? First and foremost, we must recognize the limitations of the current system, including that which it excludes, ignores, and minimizes. Once we are aware of these, we may then take a whole series of small and practical but significant actions. For instance, we can teach teachers how to recognize *kairos* moments, so that they may respond in these moments in such a way that they can facilitate the possibilities these moments open up rather than view them as nuisance interruptions to their lessons. In part, this requires returning to a nuanced understanding of pedagogy, one that is philosophically informed rather than instrumentalist. We can also foster in parents and teachers alike an appreciation for the educational value of non-prescribed moments, re-asserting their primacy in education. We can build space in our lesson plans and required curricula so that, when such moments occur, teachers may be able to respond to them with the full and unique amount of time each requires, not cutting them short in favor of the system's structural operations. We can also facilitate in parents, teachers and administrators an appreciation for childhood experiences, including their unique experience of time as the living now through exploring non-instrumentalist activities such as art, reverie, exploration, and play. This will not only improve our responsiveness to children and support youth's engagement with the world, it may also enrich our own lives. And, finally, we can continually question the various purposes of education and how our individual actions support or undermine them: Is our goal to make effective future workers for a global, capitalist system? Or should we be concerned with preparing the next generation to participate in creating a better world no matter what that world might look like?

Notes

1 The pejorative attitude toward training is also reflected in how we speak of the individual imparting the specific knowledge. In the context of primary and secondary education,

'instructors' train while 'teachers' teach. The much valued title of 'educator' in turn supersedes the teacher by being highly skilled in teaching. The educator not only successfully imparts knowledge, they are also highly effective in promoting human development.

2 For the sake of space, the account has been abridged.

References

Aoki, T., 2005. Teaching as indwelling between two curriculum worlds. *In*: W. Pinar and R. Irwin, eds. *Curriculum in a new key: The collected works of Ted T. Aoki*. Mahwah, NJ: Lawrence Erlbaum Associates. https://doi.org/10.4324/9781410611390

Bachelard, G., 1969. *The poetics of reverie: Childhood, language, and the cosmos*. Translated by D. Russell. Boston: Beacon Press.

Foran, A. and Robinson, D.B., 2017. Mollenhauer's representation: The role of preservice teachers in the practices of upbringing. *In Education*, 23 (2), 3–24. Available from: https://ineducation.ca/ineducation/article/view/354/944.

Goble, E., 2017. *Visual phenomenology: encountering the sublime through images*. New York: Routledge. Available from: https://doi.org/10.4324/9781315459295

Heidegger, M., 1977. *Basic writings from being and time (1927) to the task of thinking (1964)*. Edited by David Farrell Krell. Reprint New York: HarperCollins Publishers, 2008.

Jansson, T., 1968. *The sculptor's daughter: A childhood memoir*. Translated by K. Hart. New York: HarperCollins Publishers.

Lippitz, W. and Levering, B., 2002. And now you are getting a teacher with such a long name . . . *Teaching and Teacher Education*, (18), 205–213. Available from: https://doi.org/10.1016/S0742-051X(01)00064-6

Maitra, S. and Maitra, S., 2014. Tapping into the 'standing-reserve': A comparative analysis of workers' training programmes in Kolkata and Toronto. *Studies in Continuing Education*, 37 (3), 317–322. Available from: https://doi.org/10.1080/0158037X.2015.1043988

Marion, J.L., 2002. *In excess: Studies in saturated phenomena*. Translated by R. Horner and V Berraud. New York: Fordham University Press.

Merriam Webster Dictionary, 1994. *The Merriam webster dictionary*. 3rd ed. Springfield: Merriam-Webster Incorporated.

Van den Berg, J.H., 1972. *A different existence: principles of phenomenological psychopathology*. 19th ed. Pittsburgh: Duquesne University Press.

Van Manen, M., 2015. *Pedagogical tact: Knowing what to do when you don't know what to do*. Walnut Creek: Left Coast Press.

Chapter 15

Educational possibilities

Teaching toward the phenomenological attitude

Marcus Morse and Sean Blenkinsop

Introduction

Phenomenology has long been advocated for by educational researchers (Langeveld 1983, Saevi 2011, van Manen 1982, 1997) as a methodology through which both researcher and teacher can better understand student lifeworlds (Husserl 1936/1970). Phenomenology is a search for the lived perception of the world or as van Manen (2017) suggests, 'the study of the life world – the world as we immediately experience it pre-reflectively rather than as we conceptualize, categorize, or reflect on it' (p. 2). Methodologically, it provides a framework through which to gather information about, research and interpret lived experience: 'the descriptive investigation of the phenomena, both objective and subjective, in their fullest breadth and depth' (Spiegelberg 1960, p. 2), or, as Heidegger (1962) asserts, 'to the things themselves' (p. 58)! Phenomenology, then, begins with the lived experience of a world within which we are inextricably involved.

Sadly, this positioning of human as immersed in and in relationship with the surrounding world is not the presumptive position of the neoliberal modernist Capitalocene (Haraway 2016). For some theorists it is quite the contrary (Livingston 2007, Naess 2002, Plumwood 1997). Powerful political agendas seek to isolate the individual from themselves, their communities and the more-than-human in order to allow for a level of consumption that is rapidly decimating the planet. We believe that education can, in many ways, further such alienated, anthropocentric, colonial and consumptive ways of being through increasing measures of external control (for example, standardized curricula, individualizing competitive testing, increased measures towards accountability and efficiency, and a constant prioritizing of the 'objective', 'measurable' and 'abstract') (Jickling *et al.* 2018). And that the phenomenological attitude, proposed herein, might provide opportunities for the development of empathy for others and extend one's understandings of the complexity of lives lived. We suggest that through experiences of relationality it can become easier to recognize oneself, not as the top of a competitive hierarchy but, rather, as a member of a community filled with a multitude of talents and differences – while also bringing the more-than-human world into focus in ways that cannot deny its agency and self-willed interests.

There is a sense in educational phenomenological literature that the emphasis on the abstract and objective in education needs to be, at the very least, brought into balance with the subjective, relational and personal. Phenomenological descriptions of lived experience provide insights that enable an improved understanding of pedagogical possibilities by reflecting on that which might ordinarily go unnoticed. Such educationally focussed research takes a variety of forms. Phenomenological researchers often work with students' lived experiences and this work can then be translated into teacher education programs: discussions about pedagogy and curriculum and works relating to theories of education. Posited from a position that claims the experiential lifeworlds of students are rich, unique and never wholly understood, advocates for phenomenology often encourage teacher-researchers to develop a *phenomenological attitude* as raised by Husserl (1931). In developing this attitude, teachers and teacher educators deepen their understandings of the unique lives and experiences of their students, and thereby assist in the generation of curriculum and pedagogy that responds to student needs.

Intriguingly, given the profound and, we think, deeply ethical positions that much educational phenomenological literature has taken with regard to the incompleteness of knowledge, unique and diverse nature of students' lived experience and abstractions being centralized in education writ large, there has been little written suggesting that part of the teaching project might also be to help students develop their own phenomenological attitude. In other words, although the development of a phenomenological attitude for teachers and researchers might be considered an imperative, the benefits to the students, beyond a more responsive educational experience, seems to be ignored. The phenomenological attitude is often situated in the context of better understanding the lived experience of students' lives and thereby pedagogical possibilities. But if developing such an attitude is useful to understanding the lives of others and, by extension, is useful in the personal lives of the teachers and researchers, then surely having access to the skills which generate these insights might also be useful in the lives of students becoming adults within the world. We suggest through this chapter that individual students are capable of developing a phenomenological attitude aided by careful pedagogical and curricula approaches.

Phenomenological researchers stress the importance of describing and reflecting on one's own lived experiences. This is done in light of making the familiar unfamiliar, attending to that which is often taken-for-granted, and involving deep consideration of one's own body and relationships to the myriad things in one's community. Students too have experiences, relational bodies and lifeworlds that are unique, interesting, and worthy of attention both in terms of their own reflectively lived lives and with regard to the project of education.

We also suggest there is an additional ethical responsibility to provide opportunities for students to develop a phenomenological attitude and thereby potentially reconsider one's relationality within a more-than-human world. This has to do with the environmental and social crises that can no longer be ignored, and which are going to require much more substantive change than mere tweaking around the edges of education if the Intergovernmental Panel on Climate Change (IPCC 2014, 2018) and myriad other commentators are to be believed. We believe that teaching toward the phenomenological attitude might provide a relationally focussed way of responding to the ecological and social crisis of our time.

Phenomenological attitude and relationality

In his book, *Phenomenology of Practice*, van Manen (2014) notes that there is a certain disposition that prefigures phenomenological work; that of the phenomenological attitude. And it is to the characteristics of that disposition that we now turn. To do so we begin with a descriptive piece of research conducted with a grade 3 teacher (named Patrick for the purposes of this research), who was enrolled in a Graduate Diploma in Nature-based Experiential Learning in Canada. This was personal work done in response to a course directive to spend significant amounts of time in a local natural space, consider that place a site for learning, and find ways to involve its more-than-human (Abram 1996) denizens as co-teachers (Blenkinsop and Beeman 2010) in the lesson planning process.

> *On my second trip . . . I was joined by my two-year-old daughter. . . . As my daughter crunched through the leaves in early August, the volume of dry brown and yellow leaves on the ground struck me. Walking through the forest, I noticed mostly Red Alder, Big Leaf Maple and, upon further inspection, what I think to be black cottonwood trees. The thought occurred to me that it seemed early for this many leaves to be on the ground. I would expect to see this many in late August or September but not in the middle of summer. . . . I have seen this before at the very end of summer, or in drought conditions, but this was the middle of summer and it has not been exceptionally dry. When I asked my boss, who is an experienced landscaper, he mentioned that this often indicates that trees have been through three or four years of poor growing conditions.*
>
> *When I walked with Pearl, I thought less about the task at hand* (to prepare lessons for his grade four class that were co-constructed with place), *which trails needed to be explored, and focused more on her interests and wants. We travelled as far into the woods as she was comfortable. . . . I began to look for a place we could use as an outdoor classroom, instead of constantly moving through the trails. A place that was large enough to fit a class and have enough spots of interest that they could spread out, while still being in sight and hearing distance of one another and myself. I found an open spot with a dry creek bed and a log that crosses the now*

dry creek that I think will be perfect for a lot of our activities. Bringing my daughter along for a second visit helped to not only think about the activities I might want to do with my class, but what they would experience by taking part in this unit. I was able to inquire just by being in the place and then by watching my daughter react to the place — now I feel better prepared to visit with my class.

In considering aspects of a phenomenological attitude, we highlight here two related ideas. The first is a certain thoughtfulness triggered by a sense of wonder. Something unfamiliar, even earthy, to paraphrase Heidegger (1962), jutting through the familiar encourages Patrick to renew his attention in a particular direction. In other words, we highlight here the way in which 'an attentive attitude that meets the world with an open mind' (van Manen 2014, p. 218) is part of a phenomenological attitude. The second, is the role the child plays in all of this. The way the child relates to the world, how her 'interests and wants' push her father out of a particular mindset and to move differently through space, time and relationality and the way wonder permeates her encounters. Pedagogically, this process of changing surroundings, of allowing time to discover and encounter, of recognizing differences in what might draw one's attention, of noticing and turning toward those moments of the unfamiliar are important to a becoming phenomenological attitude. For Patrick this process was provoked by the requirements of his schooling, the realities of his daughter, and, we suggest, the living and changing environment surrounding him.

A second exercise that Patrick was asked to engage with was to actively reflect on a series of capacities that the designers of the graduate diploma felt were important to a nature-based and experiential learning pedagogy. In his reflection on the capacity 'to thrive amidst the opportunities and challenges brought about by the current ecological crisis and its implications for a changing educational context,' Patrick notes:

This may seem like a stretch for this topic, but as I read through the program capacities I was drawn to the word thrive. I would like to thrive as an individual. I believe that as long as I am thriving and overflowing that my students, family, and community at large will benefit. I think that part of me thriving must include knowing how to hold myself so as to learn what can be taught by the world around me. To be attached to the natural world in a way that, if it is harmed, then so am I. My ability to thrive is tied to that of the people around me and the environment that holds us. If any part of this chain is broken, then no individual can succeed and thrive. This is an attitude and a posture. I hope that I can learn to be slow at times, take in what is around me, and learn to learn from my surroundings. I think that would go a long way to fostering the students in my care.

Patrick uses a metaphor of attitude and posture without being directed. We suggest that the deliberate educational activity — paying attention to the natural world, thinking about it differently (as co-teacher in this case), and returning again and again to the same place, for example, might assist in the project of developing one's phenomenological attitude. To paraphrase Thoreau (1908) it is in the encounter of the other, wildness, that one sees oneself and one's possibilities.

Intriguingly Patrick lands on several of the important existentials van Manen (2014) identifies in his discussion about how to assist research subjects to reflect on their lived experiences. Van Manen names five, acknowledging that there are many more: 'the existentials of lived relation (relationality), lived body (corporeality), lived space (spatiality), lived time (temporality), and lived things and technology (materiality)' (p. 303). For van Manen, the phenomenological researcher can ask questions with respect to these existentials, which can then draw forward a richer more complex picture of the lived experience of the person being interviewed. We highlight through this chapter what we believe is an ethical need to provide students with opportunities to develop a phenomenological attitude by reconsidering one's relationality within a more-than-human world. As van Manen (2014) suggests of relationality:

> The existential theme of relationality may guide our reflection to ask how self and others are experienced with respect to the phenomenon that is being studied. To explore relational aspects of a phenomenon is to ask: How are people or things connected? What meaning of community? What ethics of being together?
>
> (p. 304)

Facilitating a phenomenological attitude

One path for facilitating a phenomenological attitude with students is to focus on the application of methods. We highlight this because, at least in part, it is through our own everyday practices and methods that we can affirm a phenomenological perspective. As Merleau-Ponty (1962) writes:

> We will find the unity of phenomenology and its true sense [sens] in ourselves. It is less a question of counting up citations than of determining and expressing this phenomenology for us, which has caused – upon their reading of Husserl or Heidegger – many of our contemporaries to have had the feeling much less of encountering a new philosophy than of recognizing what they had been waiting for. Phenomenology is only accessible to a phenomenological method.
>
> (p. xxi)

Phenomenological researchers are provided insights into the lived experience of others. Yet we can also be struck by a second chord of the research process: the gift provided to us by exercising a phenomenological attitude. Such a gift can include an affirmation of the primacy of lived experience, meeting the world with openness and a sense of being already always within the world. Is it, then, possible to gain such gifts without a prior philosophical understanding? Van Manen (2014) warns against being seduced by a potentially incomplete introduction to, or application of phenomenology (p. 19), but also alludes to a potential stepping-stone that might guide others toward a phenomenological orientation through the appreciation of a phenomenological attitude. One that we believe might be applied to pedagogical approaches with students. Van Manen is clear:

> Perhaps, a new direction needs to be sought: an agogical approach to phenomenology, as Spiegelberg urged. The term agogic derives from Greek, γωγός, meaning leading or guiding. It is the root word of pedagogy and andragogy – agogy means pointing out directions, providing support. Agogical phenomenology aims to provide access to phenomenological thinking and research in a manner that shows, in a reflexive mode, what the phenomenological attitude looks like.
>
> (p. 19)

In this way, it is through the very doing of phenomenological methods that a phenomenological attitude might become available. Thus, we are advocating for a *phenomenology as pedagogy* approach by keeping at the forefront of our thinking and doing the notion of student-as-phenomenologist. We propose to use this final section to investigate some aids that might facilitate the development of the phenomenological attitude with students and to ponder, briefly, what a pedagogy of lifeworlds might look like if we took such an idea seriously.

Aids for teaching toward a phenomenological attitude

For the most part, students are in a good position to begin to identify, write into, and reflect upon their lifeworlds, and those of their peers. They have an ability to locate wonder in the everyday, expanding their own range of possibilities for who they might become, and for recognizing their lives as a creative project in which they play an important role. The phenomenologist Patočka (1998) suggests that phenomenology should 'bring out the originary personal experience. The experience of the way we live situationally, the way we are personal beings in space' (p. 97, as cited in van Manen 2014, p. 15). This, then, is an important component of the educational project. For Patočka, originary experiences are those that occurred before reflection, cultural systems, and abstract interpretation took over. They are, if noticed, windows into the lifeworld of the individual; unique encounters with oneself and others (including other-than-human). Although Patočka is describing here the importance of this practice for the educational researcher, we think it might also be extended toward students. A phenomenological attitude has the potential to become one of a series of lenses that a student can adopt in order to better understand who and how they are in the world thereby expanding the range of possibilities with regard to who they might become.

Furthermore, van Manen (2014) suggests that phenomenological practice requires a reflective process. This involves 'attempting to recover and express the ways we experience our life as we live it – and ultimately to be able to act practically in our lives with greater thoughtfulness and tact' (p. 20). This is an important goal for all students, especially given that *tact* is understood to be a pathic understanding of the sort that is situated, relational, embodied and enacted in conjunction with forms of non-cognitive learning and knowing. Thus, if phenomenology is the study and theory of lived experiences and learners are having lived experiences, then why not offer them the tools to study it and, better yet, encounter the research results of their peers as well? How might this look in schools and other educational settings?

We recognize there are a multitude of possibilities for teachers in terms of developing a phenomenological attitude in students, and many teachers will already employ some of these. Given the critical nature of this task, though, we believe there is value in explicitly discussing pedagogical approaches available and we briefly offer some possible aids and provocations in the following sections.

A) Prioritizing aesthetic components of experience

Quay (2013) asserts the crucial importance of pre-reflective aesthetic experience in providing educational opportunities for building ways-of-being in the world, by highlighting that any reflective experience has foundational components of aesthetic experience. In other words, when we reflectively position ourselves in relation to others (in a more-than-human world) we are, at least to some degree, reliant on aesthetic components of experience. Kohak (1992), as well, asserts the importance of pre-reflectively *perceiving* worth within the world, through lived experience, rather than simply post-reflectively *conceiving* of worth – because ultimately the latter is not possible without the former being implicated: 'I am persuaded that the ability to formulate an adequate and efficacious *conception* of value is contingent on a prior, prereflective *perception* of value' (p. 173). Considered in this way, facilitating opportunities for aesthetic experience and representing ways of coming to know the world become pedagogically and ethically important.

For Patrick, as he explored the local forest with his daughter, there is a deep sense of this being a sensorial, immersive and full-bodied experience. Even as readers we are engaged physically – memories of our own times spent outdoors with and without children are triggered. We feel a breeze, see the trees and glades, encounter a frisson of sadness at the stressed trees. According to educational theorist, Egan (1997), this gathering of thinking, feeling, and perceiving is educationally significant. Thoughtfully gathering all three into one's pedagogical approach with children can make the learning more memorable and expand one's imaginative capacity (Egan 1997). For us, thinking about how any lesson might provide the combination of all three provokes opportunities for prioritizing meaningful aesthetic experiences, and provides important grist for phenomenological work.

B) Applying the reduction: returning to lived experience

As Hay (2003) suggests, 'the point of phenomenology, after all, is to suspend theory so that Being can be met, unmediated' (p. 247). One way that phenomenology does this, in its search for the return to the lived experience, is through *reduction*. Phenomenologically, reduction does not mean to make smaller; rather it is derived from *re-ducere*, meaning to 'lead back to' (van Manen 2014, pp. 215–235). Phenomenological reduction, then, means attempting to return to, or connect with, lived meaningful experience. As van Manen (2014) suggests:

> the reduction is not a technical procedure, rule, tactic, strategy, or a determinate set of steps that we should apply to the phenomenon that is being researched. Rather, the reduction is an attentive turning to the world when in an open state of mind.
>
> (p. 218)

How, then, might this look for the educator seeking to support the development of the phenomenological attitude with their students? Applying the reduction could, for example, begin by actively encouraging openness; noting and recognizing when moments of openness occur, building a classroom community that allows for the kind of vulnerability which allows students to listen more carefully to themselves and others. Reminding students to slow the quick move toward reflective interpretation and to attempt to stay with the lived encounter. This might also involve creating and allowing for the kinds of situations where learners encounter diverse and different ways of being and acting. But also giving students the opportunity to interrogate their individual experiences and try doing it beyond the limits of their implicit and explicit categories, metaphors and language. In other words, at times, by deliberately naming personal and cultural preconceptions of experience, students might be encouraged to re-examine their own, and others', original lived experience. And, finally, for Patrick, as he walks with his daughter, giving students the opportunity and the time to increase their attentiveness through careful study and close observation. One might think of this as developing the observational skills of a field biologist, artist or naturalist.

C) Asking phenomenological questions

Learning how to ask good phenomenological questions is an important part of phenomenological research (van Manen 2014, p. 297). Such a practice can also be a part of one's pedagogy both as a questioner, to encourage students to think more deeply into their originary experience, and as a teacher of students learning to ask phenomenological questions, so that the skill is transferred. Pedagogically, an example is to create situations where students do projects that are phenomenological in nature and include questions as key points of departure. For example, a lesson outdoors might involve questions: 'what is the experience of walking through the forest with others'; 'what is the experience of leaving the indoors behind'; or even 'what is it like to be a part of the community where these birds live?' This would give students the chance to do a kind of phenomenological research through a questioning of the world 'that comprise an element of wonder: discovering the extraordinary in the ordinary, the strange in the taken for granted . . . asks what is given in the immediate experience . . . asks what a possible human experience is like' (van Manen 2014, p. 15)? It might also allow the teacher to help the learner to see when their questions are pushing the subject into interpretations that are layered with cultural, communal and systemic norms (and then focus on bracketing those things out in search of pre-reflective experience). As such, there is a layer of criticality being explored as students encounter their own implicit beliefs and habits. This also offers a further opportunity to hear from and to be heard by others, building relationships and, one hopes, an empathetic attitude.

D) Engaging with phenomenological literature

Another important possibility here might be exposing students to a wide range of literature, but with a particular focus on those forms and writings that focus expressly on lived experiences. In Canada, for example, it would be wonderful to have students reading some of the outstanding nature poets (e.g. Jan Zwicky, Don McKay, and Dennis Lee). Within this form of writing are attempts to communicate through metaphor and image non-cognitive and immersive relationships with the natural world while at the same time engaging in a reflexive process that queries their chosen language and cultural realities of alienation. These are writers wrestling directly with the sense that they are always and already in the world and that much of the standard English prose assumes the opposite. What we want to note here is that this work would not just be about aiding the development of the phenomenological attitude but, more importantly, about bringing an orientation to the world that sees us as being part of, rather than detached from, the world. A pedagogy that places importance upon the lifeworlds of our students, our communities and ourselves.

Depending on the age and receptivity of students, they might also be encouraged to read both foundational phenomenological literature and/or a range of examples of produced by research. This process then can challenge them to explore their own writing, form and content, explicitly and carefully. This latter point is of some importance to phenomenological readers as they see the work of writing phenomenologically as being very challenging and requiring a great deal of care and effort. In the context of teaching writing and reading as an aid to the phenomenological attitude there are quite a few opportunities made available to the teacher. Having students offer full write-ups of their own research work, challenging them to write in myriad voices, and working with them to develop their own skills as readers, writers and phenomenological interpreters.

E) *Non-linguistic methods*

How might we attempt a return to a lived moment with students, while limiting cognitive reflection that often primarily use words and pre-formed cultural constructs to describe what, for many people, are complex, mysterious and/or ineffable experiences? How might we apply careful interrogative reflection to the descriptions of experience? We suggest here exploring creative methods that de-privilege cognition and attempt to re-present aesthetic and embodied components of experience in ways other than through language. Such approaches can include artistic, imaginative and creative representations of lived experience. In a recent study (Morse and Morse 2019), involving students on five-day outdoor journey on a river in Australia, participants' lived experiences were explored via creative methods such as painting and printmaking. This use of creative artefacts (combined with interviews) from which to build phenomenological descriptions brought to the fore a sense of students themselves developing a phenomenological attitude through practice.

The practice of *en plein air* painting, for example, an outdoor form of painting involving looking at and sensing the subject directly and used on the river journey, demands a particular form of attentiveness, attitude and even deliberate posture. Such an attentiveness can reawaken a noticing of that which might under many circumstances be taken for granted. As one artist/teacher on the journey suggested, 'paint what you can see, not what you think you can see.' These guiding words provided a moment of pause and provocation to look anew at the riverscape and see the vibrant colous and textures of the riparian vegetation and feel the relentless movement of the river. Not only did students comment on a feeling of returning to being in the river while they painted, but there appeared a sense of careful interrogative reflection. As Noë (2000) argues; [art] 'can teach us about perceptual consciousness by furnishing us with the opportunity to have a special kind of reflective experience. In this way, art can be a tool for phenomenological investigation' (p. 124). While it is never possible to fully return to the lived experience – art can offer possibilities for non-linguistic intensifications of experience as a form of reflection:

The everyday notion of representation could mean 'to depict,' or 'to present again' (re-present), but Jean-Luc Nancy asserts that the 're- of the word representation is not repetitive but intensive . . . mental or intellectual re presentation is not foremost a copy of the thing,' but an intensified presentation. It is 'a presence that is presented' (Nancy 2007, p. 36). The re- in represent is, in other words, an amplification; to represent is to present more of what is.

(Stern 2018, pp. 18–19)

Concluding thoughts

We have highlighted through this chapter a pedagogical impetus and suggested aids that might enable students to deliberately acknowledge, experience and develop a phenomenological attitude. For van Manen (1982):

> the phenomenological attitude towards the concerns of our daily occupation as teacher-researchers compels us to constantly raise the question: what is it like to be an educator? What is it like to be teacher as pedagogue? And in order to ask the questions what it is that makes it possible to thinking and talk about pedagogy in the first place, we ask, what is it about that form of life (being an educator) which makes a pedagogic existence different from other pursuits?
>
> (p. 297)

By extending this to students the pool of questions shifts and expands: what is it like to be a student? What is like to be a child growing into adulthood? What is like to be me? What is like to be my peer who is sharing with the class right now? What is it like to be part of a larger community? Our sense is that these questions can then lead to further interpretive work as the learner recognizes their own implicitly accepted limits and comes into contact with the possibilities of fellow students. This then expands their range of possibilities with regard to how they can be in the world.

We also highlight what we believe is an ethical responsibility, to both our students and the world of which they are a part; to bring to bear a renewed acknowledgment of relationality within the world. This is critical for where we are in the world right now. The rapidly accelerating environmental and social crises urgently demands a response from us all – and educationally this must include opportunities for being differently with oneself and in the world. It is our assertion that the phenomenological attitude can provoke a creative flexibility toward an individual's way of being in the world. There is, we suggest, a necessary humility that comes from understanding that we cannot know everything about something by breaking it down into objective parts. We suggest also that there is a kind of creative engagement that comes with developing a thoughtful awareness that actively notes and responds to moments of wonder – an engagement that challenges the individual to look further for possible responses, to not be restricted to the cultural *status quo*, and to step outside, if possible, positivistic norms of the systems in which they are immersed. And finally, that there is commitment to co-construction and relationship that is deepened as one encounters others in rich and tactful ways and sees the value of their ideas and ways of being. We believe these *skills* are in fact necessary if the coming generations are going to have any chance to respond to the damages wrought by their predecessors. So maybe the phenomenological attitude, developed through deliberate practices, becomes more than just a lens among many but becomes a necessary posture for survival.

References

Abram, D., 1996. *The spell of the sensuous: Perception and language in a more-than-human world*. New York: Vintage Books.
Blenkinsop, S. and Beeman, C., 2010. The world as co-teacher: Learning to work with a peerless colleague. *Trumpeter*, 26 (3), 26–39.
Egan, K., 1997. *The educated mind*. Chicago, IL: University of Chicago Press. doi:10.7208/chicago/9780226190402.001.0001
Haraway, D., 2016. *Staying with the trouble: Making kin in the Chthulucene*. Durham: Duke University Press. doi:10.1215/9780822373780
Hay, P.R., 2003. Writing place: Unpacking an exhibition catalogue essay. *In*: J. Cameron, ed. *Changing places: Reimagining Australia*. Double Bay: Longueville Books, 272–285.
Heidegger, M., 1962. *Being and time*. New York: Harper.
Husserl, E., 1931. *Ideas: General introduction to pure phenomenology*. London: George Allen and Unwin.
Husserl, E., 1936/1970. *The crisis of European sciences and transcendental phenomenology: An introduction to phenomenological philosophy*. Evanston, IL: Northwestern University Press.
Intergovernmental Panel on Climate Change, 2014. *Climate change 2014: Synthesis report. Contribution of working groups I, II and III to the fifth assessment report of the intergovernmental panel on climate change*. Geneva: IPCC. Available from: www.ipcc.ch/report/ar5/syr/ [Accessed 23 Mar 2019].
Intergovernmental Panel on Climate Change, 2018. *Global warming of 1.5°C, an IPCC special report on the impacts of global warming of 1.5°C above pre-industrial levels and related global greenhouse gas emission pathways, in the context of strengthening the global response to the threat of climate change, Sustainable development, and efforts to eradicate poverty*. Geneva: IPCC. Available from: www.ipcc.ch/sr15/ [Accessed 23 Mar 2019].
Jickling, B., Blenkinsop, S., Timmerman, N., and Sitka-Sage, M., 2018. *Wild pedagogies: Touchstones for re-negotiating education and the environment in the Anthropocene*. London, UK: Palgrave Macmillan. doi:10.1007/978-3-319-90176-3
Kohak, E.V., 1992. Perceiving the good. *In*: M. Oelschlaeger, ed. *The wilderness condition*. San Francisco: Sierra Club Books, 173–187.
Langeveld, M., 1983. Reflections on phenomenology and pedagogy. *Phenomenology + Pedagogy*, 1 (1), 3–5. doi:10.29173/pandp14870
Livingston, J., 2007. *The John Livingston reader*. Toronto: McClelland & Stewart Publishing.

Merleau-Ponty, M., 1962. *Phenomenology of perception*. London: Routledge and K. Paul. doi:10.4324/9780203981139

Morse, M. and Morse, P., 2019. Representing experience: Creative methods and emergent analysis. *In*: B. Humberstone and H. Prince, eds. *Research methods in outdoor studies*. New York: Routledge, 229–242. doi:10.4324/9780429199004-22

Moustakas, C.E., 1994. *Phenomenological research methods*. Thousand Oaks: Sage Publications. doi:10.4135/9781412995658

Naess, A., 2002. *Life's philosophy: Reason and feeling in a deeper world*. Athens: University of Georgia Press.

Nancy, J., 2007. *The ground of the image*. New York: Fordham University Press. doi:10.2307/j.ctt13x06f6

Noë, A., 2000. Experience and experiment in art. *Journal of Consciousness Studies*, 7 (8–9), 123–136.

Patočka, J., 1998. *Body, community, language, world*. Translated by E. Kohák. Chicago, IL: Open Court.

Plumwood, V., 1997. *Feminism and the mastery of nature*. New York: Routledge Press. doi:10.4324/9780203006757

Quay, J., 2013. More than relations between self, others and nature: Outdoor education and aesthetic experience. *Journal of Adventure Education and Outdoor Learning*, 13 (2), 142–157. doi:10.1080/14729679.2012.746846

Saevi, Tone., 2011. Lived relationality as the fulcrum of pedagogical-ethical practice. *Studies in Philosophy and Education*, 30 (5), 455–461. doi:10.1007/s11217-011-9244-9

Spiegelberg, H., 1960. *The phenomenological movement: A historical introduction*. The Hague: Martinus Nijhoff. doi:10.1007/978-94-017-5920-5

Stern, N., 2018. *Ecological aesthetic: Artful tactics for humans, nature and politics*. Hanover: Dartmouth College Press.

Thoreau, H., 1908. *Walden, or, Life in the woods*. London: J.M. Dent.

van Manen, M., 1982. Phenomenological pedagogy. *Curriculum Inquiry*, 12 (3), 283–299. doi:10.2307/1179525

van Manen, M., 1997. *Researching lived experience: Human science for an action sensitive pedagogy*. 2nd ed. London: Althouse Press. doi:10.4324/9781315421056

van Manen, M., 2014. *Phenomenology of practice: Meaning-giving methods in phenomenological research and writing*. New York: Left Coast Press. doi:10.4324/9781315422657

van Manen, M., 2017. Phenomenology and meaning attribution. *Indo-Pacific Journal of Phenomenology*, 17 (1), 1–15. doi:10.1080/20797222.2017.1368253

Part 4

To have been educated

Patrick Howard

It is one thing to be actively involved in education – as a teacher, a parent, or a student – but yet quite another to ponder on the traces education leaves behind in the lives of those involved. In the final part of the book, we ask what education should 'do' to people, less so in terms of being in an educational relationship, but more in relation to the longer term 'impact' (which is actually a far too strong and too mechanistic term for what we have in mind). What is the experience of having been educated? How do we understand education as it is currently conceived and organized and its role in forming the next generation? What does it do to the self and with the self? How do we come into being while being with others? Where does education constrain and limit and how and when does that become visible? What do we carry with us from our education throughout our lives? How does what we carry forward influence our lives and the world in which we live? These are big educational questions and like all questions related to authentic human interaction, they are necessarily challenging, yet somehow, inherently hopeful.

In his chapter "Deceptively Difficult Education: A Case for a Lifetime of Impact," Alan Bainbridge excavates layers of cultural and historical sedimentation to reveal educational processes evident today that have evolved over a long sweep of time and space. Neoliberal assumptions about education have become normalized in just a few short decades and, according to Bainbridge, these assumptions represent ancient human preoccupations with control and imposing meaning and predictability on a contingent and anxiety-producing reality. By drawing on psychoanalytic theory and deep ecology Bainbridge traces the educational impulse as instrumental to the constant cycle of world-building as an existential human desire to act on and change the world around us. For humans, to educate or to bring up the next generation to adapt to this world grows ever more complex. We need only to look to the current discourse of twenty-first-century teaching and learning to see, as Bainbridge argues, the paradoxical conundrum that preparing the next generation to supposedly flourish, from a neoliberal perspective, hastens and "is complicit" in increasing the uncoupling of human beings from the conditions of life on which we wholly depend. Bainbridge takes issue with the "fantasy that education will save us" as a premise that is untenable while education is in the service of fulfilling the relentless desire for continual self-improvement and the lack that drives ever increasing complexity and ambitious world-building.

Bainbridge challenges his readers to ask, "What impact do we want from education?" The education he proposes is antithetical to the controlling, technical rationalism and hegemonic economic imperative of a neoliberal educational perspective. Uncovering through dialogue and a close attention to language and individual human experience as they are revealed through the complex relationships in community can assist us to re-discover for *what* do we want to educate, and thereby re-imagine what we mean when we say to "have been educated."

Dylan van der Shyff joins the excavation undertaken by Bainbridge and opens new seams by placing current neoliberal educational processes in the arc of modernity and postmodernity. In his chapter "Focal Practices and the Ontologically Educated Citizen," van der Shyff argues that a phenomenological orientation provides a way in which dominant and deeply held assumptions, what Giroux has called a neoliberal common sense, may be bracketed making the familiar unfamiliar. In doing so, space is made to explore other ways to understand our current reality. Van der Shyff, like Bainbridge, also takes up the concept of humans as world-makers, yet how the world-making is enframed determines what the world will be. Van der Shyff believes that phenomenology and conscientization in the Freirean tradition of critical pedagogy enacted through art-based and creative praxis serve as powerful educational responses to challenge the increasingly normalized understandings of how we educate into the twenty-first century. The stultifying effects of decades of neoliberal approaches and constraining education to economic concerns linked to job preparation supported by the control mechanisms of standardization and testing eradicates imagination and cabins human potential. Creative praxis and focal practices as described by van der Shyff open opportunities for humans to explore the myriad possibilities for how we can "be" in this world. The quantification, commodification, and standardization of the educational experiences of the young can be resisted through educational models concerned with creative practice and the creative world-making that has the potential to ontologically shift education by representing new stories and providing a language to recognize how we may live and flourish outside *the neoliberal common sense*.

In "Education as Pro-duction and E-duction," Stein M. Wivestad pays close attention to language to further connect us with the former life of words that have lost much of their original meaning over time. Neoliberalism's juggernaut is the unrelenting logic of globalization that has seeped deep into cultural consciousness as it disappears into a current reality defined by the unquestioned "good" of commodifying virtually everything and the myth of the primacy of the self-maximizing individual. Wivestad works to re-animate the lived meaning of what it means to educate. He methodically opens up the concept of e-duction, a word that has fallen away over time, and connects e-duction with the lived experience of upbringing as *paideia* – an ancient concept related to rearing and Bildung – to what is good not only for humans, but generally good for all. He contrasts this understanding of e-duction with education as pro-duction, especially in the form of intergenerational world-making that, according to Wivestad, is doomed to fail.

By putting the reader in touch with original meanings and usages largely lost to time the author is calling forth another way of being, and of understanding what it may mean to educate that is very different from current practice. The challenge to the hegemony of neoliberal regimes of control and conformity will come through language and the ability to imagine another way of being. The objectifying language of neoliberalism reflects the lived experience of despair as education is stripped of its connection to the vitality and dynamism of human possibility. By putting the reader in touch with the ethos and lived experience of another way to think about and *live* the education of the young, Wivestad makes an important contribution to awakening our capacity to understand what it means to be educated comes out of a deep, rich, and vital tradition with which the moribund neoliberal view of education has little in common.

In the final chapter Patrick Howard employs phenomenological methods to inquire into the experience of "having been educated." In "Between Having and Being: A Phenomenological Reflection on Education," he illuminates the differences apparent in *having* an education as opposed to *being* educated. As is recognized by previous authors, Howard pays close attention to everyday language through which the unreflective, natural attitude is communicated and to a method by which the familiar can be made unfamiliar. Phenomenology can make an important contribution to challenging what Henri Giroux calls neoliberalism's most powerful weapon – "its claim that its worldview is self-evident and that any analysis is irrelevant" (Giroux 2019, p. 28). In this chapter the phenomenological methods of lived experience description, paying close attention to language and idiom, narrative and literature Howard, like van der Shyff, demonstrates how the everyday, concrete, lived experience can serve to enliven dialogue and contribute to a renewed language that is felt as it stands in contrast to an abstract, objectifying language that deflects from scrutiny that which is represented as normalized and beyond serious inquiry. Howard shows that education is a transformational, existential undertaking not acknowledged in current educational discourses that sweep away any sense of education as being and becoming. The objectification of education as something one *has* reflects the present day neoliberal preoccupation with quantifying and com-modifying educational experiences characterized by the pulverizing of learning into innumerable outcomes and the primacy of repressive standardization and accountability regimes. Being educated and the language that describes it rec-ognizes the unique lives of people with a pedagogical sensitivity that connects us in a shared experience toward understanding and growth, while presenting very different stories of what it means to have been educated.

Reference

Giroux, H., 2019. Neoliberalism and the weaponising of language and education. *Race & Class*, 61 (1), 26–45.

Chapter 16

Deceptively difficult education
A case for a lifetime of impact

Alan Bainbridge

Introduction

The suggestion that education might not follow empirical rules of cause and effect is not a stance welcomed in a world where measurable educational outcomes are publicly reported in local, national and global competitive league tables. In England, at least, this process now starts with 'baseline' assessments of four to five-year-old children in Reception classes, continuing into higher education when the 'destination of leavers' metric is used to report on 'teaching quality' measured by employment type and salary. The view of education offered here rejects this approach, along with other similar neoliberal technologies as acts of anti-educational violence (Bainbridge *et al.* 2018). I seek to expose this sham by casting an imaginative hypothetical net far and wide, across space and time, to catch a glimpse of educational processes encountered from our human ancestral past up to the present. This archeological exploration of the human mind (Lent 2017) offers novel ways of imagining why humans engage in education and what outcomes might emerge from considering an expansive ecology of human experience.

In particular, I draw on the work of Stephen Frosh (1991/2016, 2018) and his syntactic and semantic analysis of human behaviour. Frosh is critical of mainstream psychology for being overly concerned with establishing the syntax of human behaviour through the establishment of general rules and principles. This, he contrasts with psychoanalytic principles that seek to identify how individual meaning can be constructed and personal agency understood. In the context of this publication, Frosh's stance and critical lens also allows us to position neoliberal assumptions and mechanisms within the realm of syntactic thinking while highlighting the obsession to value rules and principles beyond what the individual may be experiencing and how they make meaning of their lives. Equally, this is reflected in the dominant contemporary view that education can be understood, managed and measured, while neglecting the possibility of a more unpredictable and yet more meaningful semantic educational experiences.

I shall consider the aspects of disruption and desire as central to ancestral and current human experience, a discussion of how this might be experienced will offer provocative and insightful possibilities as to why and how humans engage with education and what its outcomes might be. Of particular interest is Capra's (1996) holistic 'deep' ecological view that builds on Maturana and Varela's (1987) theory of structural coupling integrating aspects of physical, biological, social and political systems. From this deep ecological perspective the experience of being alive is to be at all times connected and yet in continual flux.

For non-human animals this can be conceived as a learned adaptive response, where changes in one part of the system require an individual behavioural or genetic response ensuring continued adjustments to maintain structurally coupled equilibrium and hence survival. These subtle adaptive 'couplings' not only maintain individual survival but also the integrity of the ecological system. I have previously proposed (Bainbridge 2019) that the impulse to educate has its genealogy in an ancestral experiential shift, probably driven by ecological change of sufficient magnitude, permanently disrupting the complex but synergistic structural coupling between the human and what Abram (1997) refers to as the more-than-human world. Within this context acts of education represent an interactive process of human physical, psychological, social and political world building motivated by the existential desire to 'return to' ecological equilibrium and hence a meaningful structurally coupled experience. Additionally, such human world building activity will be considered from Berger and Luckmann's (1966) social construction concept of closed and open worlds. In closed worlds all aspects are harmoniously coupled (adapted) in a relatively stable ecological system. This contrasts with un-coupled open worlds that to support human flourishing require constant construction.

The second section focuses on the role of language within the experience of education. Central to this discussion is an understanding that the origin of the motivation for language is the same as it is for education. Mollenhauer (2013) admits to not being sure what this impulse might be while also noting that there is something about being human that irresistibly and unmistakably draws towards 'upbringing' and an encounter with a novice who possesses 'self-activity'. Drawing on a consideration of a distant ancestral past will always be hypothetical, but Howard-Jones (2014) combines neurology and evolutionary biology to suggest that language involving symbols can be assumed to have emerged at a similar time as early humans stood upright, became hands-free, started to fashion tools and leave artworks on cave walls. Capra (1996) draws to our attention that human infants are distinctive in their immaturity at birth. Not being born 'ready' and the development of a disposition to craft tools and use art, support the suggestion that humans experience an 'open' world waiting to be acted on and fashioned towards the possibility of a 'closed' structurally coupled existence.

It is possible that the serendipitous ecological changes favouring upright tool making artistic humans, alongside the birth of very immature infants provided the selective pressures for prolonged nurturing and language development (Laland 2017). It is my supposition (Bainbridge 2019) that the ancestral 'ghosts' resulting from a disruption of synchronized and intimate structural coupling with the external world evokes feelings of existential loss. The response to which has been the language driven human proclivity towards world making. Consequently, that which brings us to language, shall also bring us to education and the desire to continue to act on and change the world we live.

It should be noted that language is semantic and distinguished from syntactic linguistics and shown to be central to supporting education through the communication of individual meaning. Additionally, it is argued that Maturana and Varela's (1987) conception of languaging, or communication about communication – supports the development of abstract concepts and semantic meaning making. In recognition of this, Searle's Chinese Room thought experiment is discussed to highlight the importance of distinguishing between syntactic and semantic communication. It is noted that an unintended consequence of an ancient desire towards meaning-making provides the human motivation to repair a lost ecological relationship, ultimately leading to an unforeseen increased negative impact on the more-than-human world. Education will be shown to be complicit in this act as it struggles to contain feelings of loss alongside being overwhelmed by an ever-increasing complexity of human manufactured knowledge and skills.

The final section acknowledges what it means to have been educated by considering the role education has played in the construction of an increasingly abstract, sufficiently complicated and often destructive world that it may become too difficult to think about. The thesis presented in this chapter suggests that education has its origins in an ancestral past as a response to the lived experience of 'structural un-coupling' and a disruptive shift from closed world to open world experience. Paradoxically, the long-term evolutionary outcome of education has led to further uncoupling (Bainbridge, 2019) and increasingly complex social, cultural and knowledge systems. The human desire to re-connect, or re-couple with deep ecological systems, provides the motive for the accumulation and transfer of knowledge and skills through generations, world building and the development of cooperative social systems. Mollenhauer (2013) would recognize this in the educational dilemma of what should be re-presented and to who, which to some extent in recent times the hegemonic influence of neoliberal thinking has attempted to solve.

Bainbridge et al. (2018) argue that the artifacts of neoliberal accountancy thinking have arisen as a cultural response to education and social systems of such complexity that they are too difficult to think about. Indeed, the complexity of what knowledge should be re-presented, to which individuals, at what age, through what type of education system, offers so much confusion that simplistic syntactic neoliberal accountancy technologies representing Klein's (1931/1985) split thinking have come to dominate education policy. Additionally, Frosh (2018) suggests, from a neoliberal perspective, principles of interconnectedness and interdependency are perceived as weak and therefore attacked and rejected. The language and practices of neoliberalism in education have been explored by Bainbridge et al. (2018) exposing the inherent violence, for example in the language of league tables, good/bad schools, excellence and school improvement. Using such language immediately closes down thinking about educational purpose only to be replaced by competition, winners, losers and a commodified education that can now be bought, sold and ultimately fetishized.

Consequently, this can lead to simplistic good/bad binaries supported by defensive unconscious processes, such as the 'splitting' of thinking where syntactic rules and processes are promoted ahead of the need for meaning and semantics. The work of Frosh (1991/2016, 2018) calls for a return to psychoanalytically informed principles of interpersonal (educational) dialogue of 'giving and receiving' where individual meaning and authentic life choices can be explored with an 'other'. Such dialogue will be shown to expose, and ultimately alleviate, the violence of a neoliberal induced Freudian and Marxian fetish on the process of education. Finally, the deceptively difficult educational question – 'Why did a particular Jill learn or not learn'? – can be answered.

Disruption and desire

The human mind leaves no fossil record and the following can only be hypothetical conjecture but if the discussion helps us to re-position and re-imagine education in times of technicist stultification, it may also lead to a more empowering and democratic educational mindset. The fundamental suggestion is that very early human experience has been disrupted and humans no longer experience structurally coupled equilibrium. The outcome of 'de-coupling', of not being in harmony in an ecological system for early humans is likely to have been experienced as a threat to survival, where the human niche, previously part of a complex inter-connected ecological system, no longer supported human flourishing. Such disruption represents a shift from relatively supportive and stable relationships to an open world system that requires continual reconstruction (Berger and Luckmann 1966) to provide the conditions for human flourishing. Therefore driving the need to act more directly on an open and unpredictable world, leading not only to the motive to manage and control the external environment (Odling-Smee *et al.* 2003) but also a search for meaning (equilibrium).

Ancestral acts of education can be positioned in the compulsion to manage the complex ecological open world in an attempt to control biological, physical, social and even political aspects. Yet, paradoxically, acting on an open world to re-engage with a closed world experience of synchronized coupling, has only led to humans becoming less aware of harmonious and meaningful ways of being. Humans therefore are confronted and disrupted by the more-than-human world, themselves, disrupting it and in return are continually increasing the gap between the experience of ecological equilibrium and existential threat (Flynn *et al.* 2013). Consequently, the human constructed world is now of such complexity as to be compelled, one generation to the next, to accumulate and transfer knowledge in what Mollenhauer (2013) refers to as 'upbringing'.

Current cultural expectations are for children and all novices to be deliberately interrupted by more experienced others re-presenting what is generally agreed to be the important knowledge and skills required for successful living. In England, this can be experienced in the compulsion to start formal schooling in the *academic year* a child is five years old (some children will only just be four) and learning complex grammar at the expense of creative subjects. While in higher education the need to make links between academic subjects and employability increasingly impacts the curriculum. Few other animals make such a commitment to designing the process and content of formal education settings and significantly very few other animals invest such time and resources into elaborate teaching activities (Fogarty *et al.* 2011).

It is my contention (Bainbridge 2019) that the considerable efforts to engage in education are an attempt to re-experience a more meaningful structurally coupled existence, however human world building behaviours only serve to further disrupt and interrupt. Throughout millennia the human motivation to manage and control what has become an ultimately unknowable open world has persistently confronted human flourishing; evidenced no more clearly than in the current climate change crisis, resource depletion, biodiversity collapse and mass migration of peoples from areas of war and extreme poverty. Lent (2017) argues that the continuation of destructive human ambition represents a root metaphor originating in ancestral experience. Whereas Frosh (1991/2016) would recognise such destructive behaviours emanating from the trauma of loss and mourning that have left archives of damaging behaviours throughout generations. I offer the possibility (Bainbridge 2019) that the feelings of loss reflect unconscious desires mourning the loss of an ancestral meaningful structural coupling with the more-than-human world. It should be noted that the urge to educate, to become involved in 'upbringing' (Mollenhauer 2013) is to some extent unconscious, for we cannot *not* continue to engage in knowledge accumulation and transfer to support continual world-building activities.

There is one final twist to consider before this section can be brought to a close and that is that Frosh recognizes the move to language – which for the infant and additionally in our context, the ancestral human being – is both helpful and harmful. Perhaps, there is an unconscious ancestral ghostly fantasy that education will save us – yet the damaging impact of some human activity indicates that something dark and harmful lurks in the shadows in the move to language and hence education. The following section will explore what it might mean to experience the impulse to move towards language, how language might be experienced as an education, and what the short- and long-term impact of language, and therefore education might be.

Experiencing language and education

What is it like to experience language/education? The curious question still to be addressed is how and why this evolutionary and existentially unsatisfactory long-term human behaviour pattern has persisted. It was Mollenhauer who noted that the motive to learn, to have self-activity, is the result of being interrupted by the expectations of others, confronting the learner with what they are not. A confrontation that occurs within a dialogical relationship where there is a call and response interchange reflecting very closely the dialogical conditions for what Maturana and Varela (1987) refer to as 'languaging', or communication about communication. They distinguish between communication that involves the linguistic interchange of symbols and a process of languaging that facilitates structural coupling by supporting abstract thinking (Capra 1996). Additionally, Frosh (1991/2016) argues that the role of language (Languaging for Maturana and Varela) in psychotherapy is to enable internal anxieties to be named and therefore dealt with in a shared external world. This is an educational moment, when the particularities of an individual embedded in a relational biography can be thought about dialogically, providing an opportunity for personal change.

In an attempt to understand human agency, Frosh (1989) asks a deceptively difficult question, 'Why did Jack hit Jill?' His analysis is that psychology is unable to answer such questions, based as it is to discover what conditions can be identified that might predict certain human behaviours. If psychology assumes that the mind and meaning are only features of cognitive systems, explanations will always be governed by syntactic rules and can never fully know, in Bainbridge and West's (2012) re-framing of the deceptively difficult question – 'Why Jill does or does not learn'. To answer such questions, Frosh argues, requires experiential insight and not just a suggestion of predictive conditions that may, or may not have brought about such action. He turns to Searle's Chinese Room thought experiment and the role of language to show that semantics are essential components of human mental functioning and as presented in this chapter – education.

Details of Searle's thought experiment are available elsewhere (Searle 1980), but as a summary, a closed room contains an English speaker who receives instructions to complete a task through one hole and is required to post their response out through another. In the first condition, questions written in Chinese are posted into the room, fortunately there is a codebook and the inhabitant is sufficiently skilled in its use and therefore is able to post the correct answers to the outside world. To Chinese speakers on the outside, the person in the room is assumed to understand not only Chinese but also the task – in fact they can do neither. The second condition is the same but this time English tasks are posted in and the correct answers are posted out. Now those on the outside correctly assume the inhabitant can understand the nature and meaning of their tasks. Frosh notes that in the first example syntactic rules within the codebook have been used to produce a correct answer but the situation is devoid of meaning. Whereas in the second example, as the language provides semantic meaning, the task is understood without the need to resort to a codebook.

Frosh uses this as a basis to understand how interventions such as psychotherapy may work, explaining that the 'talking cure' takes place in a dialogical relationship based on language infused with particular shared semantic meaning.

During the therapeutic encounter feelings previously unnamed are named, spoken and available for being thought about together. Likewise, Bainbridge and West (2012) suggest that the success or not of a meaningful education should not only be discussed in the context of syntactic rules, but to understand why Jill does or does not learn requires a consideration of a particular experiencing semantic Jill. Indeed, in the context of the Chinese Room, Jill may score highly in tests, complete homework on time and even understand how to use blends, digraphs and trigraphs. But, like the English-speaking successful Chinese decoder, even though Jill can complete the task – success is not an indication of making meaning and understanding. Jill's 'learning' is potentially hollow and without meaning. Equally, those schools occupying high positions in league tables are not necessarily those settings that provide a 'quality' education. It is unfortunate that current neoliberal accountancy measurements mirror the Chinese Room thought experiment by promoting syntactic anti-educational measures. This is not to suggest that all that happens in formal education settings is devoid of meaning and understanding, rather that simplistic syntactic assumptions are encouraged to thrive at the expense of an individual meaning making.

It is not yet clear how the use of language supports particular individual meaning making and how the deceptively difficult question – 'Why Jill did or did not learn?' – can be answered. To make this next step, I return to Capra (1996) and Maturana and Varela's (1987) conception of structural coupling and languaging. So far, it has been argued that the use of language in human mental functioning has been related to particular individual meaning making. In Capra's (1996) deep ecological understanding, multi-faceted systems become structurally coupled as a result of each constituent member being sensitive to and responding to continual flux, with most parts of the system achieving this via syntactic linguistic communication. One of the examples given by Capra is the dance performed by bees to direct other workers to a valuable nectar source; although regarded as communication, it is not language but instead linguistic, as information transfer is largely technical and syntactic. For example, 'Fly south by southwest for 120 metres' is a series of simple and limited instructions.

In contrast humans maintain coupling through a dialogical process of languaging, or communication about communication. Semantic patterns can emerge through languaging where external objects can become abstract concepts and inner worlds can be named and externalized. Maturana and Varela (1987) offered languaging as a medium for semantic patterns of meaning to be made available to others via thoughts represented as words, organized into statements that transmit meaning throughout the human aspect of a system. Using the earlier example, the hunt for a nectar source could now be re-imagined as – 'I was flying around this morning and my attention was drawn to a fantastic yellow flower with dark bits in the middle. Well, it's a bit wobbly and lots of other bees want to get inside but it is worth the effort. Go and see if you can find it. It's at the end of the hedge where the dog sleeps.' Similarly, education is not simply the presentation and insertion of knowledge or passing on of skills (Aldridge 2019).

The representation of internal and external objects using complex and abstract symbols of language has also been considered by Frosh (1991/2016) and although he does not use the term structural coupling, what can be recognized as similar is the intimate dynamic between mother and infant. Frosh describes a dialogical relationship of attuned giving and receiving where the infant's experience is bonded to words and phrases used by the (m)other. Hence, words infused with affect and meaning, passed down through generations, can now be appropriated by the infant in a primal act of education where the unknown is made known. As expected from Frosh's psychoanalytic stance, he goes one step further, arguing that the impulse towards language is rooted in the experience of anxiety. Further, Bainbridge and West (2012) would also acknowledge the role of anxiety in the impulse to education; not the debilitating anxiety that may consume and lead to mental ill health, instead an understanding of anxiety as an everyday feature of our lives, representing the playful and imaginative tensions of how an individual may wish to respond to psychological, social and cultural expectations.

My intention is to propose that disruption, either from an ancestral past or an experience in the present, results in a level of existential upheaval where the individual is confronted with questions about who they are in the world and how they should respond. Language has developed as a mechanism to manage these anxieties but what can also be learnt from Mollenhauer (2013) and Frosh (2018) is that what is not immediately available to awareness, which has therefore not been named and converted into language, can continue to influence experience. Therefore the unconscious, or unknown, contains unresolved hopes, fears and desires, all with the potential to subtly influence mental process and decision making. The following section will consider what the long-term impact of education might be and offer some initial insight into the particular human dilemma of living in an increasingly open world.

Impact of language/education

It is always dangerous to discuss ways of being human in an essentialist manner but irrespective of how the human/more-than-human relationship is conceived it is difficult to argue against the impact human activity now has on the planet. Some even go so far as to suggest that human activity has defined the current geological epoch labeling it as the Anthropocene. I offered an ecol-agogical hypothesis (Bainbridge 2019) that the continual process of human world making and the accumulation of educationally driven human knowledge has led, not to a re-connection with a lost ancestral niche, but instead to the paradoxical continued decreased awareness of a synchronized structurally coupled system. Nevertheless, the desire and motive to persist with educationally influenced world building continues. It is after all, what makes us human. Therefore, education will never be a finished project as it will never be able to build a closed world to satisfy an existential awareness of loss and mourning for an ancient structurally coupled experience.

The narrative presented so far may indicate that language and the impulse to educate have only led to anxiety ridden people living with the possibility of imminent world destruction. But this is unfair, language and education do offer us something more hopeful. It is after all the hope for a better world, a better personal experience that drives the desire to both engage in upbringing and self-activity (Mollenhauer 2013). Importantly, the human experience is not a solitary solipsistic war of attrition to survive one day at a time, for one of the early – for infants and our human ancestors – and longest lasting impacts of education is the shift from a subjective uniqueness to intersubjectivity in a shared world.

Mollenhauer recognizes this in the historical development from pre-modern to modern thinking and the move from having a world presented to novices, to one in which the more experienced need to make decisions about what should be presented to the novice. There are tensions between individual and community needs that Frosh (2018) argues can be resolved by acknowledging that these, largely unconscious, unknown desires are not individually owned. Instead, they are passed down through generations and that psychoanalysis has language and metaphors that can encourage interconnected complex thinking, resisting unhelpful binaries of good/bad, desirable/undesirable or even inner/outer. It is from this position that, unlike psychology looking for syntactic cause and effect, psychoanalysis encourages individuals to consider their particular context and motives, and to use this knowledge to make self-determined responses, resisting being trapped by archives of the past or fantasies of the future. This, of course, is the educational act.

Although from different traditions Biesta (2013), Klein (1931/1985) and Tomasello (2008) all suggest a similar outcome of successful education. Tomasello's work on an evolutionary understanding of how human mental functioning developed suggests that what distinguishes humans from most other animals is the existence of social cognition and thinking based on shared intentionality. The emblematic human behaviour for Tomasello is that one individual can have a conception of another's mind and act accordingly. Similarly, Biesta contends that the mature outcome of education is that of subjectification and the ability to distinguish one's own desires from those of others and to respond in such a way as to take their life and the life of others into account. Finally Melanie Klein's seminal psychoanalytic theory suggests that thinking takes place within two positions; the first represents a very early position where an infant is ego-centric and experiences the world as attacking and loving. 'Splitting' thinking into extremes of good and bad, dangerous and supportive. The more mature (educated) position is one from which the infant becomes aware of complexity and acknowledges that good and bad can reside in the same object.

Each of these theoretical approaches offers the hope that the outcome of education is an appreciation of the self in relation to the other. Frosh (2018) argues that in the present political, economic and environmental climate, riven with divisions and dissent, the ability to think beyond syntactic boundaries and to celebrate interconnectedness might be the achievement of a semantically infused language and education.

The final section of this chapter will consider how language informs and influences educational policy, exposing both harmful fetishized aspects, such as how neoliberal attacks have conspired to act against educational purpose, and more helpfully what can be done to return to an education that can support human and planetary flourishing.

To have been educated

That learning has become a fetish in education can be regarded as a response to syntactic commodification and a loss of educational purpose operating to distract from the existentially risky nature of engaging with deceptively difficult education (Bainbridge *et al.* 2018). The Marxian fetish originates from the commodification of education and conflation between use and exchange value. Marx contends that the magic trick of capitalism takes place when a commodity is perceived in relation to its monetary worth (exchange value), rather than their material properties (use value). In an educational context such a magic trick replaces the difficult and disruptive intellectual labour required to become educated with a focus on outcome, irrespective of process. From a Freudian perspective, the fetish becomes apparent through the disavowal of the loss of a loved object, resulting in the fetishist behaving in a manner that they know is not fit for purpose; for example, to persist in promoting testing and the importance of league tables, while still able to acknowledge that such practices have little to do with education.

In both contexts the complex and troubling nature of education is avoided and replaced with language that attempts to sanitize and control an education inherently messy and resistant to being restrained. Finding a way out of this violence and returning to education with educational purpose and answering the deceptively difficult question will bring this chapter to a close.

The task to arrest the slow death of education in the machinery of neoliberal accountancy measures will be to reclaim a language of education and to provide new metaphors that offer hope and resilience in troubling times. Lent (2017) encourages us to be culturally mindful and to be aware of the meanings that culture has created, while Bainbridge *et al.* (2018) called for the fetish to be 'named', to re-enter our language, as only then can it and its effects be thought about and challenged. This is not to suggest that simply by engaging with symbolic language some mystical transformation of thinking will occur. Frosh (1991/2016), writing about why psychotherapeutic talking 'cures' can take so long, makes this clear suggesting that a return to dialogue, or languaging, involves giving and receiving, being sensitive to the experiences and thoughts of others, communicating about communication in complex dialogical relationships.

Returning to the deceptively difficult question – 'Why Jill did or did not learn' – is to return to Frosh's earlier distinction between syntax and semantics. Here, Jill is a particular Jill confronted with a particular something, in a particular relationship for a particular purpose. There are resonances with Biesta's (2013) three purposes of education that highlight the importance of being taught *something* by *someone* for *some purpose*. It is important to note that Jill is not simply a brain with identifiable and predictable cognitive functions, or a woman from a known social background with predictable expectations. She is not necessarily motivated by the shame of failure any more than the pleasure of success; she does not yet know what she wants her future life to be but does know that she would like to have the opportunity to decide when she is ready.

The accountability technologies of syntactic and simplistic neoliberalism have no place for Jill, or answer to her desires. Jill's 'Jill-ness' is violently removed from awareness and can only be construed as (say) a 14-year-old female with an average IQ from a single parent working class background who achieves average test scores. There is a mystery to how education plays out in the lives of individuals; Mollenhauer (2013) is correct in his observation that the language of science, of syntax, does not make education any less mysterious. Surely what is important is that those of us engaged in education, in upbringing, can sit with this mystery a little longer. Long enough for Jill to come to an understanding of what her desires are and if they are desirable to others and the world she inhabits and to not simply invest in and hoard a series of levels, certificates and positions on league tables.

To sit together, dialogically, with Jill's desires, requires the ability to stay in uncertainty and to reject the dominant metaphors of developmental stages, monitored test progress and the certitude that exam success leads to professional success and a lifetime of wealth and personal fulfillment. Psychoanalytic theory would frame this stance as one that 'holds' anxiety, offering a time for personal reflection and the possibility of dialogue, using apposite language to stir something from the unconscious, that can be named and thought about (languaged) together. A holding space such as this can be a space that has educational purpose allowing for the possibility of personal transformation.

Attempts to employ neoliberal technologies to manage and control education are the actions of the person who digs their own grave, only serving to destroy the very thing it claims to support. This is the power of the fetish, disavowal and the capitalist's magic trick. This is where Jill no longer exists but for a test score. But there is hope as new metaphors can initiate new thinking. There is also the hope of a return to an education that has a more human and humane educational purpose, for it will be this education that brings forth a world that can be shared and not destroyed, a world that can consider and value both interconnectivity and interdependence. It will be an education that does not destroy itself and is sustainable, it will be an education that can exist in harmony and sustain the world in which it operates. It will be an education where a very particular Jill can be Jill.

References

Abram, D., 1997. *The spell of the sensuous.* New York: Vintage Books.

Aldridge, D., 2019. Cheating education and the insertion of knowledge. *Educational Theory,* 68 (6), 609–624. doi.org/10.1111/edth.12344

Bainbridge, A., 2019. Education then and now: Making the case for ecol-agogy. *Pedagogy, Culture and Society,* 27 (3), 423–440. doi:10.1080/14681366.20181517130

Bainbridge, A., Gaitanidis, A., and Hoult, E., 2018. When learning becomes a fetish: The pledge, turn and prestige of magic tricks, *Pedagogy, Culture and Society,* 26 (3), 345–361. doi:10.1080/14681366.2017.1403950

Bainbridge, A. and West, L., 2012. Introduction: minding a gap. *In*: A. Bainbridge and L. West, eds. *Psychoanalysis and education: Minding a gap.* London: Karnac, 11–36.

Berger, P.L. and Luckmann, T., 1966. *The social construction of reality: A treatise in the sociology of knowledge.* London: Penguin.

Biesta, G.J.J., 2013. *The beautiful risk of education.* Boulder, CO: Paradigm Publishers.

Capra, F., 1996. *The web of life: A new scientific understanding of living systems.* London: Harper Collins.

Flynn, E.G., Laland, K.N., Kendal, R.L., and Kendal, J.R., 2013. Developmental niche construction. *Developmental Science,* 16 (2), 269–313. doi.org/10.1111/desc.12030

Fogarty, L., Strimling, P., and Laland, K.N., 2011. The evolution of teaching. *Evolution,* 65 (10), 2760–2770. doi:10.1111/j.1558-5646.2011.01370.x

Frosh, S., 1989. *Psychoanalysis and psychology.* London: Macmillan.

Frosh, S., 1991/2016. Subjects and objects: Psychoanalysis and psychology. *Psychotherapy Section Review,* 57, 4–14. Leicester: The British Psychological Society. (Originally published in *Psychotherapy Section Newsletter,* No. 10, June 1991).

Frosh, S., 2018. Rethinking psychoanalysis in the psychosocial. *Psychoanalysis, Culture and Society,* 23 (1), 5–14. doi.org/10.1057/s41282-018-0072-5

Howard-Jones, P.A., 2014. Evolutionary perspectives on mind, brain and education. *Mind, Brain and Education,* 8 (1), 21–33. doi.org/10.1111/mbe.12041

Klein, M., 1931/1985. *Love, guilt and reparation and other works, 1921–1945.* 1985 ed. New York: The Free Press.

Laland, K.N., 2017. The origins of language in teaching. *Psychonomic Bulletin and Review,* 24 (1), 225–231. doi.org/10.3758/s13423-016-1077-7

Lent, J., 2017. *The patterning instinct: A cultural history of humanity's search for meaning.* New York: Prometheus Books.

Maturana, H.R. and Varela, F.J., 1987/1998. *The tree of knowledge. The biological roots of human understanding.* Revised ed. Boston: Shambhala.

Mollenhauer, K., 2013. *Forgotten connections: On culture and upbringing (Theorizing Education).* Abingdon: Routledge.

Odling-Smee, F.J., Laland, K.N., and Feldman, M.W., 2003. *Niche construction: The neglected process in evolution.* Princeton, NJ: Princeton University Press.

Searle, J., 1980. Minds, brains and programmes. *Behavioural and Brain Science,* 3 (3), 417–457. doi.org/10.1017/S0140525X00005756

Tomasello, M., 2008. *Origins of human communication.* Cambridge, MA: The MIT Press.

Chapter 17

Education as pro-duction and e-duction

Stein M. Wivestad

Introduction

It is inherent in our everyday language that education should move us in a desirable direction: the Americans 'raise', the Germans 'erziehen', the Norwegians 'oppdrar' and the French 'éleve' their children (Wivestad 2013, p. 56). Richard Stanley Peters compares the concepts of 'reform' and 'education'. We use 'reform' about 'a family of processes whose principle of unity is the contribution to the very general end of being better'. Education is a similar concept. It 'suggests a family of processes whose principle of unity is the development of desirable qualities in someone' (Peters 1970, p. 5). When the process of 'pro-duction' and the process of 'e-duction'[1] lead to desirable consequences, they can be combined. However, these processes are different. My main question is this: which kind of process ought to have the governing position in education?

With 'education as pro-duction' I understand how education may *producere* (lead forward to or up to) a desired future product, and with 'education as e-duction', how education may *educere* (lead out of) initial conditions that are seen as insufficient or bad. A process of e-duction is implicit in metaphors like getting 'out of the cave' (Plato) or out of a position 'occupying the center of the world' (Meirieu). E-duction aims at a good life for all – human beings included. We present the aim as sketches and narratives and must actualize and concretize it in each new and unique situation, as long as we live. Processes of pro-duction have the creation of a product in focus, for instance the ability to perform well on a certain reading test. When we create a product, we specify beforehand the criteria for a perfect result and attempt to get as much control over the process as possible. However, the value of the product depends on a hierarchy of goods ordered by an understanding of what is universally good. The critical question to any product, including a perfect performance on a reading test, is this: what is the product good for? A pro-duction process is unlike an e-duction process. The latter realizes something good in itself; the good is inherent in the process.

This chapter differentiates between two versions of education understood as pro-duction. The first version is the economy-oriented version that has dominated educational reforms during the last 30 years. Such education trusts competition as the key to progress both within and between the nations and tends to reduce the human being to a resource in the production of goods and services. Production metaphors have had a dominant position in education before 1990 as well. The second version of education as pro-duction is broader oriented. It wants to produce general human growth or development. I endorse its critique of the economy-oriented version but think that attempts to produce or create the ideal human being and the ideal society are bound to fail. The 'producers' (the older generation) are not perfect, and the 'products' (the new generation) are not primarily resources for use but persons to live in relation with.

My alternative to the variants of education as pro-duction is an education governed by processes of e-duction, understood as upbringing or *paideia*. Here the ideals function as guiding stars for the whole life, and production goals are subordinate to the aims of e-duction. The products must be legitimized as conducive to what is generally good, not only for human beings. I argue for a realistic and humbling understanding of our situation as human beings in the world. The production of specific skills ought to serve what is desirable. An awareness of general imperfection in what is attainable, can open for the perfect as a gift.

Education as pro-duction

The title of this section of the book, 'To have been educated', uses the verb in perfect tense representing 'education' as an activity that has been ended. This connects 'education' to a usual type of formal education, which ends with an evaluation and a written diploma, or with other documentation.

Economic oriented pro-duction

Such 'education' ends with a 'product' that has economic value. Predefined learning outcomes have been formulated in attempt to specify the knowledge and the skills that the participants ought to have acquired by the end of the education. A grade indicates the value of the product. When the school and the teachers function as 'producers', students and parents become 'customers' and may become 'co-producers':

> When parents allocate time watching children at play in a day care center, supervising high school students at a sports event or working with a group doing their math homework, they are 'co-producing' education with the public staff hired by a school to train and watch children enrolled in public schools. Further, educational achievements cannot be obtained without the co-production of the students.
>
> (Ostrom 2012, p. xv)

Their situation may be compared with those who make themselves comfortable in the Platonic 'cave' of superficial understanding and illusions. The individuals are rivals on arenas instead of fellow beings seeking the common good. Everyone competes with the others to maximize one's own preferences, even if these are irrational. Preferences are determined by individual feelings, and the feelings are formed by the culture industry, sports, advertisement, social media and mass media. In order to survive, the educational institutions produce competencies that are desired by the market. This is supported by the national governments. They are afraid of losing out in the economic competition with other nations. The result is superficial deliberation of what is desirable for living a good life and acceptance of self-centered acquisitiveness. Governments support research and studies that may be relevant for paid work, and national curricula and tests reinforce adaption to the predefined goals and standards of excellence. The younger generation learn to be useful and flexible products, accountable to those in power, with a constant fear of being disliked, unemployed and unable to pay back debts. Economy-oriented education has been accepted by supporters of capitalism and liberalism as well as supporters of communism and socialism. Both Adam Smith and Karl Marx were focused on production. The latter sketched the concept of production as the 'fundamental movement of human existence' (Baudrillard 1975, p. 32) and thought that human beings recognize themselves in the mirror of production (p. 19).

Broader oriented pro-duction

What are the products good for? Should all outcomes be economically relevant? The version of educational pro-duction mentioned earlier may be replaced by variants that avoid the economic focus. John Dewey (1988, p. 20) saw education as production of 'continuing growth'. Richard Stanley Peters (1965) understood education as production of development: initiation into a form of life considered to be desirable. Elliot W. Eisner wanted more emphasis on the *process* of education and a more nuanced understanding of the outcomes: 'The dominant image of schooling in America has been the factory and the dominant image of teaching and learning the assembly line. . . . Education becomes converted from a process into a commodity, something one gets and then sells' (Eisner 1994, pp. 361–362). Obsessed by selling, one ends up selling oneself, like Willy Loman in *The Death of a Salesman* (Schlöndorff 1985). 'If you are selling yourself . . . you make yourself into an object . . . and so it makes entire sense that they should say at his grave, "He never knew who he was"' (May 1991, p. 141). In addition to 'subject specific outcomes' measured by tests at the end of the 'assembly line', Eisner wanted education to produce 'student specific outcomes', 'teacher specific outcomes' and 'expressive outcomes' that attend to 'personal purposing and experience' (Eisner 1994, pp. 185, 119). Dewey asked educators to be aware of 'collateral learning in the way of formation of enduring attitudes, of likes and dislikes' (Dewey 1988, p. 29). He contended that 'the ultimate aim of education is nothing other than the creation of human beings in the fullness of their capacities' (Dewey 1984, p. 297).

A description of human capacities must be a sketch of initial human conditions, a description of the potential of the human species and of each individual human being. However, this 'fullness of . . . capacities' cannot be specified in detail beforehand, and cannot be created like products, with the notions of perfection and control that production entails. Children have a capacity for self-directed action. They can be encouraged to such actions, but it would be a contradiction in itself to control the production of a specified list of 'independent' behavior. I see 'the creation of human beings' as a futile and arrogant educational program. The older generation of human beings, who are not perfect, has never been able to create a perfect new generation, and attempts to control the production process deny human freedom either openly or in a hidden way.

Despite good intentions, formal education as pro-duction can be experienced as having bad consequences by those who 'have been educated'. Why did Pink Floyd sing 'We don't need no education'? It is important to study what we 'carry with us' after we have finished an educational 'curriculum' or 'course to be run' (Eisner 1994, p. 25). Experiences that lead to 'callousness', rigidity, confusion or 'lack of sensitivity', will be 'mis-educative' (Dewey 1988, pp. 11, 12, 31). *All* education that creates difference and strife between people can be 'eternally understood' as *Misdannelse* (mis-education) (Søltoft 2000, p. 22, Kierkegaard 2012, SKS 27, p. 455). Only love can *unite* despite differences.

Education as e-duction

Education becomes one-sided if we solely focus on outcomes – intentional movement toward a *future* condition. It is therefore meaningful to explore the possibilities of understanding education as e-duction, a movement out of *initial* conditions. Three relevant Latin words are all starting with *e* or implicit *ex* (out of): *eductio, eruditio* and *educatio*.

Eductio, eruditio and educatio

E-duction is no longer common in everyday English. According to *Oxford English Dictionary* (2007) it was used in 1842 in this way: 'It is the eduction of the pupil's nature which constitutes the education of the pupil.' S. T. Coleridge wrote in 1816 that 'education . . . consists in educing the faculties, and forming the habits.' Here the initial conditions are open or positive ('nature' and 'faculties'). E-duction may also be used about a leading out of disorder, inadequate understanding and bad habits.

A parallel word to e-duction is erudition, which has been used about all kinds of instruction and teaching, and of the outcomes of such processes as well. Now erudition may be used sarcastically about persons who are scholarly erudite, learned or literate. The verb *erudire* meant getting out of a rude or raw condition, a transition from an immature potential to a realization of something good. Today, when something or someone is called 'raw', it may be used as a praise of strength.

Education is a word on everybody's lips, but the meaning of the word and the aims of education are often taken for granted. I have found it interesting that Thomas Aquinas in the thirteenth century used the word *educatio* about what is good for the human being as an animal: 'those things are said to belong to the natural law which nature teaches all the animals, i.e., the union of male and female, the education [*educatio*] of offspring, etc.' (Aquinas 2018, Part 1–2 94,2). He does not discuss the concept, but his use of *educatio* implies that both parents take responsibility for the existence (rearing) and upbringing of the child – from the very beginning and in the later stages. Parents have the responsibility and the primary mandate in the *educatio*, even when they belong to a minority culture. 'It would be contrary to natural justice if, before a child has the use of reason, he were taken away from the care of his parents or something were ordained for him against his parents' wishes' (Part 2–2 10,12). This corresponds with the principle, 'Parents have a prior right to choose the kind of education that shall be given to their children' (UN 1948, Article 26, 3). A broad concept of education is 'upbringing' (White 2008, p. 195). 'Upbringing' can probably connect the content of *educatio, eductio* and *eruditio*.

Upbringing as progress

When the use of a word is deemed 'obsolete' in a dictionary and marked with a cross, it means that a certain way of thinking is not alive. I am interested in obsolete uses of words because they can disclose and challenge our contemporary prejudices. The language changes over time and so does 'common sense'. The saying: 'We live in the twenty-first century' is a superficial argument against the experiences of people in previous centuries. We cannot presuppose that historical changes necessarily entail progress. Many of the technological inventions during the last five hundred years are examples of progress but not the atomic bomb and the weapons of mass destruction. Today, communication technology may be used as weapons of 'mass distraction' (Bohlin 2018) and lead to a flight from the real human world of cooperation in solidarity and liberty (Meirieu 2009, pp. 286-287).

Knowledge and skills must be ordered within a universal understanding of what is conducive to the good life. Jan Amos Comenius reminded his contemporaries in the seventeenth century of this saying: 'He who makes progress in knowledge but not in morality, . . . recedes rather than advances.' Comenius insisted on seeing intellectual, moral and religious education as a whole, using language teaching built on sense experiences as basis for a general understanding of how things in the world are ordered: 'How wretched is the teaching that does not lead to virtue and to piety!' (Comenius 1907, Ch. X 17, p. 74). As an alternative to a naïve belief in progress, it is reasonable to attempt a disclosing of and questioning of our own prejudices. It is easy to become trapped in 'prejudices that inform widely shared judgments in the culture that we inhabit' (MacIntyre 2016, p. 112). However, we must do the inquiries into current prejudices with our present language. It is always possible to be seduced by the *idola fori*, the conventions of the marketplace (Gadamer 1979, p. 313).

Upbringing as paideia

A broad concept of education as e-duction has historical roots in the antique concept of *paideia* (rearing, upbringing, erudition, culture and *Bildung*). It combines a movement of bringing human beings out of or up *from* an imperfect condition – and up *to* a more perfect one. This model implies an awareness of negative possibilities and the necessity of lifelong struggles to avoid them. Neither education as pro-duction nor as e-duction can guarantee that we live good lives, but the chances are better if we don't ignore the negative possibilities. Real education implies a constant challenge. 'To be educated is not to have arrived at a destination; it is to travel with a different view' (Peters 1965, p. 110). Plato and Aristotle understood *paideia* as upbringing to 'find enjoyment or pain in the right things' (Aristotle 1985, 1104b12). Thomas Aquinas follows up: 'the first precept of [natural] law is that good ought to be done and pursued and that evil ought to be avoided' (Aquinas 2018, Part 1–2 94,2). How ought we to live as human beings in the world, and how ought we *not* to live? What is our ultimate end as human beings? These are big questions, but we should at least raise them.

The human being in the world

A classical understanding of the human being in the world is expressed in narratives of e-duction. The stories tell about liberation from an unfree situation and enlightenment by the beautiful, true and good as the foundation for being human and acting in a desirable way (Wivestad 2013).

Plato's cave allegory

Plato's well-known allegory of the Cave is a story about how *paideia* and lack of *paideia* have consequences for human beings and their actions. In book six of *The Republic* he makes comparisons of natural and human phenomena. The sun (the Good) gives light (truth) by which we can see clearly (know) what is in the dark. Book seven starts in this way: 'If we are thinking about the effect of education [*paideia*] – or the lack of it – on our nature, there's another comparison we can make' (Plato 2000, 514a, p. 220). The background of the Cave story is Plato's experience of how his friend Socrates was killed by unjust political leaders. Plato underwent an existential dizziness and crisis. His dedication to 'right philosophy' led him to declare that there would be 'no cessation from evils until either the class of those who are right and true philosophers attains political supremacy, or else the class of those who hold power in the States becomes, by some dispensation of Heaven, really philosophic' (Plato 1966, Letter 7, 326a-b). In this story, liberation and upbringing (*paideia*) help the human being to get out of the cave. This is necessary to see things as they really are and then return into the cave to help others.

Comenius' labyrinth story

Less well-known in English-speaking contexts is the story 'The labyrinth of the world and the paradise of the heart', written in 1621-1623 after the start of the terrible Thirty Years' War. Comenius lost his wife and two children and most of his books and manuscripts. He had to flee for his life. In this situation he wrote a story that has become a classical work in Czech literature. It is about a pilgrim who wants to investigate 'all human affairs under the sun', compare them and choose a pleasant and peaceful form of life (Comenius 1901, I.5). Everywhere searching for 'the highest good (*summum bonum*)' (To the reader) his experience again and again confirms this: Nothing is totally good. Everywhere 'the futility [*Nichtigkeit*] of the human self-confidence is disclosed to him' (Schaller 1962, p. 186). Comenius was contemporary with Descartes but thought that 'ego cogito, ergo sum' would be a weak foundation for human life. Real existence is necessary for thinking. However, many have followed Descartes and have had their hope for the future in the individual's cognitive mastery of the world and the possibilities it gives the market and the state to utilize the special competencies of the individuals. The schools' central purpose has become 'to promote economic competitiveness through the production of skilled workers' (Katz 2009, p. 107). Jan Patočka (1971) a Czech phenomenological philosopher, characterizes this as 'Lebensverzehrung durch Arbeits- und Leistungsvorbereitung' (p. 55), life-destruction through preparation for labor and performance.

Patočka has given a humanistic interpretation of Comenius' story. Acknowledgment of human limitation and despair in 'the labyrinth' opens a cry for help and a readiness to listen to the call: wake up, let yourself be helped and cooperate! This call is 'the e-duction or drawing out of the human beings from the stance of their misery: an *educatio*. It is by this that the human being really becomes human' (Patočka 1971, p. 18).[2]

In Comenius' story the pilgrim who calls for help hears a voice saying: 'Return to the place whence you came, to the home of your heart and shut the door behind you!' (Comenius 1901, XXXVII.2). In his own heart there is darkness and disorder. Here he encounters Jesus Christ and gets help to order his heart, to live in the labyrinth, and to help others. Christ says: 'have your mind ever lifted up to me as constantly as you can, but condescend to your neighbors as low as possible. . . . Be sensitive to the sufferings of your neighbors, but inured to the wrongs inflicted upon yourself' (LIII). The heart of the pilgrim is no longer possessed by the vanity of the labyrinth. He can endure a life in the imperfect world and do something good – living in the shadow of death (in the labyrinth) *and* in the light of love (in Christ).

Patočka interprets Jesus as the first or archetypal educator (*Urerzieher*) because he challenges us without removing our responsibility. He sees the call from and the encounter with Jesus as a metaphor for the possibility of getting 'out of the labyrinth' – out of a fragmented, superficial and restless life as a particularistic being (*Partikularwesen*) – and up to living as an integrated world being (*Weltwesen*) or universal being (*Universalwesen*) open to life as a whole, refusing to assign absolute value to oneself or other parts of human existence (Patočka 1971, pp. 18-19, 14). However, what is the whole life? If we love our finite world and let this world be the center of our life, are we then open to a whole life which has God in the center?

Possible improvements

The world is a planet in the universe with a definite physical structure. It is inhabited by living beings including the human species. Though the universe exceeds our comprehension, our language gives us a possibility to name 'all the animals' and all that exists, and to study how it all hangs together. This makes us responsible for the culture of the earth and all life, of ourselves, of the social structures and of the power that order the world. Human beings have told many different stories about this and how we ought to live. No one has a perfect position outside all the stories to compare and judge them. We must explore the different stories with the language we belong to and the prejudices of the story that we presently are living by. But we ought to put our prejudices at risk and open for improvements of ourselves in the encounter with other stories.

If I put myself in the center of the world and attempt to master the world, I am not open to 'let the world speak on its own terms, as a world that addresses me, speaks to me, interrupts me, limits me, and de-centers me' (Biesta 2017, p. 31). Therefore, children should be led out of addictions to solitary and self-centered activities and be engaged in direct play with others and in necessary tasks in the family, the school class and the voluntary groups they belong to.

A task for adults is to prioritize rightly our own activities. 'The one thing needful' is not primarily 'the wisdom of the Head' but the 'wisdom of the Heart' (Dickens 1989, pp. 1, 297). Adults cannot avoid being exemplars for the children, and 'example is more effective than words' (Aquinas 2018, Part 1–2, 34,1). In the family, children who are included in the daily activities and challenges, can gradually get more freedom and responsibility. In the school, we never 'get enough time' – we have to 'take time' – to study, converse on and celebrate what is important in life. And in all settings, we should look up to children as authorities on humility. They can show us how to be open for doing new experiences, receiving help and living in a playful way without stress and complete control. The ideal school should *not* be an arena for fighting or competitive running, but rather be like 'a small Garden of Eden, full of delights and lovely by-ways and stage-plays and discussions' (Comenius 1986, p. 65). In such contexts, production of important skills can be integrated in disciplines and 'practices' that realize 'internal goods' (MacIntyre 1985, p. 187), goods that require cooperation and is oriented toward the good life for all.

Children can be brought up to 'live in the world, without occupying the center of the world' (Biesta 2017, p. 9), living as free subjects, each with a unique possibility to make small corrections and improvements of what is going on in the world. Biesta hopes for 'the impossible possibility' (p. 98) 'which cannot be *foreseen* as a possibility' – that education with the best intentions and reasonable actions will be able to interrupt and liberate us 'from our being-with-ourselves' (p. 83). I understand this as a belief in the possibility of changing human beings in a positive direction through education. All are challenged to contribute to what is good and avoid what is evil for 'the whole world'. Relative improvements are important. However, massive experiences in human history tell us that such changes will be imperfect.

The imperfect and the perfect

The Dark Side of the Moon by Pink Floyd, published in 1973, starts with the sound of a pumping heart and describes the struggle between the life force (symbolized by the sun) and the death force (symbolized by the moon). The last song, 'Eclipse' (Waters 1973), starts with a recitation on one persistent tone which is heightened a half tone and then falls again. The text is about all things in the world – all that you touch, taste, feel, love and hate – everything present and in the future. Everything in life seems to be in tune. However, there is a shadow that darkens everything. Roger Waters (1982, interviewed by Nick Sedgwick, p. 13) has mentioned 'some dark force in our nature that prevents us from seizing' the good things. Søren Kierkegaard contends that human 'despair' is our 'sickness to death'. We forget, or dare not, or will not believe that 'for God everything is possible' (Kierkegaard 1980, p. 38). We trust in imperfect educational and other efforts and are not open to let ourselves be transformed by what is perfect. Simone Weil gives this advice:

> It is not for man to seek, or even to believe in, God. He has only to refuse his love to everything which is not God. This refusal does not presuppose any belief. It is enough to recognize, what is obvious to any mind, that all the goods of this world, past, present, or future, real or imaginary, are finite and limited and radically incapable of satisfying the desire which burns perpetually within us for an infinite and perfect good. . . . It is not a matter of self-questioning or searching. A man has only to persist in this refusal, and one day or another God will come to him.
>
> (Weil 1968, p. 158)

There is hope in acknowledging the limitations, both of ourselves and the world. Leonard Cohen (1992) sings: 'There is a crack, a crack in everything . . . that's how the light gets in.'

Education governed by e-duction

Pro-duction and e-duction processes are different. Which process ought to have the governing position in education? Contemporary education dominated by economy-oriented pro-duction appeals to individual and national competition and self-centered acquisitiveness, and it has a one-sided focus on knowledge and skills. It reduces human beings to useful resources and is not conducive to a good life for all. A concept of pro-duction broadened to 'creation' of perfect human beings seems to be both futile and arrogant. Human growth cannot and should not be defined completely beforehand by the old generation. Education as e-duction can describe the interaction between the generations in the whole life cycle. As a normative challenge, struggles are important at all stages in the cycle. In the twentieth century, hope has been attached to the beginning of life (Key 1909). Today, I think adults should struggle against being possessed themselves by all the things they *try* to possess, and struggle to be humble exemplars for the new generation. This means that metaphors of e-duction ought to have the governing position in education - in combination with pro-duction that contributes to the e-duction.

If we follow Aquinas and Comenius, e-duction starts with *educatio* (rearing) - responsible adult preparation for welcoming a potential offspring - continues by leading the actual child up *from* dependency - and up *to* taking full adult responsibility for all further e-duction and erudition. Part of this e-duction process is effective production of desirable knowledge and skills. This should be done in active cooperation with the global community of workers and citizens, pursuing the constant task of educing ourselves and all others *out of* injustice and discord - and *up to* justice and peace. Experience tells us that the creation of perfect human beings, perfect communities and a perfect world is above human capacity. I see the perfect as a gift and the conditions for receiving the perfect gift as gifts as well (Wivestad 2011). The ultimate end of the e-duction is to let oneself be led out of despair - and into faith, hope and love - in confrontation with death.

Notes

1 I write the words with a hyphen to highlight the prefixes and to avoid that the uncommon word e-duction is read as education.
2 dieser Aufruf, . . . ist das Herausziehen des Menschen aus dem Grund seines Elends: eine *educatio*; diese erst ist es, die ihn in der Tat zum Menschen macht. Patočka does not differentiate between *eductio* and *educatio*.

References

Aquinas, T., 2018. *New English translation [in progress] of St. Thomas Aquinas's Summa Theologiae*. Available from: https://www3.nd.edu/~afreddos/summa-translation/TOC.htm

Aristotle, 1985. *Nicomachean ethics.* Indianapolis, IN: Hackett.
Baudrillard, J., 1975. *The mirror of production.* St Louis: Telos Press. Available from: https://monoskop.org/images/b/ba/Baudrillard_Jean_The_Mirror_of_Production_1975.pdf
Biesta, G., 2017. *The rediscovery of teaching.* New York: Routledge.
Bohlin, K., 2018. Virtue, vice and verse: Why poetry matters. *Educating character through the arts,* 19–21 July 2018. University of Birmingham Conference Centre: The Jubilee Centre for Character and Virtue.
Cohen, L., 1992. Anthem. *The Future.* Available from: www.youtube.com/watch?v=mDTph7mer3I
Comenius, J.A., 1901. *The labyrinth of the world and the paradise of the heart.* New York: E.P. Dutton. Available from: http://babel.mml.ox.ac.uk/naughton/labyrint/labyrinth_frame.html
Comenius J.A., 1907. *The great didactic of John Amos Comenius translated into English and edited by M. W. Keatinge: Part II Text.* London: Adam and Charles Black. Available from: https://archive.org/details/cu31924031053709
Comenius, J.A., 1986. *Comenius's Pampaedia or universal education.* Dover: Buckland Publications.
Dewey, J., 1984. Philosophy and education. *In*: J. A. Boydston, ed. *The later works, 1925–1953,* vol. 5. Carbondale and Edwardsville, IL: Southern Illinois University Press, 289–298.
Dewey, J., 1988. Experience and education. *In*: J.A. Boydston, ed. *The later works, 1925–1953,* vol. 13. Carbondale/Edwardsville, IL: Southern Illinois University Press, 1–62.
Dickens, C., 1989. *Hard times.* Oxford: Oxford University Press.
Eisner, E.W., 1994. *The educational imagination: On the design and evaluation of school programs.* 3rd ed. New York: Macmillan College Publ. Co.
Gadamer, H.-G., 1979. *Truth and method.* 2nd ed. London: Sheed and Ward.
Katz, M.S., 2009. R. S. Peters' normative conception of education and educational aims. *Journal of Philosophy of Education,* 43 (s1), 97–108.
Key, E., 1909. *The century of the child.* New York: G. P. Putnam's Sons. Available from: www.gutenberg.org/ebooks/57283
Kierkegaard, S., 1980. The sickness unto death: A Christian psychological exposition for upbuilding and awakening. *In Kierkegaard's writings.* Princeton, NJ: Princeton University Press.
Kierkegaard, S., 2012. Indbydelse til forelæsninger og til subskription: Papir 382. *In*: N.J. Cappelørn, J. Garff, J. Kondrup, T. Aagaard Olesen, and S. Tullberg, eds. *Søren Kierkegaards Skrifter* (SKS) Vol. 27. Available from: http://sks.dk/p381/txt.xml
Macintyre, A., 1985. *After virtue: A study in moral theory.* 2nd ed. London: Duckworth.
Macintyre, A., 2016. *Ethics in the conflicts of modernity: An essay on desire, practical reasoning, and narrative.* Cambridge: Cambridge University Press.
May, R., 1991. *The cry for myth.* 1st ed. New York: Norton.
Meirieu, P., 2009. *Lettre aux grandes personnes sur les enfants d'aujourd'hui.* [S.l.]: Rue du monde.
Ostrom, E., 2012. Foreword. *In*: V.A. Pestoff, T. Brandsen, and B. Verschuere, eds. *New public governance, the third sector and co-production.* New York: Routledge. Available from: Google books.
Oxford English Dictionary, 2007. Oxford: Oxford University Press. Available from: www.oed.com/
Patočka, J., 1971. *Die Philosophie der Erziehung des J. A. Comenius.* Paderborn: Ferdinand Schöningh.

Peters, R.S., 1965. Education as initiation. *In*: R.D. Archambault, ed. *Philosophical analysis and education*. London: Routledge & Kegan Paul, 87-111. Available from: https://archive.org/details/philosophicalana0000arch

Peters, R.S., 1970. Education and the educated man. *Journal of Philosophy of Education*, 4 (1), 5-20. doi:10.1111/j.1467-9752.1970.tb00424.x

Plato, 1966. *Letters*. London: William Heinemann. Available from: www.perseus.tufts.edu/hopper/text?doc=Perseus:text:1999.01.0164

Plato, 2000. *The republic*. Cambridge: Cambridge University Press.

Schaller, K., 1962. *Die Pädagogik des Johann Amos Comenius und die Anfänge des pädagogischen Realismus im 17. Jahrhundert*. Heidelberg: Quelle & Meyer.

Schlöndorff, V., 1985. *Death of a salesman*. [DVD 130 min.] USA/West Germany: Punch Productions/Roxbury Productions.

Søltoft, P., 2000. To let oneself be upbuilt. *In*: N.J.E. Cappelørn, H.E. Deuser, and J.E. Stewart, eds. *Kierkegaard studies: Yearbook 2000*. Berlin: Walter de Gruyter, 19-39.

UN, 1948. *Universal declaration of human rights*. United Nations. Available from: www.un.org/en/universal-declaration-human-rights/index.html

Waters, R., 1973. *Eclipse*. Available from: http://www.pink-floyd-lyrics.com/html/eclipse-dark-lyrics.html

Waters, R., 1982. *Pink Floyd lyric book: Lyrics by Roger Waters*. London: Chappell Music Ltd.

Weil, S., 1968. *On science, necessity, and the love of God*. London: Oxford University Press.

White, J., 2008. Education. *In*: G. Mcculloch and D. Crook, eds. *The Routledge international encyclopedia of education*. London: Routledge.

Wivestad, S.M., 2011. Conditions for 'upbuilding': A reply to Nigel Tubbs' reading of Kierkegaard. *Journal of Philosophy of Education*, 45 (4), 613-625. doi:10.1111/j.1467-9752.2011.00823.x

Wivestad, S.M., 2013. On becoming better human beings: Six stories to live by. *Studies in Philosophy and Education*, 32 (1), 55-71. Available from: http://link.springer.com/article/10.1007/s11217-012-9321-8

Chapter 18

Focal practices and the ontologically educated citizen

Dylan van der Schyff

Introduction

The twenty-first century offers numerous possibilities and experiences that would have been all but inconceivable even one hundred years earlier. Digital technology allows us to organize our finances, plan meetings, shop for the latest products, and communicate over enormous distances all with the touch of a few on-screen 'buttons'. We share the most mundane and momentous moments of our lives on social media, and have immediate access to a mind-boggling amount of information and creative content anytime we want it. Developments in global systems of production and exchange mean that we can now go into our local grocery store and acquire foodstuffs grown and raised on the other side of the planet. Or, if we don't feel like cooking, we can simply select from an array of prefabricated meals that require only heating to prepare. On the surface of things, it seems that life has never been better, at least for those of us who are lucky enough to reside in the West.[1]

A closer look, however, suggests that things might not be quite so rosy. There is a growing suspicion that our fascination with social media may in fact be doing more to isolate us than bring us together. And as people increasingly consume products that are produced in factories or in remote locations and that are sold in corporate chain stores – and as they spend more time shopping on-line – their economic lives lose the connection to place, as well as the social significance that characterized the face-to-face forms of exchange of previous generations. For most of us, the things we use in our daily lives are not made by us or for us by people we know. Rather, they are manufactured by anonymous people for anonymous people. Accordingly, the social detachment produced by modern technological and economic progress risks instrumentalizing workers and consumers, rendering them as mere cogs in the neoliberal economic machine. In all, we currently appear to be suffering from a crisis of meaning where the significance of human being-in-the-world hangs in the balance. This has profound implications for the future of education, which now more than ever must enable students and teachers to see through the glare of technology and the modern corporate world view to re-examine the possibilities of what human life can entail.

If we believe that what it means 'to have been educated' should involve more than producing workers properly trained and conditioned for the global economy, then it seems crucial for students and teachers to explore ways of perceiving, thinking, communicating, knowing, and being that can help them see beyond the taken-for-granted attitudes that often prescribe our experience of self and society. This, however, is no easy task. How we think about and do education in the modern world has been strongly influenced by the more general assumptions associated with the emergence of 'modernity', which supplanted the old forms of conjecture, belief, and superstition that guided pre-modern thought. The modern orientation asserted humankind's ability to shape the world and its own destiny through the power of reason, the acquisition of objective knowledge, and the forms of scientific and technological progress that would result from this. This new worldview produced many outstanding achievements, but its ideals of progress and discovery soon became focussed through the lenses of the same industrial society it gave birth to, leading to a culture of production and consumption – where technological advancements were increasingly employed to optimize the gathering, management, and processing of resources (both human and 'natural'), to organize the channels of distribution and exchange, and to manufacture desire within the free-market economy.

By the early twentieth century, some thinkers began to warn that these developments had resulted in a de-humanizing 'technologically enframed' world view (Arendt 1958, Heidegger 1977[1954]), where existence was now disclosed largely in terms of the instrumental forms of categorization and transformation that serve a corporate techno-culture. By this light, the ontological status of trees, rivers, animals, people, and environments are reduced or obscured; and the 'being' of entities – what they are and what they mean – is revealed primarily in terms of their economic utility. Today, this instrumental conception of being extends to every corner of life, including education. This has been discussed by a range of pedagogical thinkers who have noted how education in the modern era has involved a kind of depersonalized 'production line' approach (Sawyer 2007). Here students study and are tested essentially in isolation according to standardized criteria – where 'teaching' and 'learning' often involves getting students to memorize and reproduce pre-given facts and techniques; and where education itself becomes a kind of technological procedure. Critics argue that this orientation negates the exploratory, creative, and social-collaborative aspects of learning; and that it therefore downplays the creative potentials of both teachers and students as active world-makers (Kincheloe 2003).

My aim in this chapter is not to argue that education should adopt a luddite ideology that strives to do away with modern technology altogether. Rather, I explore the role arts education can play in fostering the kinds of engagements, experiences, and practices that afford richer understandings of what it means to be and become a human being – which necessarily includes our nature as technological animals. I begin by drawing out connections between phenomenology, critical pedagogy, and arts education, showing how they can support one another in pedagogical contexts. Following on from this, I then examine the critique of modern technology provided by phenomenological thinkers. Here, I suggest that a revised understanding of arts education in light of the idea of 'focal practices' (Borgmann 1984) could help teachers and students recognize and better understand the activities and relationships that imbue life with meaning, and that this may help them lead fuller lives as educated citizens.

Phenomenology and critical pedagogy

Although phenomenology has antecedents in a range of ancient and modern philosophical traditions, it is generally understood to begin with the work of Edmund Husserl. Writing in the early twentieth century, Husserl became concerned that the successes of the positive sciences had resulted in a worldview that was increasingly focused on technological progress, thus obscuring 'the questions which are decisive for a genuine humanity' (1970, p. 10 [1936]). In response to this he sought to re-establish the human element by developing a new 'science' that takes human experience as its explicit basis. Phenomenology has been adapted and transformed in various ways to explore a wide range of phenomena (Kaufer and Chemero 2015). However, a common aspect of phenomenological inquiry involves an attempt to 'suspend' or 'bracket' (*epoché*) assumptions and judgments and attend to experience in the most open and direct way possible. This process reveals that many of our perceptions and understandings are in fact the products of ways of attending to the world that have become so ingrained that they appear to take on a fixed reality of their own. This results in the development of so-called 'natural attitudes' (Merleau-Ponty 2002[1945]) towards the things, activities, and relationships that characterize our lives – attitudes we often simply take-for-granted as the way things are. Phenomenology examines such assumptions in terms of the processes of historical (personal and cultural) 'sedimentation' that give rise to them so that new understandings and possibilities may be revealed. In other words, phenomenological inquiry highlights the active, adaptive, exploratory, ecologically situated, embodied, and creative nature of perception and consciousness; and it shows how through sustained reflective analysis we may build up deeper understandings and open new possibilities for thought and action.

While examinations of basic forms of sensory experience are an essential starting place for developing a phenomenological attitude, phenomenological inquiry can also take us further to explore and critically rethink our experience of the cultures, places, and institutions we live through. Importantly, the phenomenological stance also challenges many standard Western pedagogical assumptions, most centrally the idea that learning and 'knowledge' can be reduced to the depersonalized transfer of pre-given (objective) facts and procedures from teacher to student. And indeed, a phenomenological attitude has guided the thinking of many critical scholars who problematize this assumption (Arendt 1993[1961], Greene 1992, Thomson 2001). This includes Paulo Freire (2000[1968]), whose concept of 'critical consciousness' or 'conscientization' draws on phenomenological insights.[2]

Freire examines the varieties of social consciousness and discovers that they may be organized into three main categories. These involve, first, the 'semi-transitive' state associated with thinking that is dominated by social conditioning. This level of consciousness is characterized by its quasi adherence to an assumed objective reality – its epistemic possibilities are prescribed by that imposed reality, and thus it does not possess the critical distance to authentically engage with reality, to act on it in order to transform it. Second, Freire suggests a 'transitive-naïve' consciousness that exhibits, among other things, a tendency for facile explanations and over-simplification in the interpretation of problems; as well as a preference for rhetoric and reification over dialectic. Third, he posits what he refers to as 'transitive-critical' consciousness. This form of consciousness affords the development of richer structural perceptions; it allows us to look beyond taken-for-granted or imposed ways of perceiving and thinking, and engage with experience in new ways.

Developing transitive-critical consciousness is liberating when it allows us to see that 'the epistemological cycle does not end at the level of the acquisition of extant knowledge, but continues through the stage of creation of new knowledge' (Freire and Illich 1975, p. 28). This orientation lies at the heart of critical pedagogy, which seeks to identify and decenter the assumptions and power relations that obscure possibilities for thought and action, and to therefore reveal education as a process of self and world-making. By this light, education may only be understood as authentic when it engages and empowers the critical and creative potentials of the human mind – 'when the practice of revealing reality constitutes a dynamic and dialectic unity with the practice of transforming reality' (Freire and Illich 1975, p. 28).

Education and arts praxis

Following the thought of Freire and other critical pedagogues (e.g., Giroux 2011, Kincheloe 2003), a number of writers have demonstrated the enormous role the arts may play in realizing the educational potentials discussed here (see Elliott and Silverman 2015, Greene 1992). While critical pedagogy, phenomenology, and creative practice in the arts are not simply synonymous, they do overlap and reinforce each other in important ways, with each seeking richer, transformational understandings of human experience. As Don Ihde (1977) notes, the arts practice their own forms of *epoché* (ways of suspending taken-for-granted attitudes and perceptions). And indeed, if perception is understood as the foundation of knowledge, then the arts may also be understood to explore and illuminate the most basic ways we make sense of the world. However, because the arts also extend into the cultural and historical worlds we inhabit, it follows that the cultivation of a phenomenological attitude through arts pedagogy would support the development of the transitive-critical consciousness and social conscientization discussed by Freire (2000[1968]).

The arts may initiate, reflect, and extend phenomenological and critically transitive insights when they transform the mundane, introduce new perspectives, and thus challenge taken-for-granted ways of perceiving, knowing, and being. Maxine Greene (1992) discusses how the arts have the power to 'shock' us out of our complacent attitudes – to 'release the imagination' so that we may engage more fully with the possibilities of our own experience, and thereby develop more open, reflective, and empathetic relationships with ourselves and the socio-material environments we inhabit. Likewise, other theorists (e.g., Smith 1979) have suggested phenomenologically inspired frameworks for education that begin with students' analyses of direct perception, that proceed through the development of theoretical concepts, often involving critical discussion and guidance from teachers, peers, and other sources, and that then involve the integration of new concepts with existing understandings. From this perspective, new knowledge and categories are not imposed, but rather emerge through phenomenological analysis and collaborative *praxis*. It is also important to note the relevance of this last concept, *praxis*, which looks beyond the idea of the arts simply as something one does to achieve a specific end. Rather, a *praxial* approach involves the integration of a range of technical, theoretical, cultural, and social understandings to reveal arts education as 'a socially rooted, complex, coherent, and cooperative activity that grows over time into its own ethical world' (Higgins 2012, p. 224). Importantly, *praxial* pedagogical approaches take the unique lived experiences of students and teachers seriously as a central aspect of any curriculum (Elliott and Silverman 2015).[3]

An important perspective that begins to demonstrate the mutually influencing relationship between arts *praxis* and critical pedagogy comes from the late educational theorist Joe Kincheloe (2008), who relates how his thinking about education was transformed by his early encounters with a community of improvising jazz and blues musicians. Here, Kincheloe discovered a way of learning that was centered around a shared activity (a *praxis*) – one that was shaped by the participants themselves, who learned with and from each other. These experiences inspired alternatives to prevailing pedagogical models, leading to his *critically ontological* approach to education. Briefly, this orientation examines the mechanistic and depersonalizing assumptions that have guided conceptions of being and knowing in the modern era; and it develops new ethical perspectives on education grounded in the self- and world-making possibilities of students and teachers (Kincheloe 2003, 2008).

Let us now expand on these ideas and insights by considering how a critical, phenomenologically inspired approach to arts pedagogy might respond to the challenges posed by contemporary culture. To do this, I explore another concept associated with phenomenological philosophy that can help us distinguish the special kinds of experiences afforded by creative *praxis* in the arts: the idea of 'focal practices'. First, however, it will be useful to develop the concerns introduced at the outset through the lenses of the phenomenological critique of modern technology – this will situate the concept of focal practices within the phenomenological tradition and help clarify its relevance for arts education in the twenty-first century.

Heidegger and Borgmann on culture and technology

The concept of focal practices was developed by Albert Borgmann (1984) as part of his response to Heidegger's (1977[1954]) critique of technology. Most centrally, this involves a re-examination of the Heideggerian notion of *Gestell*, which refers to the technologically 'enframed' mode of being that prevails in the modern world. Heidegger sees the *Gestell* as a Western historical development that was preceded by a series of other epochs, each characterized by their own ontological perspective. For example, the early Greek culture based its understanding of being on *phusis* – a term that refers to the ways the entities of nature appear or 'surge up' on their own. Later, the emergence of the great political and artisanal culture in Greece brought the notion of *poiēsis*, which describes the process of 'nurturing' whereby things are helped to come forth – as in friendship, education, child-rearing, and art-making. A third transformation occurs in the Roman era with its focus on being finished works (e.g., infrastructure, architecture, and so on), which reflected that culture's interest in empire building. This was overtaken with the rise of Christianity where all being came to be understood in terms of creation by a divine all-knowing God. Yet another shift happens in the Age of Reason and Enlightenment with its modern focus on human reason and progress. This involved the instantiation of a hierarchical and dualistic schema of 'man over nature' or 'rational subjects over and against objects' – where the things of the world were organized to serve the interests and desires of human agents. According to Heidegger, this led to a final stage – the *Gestell* – where humans dominate and objectify all other beings through the use of technology.

In brief, Heidegger's historical ontology describes how the understanding of being in a given epoch guides how people live through the worlds they inhabit. As Dreyfus and Spinosa (2017[1997]) write, 'each such world makes possible a distinct and pervasive way in which things, people, and selves can appear and in which certain ways of acting make sense' (p. 199). However, Heidegger argues that the technological understanding of being that characterized life in the mid-twentieth-century was something entirely new that also posed certain unforeseen dangers. That is, it threatened to distort or destroy our fundamental nature as creatures who, through our shared practices and contextual use of 'equipment', open meaningful realities for ourselves in various environments. According to Heidegger, the challenge of the modern world involves finding ways of living with technology that does not distort or 'lay waste' to the fundamentally world-disclosing nature of human being-in-the-world. Indeed, for thinkers like Heidegger and Borgmann, modern technology threatens to warp or even erase the subject–object distinction that characterizes the modern worldview. Heidegger (1977[1954]) sees this in terms of the trend toward the evermore efficient marshalling of resources for its own sake – where everything eventually becomes objectified and 'is ordered to stand by, to be immediately at hand, indeed to stand there just so that it may be on call for further ordering' (p. 5)

Borgmann (1992) adds to this critique in an interesting and somewhat ominous way. He argues that where modern technology was characterized by the production of rigid devices, objects, and structures that enabled us to control and transform nature, postmodern technology poses a new set of possibilities and problems. This, as I mentioned earlier, is shown in the geographically and socially detached fabrication and consumption of a dazzling array of hi-tech products. But it also involves a growing shift toward the fascination with information, the increasing prevalence of internet culture, and the emergence of virtual reality. According to Borgmann, this leads to a situation where we no longer need to concern ourselves with overcoming the limitations imposed by material reality. Instead, natural and material objects are replaced by (on screen) virtual simulacra (e.g., those associated with on-line worlds and virtual reality), offering the promise of an improved reality over which the subject now has total control. While some proponents of information technology in the 1990s saw this last possibility as indicative of a coming digital utopia, Borgmann warned that the elimination of the resistance of nature and rigid objects would reduce the subject to a bundle of 'arbitrary desires', effectively doing away with the long-term identities and relationships that characterized all previous epochs. Similar analyses have been offered by other late twentieth-century thinkers (Lifton 1995, Turkle 1995) who noted how postmodern life was increasingly characterized by a desire for ever new connections in on-line virtual worlds, which would lead to protean, multiplicitous selves, as well as fluid conceptions of knowledge and culture.

Today, the fluidity brought about by information technology can be seen both in terms of its great possibilities, as well as the source for the crisis of meaning I mentioned at the outset of this chapter. For example, Zygmunt Baumann (2007) discusses the implications of 'liquid modernity', which describes how we now have less connection than ever to the political and economic forces that govern our lives in the global 'community'. Likewise, we have recently witnessed the troubling emergence of fake news and surveillance capitalism (Zuboff 2019) both of which are products of the rapid development of information culture. Problems have also arisen with the growing prevalence of short-term or 'temp' employment, as well as an increasing reliance on depersonalized forms of on-line education that are designed to continually re-educate workers for new posts. Despite the convenience and utility of these courses, they arguably bear little or no connection to the conception of education as *praxis* discussed earlier. Rather, they involve the accumulation of fixed knowledge (facts and skills) acquired in relative isolation.

In all, the worry is that as this instrumental and corporate attitude toward education, work, and life normalizes itself within contemporary society, we risk losing sight of the full possibilities of human being-in-the-world. As everyone and everything becomes sucked up into the pool of resources Heidegger (1977) refers to as the 'standing reserve' we become blinded to *phusis* and *poiēsis*, and to the world-making nature of human being and knowing – meaningful identities and relationships become difficult to maintain; and the transitive-critical consciousness advocated for by Freire becomes an increasingly distant potential. With these concerns in mind, let us now turn to examine the idea of focal practices and its relevance for education and life in the twenty-first century.

Focal practices

Borgmann's (1984) conception of 'focal practices' owes a great deal to the ideas offered by Heidegger in 'The Thing' and 'Building, Dwelling, Thinking' (see Heidegger 1975). In these writings, Heidegger examines the kinds of events and practices that bring people together in meaningful ways. Such gatherings have significance on broader cultural levels, but can also involve local interactions that set up local worlds. And, as he notes, these local worlds are often centered around a 'thing' (the appreciation or creation of a work of art or an artefact and the creative interaction with tools and materials; the undertaking of a task that is relevant to a community; the preparation and enjoyment of a meal and so on). It is these shared activities around things that Borgmann refers to when he uses the term focal practices – activities that reveal shared concerns, possibilities, experiences, and meanings in specific contexts. However, he also sets up an opposition between focal practices and what he refers to as the 'device paradigm' that characterizes modern life, where he sees the latter obscuring the former.

Briefly, Borgmann (1984) conceives of modern technological devices as purely instrumental features of contemporary life that replace the skills and activities required previously to nurture or craft various things. He argues that modern technological devices tend to disperse or 'disaggregate' focal practices when they are used to satisfy our immediate desires as quickly as possible.[4] These concerns pose serious questions regarding the role of technology in education: In educational practice, should we retreat into modes of activity that do not involve or at least minimize the use of modern technological devices? Or might it be possible to foster a richer understanding of modern technology through education? And what of the fluidity and multiplicity of postmodern life? What role can focal practices play in these worlds?

One way to begin to answer these questions is to reconsider the possibilities afforded by arts pedagogy. More traditional types of arts education – such as participating in standard musical ensembles – offer students the chance to experience forms of focal practice that can make significant contributions to their social and cultural development. Important as they are, however, these activities tend to be more formalized in nature and do not always fully engage with the kinds of challenges posed by contemporary life. What is also required, I argue, are arts education models intended to foster the kinds of phenomenological and critical-transitive attitudes discussed earlier. Such models are not only concerned with the reproduction of pre-given material and traditional modes of practice, but also with collaboration and the creation of original work – where students and teachers work together across disciplines to create their own shared goals and to negotiate how they will be achieved. Here a variety of skills are developed and deployed contextually, and students learn to take on different roles as the situation requires. Importantly, the kinds of processes involved in these educational environments could help refocus the epistemic and ontological challenges of postmodernity in positive ways by highlighting the shared agency of students and teachers.

An example of cooperative *praxis* taken from my own experience as a musician (drums, percussion) might help to illuminate these potentials. Over the past three decades I have been involved in numerous long-term collaborations with other musicians, as well as many cross-disciplinary projects with choreographers, experimental filmmakers, theatre groups, and visual artists. For instance, in 2015 I participated in a project entitled 'Time Machine' presented by the MACHiNENOiSY dance company in Vancouver, Canada.[5] This work was a multimedia, cross-disciplinary collaboration between eight children – aged eight to 13 – two choreographers, three musicians, a sound designer, a lighting-video designer, and a sculptor/costume designer. Notably, the children were integral collaborators in the development of this work, which also entailed a good deal of improvisation in performance. The project afforded an opportunity to collaborate, solve-problems, and to exercise our imaginations in new ways. In doing so, we explored and disrupted simple ontological and epistemic assumptions associated with youth vs. age, naiveté vs. experience, preparedness vs. spontaneity, technology vs. life, all through the lens of the active sense-making body in its social and material environment. For me, participation in projects like this has revealed the pedagogical possibilities for collaborative arts *praxis* – highlighting the ways focal practices can help us to see beyond sedimented attitudes and reconnect with our creative potentials.

Collaborative learning through creative arts *praxis* can offer important opportunities for students and teachers to experience and reflect upon the enactment of their own shared worlds of meaning – worlds in which they stand not merely as 'resources', but rather as active co-creators. Accordingly, these kinds of activities can help re-reveal the self-organizing or emergent dimension of *phusis* in the context of contemporary life. Such possibilities have been explored by Freya Mathews (2008), who argues that embodied, empathic, and 'synergistic' activities such as dance and music making can open richer and more compassionate perspectives on all life – revealing the continuities between human and 'natural' worlds as dynamic, self-organizing systems. Likewise, arts pedagogy can also revive the nurturing dimension of *poiēsis* within our field of possibilities as technological beings. *Poiēsis* may be revealed, for example, by encouraging activities such as cooking, gardening, woodworking, and other forms of engaged craftsmanship in pedagogical contexts – 'nurturing' activities that bring forth focal events and things. However, this reengagement with *poiēsis* can also be extended toward a critical re-evaluation of our relationship to today's technological devices, which need not be seen only as disaggregating 'means to ends' as Borgmann (1992) suggests. Rather, they may be revealed as central aspects (focal things) within, for example, the new creative multimedia environments where people gather.

Indeed, the kinds of focal practices made possible by contemporary technological equipment are not characterized by the stability found in traditional forms. And it is just this fluidity that may afford aesthetic modes of inquiry that allow aspects of contemporary human experience to be examined from shifting vantage points. As with the Time Machine project, this could provide opportunities for students and teachers to examine and express the changing worlds they inhabit through the development of creative projects that explore critical themes – where the collaborative use of multimedia technology could become a central 'nurturing' component for the new kinds of creative practice that disclose the character and possibilities of contemporary life. Additionally, the flexible nature of these new postmodern forms of focal practice could offer more inclusive 'gathering environments' – an advantage over previous kinds that tended to be more rigid and thus more socially and culturally exclusive.[6]

In connection with this last point, I conclude this section by considering an example that speaks to the relevance of focal practices in the arts for another challenging aspect of life in the twenty-first century: migration and multiculturalism. The Meet4Music (M4M) project at the University of Graz, Austria, is a community arts project that involves weekly sessions in musical and dance improvisation. Each session is guided by a facilitator, but the activities are driven chiefly by the collaborative work of the participants. The sessions are free and open to everyone in the community, regardless of age or experience. But a special effort is made to include recent immigrants and refugees. The collaborative and improvisational nature of this program provides a way for established residents and newcomers to interact, develop embodied and emotional forms of communicating, and thereby build trust and friendships even when spoken language is difficult or impossible (see Schiavio *et al.* 2018). This demonstrates the tremendous potential improvisational forms of focal practice can have for fostering an openness to difference and for initiating new shared cultural perspectives. It seems likely, then, that initiating similar projects in pedagogical settings could also serve the critical project of conscientization, offering transformational experiences that begin to dissolve acquired fears and dehumanizing assumptions associated with social and cultural 'othering'.

Conclusion

The issues, ideas, and examples I have introduced in the previous sections are intended to offer a starting place for thinking more deeply about the character of life in the twenty-first century and the role of arts education in it. I have attempted to show how phenomenological insights can help us better understand the taken-for-granted attitudes that guide our experience of the world, and in doing so, open new perspectives and possibilities. Importantly, this does not mean turning away from technology or the fluid, multiplicitous, and multicultural nature of the postmodern world in which we find ourselves. Rather it entails an awakening to both the dangers and possibilities of contemporary life, as well as a pioneering attitude toward exploring those kinds of practices through which we may preserve our nature as world-disclosing beings. This aligns closely with the phenomenological and critical-transitive modes of consciousness advocated for by critical pedagogy, where new positive options for technology and human life may be revealed through creative arts praxis.

By learning with and through focal practices, students and teachers can become empowered by experiences of engaged social and cultural agency and will therefore be able to see themselves and each other as more than mere consumers and workers (and the world as more than a pool of resources). In line with this, arts pedagogy can make an important contribution to a critically ontological understanding of what 'having been educated' entails. Most centrally, this means that educated citizens will have acquired the aesthetic, critical, and social tools to look beyond the *Gestell* – to engage with technology, work, and culture in positive, world-making ways; to better understand the meaning of those creative activities that imbue their lives with meaning; and, more generally, to enjoy richer understandings of what kinds of beings they are and therefore be able to explore their potentials to the fullest. Taken together, arts education, critical pedagogy, and phenomenology provide important avenues for thought and action that could help us realize these goals.

Acknowledgments

Earlier versions of the sections 'Phenomenology and critical pedagogy' and 'Education and arts praxis' appeared in a paper published in *Interference: A journal of audio culture* (van der Schyff 2016). Copyright of this article is owned by the author.

Notes

1 It should be noted that the term "West" is used here not simply as a geographical descriptor. Briefly, it now signals and implies notions of modernity, which are framed according to a set of ideals and beliefs such as democracy, free-markets, technological progress, economic growth, consumerism and so on. Importantly, because of the pressures of cultural

and economic assimilation associated with globalization, the assumptions and practices associated with the term have been adopted widely and are now part of the current historical conditions of postmodernism or late modernism.
2 For a discussion of this see Torres (2014).
3 This conception of *praxis* also resonates with other phenomenologically informed perspectives on education – most notably perhaps with the idea of 'education as formation' or *Bildung*. This concept has been developed in several ways, however it essentially involves 'a creative process in which a person, through his or her own actions, shapes and develops himself or herself and his or her cultural environment' (Silander, Kivelä, and Sutinen (2012), p. 3).
4 This perspective is summarized well by Dreyfus and Spinosa (2017[1997]) when they write: 'Before the triumph of technological devices, people primarily engaged in practices that nurtured or crafted various things. So gardeners developed the skills and put in the effort necessary for nurturing plants, musicians acquired the skill necessary for bringing forth music, the fire place had to be filled with wood of certain types and carefully maintained in order to provide warmth for the family. Technology, as Borgmann understands it, belongs to the last stage in the history of the understandings of being in the West. It replaces the worlds of *poiēsis*, craftsmen, and Christians with a world in which subjects control objects. In such a world the things that call for and focus nurturing, craftsmanly, or praising practices are replaced by devices that offer a more and more transparent or commodious way of satisfying a desire. Thus, the wood-burning fireplace as the foyer or focus of family activity is replaced by the stove and then by the furnace' (p. 200).
5 http://machinenoisy.com/wp/work/time-machine/
6 This possibility was already suggested two decades ago by Dreyfus and Spinosa (2017 [1997]).

References

Arendt, H., 1958. *The human condition*. Chicago, IL: The University of Chicago Press.
Arendt, H., 1993[1961]. *Between past and future*. New York: Penguin Books.
Baumann, Z., 2007. *Liquid times: Living in an age of uncertainty*. New York: Polity Press.
Borgmann, A., 1984. *Technology and the character of contemporary life: A philosophical inquiry*. Chicago, IL: University of Chicago Press.
Borgmann, A., 1992. *Crossing the postmodern divide*. Chicago, IL: University of Chicago Press.
Dreyfus, H. and Spinosa, C., 2017[1997]. Highway bridges and feasts: Heidegger and Borgmann on how to affirm technology. In: M. Wrathall, ed. *Background practices: Essays on the understanding of being*. New York: Oxford University Press, 198–217.
Elliott, D.J. and Silverman, M., 2015. *Music matters: A philosophy of music education*. 2nd ed. New York: Oxford University Press.
Freire, P., 2000[1968]. *Pedagogy of the oppressed: 30th anniversary edition*. New York: Bloomsbury Academic.
Freire, P. and Illich, I., 1975. *Diálogo Paulo Freire-Ivan Illich*. Buenos Aires: Editorial Búsqueda-Celadec.
Giroux, H., 2011. *On critical pedagogy*. New York: Continuum.
Greene, M., 1992. *Releasing the imagination*. San Francisco: Jossey-Bass.
Heidegger, M., 1975. *Poetry, language, thought*. New York: Harper Perennial.
Heidegger, M., 1977[1954]. The question concerning technology. In: *The question concerning technology and other essays*. New York: Garland Publishing, 3–35.
Higgins, C., 2012. The impossible profession. In: W. Bowman and A.L. Frega, eds. *The handbook of philosophy in music education*. New York: Oxford University Press, 213–230.

Husserl, E., 1970[1936]. *The crisis of European sciences and transcendental philosophy*. Evanston, IL: Northwestern University Press.
Ihde, D., 1977. *Experimental phenomenology: An introduction*. New York: G.P. Putnam's Sons.
Käufer, S. and Chemero, A., 2015. *Phenomenology: An introduction*. Cambridge: Polity Press.
Kincheloe, J.L., 2003. Critical ontology: Visions of selfhood and curriculum. *Journal of Curriculum Theorizing*, 19, 47–64.
Kincheloe, J.L., 2008. *Knowledge and critical pedagogy: An introduction*. London: Springer.
Lifton, R.J., 1995. *The protean self: Human resilience in an age of fragmentation*. New York: Basic Books.
Mathews, F., 2008. Thinking from within the calyx of nature. *Environmental Values*, 17, 41–65. doi:10.3197/096327108X271941
Merleau-Ponty, M., 2002[1945]. *Phenomenology of perception*. London: Routledge.
Sawyer, K.R., 2007. Improvisation and teaching. *Critical Studies in Improvisation*, 2 (2), Available from: www.criticalimprov.com/article/view/380/626.
Schiavio, A., van der Schyff, D., Gande, A., and Kruse-Weber, S., 2018. Negotiating individuality and collectivity in community music: A qualitative case study. *Psychology of Music*. Available from: https://doi.org/10.1177/0305735618775806
Silander, P., Kivelä, A., and Sutinen, A., eds., 2012. *Theories of bildung and growth: Connections and controversies between continental educational thinking and American pragmatism*. Rotterdam: Sense Publishers.
Smith, F.J., 1979. *The experiencing of musical sound: Prelude to a phenomenology of music*. New York: Gordon and Breach.
Thomson, I., 2001. Heidegger on ontological education, or: How we become what we are. *Inquiry*, 44, 243–68.
Torres, C.A., 2014. *First Freire: Early writings in social justice education*. New York: Teachers College Press.
Turkle, S., 1995. *Life on the screen: Identity in the age of the internet*. New York: Simon and Schuster.
van der Schyff, D., 2016. Phenomenology, technology and arts education: Exploring the pedagogical possibilities of two multimedia arts inquiry projects. *Interference: A Journal of Audio Culture*, 5 (1), 38–57.
Zuboff, S., 2019. *The age of surveillance capitalism: The fight for a human future at the new frontier of power*. New York: PublicAffairs.

Chapter 19

Between having and being
Phenomenological reflections on having been educated

Patrick Howard

Introduction

> *On his way to somewhere else an old fisherman would visit my father. As a boy, I was sure to be in earshot of the kitchen table conversations. Everything about this man was strange to me; the rough spun sweaters, and the large knotted hands that dwarfed the teacup in their grasp. He was not formally educated, yet he embodied a quiet confidence, a humble self-assuredness, and an intelligence in matters related to his world.*
>
> *Invariably the conversation moved to how the "chil'ren" were doing. He was interested in the fact that my brother had finished high school and was pursuing more education at the university. "You tell him," he would direct my father, "to get all the education he can get, every bit of it. It seems you can't 'ave too much education these days."*
>
> *"Well," my father replied, "he's thinking of becoming a lawyer after he finishes university."*
>
> *"That's good then," the old man replied. "That's a good job."*
>
> *"Yes, it is. But he'll need to go on after his university degree to law school."*
>
> *"Well!" the old man replied, surprise in his voice. "More education, isn't that something!"*
>
> *"But he'll 'ave all his education then, surely? Will he? Will he have it all then, all that he can get?"*
>
> *I could sense my father's hesitation. "Well, you'd think, wouldn't you?" my father chuckled and deflected.*
>
> *On subsequent visits, the old fisherman would be sure to ask after my brother's progress and seemed amazed anew, with maybe just a hint of incredulity at the fact that my brother was still in school, still pursuing "his education."*
>
> *"How is the young fella doing? Has he got all his education yet? Tell him to keep goin', keep at it 'til he gets it all, every bit."*
>
> *My father would agree to pass on the old man's words of counsel.*
>
> *In their weekly phone calls my father would relay this message. My brother was expected to "get every last bit of education there was." It became a gentle running tease of my father's.*

This memory bubbles to the surface whenever I read or hear "getting an education," and "having an education," to mean some "thing" we acquire, that we possess, or in many instances, that we can commodify in tuition fees. To my father's old friend, education was, without doubt, a quantifiable, concrete entity that one gathers up for one's own. Having more education was good, getting or having all that is available was better.

This story came to me again when thinking about the theme "To Have Been Educated." The phrase echoes a finite-ness, an endpoint commensurate with *having* an education in a similar sense as it was understood by the old fisherman. And yet, the phrase contains an echo of *being* educated as well. *Being* educated seems to speak to something very different than *having* an education. Being refers to something denser, to experience, and for that reason it is more complex, and, in many regards, it is essentially unknowable. In this chapter I explore the experience *of having been educated* by inquiring into the uneasy tension between *having* and *being* as they relate to education.

We begin by looking closely at the phrase, "to have been educated." The words can help us get closer to the lived experience of having been educated. *Having* and *being* are the subjects of previous philosophical and psychological studies. The German social psychologist and psychoanalyst Erich Fromm (1976) wrote *To Have or To Be?* Gabriel Marcel (1949/2011) the French philosopher took up the distinct existential orientations related to *being* and *having* in a collection of writings by the same name, *Being and Having*. Then there are the famous treatises on Being written by Heidegger (1953/2010) in *Being and Time* and Sartre's (1956/1984) *Being and Nothingness* in which the most ancient of philosophical questions is posed, namely 'What is the meaning of Being?' Albeit, the concept of *Being* is different from *being*, there are interesting connections to be made in how Heidegger's Being relates to truth, authenticity, and a never-ending process of active engagement with the world. We will return to see what Heidegger, the teacher, reveals about *being* educated. These writers explore the big questions related to *having* and *being* from very different perspectives. Yet they assist in our understanding of the experience of "having been educated" by helping us reflect more deeply on what this phrase may mean.

Finally, a recent memoir helps us understand more deeply what it means to say "we have been educated." In Tara Westover's (2018) compelling book *Educated*, the author offers a powerful glimpse into the life of a person for whom, as a child and young person, formal education was outside family and cultural expectations. Westover offers fresh insight into the experience of "being educated" through vivid lived experience descriptions and reflections on those experiences.

Orienting to having and being

My father's visitor is excited that my brother is "getting his education" and acquiring a great deal of it. More is better. It is not difficult to see the old man is fully given over to the idea that education is some "thing" my brother will possess. In his kitchen table chats he does not communicate any real sense that my brother is *being* educated. It is in this way we begin to see the difference between educational attainment, the levels of education achieved, and an understanding of education that is integral to human becoming deeply embedded in the life process. The old man marvels at what my brother will "get," namely a good education, and presumably a good job.

Perhaps it comes as no great surprise that education is viewed here as an instrumental means to an end – something important to have, something once attained, as the old saying goes, "can never be taken away from you." The old fisherman reflects the popular underlying belief that "getting" and "having" are the highest goals. It may even be argued that *having* is synonymous with *being*. In a hyper-consumerist society, it is not a stretch to say, we *are* what we *have*, and a person who *has* nothing, *is* nothing.

It is obvious that having is essential to the human condition. In order to function in society and indeed to live, we must *have* things. But we are also aware, largely through the great religious traditions, that having and being represent very different orientations and fundamental modes of experience. Humans are warned away from a preoccupation with having and are encouraged to live a life not centered on having property, or things, but instead to live a life centered on becoming, on moving closer to our full potential through an experience of deep living and relatedness.

Fromm (1976) argues that our culture's current preoccupation with a having mode of existence can be traced to shifts in our language usage over the past few centuries. This shift involves the growing use of nouns and the decrease of verbs.

> A noun is the proper denotation for a thing. I can say I *have* things; for instance, that I have a table, a house, a book, a car. The proper denotation for an activity, a process, is a verb; for instance, I am, I love, I desire, I hate etc. Yet, ever more frequently an *activity* is expressed in terms of *having*; that is a noun is used instead of a verb. But to express an activity by *to have* in connection with a noun is an erroneous use of the language, because processes and activities cannot be possessed; they can only be experienced.
>
> (p. 20)

Fromm shows that this linguistic turn to substitute nouns for verbs is now firmly grounded in our contemporary language. It is quite natural for me to say, "I have a problem," "I have a happy marriage," "I have concerns," whereas previously people would more likely say, "I am troubled," "I am happily married," "I am concerned." Fromm explains that by shifting *to have* the lived experience is essentially eliminated; the *I* of experience is replaced by the *it* of possession. In this pre-reflective manner, I transform my feelings, my experiences, and myself, in a way, into a possession. Gabriel Marcel says of this, "Having as such seems to have a tendency to destroy and lose itself in the very thing it began by possessing . . . in so far as I treat them as possessions that they should tend to blot me out, although it is I who possess them" (1949, p. 179).

To follow this line of thinking then is to say, "I have a happy marriage," is empty of real meaning. According to Fromm, "To say, 'I have great love for you' is meaningless. Love is not a thing one can have, but a *process*, an inner activity that one is the subject of. I can love, I can *be* in love, but in loving I have . . . nothing" (p. 22). As acknowledged earlier, we cannot live without having. It is essential. We have food, clothing, shelter, computers, furniture. And yet, there are languages for which no word for "to have" exists. Possession is most often shown in these languages by the construction "it is to me." The focus is on *being*.

And *being*, as expected, is a little more complex. I do not presume to take up an inquiry into *being*, only to look, in a limited way, at how the word is used in our language and perhaps reveal interesting insights relevant to our inquiry. Being is used in our language in several different ways. First, *being* can be used as a simple linking verb that describes or denotes identity as in, "I am hungry," and "I am tall." Second, *being* means to *exist* that is different from description or fixing identity. Being in this sense is more than a descriptive term for a phenomenon. "It also denotes the reality of existence of who we are and what *is*; it states his/her/its authenticity, truth . . . it refers to the person's or thing's essence, not to his/her/its appearance" (Fromm 1976, p. 24).

Reflecting now on the kitchen table conversations I understand it is education as product that is assumed. It is education as a means to an end, typically a good job, and a place in a competitive, global, knowledge economy. In this way, education seems to be bounded, constrained, diminished. Marcel writes, "It should be told here that *having* is often apt to reduce itself to the fact of containing . . . the containing itself cannot be defined purely in spatial terms. . . . To contain is to enclose, but to enclose to prevent, to resist, and to oppose the tendency of the content towards spreading, spilling out, and escaping" (1949, p. 174).

Being educated

Education is deeply connected to *being* and *becoming*. Outside of psychological, theoretical and philosophical conceptualizing, education is grounded in human being and becoming. Education then is inherently an existential phenomenon. And this is the heart of the matter in describing what it means to say, "I have been educated."

The old man was not asking after the status of my brother's "being." His interest did not lie in the active development of his human powers, talents, abilities, nor in the quality of his inner activities and his work in pursuit of what is real and true. He was not interested in how my brother may be incorporating those virtues as have been described by the great wisdom traditions as belonging to an educated person namely, understanding, imagination, courage, humility, generosity and strong character among others. Although it is these qualities we look for in "educated" people, and qualities like these do appear in curriculum guides, in lists of "essential graduation learnings," and the aspirational vision statements of public school systems and universities, this was not what interested my father's friend. No, he was most impressed by the quantity of education, the number of university degrees, the earning potential and the employment opportunities that result from education. It could be argued that what is of most interest is "schooling"; my brother was certainly being schooled, whether he was being educated was another matter.

Defining what we mean by education has been a perennial pursuit taken up by many thinkers from Plato to R.S. Peters. It was Peters who, in the 1960s and 1970s, subjected the question "What does it mean to be an educated man (sic)?" to rigorous conceptual analysis. He determined there was not and could not be a consensus on what it means to be educated, but it was an ongoing process. In 1970, Peters differentiated between "the educated man" and "education" since, he argued, there is a difference between "asking whether a person has been educated and whether he is an educated man, for the former could be taken as meaning just, 'has he been to school?'" whereas the latter suggested much more than this" (Peters, in Hodgson 2010, p. 110). Peters recognized the difference between having an education (being schooled) and being educated.

Teaching as learning to let be

What does it mean today to take up an existential goal for education? To move from getting or *having* an education to the experience of *being* educated? As we have seen, education is an existential phenomenon, in that we experience the meaning of *being* a human being – to question and develop understanding, the strength of character to imagine new ways, and the courage to pursue them in a spirit of generosity and humility. Who we want as friends, neighbors, business associates, political leaders, lawyers, doctors and teachers often have little to do with the number of degrees they have, the grades they achieved, or even a concern with the content they learned. But *being* educated means something else. This is what we look for in others and something we know intuitively, pre-reflectively, about *being educated*, yet we seem to have lost this understanding.

And this inevitably leads us to the question, how do we educate for being; how do we model and teach this way? Heidegger who perhaps, more than anyone, has written about Being, thinking, questioning, actively engaging with life, and technology, all fundamental educational matters, has something to say about *how* to teach. Heidegger (1967/1998) describes an approach to teaching in the opening paragraphs of a collection of lectures compiled as *What is Called Thinking?* It is here that Heidegger reveals, in his inimitable style, something about *being* educated, or educating for *being*. It is worthwhile quoting the paragraph in full here.

> Teaching is even more difficult than learning. We know that; but we rarely think about it. And why is teaching more difficult than learning? Not

because the teacher must have a larger store of information and have it always ready. Teaching is more difficult than learning because what teaching calls for is this: to let learn. The real teacher, in fact, lets nothing else be learned than – learning. His conduct, therefore, often produces the impression that we properly learn nothing from him, if by 'learning' we now suddenly understand merely procurement of useful information. The teacher is ahead of his apprentices in this alone, that he has still far more to learn than they – he has to learn to let them learn. The teacher must be capable of being more teachable than the apprentices. The teacher is far less assured of his ground than those who learn are of theirs. If the relation between the teachers and the taught is genuine, therefore, there is never a place in it for the authority of the know-it-all or the authoritative sway of the official. It still is an exalted matter, then to become a teacher – which is something else entirely than becoming a famous professor.

(1967/1998, p. 15)

In these words, perhaps it is not surprising that Heidegger points to "being educated" and at the same time how to teach for "being" educated. Those who have traced Heidegger's approach to pedagogy show his general view of the purpose of education was grounded in the "a view (of the essence) both of 'education' and of the lack of education, both of which (as belonging together) concern the very foundation of our being as humans" (1967/1998, p. 167). And in the previous paragraph Heidegger puts before us the practice, the method, if you will, to situate education, both teaching and learning with our being-in-the-world. Heidegger turns away from conventional, thinking about how to educate. He indicates the transmission of content (*merely the procurement of useful information*), the mandating of prescribed learning outcomes controlled through high stakes testing (*the authoritative sway of the official*) undermine *being* educated which depends on a "genuine relation between the teacher and the taught." At the heart of *being* educated is the pedagogical relationship.

As important to the pedagogical relationship is the method that supports the practice – to learn in order to let be. This is the *being* orientation standing in stark contrast to the *having* orientation. *Having* is interested in the gathering up of content, of detailed lessons, of ticking off outcomes, of assessing, of tallying, grading, and reporting. All of this is done to determine if students possess what was given, and then to move on. Heidegger challenges this traditional view of how education is "done" by situating education, specifically teaching and learning with being-in-the-world. Teachers are called to re-orient their beings to *let learn* or more aptly, *to learn to let learn*. Heidegger acknowledges the difficulty in situating ourselves this way. It calls for a sensitivity to the being of the student, to what calls that student, to clear spaces, and create openings so students can respond meaningfully.

What are teachers to make of this invocation *to learn to let learn*? Riley (2011) reminds us that Heidegger created a network of word meanings connecting the word *let (lassen)* "to extend and emphasize this fundamental human relation within situations is comprised of beings engaged in some way with human beings" (p. 810). He developed words such as *belassen* (leave it its own nature); *wholenlassen* (letting dwell); *sein lassen* (letting be); *sehen lassen* (let be seen); *lernen lassen* (let learn). Heidegger's call "to let" can in no way be construed as to leave, to abandon, or neglect. But what it does signify is a relational orientation to the student in which the learner's being can show through the clearing of an opening that is sensitive to the essential freedom of the *being* of the student. As difficult as Heidegger says this is, in doing so the teacher *educates* by modeling strength of character. This *letting learn* requires meeting the student with openness and generosity. To forgo educational control (*sway of the official*) inherent in contemporary education speaks to humility, integrity, and understanding what the student needs to participate fully in the world.

Student learning in order to let be

What does *to let learn in order to let be* mean for the student, the one being taught? Students in a *having* orientation, who are *getting their education*, those thoroughly schooled in transmissive, conventional approaches may also struggle when *being educated* requires another way of *being*. I was provided a glimpse of what the experience may be like for students when I was asked by two intrepid high school teachers to assist in documenting what it was like to undertake a whole school, project-based learning activity directed by a single big question. Students and teachers across grade levels were given the freedom to determine how they would engage with the question, "What does it mean to be human today?" The focus was student-led; teachers acted as mentors and guides. Students were challenged to inquire into the question by pursuing their own interest and passions, to bring to bear an interdisciplinary investigation on some aspect of the human condition. One may argue, the whole-school project was undertaken in the spirit of *learning to let learn*. After the project, follow up interviews about the learning experience were conducted with teachers and students. One grade nine student said:

> *I really didn't like the project. I mean, especially at first. It was like "what are we going to do?" We got in small groups and had to decide on how we would answer this question. I mean we were really stuck, lost – we just sat around throwing out ideas. I thought it was pretty useless – it's like we didn't have enough direction. What was the point? Like I said, I thought it was pretty useless.*
>
> *But then we decided to look at food. What could be more human than that? Right? And then, it spun into humans' relationship to food, and then factory farming, and our relationship to animals, animal welfare. We found some excellent information; documentaries and we even had a farmer come in and some one from*

the SPCA for a panel. They both had good points – it's not an easy subject when you get into it. We all learned a lot and the presentation we did for the whole school turned out pretty awesome.

I can see this working for some subjects more than others. Like Math and Science, I don't think you have time to learn this way. You've got to be ready for tests and stuff. For sure Math and Science come into the big questions. . . . I don't know. . . . I am not as comfortable with all that freedom in certain subjects, I guess.

The student reflects on the experience of learning another way. The space to choose a path forward; the freedom to ask questions that arise from personal interest and to respond meaningfully proves disconcerting and uncomfortable. The questions are asked, "What are we going to do? How will we answer this question?" And assertions are made; "I mean, we were lost. We didn't have enough direction." "Letting learn to let be" requires of the student courage and a willingness to persevere. The creation of the space "to let learn" is interpreted as having not received "enough direction" from the teachers. The comment speaks to the importance of the pedagogical relationship and the teacher knowing how much direction to give and when to withhold to allow the student to take the lead. The comment also may speak to the doubt, fear, and confusion that is to be expected when change occurs, particularly if the student has been educated in a conventional approach oriented to *having* and *getting* that is highly prescribed, transmissive and directive. While there may be a great deal in these students' words on which we can focus, I find it interesting to ask what happened between the obvious doubt and the moment of becoming "unstuck." What occurred in the space between being *lost* and *finding a way*? It would seem something very important happens here. Dewey has written a great deal in his theory of experiential learning about the immensely valuable moments in all learning that are characterized by uncertainty, doubt and confusion. He points to the space between the interruption in experience and our finding a way out of a difficult encounter (see English 2013). It presents itself as a liminal space of learning where I can identify where there is a potential change in my *self* and way of *being* in the world.

The teachers intentionally created the space for students to respond in a way that was sensitive and responsive to the students' own beings. It proved to be unsettling and unnerving. Yet, in the student's final comments we see the power of conventional approaches to education; the having orientation surfaces when the student observes, "this way of teaching doesn't prepare you for tests, to make sure you are ready for post secondary." The quantification of learning, *getting* an education seems to negate the experience of *being* educated. However, the student pauses and in a momentary reflective stance comments on the pre-reflective experience of undergoing discomfort and confusion in learning. "I don't know . . . I am not as comfortable with all that freedom in certain subjects, I guess," she remarks.

This conscious, albeit fleeting, turn to reflect on the rupture in experience opens the opportunity to learn from that experience. In the genuine relationship between teacher and student, referred to by Heidegger, it would be most appropriate to intentionally reflect *with* the student on what it means, existentially, to learn how to learn. To be educated in this way requires courage, a patient humility in the face of difficult and perplexing encounters with the world. A generosity of spirit is needed to receive and provide prior knowledge and experience to shape new learning, to change, to grow, to *be* differently, to *be* educated.

Being educated as interruption

Tara Westover's (2018) memoir begins with an epigram by Dewey, "I believe finally that education must be conceived as a continuing reconstruction of experience; that the process and the goal of education are one and the same thing." Westover's story is one of reconstructing a life. Born in 1986 in rural Idaho to fundamentalist Christian parents, Westover's childhood and adolescence are lived on the margins of mainstream society. There is deep suspicion of government, and most social institutions; life is dictated by an austere and literal interpretation of the Bible and Mormon teachings. The children's births are not reported; they do not attend formal schooling; hospitals and doctors are perceived as dangerous. Westover grows up working with her siblings in her father's scrap yard in difficult and dangerous conditions. Her homeschooling consists of some sporadic reading from the Bible and basic numeracy in the early years but even this eventually fades away. Any medical treatments are provided by the mother who concocts herbal remedies from roots and plants available on their remote mountain property. Tara Westover's being is formed in this environment as a child raised by a father who is mentally ill and fully imprisoned by paranoid delusions and an end-of-days, survivalist mentality that deeply influenced his children.

The memoir is riveting and heartbreaking. It serves as an undeniable account of a young woman's experience of *being educated*. In this case the education is very much a story of conversion in which the learner is required to undergo the existential pain that accompanies the abandoning of superstition, ignorance and a corrupt set of beliefs in the face of revelatory discovery. Her story is a rare lived description of being moved into the light of truth in a literal contemporary illustration of Plato's famous allegory of the cave.

Westover's account is one of rupture, discontinuity, doubt, and *undergoing* or the suffering of experience. At age 16, she is inspired by an older brother to prepare herself for the monumental task of taking a university entrance exam especially designed for home schooled students. She recalls her father's response to her brother Tyler's shocking assertion that he wanted to go to college. "College is extra school for people too dumb to learn it the first time around," Dad said. They were then subjected to a lecture about teachers as "bona fide agents of the Illuminati" and "high minded professors who think their wisdom is greater than God's." She prevails in gaining entrance to university and her memoir illustrates in the starkest of terms the meaning of undergoing, of rupture, of how we experience the world and learn from it.

From the many descriptions of disruption, one particularly stands out. Westover, now a freshman at Brigham Young University, experiences changes in all aspects of her life that are dizzying. She sits for her first quiz in American history,

> For two days I tried to wrestle meaning from the textbook's dense passages, but terms like "civic humanism" and "the Scottish Enlightenment" dotted the page like black holes. Sucking all the other words into them. I took the quiz and missed every question.
>
> The failure sat uneasy in my mind. It was the first indication of whether I would be okay, whether whatever I had in my head by way of *education* would be enough. After the quiz the answer seemed clear. It was not enough. On realizing this I might have resented my upbringing, but I didn't. My loyalty to my father had increased in proportion to the miles between us. On the mountain, I could rebel. But here in this loud, bright place surrounded by gentiles disguised as saints, I clung to every truth he had given me. Doctors were Sons of Perdition, Homeschooling was a commandment from the Lord. Failing a quiz did nothing to undermine my new devotion to an old creed, but a lecture on Western art did.

In this passage the "having an education" orientation characterizes her description. She questions whether she has "enough" education in her head. The failure on the quiz makes it apparent to her that she does not. She needs more. The turn to the "having" orientation is followed immediately by her recommitment to her former "truth" and a renewed loyalty to her father. One may argue that she equates her failure with simply not knowing the answers and for her it is primarily a cognitive shortcoming – not having enough "in my head by way of *education*." But *being educated* is not a matter of solving a problem, knowing the answer, employing clever rhetorical strategies or adhering to the rules of grammar and style. Being educated, Westover was to become painfully aware, begins with being-in-the world and depends on a sensitivity to context; it is existential and circumstantial.

Westover's shift to an orientation of *being educated* can be said to begin when she encounters an existential limit. In the previous passage, she clings to what she already knows, her father's creed, and dismisses her deficiencies as what she views as merely "answers" she has not yet gained. It is during the lecture on Western art that Westover is marked by the limits of her experience when she reflectively comes into a nascent awareness of what she does not know, cannot yet do, and does not yet understand. In that moment she is able to glimpse her way of *being* – a way of being that is essentially *how* we *are*.

In that pivotal lecture on Western art, Westover and her freshman classmates are shown images of paintings. The professor discusses composition, brushstrokes and historical significance. One image puzzles the young student: "the projector showed a peculiar image of a man in faded hat and overcoat. Behind him loomed a concrete wall. He held a small paper near his face, but he wasn't looking at it. He was looking at us." Westover consults her textbook to look closer at the same image.

> Something was written under it [the image] in italics but I couldn't understand it. It had one of those black hole words right in the middle, devouring the rest. I'd seen other students ask questions, so I raised my hand. The professor called on me, and I read the sentence aloud. When I came to the word, I paused. "I don't know this word," I said. "What does it mean?"

The word was Holocaust. And in that moment, in the reactions of the professor and classmates, in the heavy silence that hung palpably, she was awakened to *how* she *was*. After class, she describes running to the computer room to look up the word;

> I don't know how long I sat there reading about it, but at some point, I'd read enough. I leaned back and stared at the ceiling. I suppose I was in shock, but whether it was the shock of learning something so horrific, or the shock of learning about my own ignorance, I'm not sure.

It was at that moment when Westover begins the long and arduous process of finding ways to reflectively transform her experience of limits and shortcomings as rupture, and the encounter with the new, the disrupting and the alien becomes a center of interest and activity. Westover continues throughout her remarkable journey of *being educated*, to seek new understandings when the interruption in her experience is a catalyst for a desire to inquire deeply and find new ways of relating to the world despite the fear, the risk, the discomfort and the painful consequences that are inevitable.

Conclusion

Education is a transformational, existential undergoing wherein, as Dewey wrote, "the process and the goal are one and the same thing." Taking some time to think about the inherent differences in understanding education from a *having* orientation and a *being* orientation creates openings for further reflection. Current educational discourses tend to forget education as a *being and becoming* in the limiting, present-day neoliberal preoccupation with the quantification and commodification of education in discrete, lock-step levels that dissect educational experience into innumerable predefined learning outcomes.

Being educated is an orientation that preferences openings and possibilities. It embraces the difficulties, disruptions and struggles inherent in the liminal, and potentially transformative, spaces between old and new. To have been educated and the teaching it requires recognizes the unique *being* of learners and supports, with pedagogical sensitivity, the development through struggle and disruption of *being* that moves toward understanding, courage, humility, generosity and strength of character.

References

English, A., 2013. *Discontinuity on learning: Dewey, Herbart, and educational transformation*. Cambridge, UK: Cambridge University Press.

Fromm, E., 1976. *To have or to be?* New York: Bloomsbury Publishing.

Heidegger, M., 1953/2010. *Being and time*. Translated by Joan Stambaugh. Albany, NY: SUNY Press.

Heidegger, M., 1967/1998. *What is called thinking?* Translated by J.G. Gray. New York: Harper & Row Publishers.

Hodgson, N., 2010. What does it mean to be an educated person? *Journal of Philosophy of Education*, 44 (1), 109–123.

Marcel, G., 1949/2011. *Being and having*. Charleston, SC: Nabu Press.

Riley, D., 2011. Heidegger teaching: An analysis and interpretation of pedagogy. *Educational Philosophy and Theory*, 34 (8), 797–815. Available from: https://doi.org/10.1111/j.1469-5812.2009.00549.x

Sartre, J., 1956/1984. *Being and nothingness*. Translate by Hazel E. Barnes. New York: Washington Square Press.

Westover, T., 2018. *Educated*. Toronto: Harper Collins, 157.

Index

Note: Page numbers in italic indicate a figure and page numbers in bold indicate a table on the corresponding page. Page numbers followed by 'n' indicate a note.

Abram, D. 90, 91–92, 97, 160, 216
active and interactive bodies 151–160
Adams, C. 145
aesthetic experiences, prioritizing 203–204
Agamben, G. 9, 35
agency: attributes of 24; of love 27
agogical phenomenology 202
Alcibiades I 81
Alerby, E. 113, 140, 146
Alexander, C. 164, 170; pattern language 170–171
Alexander, T. 26
alphabetization 89, 90–91
alternative facts 68
anticipation 116
anxiety, role in impulse to education 222
Aoki, T. 189
Apple, M. 24, 29
Aquinas, T. 231, 232
architectural and environmental design in education 164–177
Arendt, H. 9, 34, 111
Aristotle 116, 232
arts: pedagogy 240–241, 243, 246–249; praxis, education and 242–244
assessment, as part of education system 63–64
automobile technology, adoption of 89

Bachelard, G. 140, 142, 144, 146, 147, 183, 187
Bachelor of Education Program Standards 48
Bainbridge, A. 211, 215, 217, 220–222, 224

Ball, S. 25
Baumann, Z. 245
Being vs. being 253
Being and Nothingness (Sartre) 253
Being and Time (Heidegger) 118, 253
being educated orientation 213, 255–256, 260–262
being/having orientation 252–263
Bengtsson, J. 140, 141, 142, 147
Benner, D. 20
Berg, J.H. van den 186, 194
Berger, P.L. 216
Biesta, G. 7, 8, 11, 29, 38, 68, 100, 103, 104, 106–108, 142, 223, 225, 235
Bildung and embodiment 120–122
Blenkinsop, S. 114, 197
bodies, active and interactive 151–160
body schema 118–119
Bollnow, O.F. 108, 147
Bolsonaro, J. 75–76
Borgmann, A. 244–246, 248
Brinkmann, M. 112, 115
Buck, G. 116

Caesar, J. 128
Canada, pedagogical practice in 45–57
Capitalocene 197
Capra, F. 216, 221
Caputo, J.D. 28
Casey, E. 146, 167
Cervantes, M. de 66–67
chance 3
children: capacity for self-directed action 230; experience of time 187; phenomenology of reading in 90;

Index   265

physical wellbeing of 151; transition 181, 187
Chomsky, N. 24
chronos (clock time) 181–183, 185
classrooms 142–146
Climacus, J. 66, 68–69, 71
Cohen, L. 236
Coleridge, S.T. 230
collaborative learning 247
Comenius, J.A. 231; labyrinth story 233–234
communal sensibility 158–159
communication 130, 137, 217, 220
community commitment 171
community of counselling, democratic education in 122–125
Concluding Unscientific Postscript (Kierkegaard) 66, 71
concurrent learning 135
conscientization, idea of 79, 242
constitutive coingredience 167
Continental education 2–3
corporeality *see* lived body (corporeality)
counseling 123
creation, place 169, 170
critical consciousness 242
critical pedagogy, phenomenology and 241–242
Cultural Action for Freedom (Freire) 79
culture and technology 244–246
'curriculum as lived' 189
cynicism 82

Dahlstedt, M. 142
Dark Side of the Moon, The (Pink Floyd) 235
Dasein 122
Death of a Salesman, The 229
de Biran, M. 158
Democracy and Education (Dewey) 130
democratic education, in community of counselling 122–125
Deschooling Society (Illich) 38
desires: disruption and 218–219; evaluating 29; value of 30
Dewey, J. 23–27, 29–31, 129–130, 137, 229, 259, 260, 262
digital technology 239
Dilthey, W. 36
disruption and desire 218–219
distance and web-based education 145
Dreyfus, H. 244, 250n4
Duquesne University 88

economic oriented pro-duction, education as 228–229
Educated (Westover) 253
educatio 231, 233
education 1–2; approaching 34–43; arts praxis and 242–244; as commodity 4; as cultivation and subjectification 20; democratic 23, 122–125; "the educated man" and 256; educationalization of societal problems 34; as e-duction 227, 230–232; essence of 37–38; experiencing language and 219–222; freedom in 40–42; fundamental goal for 141; goals of 129; governed by e-duction 236; inward form of 36; issues of 34, 38–43; *kairos* moments in 192; language and 4; latency of 193–194; learning and 8; lifeworld existentials for architectural and environmental design in 164–166; lived experience of time in 179–196; long-term impact of 222–224; marketization and privatization of 141; measurement in 63–64; modalities of 20; neoliberal assumptions about 211; objectification of 213; as 'oppgave' (task) 59; phenomenon of 7–10; philosophy of 77; place-based 175–176; as practices 100; as process and activity 8, 67, 112; as pro-duction 227, 228–230; as production of development 229; purpose of 11, 225; reform and 227; rethinking 34–37; school and 3; school buildings and spaces 141; study of 7; temporality of 188; understanding from having and being orientation 252–263
educational events, from novel and classroom 101–107
educational moments 101, 107
educational possibilities 197–208
educational purpose, domains of 142
educational responsibility 106
educational spaces/places, relationship between humans and 140–149
educator and educandus 8
eductio 230–231
e-duction, concept of 230–232, 236
Egan, K. 204
ego 16
Eisner, E.W. 229
Elias, J. 77
embodied experiences, in practicing and learning 115–117

embodiment: Bildung and 120–122; of neoliberalism 23–25
Embryonic Society 124
en plein air painting, practice of 206
'entelecheia' (inward form of education) 36
erudition 230–231
European education 4
Evans, J. 68
events: educational moments 101–107; existential 106, 107, 119; as *kairos* moments in education 192; and time 101
existence: modes of 66; problem of 67–68, 71
existential education 2
existential events 106, 107, 119
Experience and Nature (Dewey) 26
experience, horizon of 116–117
experiential learning 175, 200, 259
extended bodies 156

Facebook 67–68
Fejes, A. 142
Fenwick, T. 36
Fink, E. 122–124
Floyd, P. 230, 235
focal practices, concept of 244, 246–248
Foran, A. 45, 145
foreignness, experiences of 119, 121
Foucault, M. 77; and life as problem for philosophy 80–83
freedom in education 40–42
Freire, P. 61, 242–243; *Cultural Action for Freedom* 79; Foucault, and life as problem for philosophy 80–83; and history of life as philosophical problem 83–86; and living non-neoliberal life in education 75–86; Marx, and requirement of transformation 78–80; philosophy and life 77–78
Froese, T. 156
Fromm, E. 76, 253, 254, 255
Frosh, S. 215, 217–220, 222–225
Fuchs, T. 156

Gadotti, M. 77
Garrison, J. 24, 27, 31
Geisteswissenschaftliche Pädagogik, tradition of 36–37
genuine time 129, 134–137
Gestell 244, 249
Giroux, H. 1, 23, 47, 212, 213
givenness, of teaching 9, 11–21; being given what they didn't ask for 18; examples of manifestation 17–20; subjectification 19–20; teaching as double truth giving 18–19
Goble, E. 114, 179
governmentalization of learning 34
Greene, M. 243
Gregorian calendar 128
Gregor XIII (Pope) 128

Harvey, D. 23
hate, and love 42–43
having been educated, experience of 213, 249, 253
having/being orientation 252–263
Hay, P.R. 204
Heidegger, M. 15, 50, 118, 122, 197, 200, 244–246, 253, 256–258, 260
Henry, M. 153, 154–155, 157
hetero-affectivity 157
Howard-Jones, P.A. 216
Howard, P. 213, 252
human behavior, syntactic and semantic analysis 215
human being in the world: Comenius' labyrinth story 233–234; imperfect/perfect 235–236; in narratives of e-duction 232–236; Plato's allegory of the Cave 232–233; possible improvements 234–235
human desire 217
human experience, as pedagogy 164–177
humans, and educational places/spaces 140–149
Humboldt, W. von 120–121
Husserl, E. 5, 15, 50, 115, 122, 140, 143, 164–165, 198, 241

'I can' expressions 153–156
identity, place 168
Ihde, D. 242
Illich, I. 38–40, 88–89
Illich Principle 89, 92
implicit knowledge 116
'impossible possibility, the' 235
incarnate subjectivity 153
Incarnation (Henry) 154
In Defense of the School (Masschelein and Simons) 39
indirect pedagogy 133, 135
individuality/individualism 68, 129–130, 137
information and communication of technologies (ICTs) 88, 97

Ingarden, R. 93
inscription 183
Instagram 67–68
institutionalized education 45, 46
intensifications 89, 95, 97, 168–169, 170
intentional arc, and school buildings 142
interactions: individuality and 130; place 168
interactive bodies 156–159
intergenerative learning, in community 124
Intergovernmental Panel on Climate Change (IPCC) 199
interplay, criterion of 120
inwardness (Kierkegaard) 66–71
Irwin, J. 76
Iser, W. 94

Jacobs, H. 176
Jansson, T. 190
Jardine, D. 160
Jonas, H. 41
Julian calendar 128

kairos 181, 190–193, 194
Kansas State University 171
Kant, I. 117
Kierkegaard, S. 9, 19, 61, 65, 66, 235; approaches of phenomenology 25–26; inwardness 66–71; phenomenological understanding of repetition 25–31
Kincheloe, J. 243
Klein, M. 217, 223
Kohak, E.V. 203
Kohan, W. 61, 75
Komisar, P. 12

labyrinth story (Comenius) 233–234
Langeveld, M.J. 143
language: and education, experiencing 219–222; Humboldt's theory of 121; impact of 222–224
learnification 8, 11, 85
learning: and Bildung 117; collaborative 247; concurrent 135; and education 8; embodied experiences in 115–117; experience of 258–259; governmentalization of 34; intergenerative 124; place-based 175; and practicing from experience 115–117; quantification of 259; and teaching 11–12, 17; and training 184
learning to let learn 258
Lent, J. 219, 224

letting learn to let be 259
life phenomenology 153, 159
lifeworld, 164, 165–166
Lincoln, A. 130
Lingis, A. 3
Lippitz, W. 59, 60
liquid modernity 245
literacy 61, 88–90, 92, 97
lived body (corporeality) 115, 117, 120, 146–147, 152–153, 154, 165–166
lived experience of time 179–196
lived others (relationality) 165–166, 199–201
lived space *see* spatiality (lived space)
lived things (materiality) 165–166
lived time (temporality) 165–166, 188
Løgstrup, K.E. 60, 103
Loman, W. 229
love: and hate 42–43; notion of 42; as way-of-being 26–27
Luckmann, T. 216

magical synesthesia 91
Manen, M. van 2, 145, 164, 191, 197, 199, 201–204, 207; five existentials 165–166
Marcel, G. 253, 254
Marion, J.-L.: *kairos* moments in education 192; phenomenology of givenness 9, 13–17, 20–21n5
Marx: fetish in education 224, 225; focused on production 229; and requirement of transformation 78–80
Masschelein, J. 34, 39, 76, 107
materiality (lived things) 165–166
Mathews, F. 247
Maturana, H.R. 216, 217, 220, 221
Mayo, P. 77
Meadowcreek studio 171–175; pattern language 172, **172**; patterns and design for path to Ripple Ridge 172, *174*; project 171; site patterns 172, *173*
measurement, obsession with 63–66, 71–72
Meet4Music (M4M) project 248
memories, in place/room 146–147
mentality and corporeality 121–122
Merleau-Ponty, M. 47, 91, 95–96, 115–116, 118–119, 140, 142, 143, 146–148, 152, 154, 201
meta-patterns 171
Mollenhauer, K. 3, 54, 216–219, 222, 223, 225
Morse, M. 114, 197
movement-sensations 115

Mr. Tourette and I (Sandstrak) 101
Mumford, L. 96, 97
Murdoch, I. 69

Nancy, J.-L. 124
natural attitude, concept of 164–165
negative experiences 112, 117, 119
neoliberalism 1–2, 4, 55, 128–129; balancing time in 189–190; in education, language and practices of 217; embodiment of 23–25; impact on contemporary educational practices 9; *kairos* moments under 193; and pedagogical practice 45–47
Nicias 82
Nietzsche, F. 26, 123
Noë, A. 206
Nova Scotia Teaching Standards (NSTS) 48, 55

Ong, W. 90
online learning 145
On the Diversity of Human Language Construction and its Influence on the Mental Development of the Human Species (Humboldt) 121
Organisation for Economic Co-operation and Development (OECD) 3, 63
organism of words 95
outdoor educational space 145

paideia, concept of 232
partnered activities 158
pathic community 158
Patočka, J. 202–203, 233–234
pattern language 164, 170–171
Peck, M.S. 27
pedagogical practice 50–55; anecdotes 51–54; Canada 9–10, 45–57; imposed government standards 55–56; neoliberalism and 45–47; reclaiming 49–50; situating 48–49; in teacher education 46; teacher's practice 47–50
pedagogical tact, moment of 191–192
pedagogy 2, 124
pedagogy of place and place making: Alexander's pattern language 170–171; five lifeworld existentials for 165–166; Meadowcreek studio (example) 171–175; pedagogical value of six place processes 169–170; place-as-process 167–169; place-based education 175–176; place, defined 166; value of phenomenology for 164–177

Pedagogy of the Oppressed (Freire) 75
perception 90–92, 94
performance, obsession with measurement 64
personal dispositions 24–25
personalized learning 156, 159
pervasive literacy, invention of 89
Peters, R.S. 227, 229, 256
phenomenological attitude: aesthetic experiences, prioritizing 203–204; applying the reduction 204; asking phenomenological questions 205; developing 198; engaging with phenomenological literature 205–206; facilitating 201–202; non-linguistic methods 206–207; pedagogical aids for teaching toward 202–207; and relationality 199–201
phenomenology 2; and critical pedagogy 241–242; of givenness 9, 13–17, 20–21n5; for pedagogy of place and place making 164–177; of place 166–167; of place-as-process 167–169; and place-based education 175–176; of reading 88–97
Phenomenology of Practice (van Manen) 199
philosophy: as aesthetics of existence 81, 82; of education 77; life as problem for 80–83; other traditions for 78–80
Philosophy and Phenomenology of the Body (Henry) 154
physical wellbeing 151
physical world (place of learning) 140–149
Piaget, J. 91, 117
Picht, G. 41
place: -based education 175–176; creation 169, 170; identity 168; intensification 168–169, 170; interactions 168–169; phenomenologies of 166–167; realization 168; release 168; six processes 167–169; and space, and people 140–149
Plato, allegory of the Cave 232–233
poiēsis 244, 248
Postman, N. 89, 93
practice: developing phenomenological attitude through 206; as form of learning 116–117
praxis 243, 247, 250n3
print technology 96
pro-duction: broader oriented 229–230; economic oriented 228–229; education as 228–230; processes of 227
Programme for International Student Assessment (PISA) 3

psychoanalysis 223
public-school teachers 45
Pueblo peoples 90

Quality Reform 2003 3
Quay, J. 203

Rancière, J. 20
reading aloud event 106
reading, phenomenology of 88–97; in children 90; entering a text 93–95; loss of embodied situation 92–93; magic of synesthesia 90–92; virtuality and reproduction of culture 95–97
reality-testing subjectivity 100–108
realization, place 168
Rediscovery of Teaching, The (Biesta) 100
reduction: to givenness 15; phenomenological 204
reform and education 227
relationality (lived others) 165–166, 199–201
release, place 168
repetition, Kierkegaard's conception of 25–31
Republic, The (Plato) 232
responsivity 119
Riley, D. 257
Roberts, P. 60, 63
Rodríguez, S. 61, 76
Romano, C. 101

Saeverot, H. 112, 128, 135
Saevi, T. 59, 62, 100
Sanders, B. 89
Sandstrak, P. 101–102
Sartre, J. 253
Saviani, D. 77
Scheler, M. 42
Schleiermacher, F. 36
school: and education 3; phenomenology of 38–40; structures 183–185; year 114, 186
school buildings, relationship with people 140–149
Schopenhauer, A. 70
Schyff, D. van der 212, 239
Seamon, D. 113, 164
Searle's Chinese Room thought experiment 217, 220
self 20, 67, 125, 167
self-knowledge 82
self-relationship 122
semi-transitive state, associated with thinking 242

Sennett, R. 29
sense of belonging 147
sensible individuality 155
Sheets-Johnstone, M. 154, 156
Simms, E.-M. 61, 88
Simons, M. 34, 39
Skourdoumbis, A. 25
Smith, S. 113, 151, 229
social consciousness 242
social-emotional learning 152
social media 67–68
social phenomenology 122
Socrates 61, 76, 77, 81–84
'Socrates of Caracas' (Rodríguez) 61, 76
space: defined 117–118; human and 140–149
spatiality (lived space) 117–120, 143, 148, 165–166; of orientation 118; of resonance and responsiveness 119–120; of situation 118–119
Spinosa, C. 244, 250n4
split thinking 217, 218, 223
stewardship ethic 171
structural coupling, conception of 216, 220, 221
students, teaching outdoors 197–208
subjectification 19
"subject-ness" 100, 104, 107, 108n1
synesthesia 91–92

teacher education: in Canada 46; pedagogical practice in 46–57; programs 46, 54–56, 136, 198; struggle in 47
teachers: challenge for 54; development of phenomenological attitude for 198; lifeworld 50; lived experiences of 48–50, 56; practice 47–50
teaching: challenge of 100; as double truth giving 18–19; as educational issue 42–43; givenness of 9, 11–21; as knowledge transmission 19; and learning 11–12, 17; as learning to let be 256–260; as non-transactive act 105; notion of 9; opening up existential possibilities 101–104; in outdoors 145; pedagogical aids for 202–207; toward phenomenological attitude 197–208; practices 25, 47–50; profession 42; time/individuality/interaction impacting 128–138; transmissive 17
Teaching and Learning International Survey (TALIS) 3

technology 88–89; culture and 244–246; digital 239; modern 245; print 96; textual 92, 94
temporality (lived time) 165–166, 188
textuality 90
textual technology 92, 94
Thoreau, H. 201
time: balancing in neoliberal system 189–190; as *chronos* 181; Dewey and 129–130; in educational situation (case study) 131–138; event and 101; forms of 112, 128; as *kairos* 181; lived experience in education 179–196; phenomenon of 111–112
Time and Individuality (Dewey) 129
"To Have Been Educated" phrase 224–225, 228, 240, 253
to let learn in order to let be 258
Tomasello, M. 223
Torgersen, G.-E. 112, 128, 135
training, and learning 184
transcendence 35
transcendental affectivity 157
transitive-critical consciousness 242, 246
transitive-naïve consciousness 242
Trump, D. 68
truth 68–69, 95
Tuan, Y.-F. 146, 147
Twitter 67–68

uncertainty 69, 70
unemployment 34
'upbringing' 216, 218, 219; liberation and 233; as *paideia* 212, 232; as progress 231–232

Varela, F.J. 216, 217, 220, 221
virtuality 94, 95–97
virtual media 96
virtual simulacra 245
virtuous disposition 30
Vlieghe, J. 9, 34
Vygotsky, L. 29, 92

Waldenfels, B. 119
Waters, R. 235
web-based education 145
Webster, S. 9, 23
Weil, S. 69, 235
'we-ness' (interactive) 156–159
West, L. 220–222
Westover, T. 253, 260–262
What is Called Thinking? (Heidegger) 256
Witte-Townsend, D. 103
Wivestad, S.M. 212–213, 227
Wolin, S. 23
writing, reading and 90

Zamojski, P. 9, 34

Made in the USA
Monee, IL
15 May 2025

17516073R00157